GOLDEN GIRLS
Forever

JIM COLUCCI

HARPER DESIGN
An Imprint of HarperCollins Publishers

Published in 2016 by
HARPER DESIGN
An Imprint of HarperCollins*Publishers*
195 Broadway
New York, NY 10007
Tel: (212) 207-7000
Fax: (855) 746-6023
harperdesign@harpercollins.com
www.hc.com

Distributed throughout the world by
HarperCollins Publishers
195 Broadway
New York, NY 10007

ISBN 978-0-06-242290-3

Library of Congress Control Number: 2015948758

Designed by Paul Kepple and Max Vandenberg at
HEADCASE DESIGN
www.headcasedesign.com

Printed in the United States of America

Seventh Printing, 2018

———— *To* ————

BEA ARTHUR,
RUE McCLANAHAN, BETTY WHITE,
and ESTELLE GETTY—

*Thank You for Being
a Friend*

————————————

NBC Entertainment

A Division of
National Broadcasting Company, Inc.

3000 West Alameda Avenue
Burbank, CA 91523   818-840-4166

Camillia Razo
Manager, Contract Administration
Program and Talent Contracts
Business Affairs

RECEIVED
APR 17 1985
ZBG

sent to Haberman

cc UTHP
Watenson-Menc
Rose
+
file

April 11, 1985

Witt/Thomas/Harris
Creative Artists Agency
1888 Century Park East
Suite 1400
Los Angeles, California 90067

Attention: Bill Haber

Re: "LADIES DAY" (aka: "Miami Nice")
     Indemnity Agreement
     _____

Gentlemen:

Enclosed please find two (2) fully-executed copies of
the above-referenced indemnity agreement for your
files.

Thank you for your cooperation in this matter.

Sincerely,

Camillia Razo

CR/ar

Enclosures (2)

cc: Ms. Kate Boyle (Enc.)

1

GETTING STARTED

"Brandon always came up with these wacky ideas, and some of them were genius and some were terrible. That's the sort of thing that happens with creative people who mine their inner child. You either get Mr. Smith, *about the talking orangutan, or you get* The Golden Girls.*"*

—GARTH ANCIER,
former head of current comedy at NBC

PICTURE IT: AUGUST 24, 1984. Two actresses "of a certain age," each currently appearing on a hit NBC show, step out onstage at the network's Burbank headquarters. As presenters at the network's fall preview special, they trade scripted patter from a teleprompter, and in the process, do more than a little ogling of a male lead in one of the peacock network's more promising new dramas. The object of their affection? None other than Mr. Don Johnson, then about to debut in the fashion- and decade-defining hit *Miami Vice*. And the gawking gals, whose performance that night would inspire NBC president Brandon Tartikoff to commission a sitcom about the active lives and loves of the over-sixty set? They are, of course . . . Selma Diamond and Doris Roberts.

What, you were expecting Bea Arthur or Betty White?

The tale of how one of the most beloved comedies of all time made its way to the small screen is not a straightforward one, nor is it very likely.

Miami Nice

◆ ◆ ◆ ◆

IN TWENTY-FIRST-CENTURY TV land, we may have more channels to choose from, but some things haven't really changed since 1985; then, as now, broadcast networks like NBC aimed their programming squarely at the advertiser-coveted 18-49 age demographic. So that night

OPPOSITE:
Before the Girls were Golden, and after Miami was Nice, one of the alternate titles briefly considered was *Ladies Day*.

Photo courtesy of LEX PASSARIS.

at the NBC presentation, when Selma Diamond, who was then appearing on the network's Thursday night sitcom *Night Court*, stopped eyeballing Don Johnson long enough to excitedly tell *Remington Steele*'s Doris Roberts that "there's this wonderful new show, all about retirees in Florida—it's called *Miami Nice*," it was obviously a joke. Or was it?

In his 1992 memoir, *The Last Great Ride*, the late former NBC chief Brandon Tartikoff remembers spending a rainy afternoon channel surfing with his seven-year-old niece until they agreed on the 1953 Betty Grable–Lauren Bacall–Marilyn Monroe movie *How to Marry a Millionaire*. Tartikoff was struck by the idea: how about a frothy comedy about a group of women sharing an apartment together, waiting to meet Mister Right? There was just one problem: other people hated the idea, especially women. When he tried to recruit female writers to work on the project, they were offended at the idea of presenting the young, independent 1980s woman as being incomplete without a man. But the idea stuck in the back of Tartikoff's mind, and later, while visiting his elderly aunt in Florida and observing her crotchety interplay with her neighbor, he had another inspiration: make it *How to Marry a Millionaire for Women over Fifty*.

"Brandon may not have shared those thoughts with us all, so I'm not sure how the *How to Marry a Millionaire* stuff ended up actually being connected to the development of *The Golden Girls*," explains Warren Littlefield, who was then the network's Vice President of Comedy Programs. But Littlefield does know that at what may have been the same time, the *Miami Nice* gag was gathering steam. "It had been the highlight of laughter in a long, boring shoot night," he remembers. "That fall preview special had all these hot young stars from other shows, but here were these two middle-aged actresses who stood up in the spotlight and *bam*! They were sharp, they were hitting it, and they made their segment pop." A week later at Los Ange-

les's Century Plaza Hotel for the network's off-site retreat, Littlefield, Tartikoff, and other executives tossed around ideas to develop into series for the 1985–86 season. As they recalled Diamond and Roberts's phenomenal performance, suddenly "Miami Nice," the shtick about the ridiculousness of a "retirees in Florida" sitcom, didn't seem so ridiculous anymore.

From that meeting, Littlefield resolved to seriously develop *Miami Nice* as a sitcom for the following season. The timing was right to be daring. Only one season after turning around its comedy fortunes with the 1984 debut of *The Cosby Show*, NBC had nowhere to go but up. And having succeeded by airing *Miami Vice*—even though testing prior to the show's debut had predicted horrendous ratings—the executives were ready to reach outside the 18–49 age group and defy convention one more time. "We felt like lightning had struck us with something," Warren explains. "We would look at those little charts in *USA Today*, and there would be some factoid like 'women over fifty have a one in eleven billion chance of remarrying.' It was always some sad statistic, and it reinforced what we were feeling about 'Miami Nice,' that somehow, these women would be there for each other, and they would take a difficult reality and make a bright picture out of it."

Although Roberts and Diamond were already committed to other NBC series, the network knew they would have no problem casting a show about older women. "We learned a lesson in casting *The Cosby Show*," Warren remembers. "If we could have cloned Bill Cosby, then we could have created five more road companies of that show, because there was just so much talent from black actors who weren't being used on television. And the same thing happened with this show. There was a large pool of wonderful older actresses who weren't doing feature films and television, who were being ignored. And when we saw how similar that situation was to *Cosby*, we knew we were on the right track."

A Gay Among Girls

* * * *

BEFORE RECRUITING A writer for the project, the network decided that *Miami Nice* would center on household life for several women, one of whom owned the house. At least one character would be older, to allow for intergenerational conflict. And there would be one more character, a gay houseboy.

Yes, in 1985—twelve years before Ellen DeGeneres and her character Ellen Morgan's courageous coming out on ABC's sitcom *Ellen*, and thirteen years before NBC's own *Will & Grace*, the first series created with a gay leading man—a major broadcast network commissioned a pilot that was to feature a gay character. "Miami at that time was such a cool, happening place, and a gay character just felt like someone you might find in that environment," Warren explains. "To us, it didn't feel bold or outrageous, but organic. These ladies are probably not on their hands and knees, scrubbing. They've had a lot of years where they'd done all that stuff, so they would hire someone to help out. And we thought the gay houseboy would be a fresh character and a fun contrast to the women."

That all sounds logical—but as we all know, networks don't always stand so tall against homophobia. In fact, just four years earlier at NBC, Tony Randall's Sidney Shorr was to have been network TV's first gay lead in the 1981–83 sitcom *Love, Sidney*, until internal network politics forced a change for the character. In the two-hour telemovie that launched the series, Sidney had been "not openly gay," explains the network's openly gay former Senior Vice President of Talent and Casting Joel Thurm. "But he was a lonely old man who had had a relationship with a man we see in a picture on his mantel, and at one point he goes with Laurie, the young single mother who with her daughter moves in with him, to an old Greta Garbo movie, so it's definitely implied."

When the *Love, Sidney* movie turned out to the development execs' liking, the future looked bright for a Sidney Shorr series. "But then," Joel remembers, "someone at the network, obviously a rabid homophobe who didn't want the project, slipped a copy of the movie to the network's sales department without authorization. And so the sales department came into program meetings and announced that because of the gay content, they couldn't and wouldn't sell it to advertisers as a series. And if the sales department is one hundred percent against a project, that's a very, very strong negative." Eventually, out of desperation as many of its other series failed in the ratings, NBC did resuscitate *Love, Sidney* as a midseason replacement series—but not before turning gay Sidney Shorr into an asexual celibate. And that photo disappeared from the mantel, too.

Julie Poll, a television writer who worked as a production assistant on the series version, remembers NBC's Standards and Practices department—a.k.a., the censors—combing through every word of *Love, Sidney*'s dialogue, eliminating any possible reference to homosexuality. "I'll never forget. Laurie had a perfectly innocent line where she gratefully said to Sidney, who had taken her into his home, 'You're my fairy godmother.' But then the network saw it, and out it went," Julie remembers.

Enter Susan Harris

* * * *

JUST A FEW years later, the proposed "Miami Nice" gay character might have suffered the same de-gayifying fate as Sidney Shorr. But, luckily for the houseboy, Littlefield got the idea through to writer Susan Harris, who had created one of TV's first gay characters, Billy Crystal's Jodie Dallas, on her first big hit comedy series, *Soap*. (Jodie may not have been *the* first regular gay character on American TV, but he was certainly the highest profile to date, since few remember Vincent Schiavelli's Peter Panama on the short-lived 1972–73 CBS sitcom *The Corner Bar*.) But even the hiring of Harris happened by happy accident.

Paul Junger Witt and Tony Thomas—two-thirds of the then-growing TV powerhouse production company Witt/Thomas/Harris—had brought one of their writers in to present a new series idea about two young sisters living together to NBC's Warren Littlefield. Littlefield had been unmoved by the pitch, but, eager to steal away the producers of such hits as *Soap*, *Benson*, and *It's a Living* from rival ABC, he offered an idea of his own: how about you go off and develop "Miami Nice?" The writer—who is probably still kicking himself to this day—was uninterested. But just after seeing their scribe out of Littlefield's office, Witt and Thomas poked their heads back through the executive's doorway. "Were you serious about that idea?" they asked. Because Paul Witt had just the writer in mind.

Although she had sworn off writing for television after burning out during the intense production of *Soap*, Witt's wife and producing partner, Susan Harris, was taken with the "Miami Nice" idea the moment her husband came home with it. "As soon as he used the word 'older,' that got me," Susan remembers. "I love to write old people, because I find that the older the character, the better the stories he or she has to tell. So that was the hook for me—that I could write about an interesting demographic that had really been ignored." Together, Witt, Thomas, and Harris, who had been a creative entity since the days of their first series, *Fay*, starring Lee Grant, for NBC in 1975, brainstormed the structure of the series: three women, a mother—and of course, that gay houseboy.

As Paul remembers, he and Susan Harris were more than happy to accede to the network's request for a homosexual about the house. He notes that he, Susan, and Tony "had all grown up knowing gay people, and felt it was absurd not to see gay people on TV." *Soap* had succumbed to cancellation after only its fourth season because, as Paul explains: "A phantom constituency [of conservatives] managed to convince Madison Avenue that they had more members than they did, and they would boycott." But far from scaring the three producers away from gay characters and storylines, the *Soap* experience had "just made it all the more attractive to do it," Paul reveals. "Not to rub anybody's nose in anything. But we had been approached by more people about *Soap*'s Jodie character because he was the first out gay person they had seen, and he had made them feel much better about themselves." So if there was indeed a risk to bringing another gay character to their new show, "it was a risk we wanted to take."

The Golden Girls

◆ ◆ ◆ ◆

A FEW MONTHS later, Warren Littlefield received delivery of a Susan Harris script, now titled *The Golden Girls*. The new name immediately started to grow on him. After all, the network had been wondering: How can we possibly risk confusing our audience by airing both *Miami Vice* and *Miami Nice*? But "girls"? "I had a moment where I wondered, 'It's the eighties. Can we call grown women girls?'" Warren remembers. "I brought that up to Paul and Tony, and they said, 'Yes, Susan says we can say "girls."' And I said, 'Okay—if she says so.'" And so, in that newly retitled script that NBC read and immediately loved, four Golden Girls named Dorothy Zbornak, Blanche Devereaux, Rose Nylund, and Sophia Petrillo were born.

*"In the beginning, Brandon Tartikoff and the people at NBC all thought,
'Let's not go the tried-and-true way and just give America a bunch of familiar faces.
Let's go to Broadway and Chicago and cast some faces they don't know.'
We thought that was odd, but we did then go out to those cities and see many,
many, women—and nobody was quite right. After all, the stars we ended up bringing
in were stars for a reason. It was just luck that they were all available for a series."*

—TONY THOMAS,

producer

TWO OF THE show's creators, Susan Harris and Paul Junger Witt, remember how these four quite different ladies—Dorothy Zbornak, Blanche Devereaux, Rose Nylund, and Sophia Petrillo—sprang forth from the pilot's pages.

Dorothy Zbornak

♦ ♦ ♦ ♦

RECENTLY DIVORCED FROM Stanley, her philandering husband of thirty-eight years, brainy ex-Brooklynite Dorothy is a no-nonsense substitute schoolteacher. "Dorothy was the easiest character for us to come up with," Susan explains. "Because Paul and I are from the New York metropolitan area. And she had a mouth on her." And, Paul adds, "A sarcastic, cynical voice we could hear fairly early."

Susan says she may have been conscious of the name Dorothy in honor of either Paul's aunt or her own childhood friend. But the origin of the character's unusual last name is much more clear: she cribbed it from her assistant, Kent Zbornak, who later became a producer on the show.

Rose Nylund

♦ ♦ ♦ ♦

A WIDOW FROM the seemingly moronic town of St. Olaf, Minnesota, naïve Rose somehow finds the wisdom to counsel others at a grief center—that is, before beginning an even more unlikely career assisting a consumer reporter at a local TV station. "Rose, too, was a fairly easy character for us to create," Susan remembers. "Because she sounded a lot like Katherine Helmond's character, Jessica Tate, from *Soap*."

Since Rose was to be of Scandinavian heritage, Susan borrowed the last name Nylund from a Swedish woman whom she and Paul had

met sailing the Yugoslavian coast. "Rose was more midwestern than prototypically Scandinavian," she says. "And there are a lot of names like that in the Midwest."

Blanche Devereaux

◆ ◆ ◆ ◆

A GEORGIA PEACH who never fails to remind her roommates that she is still ripe for the plucking, the hypersexual, über-Southern widow, Blanche, is the owner of the house in which the Girls live—all the better to entertain a steady stream of gentleman callers. "Blanche was definitely the hardest character for us," Susan says. "We wanted very distinct characters, and that's why we placed their origins in different parts of the country." Problem was Paul and Susan hailed from New York Yankee territory, and Tony Thomas grew up in Los Angeles. So the trio turned to a reliable source: Southern literature.

"Blanche is almost a literary figure in representing that classic kind of Southern femininity," Paul explains. As Rue McClanahan remembers, Susan's pilot script describes the character as "more Southern than Blanche DuBois," her obvious namesake. "It's an homage," Paul says. "And certainly a way to remember which character was the Southern one."

Sophia Petrillo

◆ ◆ ◆ ◆

AN ESCAPEE FROM the fire-ravaged Shady Pines nursing home, the eightysomething Sophia shows up at daughter Dorothy's door—and because she became so popular with viewing audiences, she never leaves. Sophia shows a tendency toward blunt honesty—caused, we're told, by a stroke that destroyed the tactful part of her brain, yet left her with more than enough mobility to cause trouble.

As former New Yorkers, Paul and Susan say they had grown up with Italian friends and neighbors, and liked the "New York sensibility," as Susan calls it, "either Italian or Jewish." "It's

all very much the same," Paul adds. "Except it's probably less clichéd to show an Italian-American mother/daughter duo than a Jewish one." Of course, this Brooklyn-bred Sicilian mama also knows her way around a knish, and her dialogue captures those cadences as well. She exhibits the best of both worlds because, as the half-Sicilian and half-Lebanese Tony explains, "The funniest rhythms in the world are Semitic. Sophia was Sicilian, but she has a lot of the comedy rhythms I grew up with as well." In naming their pan-Mediterranean creation, Susan turned to her own childhood in Mount Vernon, New York, where the family name Petrillo "is a large part of Mount Vernon history."

Age before Beauty, Brains, and Naïveté

◆ ◆ ◆ ◆

WHEN IT CAME time to find actresses to embody the four ladies, the Witt/Thomas/Harris team, working with casting director Judith Weiner, knew they had plenty of talented—and underemployed—sixtysomething actresses to choose from. And so they focused first on the character they thought would be hardest to find: feisty octogenarian Sophia.

Estelle Getty had been primarily a stage actress in local productions in Queens, New York, a late bloomer who had only recently scored her most noteworthy role playing the mother to Harvey Fierstein's Arnold Beckoff character in the actor/playwright's off-off-Broadway *Torch Song Trilogy*. As she made a name for herself in LA during the show's subsequent West Coast production, Estelle landed some small Hollywood roles, including a blink-and-you'll-miss-it appearance in *Tootsie* (costarring Doris Belack, who played her future TV daughter Gloria) and a larger role in the made-for-TV Western *No Man's Land*. (Picture it: Estelle Getty? In a *Western*?) After the end of *Torch Song*'s 1984 run, Estelle returned to New York. Never believing that true Hollywood stardom would come for her, she made a deal with her manager, Juliet Green, to come back to LA for only two months during the spring of 1985. By the end of that brief trip, Estelle had nailed the role of a lifetime.

Allison Jones, who was at the time working with casting director Judith Weiner, remembers that Estelle had auditioned on February 8, 1985, for the guest role of Michael Gross's visiting mother on NBC's *Family Ties*. Judith had seen Estelle in *Torch Song*, but "it was the first time I'd ever heard of her," Allison remembers. "I even misspelled her name 'Geddys' on the call sheet." Estelle didn't get the part—but Judith remembered admiring her talent when it came time, a few weeks later, to cast her next project.

Although Susan Harris says that she created the character of Sophia Petrillo with no physical type in mind, Juliet and Estelle remember hearing that the *Golden Girls* producers were looking for a "big, fat Italian mama with a bun." As Estelle writes in her 1988 memoir, *If I Knew Then What I Know Now… So What?*, she thought she would be reading for the role of Dorothy, and at just sixty-one, was surprised to be considered for eighty-year-old Sophia. Still, age and ethnic she could do. She had played those things before. She said even "fat I knew I could handle." When she confessed to her TV writer friend Joel Kimmel that she doubted she was right for the part, he encouraged her to "'do what you do best—make 'em laugh,'" Estelle writes. "I would play Sophia my way. I would play her New York Brooklyn."

I'm Older than Dirt

◆ ◆ ◆ ◆

ALLISON JONES REMEMBERS that Estelle had an amazing first Sophia audition for Judith Weiner in late February 1985. "I remember the way she said, 'I'm older than dirt!' with her New York accent. She made it her own, and nailed it to the extent that it was a no-brainer."

Tony Thomas recalls that on the day the producers, who had "read a lot of people

for Sophia," were seeing another group of candidates, Paul and Susan were off working on one of the company's other shows. "Estelle came in to see me, and it was actually frightening. You don't expect to hear the words jump off the page that way. It was like, 'Oh my God, this is everything we wanted!'" He set up a callback for Estelle to come in to see his fellow producers. "I told them if you don't like her, have her do it again. Don't let her out of the room until you're satisfied, because she's the one."

In her book, Estelle remembers that the audition process took over a month. "The producers seemed pleased, but there was also a reservation: they thought I might be too young." Estelle got callback after callback—"I had never auditioned that many times for one role." And each time, she was advised: don't change a thing. "I kept wondering, 'If they don't want me to change anything, then why do they keep asking me back?'" Finally, Juliet got word that Estelle had made it to the final level: reading for the network. What neither woman knew, though, was that by now, Estelle was the only candidate being considered.

It's All about the Right Purse

◆ ◆ ◆ ◆

AS SHE CONTINUED building the character of Sophia Petrillo, Estelle decided she needed some props. "The quintessential bargain shopper," as Juliet admiringly calls her, Estelle scoured the thrift stores of LA's Fairfax District, searching for Sophia-like items: a size 12 polyester dress, lace-up orthopedic shoes, a straw hat with veil, gloves, and above all, a purse. "She was very insistent about finding the right purse," Juliet remembers. And indeed, the one Estelle ended up picking out is the famous straw, top-clasping bag that her character toted around for all of the show's seven seasons. The wardrobe department even ended up having a double made, in case of emergency. "She knew that a woman that

OPPOSITE:

Betty White in *The Mary Tyler Moore Show*, 1975.

Photo courtesy of CBS PHOTO ARCHIVE.

age would have her medicines, her money, her whole life in her purse."

Juliet hired a makeup man to age Estelle's face and spray gray onto her hair. "From the time she walked through the doors at NBC and entered the waiting room, she was in character," Juliet remembers. "She walked in and said hello, and they just fell apart." Warren Littlefield agrees. "When that little woman had those barbs hurling out of her mouth, it was like, 'Excuse me, but I have to run down to the bathroom. I have no bodily control whatsoever.'"

A Rose Is a Rose Is a . . . Blanche?

◆ ◆ ◆ ◆

WITH THEIR SOPHIA in place, the production team concentrated on finding ladies to play her roommates. They ran casting sessions in New York and LA, and as Paul Witt remembers, they "saw a lot of talented actresses. Anyone of a certain age who saw the script wanted to do it."

Bonnie Bartlett, who would ultimately guest star as snooty author Barbara Thorndyke in the third season, was among the many actresses who auditioned. Another, Jo DeWinter, was among those who made it through several rounds of tryouts. Instructed to read for both Rose and Blanche, Jo says she had a unique perspective on how good the pilot's writing was. "I thought, 'This is heaven,'" she remembers. "For the first time in a long time, this was witty material—not just setup/punch line. These were real people."

Eventually, as the producers and network executives narrowed their list, they decided to cast along traditional lines, picking actresses already known for particular qualities. At the time, Betty White was most famous for her recurring 1973–77 appearances on *The Mary Tyler Moore Show* as Minneapolis's homemaker/neighborhood nymphomaniac Sue Ann Nivens. "She had played that part brilliantly on *Mary*," Paul explains. "And so we knew she could play Blanche. We didn't know if she could do the

Southern thing, but we had to assume she could do anything, she's so good."

Rue McClanahan, on the other hand, was best known to TV audiences for meeker roles, such as put-upon second-banana neighbor Vivian Harmon on *Maude* and mousy Aunt Fran on *Mama's Family*. (Having originally been promised a feistier character, Rue was miserable playing a woman so dull, and wanted out; finally, during a long hiatus, Aunt Fran was written out as having choked to death on a toothpick.) The casting team zeroed in on Rue for Rose, realizing, as Paul notes, that even if the role was not as deeply written, "Rue was someone who had always worked well in great ensembles, and always carved out a really unique territory for herself."

Both Betty and Rue had crossed paths with the Witt/Thomas/Harris key players before. Betty knew the *Girls* pilot director Jay Sandrich from their time working together on *The Mary Tyler Moore Show*. Rue had won but turned down *Soap*'s Mary Campbell role, which eventually went to Cathryn Damon; she had her heart set on playing Mary's sister, Jessica Tate, but that part already belonged to Katherine Helmond. Similarly, when Rue told her agent that she loved the *Golden Girls* script and was thrilled to audition for Blanche, she was devastated to hear she would be considered only for Rose. "My agent told me that they had Betty White in mind for the Blanche part, and my heart sank," Rue remembers. "I said, 'How could I go to work every day playing Rose?' because I knew instinctively that I was just too right for Blanche. And she said, 'Well, it's either that, or you don't do the series at all.'"

The Golden Switch

◆ ◆ ◆ ◆

NOT WILLING TO give up on making TV history—"I knew from the moment I opened the envelope and saw *The Golden Girls* written on the cover in cursive typeface that it would be a hit," she claims—Rue acquiesced; she would play Rose. But then, on her first meeting with the pilot's director, *Mary Tyler Moore* and *Soap* veteran Jay Sandrich, something historic happened. After her reading of Rose, "Jay said, 'I'm going to do something unorthodox—would you mind reading Blanche for me?'" Rue remembers. "And I said, 'If you insist.'"

"I had never met Rue," Jay explains. "After she read Rose, I said to her, 'You're really wonderful—but I don't for one second believe you're innocent.'"

A few days later, when Rue and Betty came in to read for the director together, Jay had the same surprise for Betty; knowing from the *Mary Tyler Moore Show* that "she can get a laugh doing anything," he asked her to read for Rose. "Betty had had no inkling," Rue says. "And then her eyes widened and she said, 'Rose?'"

Betty remembers how Jay broke the news to her; he felt that if she were to play another nymphomaniac, the audience was going to think it was Sue Ann all over again. Susan Harris told Betty that Rose was actually her favorite character—which Betty suspected just be a ploy to bring her around. "But then the more I looked at Rose, the more I was okay with it," she explains. "And I give Jay Sandrich full credit for helping me make it work. He said Rose doesn't have a sarcastic bone in her body, that she isn't witty or hip at all. She takes every single word literally and puts them all together and it makes perfect sense for her. And when he said that, it made sense for me."

And so, the qualities that had originally gotten each actress in the door were now thrown out the window. Rue was to be mousy no more, and Betty was to take a break from the man baiting. "Betty was hysterical as Rose," Rue says. "Her eyes went wide and stayed that way for seven years. I used to call them her Little Orphan Annie eyes—white ovals with nothing in them. The irony is that she's such an incredibly brilliant woman."

"And Rue took Blanche and went with her where I never would have had the guts to go," Betty adds. "So it just worked out beautifully."

A Bea Arthur Type

$\bullet \ \bullet \ \bullet \ \bullet$

THE LAST OF the women left to cast was Dorothy, ostensibly the lead role. Susan had created the character with only one person in mind. She had even described the character in the pilot script as "a Bea Arthur type." The problem was Bea wasn't interested.

Susan, who had worked with Bea on *Maude*—in fact, she wrote that series' most famous episode, "Maude's Abortion"—and on *Soap*, where Bea played God in a fourth-season episode, had her heart set. But with the actress refusing the role, the team was forced to move on. So NBC's Senior Vice President of Talent and Casting, Joel Thurm, suggested a Broadway favorite. As Joel recalls, "I said to Brandon Tartikoff, 'There's one other woman who I think would be very good for this. And she has a lot of the same rough edges, and she's new. No one has seen her on television, other than a British series she did for a while. Her name is Elaine Stritch.'"

Brandon Tartikoff and Judith Weiner both agreed that auditioning Elaine would be a good idea. But only after striking a "test deal" with Stritch's agent and arranging her plane ticket and hotel room, bringing her in and auditioning her, did Tartikoff fully understand just how stuck Susan was on Bea. And only Bea.

Joel's large NBC office, where Elaine's audition took place, sat sixteen people around an L-shaped couch. "And on a good day, the vibes for an actor, looking at all those faces, could be horrendous," he explains. "But that day, because Susan and Paul and Tony and some other people had the agenda in mind of accepting only Bea, the room was ice-cold. Add to that, of the NBC people, not everybody knew who Elaine Stritch was. Then when she started to read, she was really nervous and she had a couple of mis-starts. Then her reading started out okay, but it got zero reaction. So what happens to a performer when there's no reaction in the room? She starts getting bigger and bigger. It ended up being a disaster."

It was then, in that room, that Susan Harris revealed that she had written the part expressly for Bea. But never mind Bea's feelings about the role— NBC didn't want her anyway. Brandon Tartikoff worried that Bea's "Q" scores, which track a performer's standing among audience members, were exceedingly low. Undoubtedly because of *Maude*'s unabashed liberalism and TV abortion, "of those who knew her, only twenty percent liked her." For weeks, all through the development phases of *The Golden Girls*, Tartikoff had been adamant: no Bea Arthur. But now that the Elaine Stritch plan had fizzled, there was no plan B.

Finally, as the discussion became heated, Susan and Paul began to make headway with the network president. They argued that unlike *Maude*, *The Golden Girls* would be an ensemble piece. The show would not rest solely on Bea's shoulders, and thus she could win over anyone Maude Findlay had possibly alienated. Finally, the network chief gave in.

Maude and Vivian, Meet Sue Ann Nivens

◆ ◆ ◆ ◆

EVEN WITH NBC on board, Susan Harris still had to convince the actress to accept the part. So she prevailed upon Bea's former cast mate Rue McClanahan to put the pressure on. And so Rue called Bea. "And I said, 'Why on earth are you turning down the best script that's ever going to come across your desk as long as you live?'" Rue says. "And she said, 'Rue, I have no interest in playing Maude and Vivian meet Sue Ann Nivens.' I said, 'That's not the way we're going to play it, Bea. I'm going to play the Sue Ann Nivens vamp, and Betty's going to play the Vivian role.' And Bea took a beat and said, 'Now *that* is very interesting.'" And with that, the team was set. "Next thing you know, the four of us, including Estelle,

came in to read for the suits at NBC," Rue remembers. "And we laid them low. And *that's* the way they cast it."

For her part, Bea doesn't remember hesitating; she says she simply must have been the last person in town to get her hands on the pilot script. "I got a phone call from my agent, who said, 'What's this I hear about you doing a new show?' I told him I had no idea what he was talking about, and he said there was a new show I was cast in," Bea remembers. "I told him I know nothing about it, and nobody is calling me. A few days after, I did get a script, and found out that everybody in the country had auditioned for a part described as 'a Bea Arthur type.'"

Bea's contract paperwork was rushed to her house just in time on that Good Friday, April 5. The cast began rehearsals the following Monday, April 8. There was now no time to lose in fleshing out Susan Harris's leading ladies; nine days later, on Wednesday, April 17, 1985, *The Golden Girls* pilot was scheduled to be videotaped at Sunset Gower Studios in front of a live studio audience.

ABOVE:
Bea Arthur and Rue McClanahan in *Maude*, 1975.
Photo courtesy of CBS PHOTO ARCHIVE.

Casting Coco

◆ ◆ ◆ ◆

BUT THERE WAS still one more character yet to be cast—the gay houseboy, Coco, named after Susan Harris's dog.

Golden Girls casting associate Allison Jones notes that the candidates for Coco ranged all over the Kinsey Scale, including her friend Dom Irrera and another Italian American comic actor, Paul Provenza—both of whom, in real life, display far more hetero swagger than swish.

Early on, the producers began eyeing Jeffrey Jones, who had recently played a young, gay Brit in Caryl Churchill's play *Cloud Nine*, an effete emperor in the 1984 film *Amadeus*, and was generating buzz for his soon-to-be-infamous role as Principal Rooney in 1986's *Ferris Bueller's Day Off*. But as he remembers, Jeffrey spoiled his chances himself.

"I wasn't concerned about playing another gay character," Jeffrey explains. "But I didn't think this character was very realistic, but more cheap. Obvious and jokey. When I went in to read, they asked what I thought, and I naively told them: I thought that Coco brought the show in the wrong direction, away from the women. He didn't fit with the interplay of the characters and so he just seemed unnecessary. I guess I talked myself out of a job."

Although both Susan Harris and Allison Jones say there had never been a particular "type" at all in mind for Coco, both Paul Provenza and Jeffrey Jones recall being told that the casting team was thinking of Coco as a drag queen. "But they wanted an actor doing drag, not a drag queen trying to act," Paul recalls. "Still, they weren't sure an actor could really commit to being a drag queen. I said, 'Let me think about it and let you know.' With a plan in mind, Paul was referred through a mutual friend to actress/writer Hillary Carlip, who was then the lead singer of the band Angel and the Reruns. "Her entire garage was filled with costumes," Paul remembers. "So I went to her house and picked out something I thought would work. Hillary decked me out, and

a friend of ours did makeup. Rather than coming off like a big, flamboyant drag queen, I chose to look like a guy who's trying to pass for a nice, average, Beverly Hills–esque woman."

Never having done drag before, Paul showed up on the studio lot for his audition "and was having the damnedest time in those fucking heels." But his look was convincing—maybe too convincing. "On the way back to my car, I got hit on by the lot's security guard, who said, 'I've never seen you around here before. You must be new in town,' which I thought was really funny. So I didn't get the part, but I did have a fun time doing the audition."

Paul Witt remembers that the search for Coco became harder than the producers had imagined. "We wanted an actor who could play gay life with dignity," he explains. "That's very tricky." And, again at odds with Jones and Provenza's memories, Paul explains, "We didn't want to get laughs out of outrageous, campy stuff." When it came to finding the actor who could deliver all that, he says, demographics didn't matter. "It never occurred to us to cast a straight guy versus a gay guy. We just knew that we wanted the character to integrate in a way that he would be part of this family."

Enter Charles Levin

◆ ◆ ◆ ◆

IT WAS NBC president Brandon Tartikoff who suggested Charles Levin, who had three years earlier begun a groundbreaking recurring gay role on *Hill Street Blues*. Charles's character, Eddie Gregg, was a flamboyant men's room hustler who formed an unlikely soul-matching friendship with Bruce Weitz's detective Belker.

Charles remembers that when he first met with the *Golden Girls* pilot's Jay Sandrich, he was surprised at the director's resistance to the same gay affectations that had worked so well in the Eddie role. "Jay told me, 'I don't want you coming in here, doing a lisp or mincing around,'" Charles remembers. "He did not want the character to be flamboyant at all—just a regular guy who was gay. The trouble was, that wasn't what was written on the page. Susan Harris had written that he was a 'fancy man' [as Sophia still calls him in the pilot to this day]. And his lines were outrageous, hilarious, and way over the top."

Charles was unnerved, but he tried to follow Jay's direction. "But it really threw a wrench into my plans," he says. "I didn't feel comfortable just coming in and 'playing it straight.' I needed that mask of whatever I chose to do to portray a gay person." When he had his big reading in Brandon's office, Charles read the lines as Jay had specified. "And there wasn't a peep in the house. They looked at me like, 'What

the hell are you doing? This isn't funny.' And they said, dismissively, 'Thank you very much.'"

Charles left the audition convinced that he had blown it—and angry with Jay Sandrich for his bad advice. "They had chosen me based on a prior character, and Jay wouldn't let me play anything like that character," he remembers. Later that night, Charles got a call at home from NBC's VP of casting, Joel Thurm. "He said, 'We don't know what you were doing, but would you please come back tomorrow and just play Eddie Gregg?' So the next day I went back and did Eddie Gregg. And with the first word out of my mouth, these people were in stitches … And I got hired right then and there."

BEING A FRIEND

A CONVERSATION WITH . . . ELAINE STRITCH

(1925–2014)

I'M NEVER IMPRESSED with sitcoms. They're not my kind of thing. I don't think my humor fits sitcoms, either. But I went out to LA and auditioned for *The Golden Girls*, and in my one-woman show *Elaine Stritch at Liberty* I told the story what the meeting was like.

I met a room full of people who were just stonewalled against me, and it was terrifying and not pleasant. Before I started to read, I tried to explain that there was some of the dialogue that didn't sit comfortably with me. And I said, "If you don't mind, I'd like to change a few things." And Susan Harris said, "Hopefully just the punctuation." And I thought, "I'm up against something here." Well, her answer didn't sit well with me, and I guess the devil came up in me. So I said, "For example, on page seven where Dorothy says, 'Don't forget the hors d'oeuvres,' do you mind if I say 'the *fucking* hors d'oeuvres?'" Well, that made her mad.

The whole thing didn't go down very well, and I was very nervous. Cut to the chase, it was so the right thing to happen. *The Golden Girls* and I did not fit. First of all, the idea really didn't appeal to me at all—three broads living together in Florida? What could be less exciting? But in retrospect, I do think the show turned out excellent—and it's amazing the life it's had. And I'm so glad it happened to Bea, making her life certainly a lot more luxurious. But I think if I'd have gotten the part and been stuck out there in LA, doing a sitcom for seven years, I might never have sobered up.

I think we can all look back in retrospect and realize that most things that happen to us happen because they're meant to. So we have to accept them one day at a time. And I get a lot of mileage from this story in my show because *The Golden Girls* is such a popular thing, and I treat my own hurt feelings about it with humor. I get laughs in the theater, and so the whole experience has served its purpose and given me what I needed—a good piece of writing in my show coming out of a very bad experience.

3

CURTAINS UP

*"Normally with new shows, they take only a few minutes' worth of clips
to show the advertisers each May. But with* The Golden Girls, *they decided
to show the whole pilot. And from what I've been told, the audience in the
grand ballroom at the Waldorf Astoria hotel laughed so loud that they ended up
missing some of the lines. Five minutes after it finished, my phone rang,
and it was my friend Grant Tinker, who was then at NBC. He said,
'Betty, don't make any plans for the next couple of years.
I think you're going to be very busy.'"*

—BETTY WHITE

ON THE NIGHT of April 17, 1985, as *The Golden Girls* was taping its pilot episode, it was immediately evident to all that a potential classic—and certainly a show with long-term potential—was being born.

The producers had known even earlier that they were on to something special. From the first time the pilot script was read aloud around a rehearsal table, Paul Witt says that "everyone there, from the performers to the craft service guy to the network to us knew it was a home run."

The Witt/Thomas/Harris sitcom methodology, developed over the decade-long span of shows like *Fay, Soap,* and *Benson,* called for two tapings of any given episode, in front of two separate live audiences. The first show, referred to as the "dress show," was used to work out any kinks; if something fell flat, it could be rewritten during dinner, where the

cast could be given new lines to perform at the "air show" later that evening. As such, *The Golden Girls* pilot was actually taped twice, in front of two different audiences. And both audiences went wild for it.

Jay Sandrich remembers the huge laughter that night when, as the actresses had cooked up onstage that week, Dorothy put Rose in a choke hold to keep her from blabbing to Blanche about the true nature of her intended husband. And there was an even bigger explosion when Sophia summed up the situation with a simple: "The man is a douchebag!" (an epithet that had to be reshot as "scuzzball" before NBC's censors would allow it.)

The show's producers were not surprised at the reaction. According to Jay, Estelle had been getting such big laughs from the start that she inspired a change to the structure of the show; now, instead of Sophia living at Shady Pines,

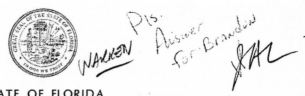

STATE OF FLORIDA

OFFICE OF GOVERNOR BOB GRAHAM

April 29, 1985

Mr. Brandon Tartikoff
President
NBC Entertainment Network
3000 West Alameda
Burbank, California 91523

Dear Mr. Tartikoff:

I read with interest an article in the Miami Herald regarding your new series entitled "Miami Nice."

This is exciting news, and I invite you to contact the Motion Picture and Television Bureau in our Department of Commerce. There are many advantages to originating and filming the series in Miami, and they are eager to share them with you.

Ample studio space, in addition to the Ivan Tors Studios where "Miami Vice" is filming presently, exists in Miami. Limelight Studios is new and quite large and available. Miami also boasts a fine film processing lab which most of the majors have used and found to be on a par with labs in Los Angeles.

There are many more reasons for filming in exciting Miami, including dinner at Joe's Stone Crab Restaurant, which is an experience in itself. Laura Kitzmiller of the Motion Picture and Television Bureau will be happy to provide details about the availability of state-of-the-art equipment and support service. She will also share names and phone numbers of producers who have used Florida's crews and locations successfully. She can be contacted at Bureau of Motion Picture and Television, Department of Commerce, Collins Building, Tallahassee, Florida 32301, telephone number 904/487-1100.

Thank you for your interest in our State and City of Miami. Please contact me if we can be of any assistance now or in the future.

With warm regards,

Sincerely,

Governor

BG/rgf

and making only recurring appearances, she would be a regular character, living with the three girls after Shady Pines burns down. Sophia was now a full member of the family.

Good-bye, Coco

• • • •

AS FORTUITOUS AS Sophia's promotion was for Estelle, it ultimately spelled curtains for Coco. As Charles Levin remembers of the pilot taping, "old pros" Rue, Betty, and Bea brought down the house. But when Estelle, the one unknown, came in, "They didn't know what to make of her, and they fell in love with her." That night, not only did Estelle Getty hold her own against these three television heavyweights, but also "she sandbagged everybody. During the rehearsal, she was insecure. But like the true stage pro she is, when the lights went up, Estelle was on fire. The woman couldn't miss, and everybody saw it. It wasn't, 'Did you see what Estelle did?' It was, 'Oh my God, Estelle is stealing the show out from under three real comic pros.'"

Meanwhile, the pilot's audience had gone cuckoo for Coco, too. As Charles explains, "They'd never seen a character like him. They'd seen characters flirt with being gay or hint at it. But this guy, as soon as he opened his mouth, was way out there. So far out there, they found it hilarious and endearing." But with four other characters also getting big laughs, the house was getting a little too crowded.

All week, as the actors prepared for the taping, Charles remembers Estelle's lack of confidence. "She and I gravitated toward one another because we were the lesser knowns," he recalls. "She was certain she was going to be fired. She said, 'If it's between you and me, Chuck, you're obviously staying. I'm gone.' I didn't see it that way, and rehearsals were going so well, I didn't have those worries."

But after the taping, when the supposedly twenty-

three-ish-minute pilot clocked in at over twenty-eight, some painful cuts had to be made. "Everybody lost stuff," Paul Witt explains. And although it might be tempting to wonder whether, in the height of the AIDS panic in 1985, Coco might have been cut to appease an already *Love, Sidney*–scarred NBC, everyone insists he was eliminated for purely artistic and practical reasons.

"It really came down to that there wasn't enough room in a half hour," Paul explains. "Charles Levin was a terrific actor, and was terrific in the part, but we had too much." As Susan Harris adds, "We couldn't possibly service all five regular characters adequately. It would have been unfair." Perhaps seeing Jeffrey Jones's earlier point about Coco's storylines being somewhat off topic, the producers decided to whittle the show down to its very core—the relationships among just the four women.

In justifying the painful decision, the team admitted that maybe it wasn't a good idea anyway to have someone working for the Girls; without some housework to busy themselves with, all the actresses would be doing was sitting. And for a show about the struggles of older women living together, partly out of economic need, a live-in houseboy might suggest that they were too well-off. "We wanted people to identify with them," Susan says. "We needed the element of struggle so that the audience would worry about them."

Warren Littlefield says that far from being worried about any backlash due to airing a show with a gay character, he was actually a little reluctant to let Coco go, but he eventually yielded to Paul Witt's logic. And so, through the use of some pickup shots filmed later and additional looped dialogue, *The Golden Girls'* gay houseboy was excised from as many pilot scenes as possible. And because this was the era before "TV on DVD" gift sets, with their lost scenes presented as "extras," most of Levin's work fell forever to the cutting room floor.

OPPOSITE:

As production ramped up for the much-buzzed-about new series, Florida governor Bob Graham made a pitch for the *Girls* to film on location in the Sunshine State.

Photo courtesy of LEX PASSARIS.

*"Back then, Saturday was a night where no one was dominating.
So the way that Brandon looked at it was that we could dominate if we found the
right shows. He thought that the reason the HUT [households using television]
level was down on Saturday was because nothing good was on."*

—GARTH ANCIER,
former head of current comedy at NBC:

Saturday Night Dead

◆ ◆ ◆ ◆

ON ITS SEPTEMBER 14, 1985 debut, *The Golden Girls* earned golden ratings—and did so on a night where successful sitcoms have been rarer than platinum. Although Saturday night had once been home to CBS's classic 1970s comedies—*The Mary Tyler Moore Show*, *The Bob Newhart Show*, *All in the Family*, and *The Carol Burnett Show*—the powerhouse programs had since been shifted to shore up the network's other flagging nights. By 1985, Saturday had been all but abandoned. So when they heard that their promising new show was to air Saturdays at 9:00 p.m., the producers of *The Golden Girls* feared the worst.

But NBC had research to justify the bold decision. After all, the show's presumed target audience—the older set—is often the only group home during prime weekend partying hours. Through testing, the network had learned something else: beyond anyone's prediction, the pilot showed just as much appeal to just about all other age groups, too, including young adults, teens—even kids. Test audiences predicted that *The Golden Girls* would be an across-the-board hit. And with a hit early enough on Saturday night, NBC could draw people over fifty as they settled in for the night with the kids and grandkids, as well as those between eighteen and forty-nine before they decided which movie to rent or club to attend. And hopefully, the network could keep them around through the 1:00 a.m. end of *Saturday Night Live*.

Premiering just before the rise of cable TV, *The Golden Girls* became one of the last of the old-school broadcast network hits. With little Saturday night competition, the Girls routinely drew a thirty-plus "share," meaning that 30 percent or more of the television-viewing audience was tuned in to the show; producers of today's shows are ecstatic if they draw a share in the double digits. In all parts of the United States— red states and blue—*The Golden Girls* was a watercooler hit, unifying people of varying demographics and geographics if only for a half hour every Saturday.

Golden Appeal: Why People Love The Golden Girls

♦ ♦ ♦ ♦

EVER SINCE *THE* Golden Girls went off the air in 1992, Saturday night has been abandoned again. The broadcast networks have once again hung the GONE FISHIN' sign, airing no original scripted programming. But for so many of us who remember the show fondly today, *The Golden Girls* ushered in a comedy tradition, a comfortable world of funny grandmas and cheesecake to snuggle into on a Saturday night. Harkening back to the wholesome early days of TV, here was a show about grandparents you could watch *with* your grandparents. It aired on a night when bedtimes were relaxed and extended families might be together. It was witty enough for adults, while research showed that kids related to brash little Sophia.

For generations X and Y, Blanche, Dorothy, Rose, and Sophia became regular babysitters, seeing kids and young teens through Saturday nights at home while parents and older siblings might be out on dates; thirty years later for those grown-up kids, reruns on cable carry an air of nostalgia. For older viewers, *The Golden Girls* was the rare network show centered on relatable women "of a certain age," bringing dignity and visibility to an otherwise-ignored bracket.

And right from its start, *The Golden Girls* was a watershed show for the LGBT community as well. Just as gay people often build surrogate families of their friends, the Girls choose to be together, even to the point of eschewing contact with their biological relatives. Instead of hang-

> *"I feel that* The Golden Girls *is the granddaddy—or grandmammy—of all female ensemble shows, and that's because of the purity with which Susan created it. She took the three qualities that make up human beings and devised a character around each, of course with additional flourishes. If you consider Sophia off to the side and look at the other three, Dorothy is the intellectual, Rose the emotional, and Blanche the physical. It was so beautifully constructed that their points of view were always so different. And you knew how they were going to react in any given situation."*
>
> —MARC CHERRY, writer

ing out with kids who would treat them like helpless old ladies, they've built the fantasy family any fan would yearn for, founded on the acceptance for which so many gay and lesbian viewers yearn.

But the big draw for viewers of all ages was always the show's impeccable writing. Working from a template designed by the revered Susan Harris, the show deftly managed a delicate balance of compelling, moving storytelling with razor-sharp jokes. As the only show on the air with such mature leads, *The Golden Girls* had the advantage of "owning" certain subject areas—and it mined them brilliantly for every vein of their inherent humor. What other show could bring four old ladies to a nudist colony— and wring a laugh out of their every cringe? Or have them arrested as Miami's unlikeliest hookers? As it packed on the clever wordplay and double entendre, *The Golden Girls* far surpassed the IQ level of its 1980s peers and enticed veteran comedy writers and talented newcomers to join its writing staff. By the end of its run, the show had become a training ground for some of today's hottest writer/creators, including Mitchell Hurwitz of *Arrested Development*, Marc Cherry of *Desperate Housewives* and *Devious*

Maids, and Christopher Lloyd, one of the executive producers of *Frasier* and co-creator of *Modern Family*.

The Power of Four

◆ ◆ ◆ ◆

THE GOLDEN GIRLS defined a generation's view of older women, and single-handedly resurrected comedy during prime time on Saturday night. But perhaps the show's most lasting innovation is the comedy formula it pioneered. Call it the Golden Rule of Four.

"Four points on a compass," as Betty White aptly describes them, the characters of Dorothy, Blanche, Rose, and Sophia match up to four classic comedic types: respectively, the Brain, the Slut, the Ditz, and the Big Mouth. Comedy duos are a classic tradition, but a completely different animal. And while it's certainly true that three women can work, especially in film — think *9 to 5* — having three lead characters in a sitcom might leave one character having to carry the B plot on her own.

But four leaves us with infinite possibilities. Rose takes Dorothy's night-school class in order to earn her diploma, while Blanche and Sophia compete for a suave Latin lover. Or Blanche and Rose try out for the road show of *Cats* while Dorothy tries to prove that her mother is faking her injury.

Having popularized the Golden Rule of Four,[1] *The Golden Girls* is the thematic ancestor of many shows that followed. Only one year after the *Girls'* premiere, along came the Southern version (*Designing Women*), followed in the 1990s by the black version (*Living Single*) and the urban version (*Sex and the City*). In recent years, the formula has shown a resurgence in popularity, spawning a suburban version (*Desperate Housewives*), a middle-aged version (*Hot in Cleveland*), a Latina version (*Devious Maids*),

and, inevitably, more than one gay version (*Noah's Arc* and *Looking*).

In *Designing Women*, which launched in 1986, vain Southern beauty queen Suzanne Sugarbaker would certainly sense sisterhood with Blanche. And apart from the difference in accents, Charlene Frazier's hometown of Poplar Bluff, Missouri, could easily be mistaken for Rose's birthplace of St. Olaf, Minnesota. Suzanne's older sister, Julia, is clearly the Dorothy of the group — smart, opinionated, and prone to speak her mind. Only Annie Potts's character of Mary Jo Shively is no easy match to a Golden Girl, perhaps because at the start, Mary Jo was the show's least defined character. Over seven seasons, Mary Jo grew from a sheltered, naïve Rose-type into essentially a mini Julia, another Dorothy. So it's no surprise that after his initial appearance in an early first-season episode (and also after actor Meshach Taylor's small role in the *Golden Girls* pilot), *Designing Women* quickly promoted African-American delivery man Anthony Bouvier to regular status; like Sophia, he provides needed commentary from an outsider's perspective (this time due to race and gender rather than age).

"There were so many pop culture references in The Golden Girls *— and when you look back, many of them don't hold up. But that also gave the writers opportunity to constantly be dogging* Designing Women, *putting in jokes to bash that show. I remember one example, from the fourth season, in the episode 'Stan Takes a Wife.' As Sophia is in a hospital bed, recovering from pneumonia, she tells the Girls, 'I survived war, disease — and two seasons of* Designing Women*!'"*

— RICK COPP, writer

---

[1] It's unclear whether we should credit the 1979–88 NBC sitcom *The Facts of Life* as a pre-*Golden Girls* inventor of the Rule of Four. Set at the fictional Eastland Academy in Peekskill, New York, the show originally centered on a larger group of young girls, and did not pare its cast down to just four — plus older house mother Mrs. Garrett (Charlotte Rae) — until its second season, beginning in 1980.

Starting in 1993 on Fox, *Living Single* was almost a direct copy of *The Golden Girls*—and in fact, as *Golden Girls* writer Kevin Abbott explains, the show's creator, Yvette Lee Bowser, even asked him for a copy of the *Golden Girls* pilot script to use as a template. *Living Single*'s characters of Khadijah and Synclaire James and Regine Hunter fit perfectly into the molds established by Dorothy, Rose, and Blanche, respectively. Again, only the Sophia role seems hard to fill, perhaps because when creating a show about young black women, there's no obvious parallel for an old lady. But Erika Alexander's character, Maxine Shaw, comes pretty close; in her flirtatious banter with upstairs neighbor Kyle, she can be the most outrageous and outspoken of the four friends.

In HBO's hit *Sex and the City*, it's obvious which of the characters is "the slut" and which one is a little bit naïve. And while both Miranda Hobbes and Carrie Bradshaw have moments of Dorothy-like cynicism, it's Miranda who is the true master of the form. Although not a perfect fit in the Sophia role, obviously younger and sexier Carrie does share some of the old woman's characteristics; in diner scenes (the show's equivalent of cheesecake scenes) Carrie is often the character to sum up the situation, even at her friends' expense. And just as Sophia recaps her roommates' problems with pithy one-liners, Carrie literally narrates the travails of her friends, typing them on her laptop screen.

Inevitably, in 2005 came the first gay take on the formula, Logo's *Noah's Arc*. "I didn't set out to make a *Golden Girls*," says the show's creator, Patrik-Ian Polk. For one thing, instead of a multicamera sitcom about women, *Noah's Arc* was a single-camera, serialized drama about men. "But I did want to do a show about four black gay men, and so there are obvious parallels" to the Girls with his characters: sweet, naïve Noah, sexually voracious Ricky, sarcastic Chance, and outrageous Alex. "There were times when we'd have a funnier scene coming up with the four guys together, and I would say to them, 'Think of

this as a real *Golden Girls*–type scene.' And they'd immediately get it."

In 1990, during the *Golden Girls'* run, one of the show's writer/producers, Gail Parent, landed her co-creation *Babes* at Fox; but the sitcom about three overweight sisters and their elderly neighbor in a Manhattan apartment building was canceled after a single season. Ultimately it would be Gail's fellow *Golden Girls* writer Marc Cherry who would find the greatest success by tapping into the power of the Rule of Four. Having tinkered with the formula in 1994 by creating *The Five Mrs. Buchanans* for CBS, Marc brought *Desperate Housewives* to ABC a decade later, while acknowledging his debt to the four ladies from Miami. "Blanche was my favorite character to write for," he remembers. "Because the character was so selfish and vain and self-obsessed, and yet you still liked her." Marc admits, "There were a lot of traces of Blanche Devereaux in Gabrielle Solis. It's totally a credit to the actor. Like Rue McClanahan, Eva Longoria is one of those actors who is able to be likable when she is doing some unlikable things."

Otherwise, though, Marc says that although his training comes from *The Golden Girls*, the construction of *Desperate Housewives* was more akin to that of one of its older siblings under the Golden Rule of Four, *Sex and the City*. Thus, his Lynette Scavo equaled Miranda, Bree Van De Kamp was Charlotte, and lead character Susan Mayer was akin to lead character Carrie. In creating Susan, "I chose to make the romantic character the show's anchor instead of the common-sense one, as was done on *The Golden Girls*," Marc explains. "Susan Harris's paradigm was so successful—and indeed, Linda Bloodworth-Thomason copied it on *Designing Women*—that I just chose to emulate something else."

In 2013, Marc gave the formula yet another twist in creating his follow-up series, *Devious Maids*. It's easy to see parallels to Rose in naïve, good-hearted Rosie, and to Blanche in sexy and self-centered Carmen. And while the educated, intellectual Marisol has obvious similarities to

Dorothy, Marc points out that "the tart-tongued part of Dorothy you will find in Zoila's mouth." In creating his *Devious* characters, he says, "I kind of took Dorothy and split her up."

As Marc explains, "due to her youth and inexperience" there's no obvious singular *Golden* antecedent for *Devious'* fifth maid, Valentina; she has the naïveté of Rose, she's a daughter like Dorothy, and as one set apart by age, she could even be seen as a twenty-first-century Sophia. But Marc does acknowledge the Girls as an influence when he was conceiving the character. In speaking with real domestic workers in Beverly Hills, he reveals, "I discovered that it was not uncommon for there to be two members of one family working in a home. And because I remembered the mileage we always got from having Sophia and Dorothy in the same household, I knew how effective it would be to again have a mother/daughter connection in this new female ensemble show."

By 2012, viewers were ready for a foursome from a whole new generation, and HBO's *Girls* was born. Although the show's creator and star, Lena Dunham, didn't base her *Girls* directly on the Girls from Miami, she does see at least one obvious parallel: "I think we can all agree that [Jessa] is Blanche." As the show's executive producer Bruce Eric Kaplan further explains, Lena's creations do descend from Sophia, Dorothy, Rose, and Blanche—albeit indirectly. Addressing head-on the inevitable comparisons to its HBO ancestor *Sex and the City*, *Girls'* pilot featured not only a discussion of Carrie and company, but also a poster of the iconic nineties series on Shoshanna's bedroom wall. "We have a very clear connection to *Sex and the City*," Bruce explains. "*Girls* is an update of *Sex and the City*, much as *Sex and the City* was so clearly a modernist version of *The Golden Girls*. So I guess *Girls'* link to *The Golden Girls* is sort of transitive." Thus, he adds, *Girls* lead character Hannah Horvath may be more direct a legacy of her more immediate predecessor Carrie Bradshaw than she is of Dorothy or Sophia. But he agrees the connection is there.

Most recently, HBO debuted another fab foursome with *Looking*, a San Francisco–set comedy about the lives of three gay men and their straight female BFF. One of the show's producers, John Hoffman, explains that he and his fellow writers were so conscious from the start of their LGBT target audience's love of the Girls that as they initially brainstormed potential titles for the series, he suggested *Golden Sons*.

The proposed title didn't fly, but *Looking*'s 2014 debut season still ended up being book-ended by *Golden Girls* references. As the show was in mid-shoot of its second episode, its British-born writer/producer/director Andrew Haigh suggested a last-minute script change, replacing lead character Patrick's reference to *Friends'* Ross and Rachel with a recitation of the lyrics to the *Golden Girls* theme. As Andrew reveals, after each long day of shooting on location, he had gotten in the habit of unwinding in his San Francisco hotel room by watching *The Golden Girls*. And so was born what would become the series' running joke, which paid off in the waning moments of the first season's finale as Patrick climbed into Agustín's bed with his laptop, recommitting to their roommate tradition of watching the Girls together.

As the episode faded with "Thank You for Being a Friend" over its closing credits, it was an appropriate season ending for a series about a friendly foursome—particularly one that has obvious parallels in terms of its characters: naïve Patrick to Rose, caustic Agustín to Dorothy, and sexually charged Dom to Blanche. As the group's only female, Doris stands out as its quippy Sophia—although "for the record," notes *Looking*'s creator/writer, Michael Lannan, "our Sophia is actually our costume designer, Danny Glicker."

GOLDEN GIRLS:
THE NEXT GENERATION

"At tapings of Hot in Cleveland, *during breaks between scenes,
our warm-up comedian, Michael Burger, would often play different TV theme
songs for the studio audience. When the* Golden Girls *theme would come on,
everybody would go crazy. And even though I would usually be backstage,
that song would pull me out in front of the crowd like a magnet."*

—BETTY WHITE

IN THE SPRING of 2010, TV Land, previously known as a home for reruns of TV classics, decided to get into the business of original programming. And for a cable network looking to make a splash in sitcoms, what better show to emulate than a certain generation-spanning megahit?

The network's first and so far most successful original comedy, *Hot in Cleveland*, was the story of three aging Angelenas who decide to move to Ohio after finding they were considered more attractive in the Rust Belt, and their new house's cantankerous nonagenarian caretaker. That last role, not so accidentally, was played by Betty White. "When I was first thinking about *Hot in Cleveland*, I actually was thinking about [*The Golden Girls* and] what those women [would be like] today," says the show's creator, Suzanne Martin. "The two shows certainly did have a lot in common."

Just as had the Girls, *Hot in Cleveland*'s four leading ladies comprised a supergroup of TV comedy, with each actress already iconic from a previous TV role. And *Cleveland*'s twenty-first-century foursome hewed to the *Golden* formula so unabashedly that early on the show's stars sat down to discuss exactly who compared to whom.

"We've been trying to figure it out," admitted Valerie Bertinelli, who played *Cleveland*'s trusting and optimistic self-help writer Melanie Moretti. "I do know that I'm probably Rose." Jane Leeves, too, had a strong viewpoint about her character, the sardonic, unlucky-at-love eyebrow stylist turned private eye Joy Scroggs: "I'm definitely the Dorothy."

Meanwhile, the former Rose, Betty White, graduated into *Cleveland*'s Sophia-like part; her character, the cranky but wise Polish-born Elka Ostrovsky, was supplied not only with the wisdom that comes with age but with the show's most devastating one-liners. But, as Betty's costar Wendie Malick pointed out, Elka had a strain of Dorothy in her, too. Unlike with the oft-confused Sophia, with Elka, "Nothing gets past her."

Wendie admitted that her character, egocentric actress Victoria Chase, was probably *Cleveland*'s Blanche. "Although I think you might have to split Dorothy in half, giving some of her sarcasm to Joy and some to Victoria.

"Besides," Wendie added, "Victoria didn't sleep around as much as Joy did," which was, not so coincidentally, the same type of defense Rue McClanahan used to offer for Blanche.

Hot in Cleveland was not shy about paying homage to its *Golden* ancestor, both on- and offscreen. In March 2014, in the show's live fifth-season premiere, the star of *Cleveland*'s spin-off *The Soul Man*, Cedric the Entertainer, crossed over to *Cleveland* as his character Reverend Boyce. After Elka delivered a jab about Steve Harvey being the funniest of the Kings of Comedy, Boyce came back with a retort: "Oh, the way Rue McClanahan was the funny one on *The Golden Girls*?" Betty expertly waited out the laugh as the audience responded to the in-joke. "I never saw that show," Elka responded dismissively. (Betty would soon get a shot at revenge; immediately after the live episode of *Hot in Cleveland*, the ninety-two-year-old legend raced over to *Soul Man*'s soundstage next door to guest star on that show's live season premiere as well.)

As the fifth season of the bona fide sitcom hit was airing on TV Land, one of its executive producers, Todd Milliner, was brainstorming ways to raise money to support LA's Celebration Theatre, of which he is a board member and his partner is one of the artistic directors, along with Michael A. Shepperd. When Todd suggested a historic mashup of the *Girls* from Miami with the ladies of *Cleveland*, "Ding, we knew we had a winning idea," Shepperd remembers.

ABOVE:

The cast of the Celebration Theatre's *Golden Girls/Hot in Cleveland* mashup *(left to right):* Michael A. Shepperd, Max Greenfield, *Hot in Cleveland* stars Wendie Malick, Jane Leeves, Betty White, and Valerie Bertinelli, and Millicent Martin.

Photo by SEAN LAMBERT, *courtesy of* CELEBRATION THEATRE.

After another of Celebration's troupe members, former *Golden Girls* writer Stan Zimmerman, suggested a performance of the script for his season-one episode "Blanche and the Younger Man," the *Hot in Cleveland* stars divvied up the four iconic roles. Valerie prepared to play Rose, Wendie to play Blanche, and Jane, despite her British accent, would be Sicilian Sophia. The casting happened to fit the women's *Cleveland* characters—but the assignments were actually made based on Betty having first dibs. And this time, Betty wanted to play Dorothy.

"This is so surreal," Stan told the excited audience of the theater company's benefactors, seated on the CBS Radford lot's Stage 19 on the night of April 26, 2014. As he introduced the table read of the twenty-nine-year-old shooting script he had unearthed from his files—which included never-before-heard jokes that had been cut for time from the finished episode—Stan gestured at the chair about to be occupied by Betty White. "One of the Girls literally is here," he noted. "But I watched a rehearsal earlier today. And the *Hot in Cleveland* cast is invoking such a *Golden Girls* vibe, I feel like the other three are also here tonight."

The performance would go on to be a highlight both for the Celebration Theatre, which raised more than enough money to pay off its debt—and particularly, as former *Golden Girls* script coordinator Robert Spina noted, for Betty White. "Betty was first cast to play Blanche, played Rose for eight years [including *Golden Palace*], on *Hot in Cleveland* is essentially playing Sophia, and now has the chance to play Dorothy," he cited. "So as of tonight, Betty White has gotten to be all four of the Golden Girls."

ABOVE LEFT:

Left to right, Hot in Cleveland co-stars Wendie Malick, Valerie Bertinelli and Jane Leeves walk the red carpet for Betty's 90th birthday celebration at Los Angeles' Biltmore Hotel, January, 2012. ABOVE RIGHT: In 2010, as Hot in Cleveland began shooting its first season, Betty White scribbled a Golden Girls-themed blessing on the wall of Stage 19 at Los Angeles' CBS Radford Studios.

Photos by AUTHOR.

Rose Nylund

NAIVE SCANDINAVIAN NITWIT
from ST. OLAF, MINNESOTA

BETTY WHITE

"I love cheesecake, but I never eat on camera. I just toy with it.
But ask Rue about what she does. Because I'm telling you, if it's on camera,
it's a license to steal, as far as Rue is concerned. It has no calories.
So she'd not only eat the cheesecake, but when Sophia would
make spaghetti, she'd eat that, too."

—BETTY WHITE

AS AN ACTOR, you get so many bad scripts, but when I read the pilot script for *The Golden Girls*, I sat up and took notice. It was different from anything I'd gotten. And it was all because of the wonderful writing. The four of us get a lot of credit, but we couldn't do it if it weren't for the amazing scripts. I promise you, as an actor you can screw up a good show, but you can't save a bad one if it's not on the page.

From the first table read of the script, we knew we were on to something. Everyone was so perfectly cast that the minute you heard the lines coming out of our mouths, it was exciting. I've never had a read-through like that. All of a sudden, I'd start throwing them over the net, and I'd get them right back. We all had the same reaction. We could feel the chemistry. We could taste it.

The magic of the show was the way the writers drew our characters so distinctly. All these years I've used the analogy of four points on a compass. We balanced each other out beautifully. And not only were the lines wonderful, but they would shoot the reactions of the other characters. So pretty soon, since the audience got to know these women so well, they'd start to anticipate. "Oh, how is Bea going to react to that?" Or Rue, or Estelle. It made for a very exciting seven years.

Right from the beginning, Rue would always remark how evidently Rose and Charlie had had a very active sex life. Off camera, that was always Rue's thing: "Come on, Rose gets more action than Blanche does!" That was the beautiful part about the writing. We could get away with murder and talk about so many things. At our age, everybody knew we'd been around the block, and so the talk wasn't as salacious as it would have been with younger women. And it was funnier because we *were* our ages, rather than if we had been young enough to be participants.

I always believed that Rose was truly naïve more than dumb. I'd hear people calling her ditzy or a dumbbell, and I would defend her. Of course, she did think her second-grade teacher was Adolf Hitler, so it was a very fine line. In playing Rose, I found that the most interesting challenge was that even though as an actor I had to kind of think funny and play on things in my head I had to be careful to keep the awareness not only out of my mouth but also out of my eyes. Rose couldn't ever look like she got it. She had to be innocence personified. That was the saving grace that would allow her to get away with saying something like "Can you believe that back-stabbing slut?" about Blanche. Those were the lines where the producers would warn me: "You never get it. You're never too smart for the room." They knew coming from Rose the line would work, but coming from me it wouldn't.

Rose is like me in some ways, in her optimism and her wanting to think that life always has a happy ending. That was in the script, so I don't think I brought that to the role, but it was just something that was terribly comfortable for me. She also has a Viking temper—like me, I'm afraid—and wasn't always sweetness and light. When she got mad, she got really mad. But I'm not as prone to telling someone off. No point in getting into a confrontation—I'll just wait until they go home and then I'll bitch like mad.

From the start, seventy-five percent of our mail has always come from young people, especially in their teens and early twenties. Fans will often come up to me and quote every line of a St. Olaf story, and I don't blame them. They were brilliant. When I'd read a script and see one, I'd be thrilled. I don't do accents, but there was just an undulating rhythm to those words that I was able to pick up on. Still, some-times before work if I'd see a newspaper story with some very difficult-to-pronounce Scandinavian name, I'd think, "Uh-oh—I'm going to get it." And sure enough, it would show up in the script. I swear the other girls would make bets that I'd never make it through some of these difficult words. So when I told a St. Olaf story, I always had to look over their shoulders instead of locking eyes with any of them. Because I knew they were just sitting there, thinking, "You're going to screw up. You know you are!"

When the show premiered we were at number one, over Bill Cosby, who at that time owned the world. We felt, well, that's just curiosity, that first show. Four old broads are not going to continue to get that kind of ratings. Well, we stayed, and I don't think we were ever out of the top ten, which is such a privilege. It was just one of those things that comes along I would say once in a lifetime—but my "once in a lifetime" had already been used up with *Mary Tyler Moore*. So to get it again—and then on *Boston Legal*, with David E. Kelley's writing—I mean, how lucky can one old broad get?

"Rose, if you say ONE MORE of those stupid words..."

"OH, BLOW IT OUT YOUR TÜBEN-BLÜRBLES!"

—Rose Nylund

In an appearance on *Larry King Now* in April 2014, Betty had to amend her last state-ment from 2006 to reflect her most recent work. When Larry asked how she would like to be remembered, Betty thought for a moment. "I think for *Life with Elizabeth*, maybe, or *The Golden Girls*. And *Mary Tyler Moore!*" Betty responded. "How lucky can you get? To get one big series or maybe two—but to get three, and now, with *Hot in Cleveland*! We're having a ball."

After *The Golden Girls* ended, the then-seventysomething Betty kept busy not only with a season of the doomed CBS sequel series *The Golden Palace*

(1992–93), but by appearing in a variety of TV guest spots, plus in regular roles in the short-lived sit-coms *Bob*, opposite Bob Newhart, on CBS (1993); ABC's *Maybe This Time* with Marie Osmond (1995–96); and CBS's *Ladies Man* (1999–2001), playing the mother of Alfred Molina's title character. After several guest appearances on ABC's legal drama *The Prac-tice*, Betty brought her secretary character, Catherine Piper, to the cast of its spinoff series, *Boston Legal*, where she appeared from 2005 to 2008. During much of that same period, from 2006 to 2009, she also popped up on CBS's daytime soap *The Bold and the Beautiful* as Ann Douglas, the long-lost mother of that show's matriarch Stephanie Forrester; the ever-energetic Betty ultimately outlived Ann, who died on the soap in November 2009.

Betty's big-screen career blossomed as well, with hilarious roles as a foul-mouthed, alligator-loving old lady in 1999's *Lake Placid*, and in 2003, as racist busy-body neighbor Mrs. Kline in *Bringing Down the House*.

But 2010 turned out to be Betty's banner year; just as she turned eighty-eight, her career suddenly burned hotter than ever. In January of that year, she accepted the Screen Actors Guild Life Achievement Award—an honor that usually comes at the end of a career, but for Betty turned out to be just the opening curtain of yet another act. That spring continued with what turned out to be a well-timed blitz, parlaying the heat from Betty's role in the 2009 Sandra Bullock–Ryan Reynolds film *The Proposal* into a buzzed-about appearance in a Snickers commercial during the Super Bowl.

A Facebook petition that built throughout the spring of 2010 landed Betty the gig hosting a May episode of *Saturday Night Live*—for which she ultimately won her sixth Emmy Award. Just over a month later, on June 16, Betty debuted in yet another hit series, TV Land's *Hot in Cleveland*.

In 2011, Betty published her seventh book, a volume of her wit and wisdom on such topics as love, friendship, animals, aging, and television called *If You Ask Me (And of Course You Won't)*; in February 2012, she became, at ninety, the oldest person ever to win a Grammy Award, beating out such competition as Tina Fey and Val Kilmer in the Best Spoken Word Album category for her reading of the book.

Also in 2012, she launched *Betty White's Off Their Rockers*; the hidden-camera comedy show, which she also hosts and executive produces, ran for two seasons on NBC before jumping over to Lifetime for its third. To mark Betty's big nonagenarian celebration in January, NBC gathered the biggest names in comedy for a tribute special. Before the cameras rolled, but after properly greeting her guests—such as Mary Tyler Moore, Valerie Harper, Ed Asner, Carol Burnett, Vicki Lawrence, Carl Reiner, Tina Fey, Amy Poehler, and her *Hot in Cleveland* costars, Valerie Bertinelli, Wendie Malick, and Jane Leeves—Betty, in a sparkly sky-blue gown, presided over a press conference in one of the ballrooms of downtown Los Angeles's Biltmore Hotel. I asked her if Betty White was turning ninety, does that mean Rose Nylund and her *Mary Tyler Moore Show* character, Sue Ann Nivens, were as well?

"Rose may very well be ninety, but if Sue Ann is, she'll never admit it," Betty replied with a laugh. "She would lie, and would knock off a couple of decades.

"My mother always told me, 'Never lie about your age. Brag about it,'" Betty added. "And when you get to this point," she said—acknowledging with a sweep of her arm the sheer size of the celebration in her honor—"you get spoiled so rotten that I love being ninety.

"And I'll see you again in ten years!"

RUE McCLANAHAN

(1934-2010)

"Betty says that I always ate the cheesecake, but it's not true.
I would actually put a bite of cheesecake on my fork and move it close to my mouth.
Then when the camera cut to someone else, I'd put it on a plate under my chair.
By the time they'd cut back to me, I would pretend to be chewing."

—RUE McCLANAHAN

IT WAS STATED from the very beginning that Blanche was more Southern than Blanche DuBois. But the accent in Atlanta where Blanche is from is very slight—hardly funny enough. So I decided to go with my instinct and make her a kind of phony. My mother had a cousin, Ina Pearl, who was from southern Oklahoma like everybody else, but put on an accent that was part extreme Southern belle and part her idea of upper-class British. It was a remarkable accent and it was really obviously hers alone. Nobody in the family knew where she got it from and although she didn't think she was being funny, I always did. So I played Blanche the way I felt Blanche. She thought an accentuated Southern accent like Ina Pearl's would be sexy and strong and attractive to men. She wanted to be a Southern heroine, like Vivien Leigh. In fact, that's who I think she thought she was.

But as we rehearsed the pilot, Jay Sandrich said to me, "No, no—I don't want to hear a Southern accent." He said he wanted just to hear my regular Oklahoma accent, which he thought was Southern. Well, there's no arguing with the director. So I sort of did what he asked and used a modified sort-of-Southern accent. When I heard we got picked up for thirteen episodes, I worried about it for a couple of months. Finally, when we came back to shoot in July, I went to Paul Witt and Tony Thomas and said, "Okay, I know I'm not supposed to play it with a Southern accent, so I have an idea: I'll do a real Mae West." And they said, "What are you talking about? Of *course* Blanche has a Southern accent!" And I said *whew!* And was thrilled I got to play it the way I wanted to in the first place.

I needed to pick a voice that wasn't Rue that would work to help me create a character. You can't just do your regular voice, your regular walk, your regular beliefs, your regular anything if you're creating a character. For example, the Blanche

Blanche Elizabeth Devereaux

(B.E.D.)

MAN-HUNGRY BELLE *from* ATLANTA, GEORGIA

"I'M JUMPIER

—————

THAN A

virgin AT A

—————

prison rodeo."

—————

—Blanche Devereaux

walk came to me very quickly after the pilot. That's not my natural walk, but it is hers. And I don't think there's anyone else on earth who walks like Blanche. Movement is very important to me in developing a role, and I think Blanche's walk showed self-assurance and her always being on top of the situation. If she was at the Rusty Anchor or on a date, she felt it was irresistible and beguiling. The shoes were a big part of it, the sound they made. I always have to know what a character is going to wear, and once I discovered the walk, Blanche always wore those slingbacks.

As self-involved as she was, Blanche also had a sense of humor about herself, if the jokes were coming from the right place. It was a delightful thing for me to discover early on that Blanche would find Sophia adorable. It's really her fault that Blanche got to be known as a slut, but Blanche would forgive her because she'd had a stroke, and find everything she said funny and endearing. So if Sophia said something particularly nasty, I'd laugh like "aw, you cute little thing," and never took offense. It helped the jokes work, because it avoided a sour note of actual hurt feelings, and kept the audience with us.

Blanche also had a conservative side that was a lot unlike me; she could be homophobic, which I'm not, and for example she was grossed out by her daughter's artificial insemination, which I wouldn't have been at all. I had to act all that. Really, none of us is at all like our character—Betty probably the least of all, because she has nothing but brains. Estelle isn't at all pushy and vitriolic like Sophia—but they both were New York funny. And because Dorothy is probably the "straightest," least eccentric character, Bea is like her in that way. They both have a very funny take on people and are quick-witted, not suffering fools gladly. But certainly Dorothy's failure in life is completely different from Bea's huge successes. And when people ask me if I'm like Blanche, my standard answer is: Just look at the facts. Blanche is a man-crazy, glamorous, extremely sexy Southern belle from Atlanta. And I'm not from Atlanta.

But in truth, I actually don't see Blanche as a slut at all. She actually had fewer dates than anybody if you go back and count. Sophia had more going on sexually than Blanche did. But Blanche talked a lot. I think that she was married to George for a long time, and she never got over him. She was always looking for a replacement; she was looking for love. She was also oversexed. I had a best girlfriend like that. They do go well together. I'm not oversexed, but I was looking for love, and I got myself into a lot of trouble that way. In fact, my memoir is titled *My First Five Husbands . . . And the Ones Who Got Away*. Maybe there is more similarity with Blanche than I've realized.

AUTHOR'S UPDATE:

Following the end of *The Golden Girls* and *Golden Palace*, Rue continued to pop up all over the small screen, in TV movies such as the 1994 made-for-TV sequel to *Nunsense*, and in guest roles on *Boy Meets World*, *Murphy Brown*, *Touched by an Angel*, and *King of the Hill*. In the fall of 1999, she played a regular role in the WB's *Safe Harbor*, as the mother of the widowed sheriff, and grandmother to his three sons; the series lasted only eleven episodes.

Rue continued to appear on the big screen as well, in key roles in independent films and in small roles in the big-budget films *The Fighting Temptations* (2003) and *Starship Troopers* (1997). Also in 1997, she appeared in the feature film *Out to Sea* as Mrs. Ellen Carruthers, the owner of a cruise ship that apparently caters to a similarly Golden geriatric set, employing Jack Lemmon and Walter Matthau as dance instructors. And that same year, Rue successfully underwent treatment for breast cancer.

With her return to New York, Rue also returned to the stage, off Broadway in *The Vagina Monologues* and in the Broadway productions of *Wicked* and *The Women* (2001). As that production's Countess de Lage, she was wont to proclaim her need for "L'amour, l'amour!" Rue then catalogued her own similar real-life quest in her 2007 memoir.

Rue's final acting role was in the Logo network series *Sordid Lives* in 2008. Although Texas matriarch Peggy Ingram had been played by actress Gloria LeRoy in the original film—in which the character died—in the series version, as embodied by Rue, she was not only alive but embarking on a secret love affair with a younger man.

The role offered the seventysomething Rue the chance both to play a still-vital woman and to support a series by her friend, out gay creator Del Shores. Rue supported presidential candidate Barack Obama in the 2008 election, and advocated for the legality of same-sex marriage. In January 2009, she appeared in the star-studded event "Defying Inequality: The Broadway Concert—a Celebrity Benefit for Equal Rights." That following November, she was scheduled to be honored for her lifetime achievements at the event "Golden: A Gala Tribute to Rue McClanahan" at San Francisco's Castro Theatre, but was forced to cancel due to cardiac problems. Following triple-bypass surgery, Rue suffered a minor stroke early the next year. After suffering a brain hemorrhage, Rue (née Eddi-Rue) McClanahan died at New York–Presbyterian Hospital on June 3, 2010, at age seventy-six.

In 2006, I sat down with Rue to conduct an interview for the Archive of American Television, a daylong discussion of the actress's life and career. At the end of the grueling shoot, I asked her how she would like to be remembered. "As alive," she quipped, before thinking more seriously about it, and turning the question back on me. "But you've got to ask me about my proudest achievement in life!" she insisted. And so I did.

"My son, Mark [Bish], the jazz guitarist," Rue replied, sounding very unlike Blanche, who always struck me as more self-involved than maternal. "He's also an artist. He builds, he paints, he draws. And he's my biggest pride. If I had done nothing else, I'd be satisfied that my life had meant something."

LESLIE JORDAN

the Actor and Author

REMEMBERS RUE McCLANAHAN

WHAT A BAD queer I am. I don't know much about *The Golden Girls*, because I did not get sober until 1997. I was too busy running the streets of West Hollywood to watch the show. I do come across it quite a bit in reruns. The first thing I notice is the sunny, pastel set that is so indicative of retirement complexes in Florida. My sisters worked for the Villages in Lady Lake, Florida, which is one of the largest retirement communities. They have so many stories; it is no wonder the show was able to capitalize on that arena.

And of course, if I had to pick a favorite Golden Girl, it would have to be Blanche. My contribution to this missive will have to be my association with the real Blanche, Miss Rue McClanahan. We worked together on the TV series *Sordid Lives,* based on the hit movie of the same name by Del Shores. It ran on Logo for one season. We were all dropped off in Shreveport, Louisiana, and had to "make do." The show was a prequel to the movie and Rue's character was already dead when the movie began, but her character was certainly alive and well in the TV series.

I could not wait to meet Rue, and just knew we would hit it off. I was right! We met in a casino in the hotel where we were staying. Rue McClanahan was so much like her character Blanche it's hard to tell where Rue ended and Blanche began. I loved the quote that Del uses about why Miss McClanahan was so eager to be a part of a project where there was not a lot of money involved. She read the script and called Del *that night*, personally, to say, "I'll do it. I never thought at my age I'd get an opportunity to play a woman in love again."

A few years after the TV series was canceled, we all went on the road with a show we called *An Evening of Sordid Comedy*. It was Rue, Caroline Rhea, Del Shores, and me. Rue was having some back problems, and had to take pills for the pain. They made her a little testy, to say the least. Del would sell tickets to a meet and greet after each of our performances. Rue loved her public, *but* she just wasn't feeling up to meeting all those people. She asked me before we went on in Dallas, "How long are you gonna go?" I said, "The same as you, Rue. We each get twenty minutes." She looked me straight in the eye. "Do *not* go over. We've got to do this damn meet and greet. I don't feel well."

Well, you certainly would not have known she didn't feel well. She walked onstage, sat down (she did sit-down comedy at her age, not stand-up comedy) and brought the house down with her stories. Trust me, she went way over her allotted twenty minutes. Then, I walked onstage and was *killing*! Twelve hundred gay Texans! What a response I was getting! But then all of a sudden the crowd *really* went apeshit. I turned around, and here was Rue marching back onstage. She walked right up to me and ran her fingers over her throat, which I took to mean, "Wrap it up!" The crowd could not get enough of her! I was livid!! But how long can you stay mad at Rue McClanahan? I miss her desperately.

Dorothy Zbornak,
(a.k.a. "PUSSYCAT")

CHRONIC FATIGUE SYNDROME
SUFFERER *from* BROOKLYN

BEA ARTHUR

(1922-2009)

"I hate cheesecake. I didn't like the cheesecake scenes, either –
I didn't find them amusing, and thought of them as just a segue.
But audiences love it, and to this day they still talk about it. And when I do my
one-woman show and talk about this, people will come backstage and say,
'Do you really love cheesecake? Don't lie!'"

—BEA ARTHUR

THE FIRST THING I noticed about *The Golden Girls* pilot was that it was a beautiful script. It had an extra character, a gay house man, who was very charming, but they cut him by the very next episode. I don't think they had any idea that just the four of us would be so strong together. And we were lucky enough to have brilliant writers on the show and a fabulous director, Terry Hughes. It was a great combination of all the elements.

I think the relationship between Dorothy and her mother makes for one of the most brilliant comedic duos I've ever known. First of all it was so ludicrous, with the fact that physically Estelle and I are so completely different. And then their love/hate relationship, where they could be so sweet yet so cutting with each other, was so real, and was just marvelous the way it was written. I also loved Dorothy's relationship with Stan. She could be so mad at him, and claim she hated him, but the lines were written to say that they obviously still loved each other. And so it became a comedic relationship that really paid off.

I remember one scene [in season 3 episode "My Brother, My Father"] where Stan is staying over, and I've made him sleep on the floor. The camera is on me, and suddenly I hear him laughing. And I have a line like, "Stanley, if you're doing what I think you're doing . . ." I remember saying to the writer, "How are we permitted to do this?" We certainly got away from the censors more than we had on *Maude*, where every third day of every week we had to read the entire script to the network and then Norman Lear would start his negotiations with them. "I'll cut that line or that section, but Bea has to say that line." It was one fight after another. And that struck me when we were doing "Journey to the Center of Attention" in the seventh season, and Rue does a thing where she sits in a guy's lap and does the "is that a gun or are you just happy to see me" joke. But it seems like that leeway came with time, because in the pilot episode, we had to change the line where Sophia calls Blanche's fiancé a "douchebag."

Sometimes rather than a written line, the writers would want a reaction shot from one of us. They and Terry Hughes were so good at knowing what was and was not going to work. People always ask me about my "slow burn." I just know that I tried to keep my reactions honest. I didn't even start out doing comedy, but I think you have to be real. So many really brilliant actors, once they are told that they're in a comedy, turn into people from another planet. There is no similarity between their characters and reality. So you just have to make sure as an actor to make everything real for yourself.

That had been easier for me on *Maude*, because we taped on Tuesdays, which meant we had a few days over the weekend of not rehearsing where suddenly it would pop into my head "I know how to do that!" But there were at least a few things about Dorothy that were easy for me to find real, because they are like me. I always tell people we're both 5'9½" in our stocking feet, and both of us have very deep voices. But we're also the same in that like Dorothy, I hate bullshit. I call it bubble-pricking. Being the great leveler, the voice of reason who brings other people back down to earth. Dorothy was the voice of reason on that show. Left to their own devices, I don't know how the other women could have survived.

I also get asked all the time if we're going to do a reunion. But the way I see it, why would we? We're not going to be any better than we were, or top some of the great shows we did. I left Maude after six years and *Golden Girls* after seven, because even then, I realized we couldn't top what we'd already done. *Golden Girls* started to strain a bit by the end, and wasn't as hysterical as it had been, so I thought it was time to leave. Today, I still have people constantly recognizing me, saying "Oh my God, it's Dorothy!" It is so sweet and so nice. Often, flight attendants will come up and say something to me when I'm traveling. After all these years, I am delighted. It is incredible when you realize, *The Golden Girls* is all over the globe.

AUTHOR'S UPDATE:

After leaving *The Golden Girls*, Bea returned once to small-screen Miami, as Dorothy Zbornak spent a two-part episode in the fall of 1992 visiting her Girls at their hotel, the *Golden Palace*. Throughout the '90s, she was in demand as a lively talk show guest, and popped up in such unscripted fare as a tribute to her former *Mame* co-star and close friend, Angela Lansbury, and as a presenter at the Tony Awards. In 2002, she appeared on both *The Daily Show* with Jon Stewart and on an Oscar-themed comedy special, *The Big O! West Hollywood Story*, hosted by that show's gay movie critic [and the author's husband] Frank DeCaro.

"MY CUPCAKES ARE

MOIST & DELICIOUS.

Men love my
CUPCAKES!"

—Dorothy Zbornak.

Bea continued to appear on TV comedies as well, with guest spots on *Dave's World* in 1997 and *Futurama* in 2001, and in recurring cameo appearances on Showtime's *Beggars and Choosers* in 1999. In 2000, Bea was nominated for an Emmy for her guest role as babysitter Mrs. White in the first season of *Malcolm in the Middle*, and she popped up again in another prominent role, as Larry David's mother, in a 2005 episode of *Curb Your Enthusiasm*.

But after finding TV fame as Maude Findlay and Dorothy Zbornak, Bea ended up being most compelling when she appeared on the small screen just as herself. At *The New York Friars Club Roast of Jerry Stiller*, televised in 1999 by Comedy Central, comedian Jeffrey Ross made a hilariously crude reference to "Bea Arthur's dick," and Bea's reaction from the dais was priceless.

Then, in 2005, it was Bea's turn to do some roasting, as she read aloud from the semi-autobiographical novel *Star Struck* by honoree Pamela Anderson, her friend and fellow supporter of animal rights. "The story concerns a blonde, very large breasted actress, imaginatively named Star, who plays a lifeguard on a hit television show," Bea deadpanned. "And she becomes actively involved romantically with a tattooed rocker. And a videotape that they have made of their sexual escapades is leaked to the public. Pam, where do you come up with this shit?!" 83-year-old Bea proceeded to read particularly tawdry passages from the book, with her elegant, Broadway-honed elocution. And she killed.

Having gotten her start in theater, Bea continued to perform on stage throughout her life, appearing in Los Angeles-area productions of Renee Taylor and Joe Bologna's *Bermuda Avenue Triangle* in 1995-96, and in Anne Meara's *After-Play* in 1997-98. Having developed a traveling act in the '80s and '90s, she continued to tour through 2006, including a 2002 New York run titled *Bea Arthur on Broadway: Just Between Friends*. A collection of stories and songs based on her life and career, the show was extended beyond its initial limited run, and was nominated for a Tony Award for Best Special Theatrical Event.

In the spring of 2008, Bea rejoined Rue McClanahan and Betty White in Santa Monica, California for the taping of the *6th Annual TV Land Awards*, where *The Golden Girls* was honored with the network's Pop Culture Award, presented to the three ladies by Steve Carell.

It was to be Bea's last televised appearance. Beatrice Arthur, née Bernice Frankel, died of cancer on April 25, 2009 at the age of 86.

At her memorial service that September at New York's Majestic Theater, her longtime friend Dan Mathews, vice president of People for the Ethical Treatment of Animals, spoke about his beloved Bea as both a force of nature and a fascinating study in contradictions. Although tall and physically imposing, he noted, Bea would often be reduced to tears by stories of animal suffering. And yet, on one afternoon at her home in California's Pacific Palisades, when Dan the ardent vegan was helping prep for a fundraising dinner, the equally ardent non-vegetarian Bea asked him to cut up some onions and press them into the meatloaf she was preparing. "And I thought, 'I'm a hardcore vegan, here at Bea Arthur's house for a PETA meeting, and I'm helping her make a meatloaf?!'" Dan remembers. "But then, I don't know if it was the look in her eye, or the knife in her hand—but I did what she said!"

BILLY GOLDENBERG

Bea's Friend and Longtime Accompanist

REMEMBERS BEA ARTHUR

*a Star Who Gave Back to the
LGBT Community*

I MET BEA in 1981, when we were asked to work together to prepare material for a benefit for the ACLU. We rehearsed for a day, and the next morning she called me up and said, "Would you come to dinner?" I said, "Of course"—and that was the beginning of a very long friendship.

It turned out we hated all the same, often very famous people. There is no bond like hating the same people! After a while we started to work on some songs together. After all, people who came to parties at Bea's house were always asking her to sing. And she knew a lot of songs and performed them well, from Kurt Weill to Bob Dylan. One day, our mutual friend Nick Perito, who was the musical director for Perry Como, urged us to do a show.

As Nick reminded us, Bea knew every funny writer in the business, so we started interviewing writers and asking them to submit ideas. But they all wanted Bea to do what they were used to from her: very campy and gay material. We wanted the show to be more personal to Bea—not necessarily autobiographical, but about things Bea thought about life. So I sat Bea down with a tape recorder, and asked her to tell every funny story she'd ever told me, with her particular inflection, and with her typically funny asides and comments. We had it transcribed, we edited it, and we had a show, which we tried out in Palm Springs during Bea's weekend break from *The Golden Girls*.

We did the show—that we had planned for 30 minutes but which turned into an hour, because of Bea's ad-libs and the audience's laughter—at the town's most presti-gious golf course, and all of the richest gay men were there. We eventually traveled the world with the show. We had our best reaction in South Africa, where I'm told *The Golden Girls* was on seven times a day. African-American audiences in particular loved Bea, too. But of course, gay men were her biggest fans. We always knew when the audience was predominantly gay, we couldn't miss.

In 2005, we did a one-night-only show in New York to benefit the Ali Forney Center, which Bea had become very devoted to, doing interviews on their behalf and whatever else they needed to serve the city's homeless LGBT youth. And throughout the years, we very often played for an AIDS audience. After the show, Bea would come out the stage door, and all these guys in wheelchairs would be waiting. Bea would talk to them, and go and kiss a couple of them. She spent hours, and they appreciated it incredibly. But Bea had a special way like that, always liking to help people.

Soon after Bea and I started doing the show together, we were invited to take it to Westport, Connecticut, to the White Barn Theater. In the first rehearsal, the director, our friend Donald Saddler, reminded me that if I was going to be on stage with Bea Arthur, people would be looking at the both of us, so I couldn't just look at my music or at the piano. He told me the first rule of performing was reacting. And so Bea and I began to try things out each night on stage. Some nights, as we walked off, she'd say, "You did something tonight—I want to know what it was." I'd tell her, and she would often say, "Okay, I think we could do something further with that," and we would invent fun little bits of interplay.

I'll always remember one of those bits: another director later suggested that before Bea would sing "The Man in the Moon Is a Lady," one of her famous songs, in the encore, she should walk over to me and whisper something in my ear. It didn't matter what she would say—it could be "fuck you"—and often was. She would then walk downstage, and I would have a line: "You're not serious." He expected we'd get a big laugh out of it. So the first night, Bea whispered in my ear, and I said my line right away—and no laugh. The second night, I tried making a disdainful face—and still nothing. So on the third night, I decided to try something. That night, I let Bea walk off almost to the edge of the stage, and then I said to her, "You're not serious." It got a huge laugh.

As we walked off stage that night, Bea said to me, "Darling, you've just discovered the secret of comedy."

I said, "What's that?"

And she said, "Waiting."

To this day, I can tell a joke better than anybody because of all the training I got with Bea. I learned from the best.

Golden "Girls": Drag Tributes to TV's Fab Foursome

◆ ◆ ◆ ◆

NEW YORK, NY

IN 2003, NEWLY dating couple John Schaefer and Peter Mac first came up with the idea of celebrating the *Girls'* appeal to gay viewers via an all-male stage production of two of the show's episodes, "Break In" and, inspired by the fun they had pronouncing the word "LES-bian" à la Rue McClanahan, "Isn't It Romantic?" As a payback to Estelle Getty for her early fund-raising to fight AIDS, their show *Golden Girls . . . Live,* which ran for sixty performances at the cabaret room Rose's Turn in Greenwich Village, raised money to fight progressive supranuclear palsy, the disease with which Estelle had been at the time diagnosed. (The diagnosis was later changed to Lewy body dementia.)

After coverage in *Entertainment Weekly,* the tiny cabaret club routinely found itself with a wait list seventy-five deep. "It was a lot like *Rocky Horror,*" Peter remembers, because the audience comprised of gay men, bachelorette parties and sorority groups "would say the lines with us. People had fun being so close to the 'Girls' who weren't trapped in that little box anymore."

Then, in the spring of 2014, writers Nick Brennan and Luke Jones reprised the idea by joining with Chad Ryan and John de Los Santos for *Thank You for Being a Friend,* an unauthorized parody musical at the Laurie Beechman Theatre featuring four characters named Dorothea, Blanchet, Roz, and Sophia as well as original odes to Miami and, of course, cheesecake.

SAN FRANCISCO, CA

IN 2006, SAN Francisco drag icon Heklina began staging a tribute to the Girls in a friend's home in the city's Lower Haight

ABOVE:

Clockwise from top: Heklina, Matthew Martin, Cookie Dough, and Pollo Del Mar as the Girls.

Photo by KENT TAYLOR.

neighborhood. Quickly outgrowing that original parlor, the show then moved to the five-hundred-seat Victoria Theatre, where it has become an annual holiday tradition. *The Golden Girls: The Christmas Episodes* stars Heklina as Dorothy, female impersonator Matthew Martin as Blanche, Pollo Del Mar as Rose, and Cookie Dough as Sophia, complete with rattan purse and shuffling gait. "It's a perfect fit," Heklina explains, "because with the clothes they wear, the situations they get into, Bea Arthur's genius comic delivery and Blanche's reputation for being a slut, the Golden Girls are all like drag queens anyway."

LOS ANGELES, CA

IN THE SUMMER of 2014, another California drag doyenne, Jackie Beat, teamed up with an import from New York, Sherry Vine, and actors Sam Pancake and Drew Droege for their own *Golden Girlz Live* at LA's underground Cavern Club Theater at the Casita del Campo restaurant. Tall Jackie, whose own home contains a room she has turned into a shrine to the four holy ladies of Miami, made for the perfect Dorothy, while Sherry essayed a vampy Blanche, Drew a ditzy Rose, and Sam a bespectacled comic Sophia in performances consisting of two episodes from the troupe's growing reper-toire of episodes, including "The Flu," "Blanche and the Younger Man," "Isn't It Romantic?" and "A little Romance." The foursome reconvened in the spring and summer of 2015, with more weekends scheduled to come. But Jackie says she's already noted some VIPs in the basement the-ater's tiny audience. When *Golden Girls* writer Win-ifred Hervey caught the show in 2014, Jackie says, "she came backstage after the show and said, 'Thank you for keeping our words alive.'"

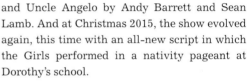

PORTLAND, OR

IN 2013, INSPIRED by Heklina's holiday suc-cess, Trenton Shine decided to round up some "Girls" of his own to reenact the Girls' two hol-iday episodes at Portland's Funhouse Lounge. After their sell-out success, the Portland Girls returned the following summer, presenting "Isn't It Romantic?" and "Sisters of the Bride" with a revised cast including Trenton himself as Doro-thy—"which people expected me to do, because I'm tall and sarcastic," he explains—and the roles of Rose, Sophia, and Blanche played by Scott Engdahl, Randy Tutone, and locally known drag queen Honey Bea Hart. By yuletide 2014, the troupe's repertoire included "My Brother, My Father" as well, with impres-sive impersonations of Stan

and Uncle Angelo by Andy Barrett and Sean Lamb. And at Christmas 2015, the show evolved again, this time with an all-new script in which the Girls performed in a nativity pageant at Dorothy's school.

All told, the productions have raised over twenty-eight hundred dollars for the antidis-crimination advocacy group Basic Rights Ore-gon, and five thousand dollars each for the human services charity JOIN and the Cascade AIDS Project. The per-formances—each of which began with a selected audience member sing-ing "Thank You For Being a Friend" as the cast acted out the open-ing credits—had a pro-found effect on their audiences as well, Trenton explains. "We've found that people are really emotionally attached to *The Golden Girls*, and will come up to us, crying, to say, 'Thank you so much for doing this.'"

NEW ORLEANS, LA / PROVINCETOWN, MA

HAVING ONCE PLAYED Blanche when Hek-lina brought her *Girls* to New Orleans, drag diva Varla Jean Merman joined her longtime friend and collaborator Ricky Graham in 2012 to mount their own hometown stage rendition. Their Big Easy production of *The Golden Gals* became such a smash, selling out its two month-long weekend runs, that Varla then decided to export the Gals to the gay summer mecca of Province-town, on the tip of Massachu-setts' Cape Cod. The summer 2014 edition, stitching to-gether the full episodes of "In

ABOVE:

The LA troupe's recreation of season 1 episode "Blanche and the Younger Man," starring Mario Diaz as Dirk, Drew Droege as Rose, Sam Pancake as Sophia, Sherry Vine as Blanche, Melanie Hutsell as Alma Lindstrom, and Jackie Beat as Dorothy.

Photo by JACKIE BEAT.

a Bed of Rose's" and "Isn't It Romantic" with one of the vignettes from "Valentine's Day," proceeded to sell out every single one of its nightly performances at the Art House theater from early June through Labor Day weekend; the Gals then returned in the summer of 2015 and beyond. Each time, the show's cast has included Varla, with her perfect impersonation of Blanche—"I've noticed that Rue as Blanche always led with her breasts, so I play it with my breasts shaking and head bobbing," she says—plus Ptown theater impresario Ryan Landry as Dorothy, Olive Another as Sophia, and Brooklyn Shaffer playing Rose. That last role, Varla explains, is always the hardest to cast, "because Rose has to be sweet and innocent, and it's hard to find a man who can play that."

BOSTON/SALEM, MA

A FEW YEARS after their first turn playing the Girls in New York, John Schaefer and Peter Mac moved west and attended Heklina's show on a weekend in San Francisco. Soon after the couple, now known as John and Peter Mac since their 2014 wedding, "decided to give *Golden Girls* fans the reunion they never really got," John remembers. And so, running for 194 performances at the Los Angeles gay bar Oil Can Harry's in 2012–13, their "Lost Reunion Episode" took place at the funeral of Blanche's uncle and Dorothy's husband, Lucas Hollingsworth, bringing all four Girls back together— and sidestepping the debacle of *Golden Palace.*

In the fall of 2014, while performing another show at the Opus Theater in Salem, Massachusetts, John and Peter were inspired by the witchy environs to write and perform a "lost" *Golden Girls* Halloween "episode," in which English teacher Dorothy visited town to research her teaching of Arthur Miller's play *The Crucible*, with the other three Girls in tow. The couple followed with a second show, *"The Golden Girls* Lost Christmas Epi-

sode," before premiering yet another original hour, "The Lost 'Shady Pines, Ma' Episode" at Boston's Jacques Cabaret the following spring. Each show, Peter explains, contained "eighty percent new material, and twenty percent classic lines fans remember."

Back in 2003, *Golden Girls . . . Live* was visited by two of the show's early writers, Stan Zimmerman and James Berg; later, producer Marsha Posner Williams caught John and Peter's L.A. show. But there were still a certain four older ladies the guys always wished would pop by. As the 2003 *Entertainment Weekly* article covering the show had noted, Rue McClanahan herself once tried to attend at Rose's Turn, but couldn't secure a seat.

John and Peter still hope to this day they'll look out one night and see Betty White in the crowd. After all, they do know for sure that Betty is aware of their act. Back in September 2003, Betty appeared on one of the earliest episodes of Ellen DeGeneres's daytime talk show, in which the host asked her if she knew about this new show in New York where four gay men played the beloved Golden Girls.

"Yes," Betty replied with enthusiasm. "And I hear they play them better than we did!"

ABOVE:

The Golden Gals at Province-town's Art House theater in 2014 *(clockwise from top):* Varla Jean Merman, Brooklyn Shaffer, Olive Another, Ryan Landry.

Photo by MICHAEL VON REDLICH.

HARVEY FIERSTEIN

the Legendary Actor and Playwright on

ESTELLE GETTY

(1 9 2 3 - 2 0 0 8)

YOU CAN'T BELIEVE everything Estelle said in that autobiography she wrote, *If I Knew Then What I Know Now . . . So What?* The book presented what Estelle wanted to show the world, her public persona. But I would love to have read Estelle's real story. As I used to say to her, if the world had known where Estelle really came from, and what magic had happened to her, they would have loved her ten times more.

Whatever stand-up Estelle had done early in her life, whatever community theater, when I met her, she was a housewife in Bayside, Queens. Named Estelle Gettleman. Later on, I would hear her telling people she was from Long Island, and I'd tease her and yell, "You're from Queens!" And she'd yell, "Long Island!" Her husband, Arthur, had a business changing automobile glass, and they were a very funny, curmudgeonly couple. Estelle was friends with Ann and Jules Weiss, who were supporters of the La MaMa theater, where I was at the time. And so Estelle used to come to see all my shows. When I wrote *Flatbush Tosca*, I cast Helen Hanft in it, but then for whatever reason, she decided not to do it. The Weisses recommended Estelle, and she came in and auditioned—but then an actress named Suzanne Smith, with whom I had done Andy Warhol's *Pork*, said she would play the role. Estelle was mad at me, but when I wrote my next play, *International Stud*, which was the beginning of *Torch Song Trilogy*, Estelle came to see it, and loved it. Same thing with the next part, *Fugue in a Nursery*. Estelle kept saying to me, "Why don't you write a mother, and I'll play her?"

So for the third part of the trilogy, *Widows and Children First!*, I did write a mother, and gave the part to Estelle. We did a reading, and she was hysterical. Estelle was ready to go legit, and to be an actress. In fact, you can tell you have a first edition of the book of *Torch Song Trilogy* by the cast list for the third act. Because just as the play was being published, Estelle called me up and said, "I want to be listed as Estelle Getty." They had to reset the print, and in doing so, her name ended up not lining up with all the other actors'.

Sophia Petrillo
(a.k.a. "MA")

SASSY STORYTELLING SICILIAN,
FORMER SHADY PINES RESIDENT

Estelle had strong opinions, and was the expert on everything. When we were rehearsing the big fight scene in *Torch Song Trilogy*, Estelle objected to the speech her character gives to mine about what it's like to be widowed. She told us, "I don't want to say that, because that's not the way it is. My sister lost her husband, and that's not the way she felt." And I said, "Estelle, just shut up and do it." The director broke up the fight between us, and gave Estelle specific instructions on what to do: "Stand here, turn, count to three, walk three steps forward, put down the bag, say the line, pick up the bag, turn, walk out the door."

She agreed to do it, but warned us: "I'm telling you it's terrible, and nobody's going to like it." At the first preview, just to prove it wouldn't work, Estelle did just as the director had instructed. As she exited, she said to the stage manager in the wings, "Did you see how badly that went? The whole audience was shuffling, and coughing. They were all bored by that speech, that's how bad it was!" Well the truth was the audience had collapsed in tears, and that noise was people getting out their handkerchiefs. Later, one of Estelle's friends came backstage and raved about how moved she was. "Oh, I know," said Estelle. "I told Harvey that speech was a winner." That was Estelle.

When we transferred the show in 1981 to the Richard Allen Theatre off-off-Broadway, the cast included Joel Crothers, who was on *The Edge of Night*. Estelle used to tease him: "Mr. Handsome! Mr. Soap Opera! Mr. Rich Guy!" Those started out as great times. Then suddenly Joel got a stomach bug that we all thought was due to a parasite he'd picked up on his last vacation to South America. When the show moved to off Broadway, Joel said he wasn't well enough to come with us. So another actor, Court Miller, came in. Court would come in to work every day with a new ailment, and we'd all laugh, thinking this man is the biggest hypochondriac of all time.

ABOVE:
Harvey Fierstein and Estelle Getty in *Torch Song Trilogy*, 1982. OPPOSITE:
Estelle backstage on tour with her *Torch Song* family, including Jonathan Del Arco *(right)*.
Photo by GERRY GOODSTEIN, *Photo courtesy of* JONATHAN DEL ARCO.

One day it was cold sweats, then stomach problems, then this, then that. Shortly after that our pianist, Ned Levy, brought in this article from a San Francisco newspaper about this newly discovered gay cancer.

We had had no idea. They didn't even know yet that it was sexually transmitted, and Court had never been to California. But very slowly, it began to dawn on us that Court was sick. It still didn't dawn on us that Joel had already been sick, one of the earliest cases before it was even an epidemic. So already, in those early days, two people whom Estelle loved had already been stricken with what we would learn was called AIDS.

When we moved to Broadway, our stage manager, Herb Vogler, was sick. We hired an actor to understudy the boyfriend in act two and the son in act three, a young man named Christopher Stryker. And again, another young man Estelle came to adore. Christopher started getting sick, and then people at my other show, *La Cage aux Folles*, started getting sick.

Torch Song had really become Estelle's family—and not in that clichéd way that most actors talk about; Estelle yelled at me the way only a mother would yell. I'd have to remind her all the time that she was merely acting as my mother. By the time the show closed on Broadway in 1985, Estelle was out in California, about to begin work on *The Golden Girls*, and was doing whatever she could to fight the disease. She had been heartbroken not to be cast in the movie version of *Torch Song Trilogy*, but she was there at its premiere, which became the first AIDS benefit ever held in LA.

So Estelle ended up being in the middle of the AIDS epidemic from day one. We were fighting that war very early on. Because this was Estelle's family. These were her kids. She loved them, and seeing them die, one by one, just destroyed her.

When she got to LA, Estelle settled into a new life as a single woman. She hadn't let Arthur come to California with her, nor were her two sons there. She lived in an apartment, and hung out with her gay entourage, her "five-fag minimum."

In 1994, I did a very short-lived series for Witt/Thomas called *Daddy's Girls*, which was shot on the same lot, so I got to see Estelle all the time; she was next door doing *Empty Nest*. I know I found acting in a sitcom very difficult, because during the dinner break between the night's two tapings, the writers could rewrite possibly the entire script. When you go back out there, you might be doing a whole new scene you'd never rehearsed. They say doing that, it's like with any other muscle; if you do it long enough, it gets easier. And certainly the other three Golden Girls, Bea, Rue, and Betty, were all veterans.

But Estelle had a different style. Doing a sitcom versus a movie versus appearing onstage is all called "acting," but they're all such different disciplines. For an actress like Estelle, in the theater, you would learn your lines, and then have them under your belt so that you don't ever have to think about them; then you can really act. But unfortunately, that's not how sitcoms are. And on top of that, Estelle was beginning to have memory issues, and for such an independent woman, that frightened the hell out of her. And then the fear only made the issue worse.

Nobody's ever going to be Estelle to me. With all our fighting and all the other dynamics that went on between us, that was a relationship that was singular in my life. I created *Torch Song* for her; I created that character for her. I owe her a large piece of my success. When I turn on *The Golden Girls* now, it's not for the guest stars. I prefer the episodes where it's just the four women. I don't care about the stories either; they're just bullshit. What you want when you turn on *The Golden Girls* is to spend thirty minutes with your friends. For me, I turn it on, and get to spend a little more time with Estelle.

AUTHOR'S UPDATE:

After appearing for a year in the *Golden Girls* sequel series *Golden Palace*, Estelle proved there was still life in the nearly nonagenarian Sophia Petrillo, bringing the character back to appear in nearly fifty episodes of *Golden Girls* spinoff *Empty Nest*. After that show's demise in 1995, Estelle continued to make sporadic TV guest appearances on such shows as *Touched by an Angel* and *Mad About You*. As her issues with remembering lines progressed, Estelle was drawn particularly to voice-over roles, where she could perform with a script; so she voiced a character in an episode of the animated series *Duckman*, and played a role in HBO's 1999 animated adaptation of *The Sissy Duckling*, written by her longtime friend Harvey Fierstein.

Having made a few movies, including *Mannequin* and *Stop! Or My Mom Will Shoot*, during the run of *The Golden Girls*, Estelle landed a few more roles on the big screen, in *The Million Dollar Kid* in 2000, and, belovedly, as the voice of the grandmother of the title mouse in 1999's *Stuart Little*.

In 1996, Estelle reunited with Betty White and Rue McClanahan,

I love you more + more - you are the BEST. Estelle

as they played themselves in a hilarious and surreal episode of NBC's *The John Larroquette Show*, written by former *Golden Girls* scribe Mitch Hurwitz, titled "Here We Go Again." A parody of *Sunset Boulevard*, in which Betty wants to stage a demented, hours-long *Golden Girls* musical in *Larroquette*'s St. Louis bus station, Estelle was Max the butler to Betty's Norma Desmond. In 2000, Estelle was reunited again with two of her Girls when, visibly frail, she was led through the door by fellow guest star Rue to make a brief appearance in the tag of an episode ("Romance") of Betty's CBS sitcom *Ladies Man*.

By the early 2000s, Estelle had faded from public view, as she battled what came to be diagnosed as Lewy body dementia. Bea, Betty, and Rue all tried to stay in touch, but it wasn't easy, as the disease took its toll. On July 22, 2008, Estelle Getty, née Scher, died at age eighty-four. The self-described "little girl from the Lower East Side" had moved west late in life, and then made it bigger than she had ever dreamed she could. She is buried in a Los Angeles cemetery, open to the public and fittingly called Hollywood Forever.

OPPOSITE LEFT:

Estelle *(center)* joins Jenna von Oÿ *(left)* and Mayim Bialik on crossover episode "I Ain't Got Nobody" of Witt/Thomas/Harris's NBC series *Blossom*, aired February 11, 1991. OPPOSITE RIGHT: Estelle and Rue join Betty on her CBS sitcom *Ladies Man*, in an episode airing May 19, 2000.

Opposite left: Photo by CHRIS HASTON/NBCU PHOTO BANK, *via* GETTY IMAGES. *Opposite right: Photo courtesy of* CBS *via* GETTY IMAGES. *Above: Photo courtesy of* ESTATE OF RUE McCLANAHAN, *estateofrue.com.*

"LET ME GIVE YOU

——

TWO WORDS

——

OF ADVICE:

ENOUGH

WICKER!"

—Sophia Petrillo

5

GOLDEN EPISODES

From its very start, *The Golden Girls* broke new ground. Over seven seasons, the ladies brought their maturity and humor to landmark episodes about homelessness, ageism, gay rights, and the AIDS epidemic. But then, as these multitalented matrons of the small screen were also wont to do, the Girls could just as easily turn a silly subplot about a piano-playing chicken into a juicy comedic nugget to last for generations. In this chapter, the show's stars, writers, producers, crew, and guest stars reminisce about the Girls' most memorable moments, both on and off the screen.

◆ EPISODE 1 ◆

THE ENGAGEMENT

(A.K.A. THE PILOT)

Written by: SUSAN HARRIS ◆ *Directed by:* JAY SANDRICH
Original airdate: SEPTEMBER 14, 1985

Blanche comes home from a date with Harry (Frank Aletter, 1926–2009) all aflutter with marriage plans. Rose and Dorothy realize that Blanche's forthcoming union will mean a change of address for them—and worse yet, Rose is struck with a sinking feeling about Harry, which Dorothy won't allow her to share. After a policeman arrives at the house to tell Blanche that she has become involved with a bigamist, the other women attempt, but fail, to cheer Blanche up. Eventually, Blanche does emerge from her bedroom, with the realization that she would be hard-pressed to find the love and support from someone else that she has found with her friends.

◆ ◆ ◆ ◆

COMMENTARY: This episode marks the sole appearance of the Girls' gay houseboy, Coco. But after heavy editing, not much remains of Charles Levin's original performance. His presence remains the strongest in the show's opening scene, which introduces Dorothy Zbornak as she comes home from a hard day of substitute teaching, complaining about the hoodlums in her class. With her roommates Blanche and Rose not having yet been introduced, and Shady Pines not yet having burned down, who else would Dorothy have to communicate to if not Coco?

The decision to eliminate the extraneous houseboy had not been an easy one to make—and then, it turned out, not an easy one to execute. The original tape night for the *Golden Girls* pilot had been magical; now, the show's editors had to make sure the laughs in any newly shot scenes matched that elevated level of audience energy. Even the prop guys had their work cut out for them. Sometime after the original pilot shoot night, the perforated soda cracker that Sophia fetches from the kitchen had ceased to be available. So to ensure that the new footage would match, the crew glued several smaller crackers together, and fed the Frankencracker to poor Estelle, who, like a trouper, nibbled on it anyway.

May 13, 1985

TO: SUSAN
      TONY
      PAUL ✓
      HARRY

FROM: MARSHA

RE: "GOLDEN GIRLS"

      I spoke with the NBC Standards & Practices guy
      this morning (Warren Ashley) about the concern
      of "mama had a stroke...."

      He said that the senior citizens test group had
      problems with the line -- his formal documentation
      for NBC about those lines will be that her problem
      was the result of a 'very rare and mild form of
      Broca's Aphasia'. In reality, she would probably
      have some speech problems, but since we were not
      grossly inaccurate, he sees no problems.

      Thanks,

      Marsha

One more noteworthy bit of trivia: this pilot episode features future *Designing Women* regular Meshach Taylor (1947–2014) as the policeman.

SUSAN HARRIS: In a pilot, you have so many problems to solve in such a short amount of time there's just so much you can do. You just hope to establish characters, their back stories, and the story that you're about to tell. That's all you've got room for in your twenty-three minutes and change.

PAUL WITT: When you're hoping that all the right talent comes together at just the right time, there's always an element of luck when you make a pilot. But we knew we had a great piece of material. Susan's script is widely considered one of the best pilots ever written. And thanks to our amazing cast, it turned out to be one of the best pilots made.

BARRY FANARO: My writing partner, Mort Nathan, and I had worked on *Benson* for Witt/Thomas, and then the company's new show *Hail to the Chief*, starring Patty Duke as the first female president. *Hail to the Chief* was irreverent like *Soap* had been,

ABOVE:
Shortly after filming this pilot episode, NBC censors tested *The Golden Girls* with viewers, paying particular attention to public reaction to the portrayal of Sophia. Although some senior viewers objected to the depiction of the effects of a stroke, ultimately, the line remained.

Photo courtesy of LEX PASSARIS.

and we loved it. While we were waiting anxiously to hear if it was going to be picked up for more episodes, Paul and Tony invited us, as well as our fellow writers Kathy Speer and Terry Grossman, to the taping of the *Golden Girls* pilot—which turned out to be one of the best pilot tapings I've ever seen. Right out of the gate, the audience knew who these ladies were, and embraced the show's central idea. Here were three beloved TV all-star personalities, and a new discovery in Estelle, and they had the audience screaming with laughter. The four of us looked at each other and said, "I hope *Hail to the Chief* gets canceled, because I want to do *this*!" And that's exactly what ended up happening.

CHARLES LEVIN: I had no concern whatsoever about playing a gay character. I grew up in the theater, and played all different parts, heterosexual and homosexual. The eighties were a more innocent time, a time of coming out. But they were also still a time of lisping, effeminate gay characters on TV. My physical type doesn't lend itself well to that stereotype, but what I could do was affect it.

Unlike my *Hill Street Blues* character, Eddie Gregg, whose life ended heroically but tragically, Coco was a gay character being played for laughs. Susan Harris has a great track record of doing that, like with Billy Crystal on *Soap*. The way she wrote Coco, he was obviously gay and loving it. Even though he was way over the top, this was a real person, and you're allowed to laugh and enjoy him without feeling self-conscious or afraid that he's gay. And he was completely acceptable to all the women in the house; that was the irony of the title, that he, too, was a Golden Girl.

Susan wanted to write a character who gave you insights as to what gay guys do—their love lives, their private lives. But as I found out during rehearsal week, that was verboten. I had a scene where I come in and announce, "That's the

last time I date a cop!" I pour my heart out to Sophia, my confidante, and she decides to cheer me up by taking me to the dog track. Well, word came down that this was offensive to NBC, who did not want any reference to what Coco was doing with other men. The scene was cut. Nobody wanted to know what he did on the outside. His only function was to be within the house, dealing with the women. I think one of the real problems was that Rock Hudson was dying of AIDS. I think it threw everyone for a loop, especially those in TV. Because now, how do you deal with gay characters when there's this threat of a horrible death hanging over their heads? So any mention of intercourse between men was just not going to be tolerated. It was too frightening.

The night of the taping, I went home on cloud nine. Over the next few weeks, as I waited for the official pickup of my "option," my wife and I were getting calls about when the limo would be picking us up for the network affiliates meeting, and what to wear. And then, two days before the option deadline, Paul Witt called and said, "Chuck, it's not going to work out." He explained that there were too many people in the show, and that they really wanted to concentrate on the women. They didn't want to have to give me less to do just to keep me in the show; it wouldn't be fair to me.

I was devastated, simply because it was such a great show. I didn't care about the money; that stuff has never been important to me. But I'd fallen in love with Bea and Estelle. I've actually never seen the pilot as it ended up airing. I refused to watch it because I remember what it was, and it's too disappointing to see how it was butchered. Basically what you see now is that I'm sort of a walk-through.

I still think back on my *Golden Girls* experience fondly, and don't have any regrets. I just sometimes grieve the loss of that character, who could have grown into something wonderful.

OPPOSITE:

An early publicity shot featuring all five of the "Girls," prior to Coco's untimely demise.

Photo by HERB BALL/NBCU PHOTO BANK *via* GETTY IMAGES.

GUESS WHO'S COMING TO THE WEDDING?

Written by: WINIFRED HERVEY ◆ *Directed by:* PAUL BOGART
Original airdate: SEPTEMBER 21, 1985

As she awaits Kate's (Lisa Jane Persky) arrival, Dorothy reveals to the Girls that she's anxious about meeting the man her daughter is bringing along. Dorothy is excited that said boyfriend Dennis (Dennis Drake) is a doctor—and even more thrilled when Kate announces that in just a few days, the two plan to wed. When Blanche and Rose suggest throwing the wedding at the house, Kate accepts—on the condition that her father, Stan Zbornak (Herb Edelman, 1933–96), also be on the guest list.

But on the big day, when Stan arrives, sporting a new toupee but without his new wife, Chrissy, Dorothy slams the door in his face. When Dorothy declares she can't bear being in the same church with Stan and plans to stay home, Blanche forces her to her feet and out the door. Later, at the living room reception, Blanche even teaches her friend a sorority trick of squeezing a friend's hand in times of stress; and so, Dorothy makes it through Stan's obnoxious toast. Sophia advises her daughter to confront Stan instead of internalizing her anger. So after the guests depart, Dorothy unloads her thirty-eight years' worth of feelings for the man she once loved, this time saying good-bye on her own terms.

◆ ◆ ◆ ◆

COMMENTARY: This episode introduces the character of Stan Zbornak, a philandering louse nonetheless played so charmingly by Herb Edelman. We'd heard about Dorothy's former husband in the series' pilot, but here we meet the man in the flesh and toupee. Stan would be back again and again, often with get-rich-quick schemes and, in the series' finale, with a blessing for Dorothy on her new marriage. The show's most frequently recurring character, Stan would

ultimately appear in twenty-five of its episodes, becoming a de facto fifth Golden Girl.

Playing Stan and Dorothy's daughter, Kate, is Lisa Jane Persky, whose movie credits include *The Great Santini*, *The Cotton Club*, *The Sure Thing*, *Peggy Sue Got Married*, and *When Harry Met Sally*.

This episode was shot as the *Golden Girls'* fourth. But "Guess Who's Coming to the Wedding?" must have been one that the producers

WINIFRED HERVEY: When I wrote the episode, we knew Stan would be tall, so as to match up to Dorothy. And we knew he was going to be bald. I think I just made up that he wore a bad toupee, and they went with it.

LISA JANE PERSKY: In this episode, when Kate hugs Dorothy, that was very genuine, and easy for me to act, because that was really me hugging someone whom I'd always admired. I grew up with liberal parents who were a lot like Maude Findlay. So it wasn't that much of a stretch for me to consider her a mother figure.

On the set, all Bea really said to me and to many people the whole day would be "Good morning, everybody," and then not much after that. When we weren't acting as Dorothy and

considered an early calling card for the series, because it was moved up on the schedule. As in any early episode of a TV series, some things are just being worked out. Rose is a little less dumb than she would come to be, and Blanche a little more grounded. The show has a few production bugs to work out as well. Take a close look at the episode's final climactic scene; at about the 22:50 mark, as Dorothy is winding up her heartfelt speech, a TV camera briefly rolls into the left side of the frame.

KATHY SPEER: When we introduced Stan in this episode, we didn't know he would become a recurring character. At one point in the casting process, I know one name that had been mentioned was Carl Reiner, but I don't think he was ever asked to play the part. Because Bea was going to have to get along with whoever was chosen, the producers asked her for her thoughts. Bea knew Herb and liked him.

TERRY GROSSMAN: Everyone liked Herb Edelman. It was always a pleasure working with him, for us and for Bea. Kathy and I just worried that maybe we found him funnier than the rest of the world did, the way he played a lovable shlub, because when he would play Stan, we would be crying with laughter.

> *"It's settled. Now call your father, and tell the dirtbag he can come."*
> —DOROTHY

Kate, she didn't really give me any advice, except she asked me not to put my arms around her neck. That made me laugh when she first said it, because I wasn't sure if she was kidding. I don't know whether she thought I was going to block her face, or whether it was uncomfortable for her, or whether she felt it wasn't right for the characters. But of course, she knew what she was doing, so I did what she said.

ABOVE:

Herb Edelman *(center)* with script supervisor Robert Spina *(left)* and assistant director Lex Passaris.

Photo by KARI HENDLER PHOTOGRAPHY.

TRANSPLANT

Written by: SUSAN HARRIS • *Directed by:* PAUL BOGART
Original airdate: OCTOBER 5, 1985

Blanche dreads the upcoming visit from her youngest sister, Virginia (Sheree North, 1932–2005). That "conniving little witch" is always out to get something of hers, a petty-sounding Blanche insists—but this time she's right. Because Virginia needs a kidney.

With their older sister, Charmaine, already deemed an ineligible donor, Blanche debates the possible sacrifice. Blanche ultimately makes the right decision, and leaves to meet Virginia in Atlanta for the surgery. But Blanche, too, is deemed unsuitable just as another donor is found: a retired Mormon schoolteacher. Blanche returns to Miami victorious, with two kidneys, a date with a handsome doctor, and a sister to love anew.

Meanwhile, Rose, Dorothy, and Sophia are consumed with caring for baby Danny, son of neighbors Ted and Lucy—all of whom we've never heard of before, and never will again.

◆ ◆ ◆ ◆

COMMENTARY: Actress Sheree North played Blanche's younger sister, but in real life was two years older than Rue McClanahan. A trained dancer whom Hollywood initially sought as a possible successor to Marilyn Monroe, Sheree ended up finding fame on TV, as Lou Grant's girlfriend Charlene on *The Mary Tyler Moore Show* in the seventies, and famously as Kramer's mother, Babs, on *Seinfeld* in the nineties. The actress had appeared in a regular role on an earlier Witt/Thomas sitcom, the short-lived *I'm a Big Girl Now* in 1980–81, and would return in a second *Golden Girls* episode, season five's "Ebb Tide," in which Blanche and Virginia clash again at Big Daddy's funeral.

This episode marks another *Golden* milestone, in a major change behind the scenes: "Transplant" became the last of four episodes helmed by director Paul Bogart. Renowned for his work in TV's earliest days and as the regular director of the landmark sitcom *All in the Family*, Bogart had a style that just didn't fit in with the *Girls*. "Paul told me that he'd gone in and told the *Golden Girls* staff, 'Just give me the show in the beginning of the week, and by the end of the week, you'll have an Emmy winner,'" remembers Jim Drake, Bogart's friend and one-time protégé who would go on to direct the following eight episodes of the show before a regular director, Terry Hughes, was ultimately hired.

Bogart's pronouncement hadn't endeared him to the *Golden Girls*' hands-on producers Tony Thomas and Paul Witt, nor did the perception that the director was trying to sway the actresses' opinions in the inevitable creative differences that followed. Indeed Rue McClanahan did initially favor Bogart, who allowed her to play Blanche with the Southern accent Jay Sandrich had discouraged for the pilot. But in the end, the director didn't have the full support of the Girls either. Just as Bea Arthur had sometimes bristled at Sandrich's softer style as evidenced in the classic *Mary Tyler Moore Show*, this time it was Betty White who had issues with the way a *Golden Girls* director wanted her to play her part. Bogart had come from the Norman Lear school of sitcoms, where arguments were loud and emotional moments played in extreme close-up. (For example, note the atypical *Golden Girls* close-up here on Blanche at the end of her dinner with Virginia.) And he wanted Betty to be bigger on-screen.

"Bea was very happy with Paul Bogart. And he was probably great for other things, but not for Rose," Betty explains. Two weeks before this episode's taping, during production of "Job Hunting" (a troubled episode that, although shot as the series' second installment, was ultimately delayed for airing until the following March) Bogart had urged Betty "to get really mad, and yell and scream," Betty remembers. But "Jay Sandrich had set such a wonderful course for the character of Rose for me in the pilot, and to me, screaming was more Paul Bogart than it was Rose Nylund. I was very uncomfortable with it."

Still, a trouper who always tries not to argue with her director—"I figure a director has a more objective view and may know more than I do,"

ABOVE:

To make her case for a kidney, Virginia takes Blanche to this fancy restaurant.

Photo courtesy of the EDWARD S. STEPHENSON ARCHIVE *at the* ART DIRECTORS GUILD.

Betty explains—she tried it Bogart's way. "But it was just so un-Rose. She was scared, but she wouldn't suddenly turn into a strong New York woman and scream. I just couldn't find an excuse for it, and I felt like I'd lost the character." Then, during a run-through of "Transplant" for the writers late in that week, Jay came back to observe the proceedings on the show he had helped launch—and noticed right away that something was amiss. Jay urged Betty to speak her concerns to Paul Witt and Tony Thomas, and when she was reluctant, he apparently did so on her behalf. Soon, Tony walked on to the set. "He told me: 'Do it the way you think you should,'" Betty remembers. "And the next week, Paul Bogart wasn't there."

TERRY GROSSMAN: Rue adored Paul Bogart, because he was a real actor's director. But from the writers' perspective, he was all about the "moments," and not the jokes. The comedy was suffering.

Just as the show's first season was starting, Susan Harris had been feeling sick, and so the production order of some scripts was changed. Kathy and I ended up being the guinea pigs, with our episode "Job Hunting" being the first to be shot after the pilot. We found Paul's working style to be territorial, gathering the cast around him and excluding the writers. That wasn't how we were used to working on *Benson*, and we complained to Paul Witt and Tony Thomas. When we shot "Transplant," written by Susan, Paul [Bogart] did the same thing again—and that was it. He was gone.

ROSE:

"Sophia, if you hated your sister, would you clean the house?"

SOPHIA:

"I'd put Vaseline on the tips of her walker."

PAUL WITT: The storyline of someone needing a kidney has been done on almost every comedy series that runs for any length of time, because it's such a natural. There's also definitely a hypochondriacal strain among the three of us—Tony, Susan, and me—and we always liked to ask ourselves, "Would you?" "What would you do if . . . ?"

LEX PASSARIS (associate director): At the time of this episode, Sheree North was suffering from some kind of neurological symptom that caused her hand to shake, but we managed to shoot around it. This was the first prominent guest star spot since the pilot, and I was excited to hear that she had been cast. Because now, for the first time, I got the sense that we were going to get to work with some really cool people on the show. With the real richness to this story, it was clear that *The Golden Girls* was going to be able to do anything it wanted to. The show could get as serious as it wanted, and as funny and as out there as it wanted, and it was all going to be okay because of the writers who balance it just right, and the actors who make it work onstage.

RUE McCLANAHAN: Sheree North had been one of my favorite actresses for a long time. I was thrilled to death they had hired her, and that we got to work together. I still have an 8x10 of us in that episode, and it looks like we really could be sisters. Working with her was a thorough delight, and I enjoyed the entire week.

In this episode, Blanche has a terrible decision to make. You'd think a person would make that decision on the spot: of course I'll help save your life! But as written, there was quite a bit of animosity between these two sisters, perhaps born of jealousy. Blanche was always worried about not being the queen bee. I think it explains here that she was the middle sister, so that might explain some of her attitudes. But I think she would have been jealous of any attractive sister, and of any sister who competed for the love of Big Daddy. When I approached this episode, I could figure out how Blanche felt based upon what we knew about her family. I myself have a sister, but the one thing I couldn't do was relate to Blanche's jealousy, because I had wanted a baby sister so badly!

Left to her own devices, Blanche tended to be less responsible than she could have been. That's why it was so good that she lived with the other women, because they often put her on the right track. Obviously Blanche was happy how this turned out: she didn't have to give her kidney. I was happy about that, too—and happy as well that she'd decided to give it.

ROSE THE PRUDE

Written by: BARRY FANARO & MORT NATHAN ◆ Directed by: JIM DRAKE
Original airdate: SEPTEMBER 28, 1985

When Blanche and Rose double-date brothers, Blanche's beau Jeffrey turns out to be a dud, but surprisingly, Rose has a great time with Arnie (Harold Gould, 1923–2010). But when Arnie invites Rose on a romantic cruise to the Bahamas, the widow of fifteen years panics at the prospect of sleeping with a man other than her first and only. A widower himself, Arnie is sympathetic, and elicits from Rose her true, deeper fear: sex with her might kill him; after all, her husband Charlie died while making love to her. The scene onboard fades with Rose and Arnie in a tender embrace. But when Rose returns home, and the Girls press her for sexy details, we learn that the physical contact did indeed go a lot further than that. And to Rose's relief, Arnie is still alive and well.

◆ ◆ ◆ ◆

COMMENTARY: This episode marks the first appearance of Harold Gould—but not as Miles Webber, Rose's longtime squeeze. (See season five, "Dancing in the Dark.") Here, he's Arnie Peterson from Plainfield, New Jersey—and equally charming as he consoles a vulnerable Rose on their cruise.

The episode would be momentous for Betty as well; it's the one from the show's first season she chose to submit for Emmy consideration in 1986. And that night, she won, becoming the first of the Girls to bring home the trophy for Outstanding Lead Actress in a Comedy Series.

BETTY WHITE: I love that in this episode they let the romance show between Rose and Arnie. Rose was so confused and reluctant, and then all of a sudden, romance won out. That was a rare chance for Rose; she didn't often get that.

JIM DRAKE: The idea in the scene with Rose and Arnie on the cruise was to put them in a small stateroom. Not so small that it becomes a scene from the Marx Brothers, but to make it seem like they're really on top of each other, and underscore how trapped Rose feels. The scene ends with a touching moment, where Rose asks Arnie to sit on the bed with her, and says, "Hold me." I give credit for that to [the show's former director] Paul Bogart. Having worked with him, I had observed how well he used more dramatic punch lines or "scene buttons." And *The Golden Girls* ended up with its share of those, too.

TERRY HUGHES: This episode was before I joined as director. But I'd heard that for a while during the week, the episode wasn't working that well. It wasn't as funny as it needed to be. Susan was getting on a plane to go to New York, so she wrote a scene on the plane and phoned it

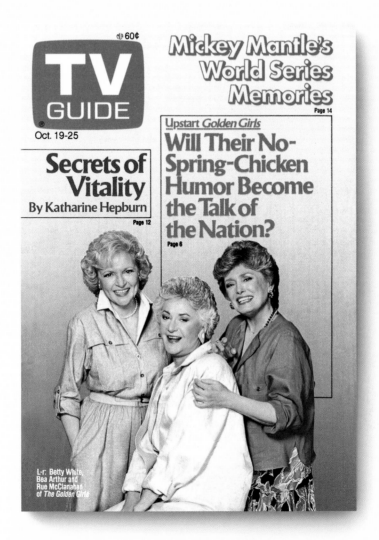

60¢

TV GUIDE

®

Oct. 19-25

Secrets of Vitality
By Katharine Hepburn
Page 12

Mickey Mantle's World Series Memories
Page 14

Upstart *Golden Girls*
Will Their No-Spring-Chicken Humor Become the Talk of the Nation?
Page 6

L-r: Betty White, Bea Arthur and Rue McClanahan of *The Golden Girls*

back in to us. That became the cheesecake scene in this episode—the series' first cheesecake scene—where Blanche discovers she's horrified about how she looks in the hand mirror, and Dorothy advises her always to use the mirror while lying on her back, so that everything falls down and into place. And suddenly, they had a second scene that was

hilarious. In fact, that scene ended up being worked in to the ten-minute sketch we performed for the Queen and Queen Mother at the Royal Variety Performance at the London Palladium in 1988.

(Author's note: the sketch is viewable on YouTube; search *The Golden Girls* on the 1988 Royal Variety Performance.)

ABOVE:

Already a hot new show, *The Golden Girls* nabbed the cover of *TV Guide* magazine's October 19, 1985, issue.

Courtesy of TV GUIDE MAGAZINE.

BLANCHE AND THE YOUNGER MAN

Written by: STAN ZIMMERMAN & JAMES BERG • *Directed by:* JIM DRAKE
Original airdate: NOVEMBER 16, 1985

Rose receives a visit from her mother, Alma (Jeanette Nolan, 1911–98), an energetic, fun-loving woman whom Rose insists on treating like an invalid. Alma takes to hanging out with bad influence Sophia; and eventually, after some late-night jai alai hijinks, Alma stops to ask for directions, and is picked up by police officers who apparently also think that she must be confused. After retrieving her mother from the station, Rose ratchets up her smothering, and a frustrated Alma decides to depart for Rose's brother's house. Only after Dorothy intervenes with advice to treat Alma as an adult does Rose reconcile with her mother, who reminds her that "keeping me from living isn't going to keep me from dying."

Meanwhile, Blanche is preoccupied with her love life, having been asked out by her young Jazzercise instructor, Dirk (Charles Hill). Blanche starves and aerobicizes herself into a weight-loss frenzy. But over a dinner of watercress salad, Dirk turns out to be a big, beefy dud—and what's worse, one who's looking at Blanche as a mother figure and not a lover.

❖ ❖ ❖ ❖

JIM DRAKE: Blanche was originally supposed to have the A story—but as rehearsals went on, it became clear that Rose's story with her mother was going to take precedence, and that meant that Blanche's would have to get shorter. But then, on the night of the taping, the Rose storyline presented a big problem. Jeanette Nolan had already appeared on *Night Court*, and later would appear again on an episode of that show that I directed. But she was getting to the point where she had become forgetful. She had been okay as long as she had the script in her hand. And through the week as we rehearsed, we figured "she's doing what Bea does," working toward being off book. And every day, she would get a little better.

Through all her radio and movie work, it's possible Jeanette had delivered her lines in small sections, and never really had to put it all together. In our scene around the kitchen table, Alma has a long speech about how she found love with a farmhand after losing her husband. In rehearsal, Jeanette performed it well. But then, in front of the audience, she appeared to forget everything. I've experienced this quite a bit with older actors, and my attitude is, no problem—we can do pickups of parts of the speech at a time, and put it all together.

Then the phone rang; it was the producers in their booth, and they insisted that we needed to get Jeanette's speech all in one take, straight through with all the other Girls' reactions. We were already up to about take six, and it wasn't getting any better. Between takes, the ladies called over to Tom Carpenter, our stage manager, and asked him to ask the producers not to do this. But as the director, I felt like I had a gun to my head. To make things worse, they tried putting a few new jokes in, hoping to make the speech fresh for her.

It was terrible, like watching someone being flagellated. You just want it to stop. Finally, somewhere around take eight, she got through it—and the audience really applauded.

STAN ZIMMERMAN: My writing partner, James Berg, and I had read a story in the *New York Times* in which Betty had said about her late husband, Allen Ludden, that not a day goes by where she doesn't think of him. So we put that in the script for Rose to say about Charlie, because we really wanted to use a real part of Betty's life. Well, little did we know how close to real life we were getting. It turned out that at the time, both Betty's and Bea's mothers were critically ill. And then, two days before taping this episode, Bea's mother died. The producers offered to cancel the taping, but Bea wanted to go ahead. Toward the end of the episode, there's a scene in the kitchen where Sophia thanks Dorothy for not treating her like an old lady, and tells her she's a good daughter. Bea had trouble doing the scene, and they had to do it a few times. And whenever I see the scene, I always choke up, because you can see Bea choking up. She can't even look at the camera, and has to look away.

BLANCHE:

"This is strictly off the record, but Dirk is nearly five years younger than I am."

DOROTHY:

"In what, Blanche, dog years?"

THE RETURN OF DOROTHY'S EX

Written by: KATHY SPEER & TERRY GROSSMAN ♦ *Directed by:* JIM DRAKE
Original airdate: NOVEMBER 30, 1985

Dorothy's ex-husband, Stan, comes to the house with legal papers for Dorothy to sign, ridding the two of the last vestige of their thirty-eight-year marriage, an old piece of Florida property they purchased on their honeymoon. The next day Stan reveals the real reason for his visit: his young new wife, Chrissy, has already left him for a younger man. Stan persuades Dorothy to take a car ride out to the swampland that had once been their retirement dream, and as sentimentality overtakes them both, they wind up in bed together. The next morning, Dorothy is shocked to overhear Stan ordering roses to celebrate their "wonderful new beginning." Dorothy takes Stan's proposed reunion seriously, and agonizes over the decision, but ultimately realizes that she could never trust him again—and it's a good thing, too. Because at Stan's hotel the next day, Chrissy (Simone Griffeth) shows up, looking to reconcile. And Stan being Stan, the moment he realizes he's out of luck with Dorothy, he chases after the young blonde anew.

♦ ♦ ♦ ♦

COMMENTARY: Character actor Herb Edelman had made his first appearance as Dorothy's ex-husband, Stanley Zbornak, in the series' fourth episode, "Guess Who's Coming to the Wedding?" At the time, Stan was not necessarily intended to become a recurring character. But as Herb immediately displayed a dynamic on-screen chemistry with Bea Arthur, the comedic potential became obvious. In fact, explains the show's later longtime director Terry Hughes, Stan soon became his and the writers' secret weapon of sorts. "If a script wasn't working, or a scene needed levity, sometimes I would say, 'We need Stan in here.'"

As much as Bea Arthur, too, loved working with Herb, this storyline of a divorcée confronting the ex-husband who'd abandoned her for a younger woman may have hit too close to home. Bea had divorced her own husband of twenty-eight years, director Gene Saks, under similar circumstances in 1978. "Apart from the episode we shot just after Bea's mother died, this was the second toughest show I worked on," says director Jim Drake.

In the beginning of the production week, when Bea first encountered the script at the table read, "you could see her face fall," Jim

DOROTHY:

"Please, Stan, no hugging, no kissing. Let's just do it and get it over with."

STAN:

"Sounds like the last few years of our marriage."

BARRY FANARO: My writing partner, Mort Nathan, and I loved Herb Edelman from all the Neil Simon plays we had seen him in on Broadway. We were always looking for the best of the Broadway character actors for TV projects. And so when we wondered who could be Dorothy's husband, he came to mind. I'm sure there were ten guys who came in to read, but Herb came in and was brilliant. And he was tall, to play against Bea. Kathy and Terry loved him and we loved him. He came in and he instantly was Stan.

PAUL WITT: The networks always seem to prefer comedies about people in their twenties and early thirties, but very few actors have gotten comedically proficient by then. But on *The Golden Girls,* we had so many great casting choices. Herb Edelman was just a dream for the part of Stan. He had a kind of forgivable quality. He was such a shlub that you couldn't help but love him. You certainly couldn't hate him, no matter how aberrant or over-the-top his behavior.

BEA ARTHUR: Herb Edelman was lovely and a wonderful funny, funny actor. I loved the relationship between Dorothy and Stan. It was just as bizarre as Dorothy's relationship with Sophia, which made for great grounds for comedy.

remembers. "At first she said, 'I'm not going to do this.'" But as Jim theorizes, "I think that once she told herself, 'I'm a professional,' she came around. And actually, the more we worked on the script, the more she was really relating to it."

Then, just as the episode looked like it was back on track, came a casting coup de grâce; the casting department found its Chrissy in Simone Griffeth, a beautiful blonde who had worked with Bea once before. The problem was Bea already disliked the young actress, who was now playing Dorothy's younger rival. "I'm not telling tales out of school here," Jim says. "Because Bea would have been the first to say that this episode was not to her liking, neither the concept nor the casting."

SIMONE GRIFFETH: One day, my agent called and said he was sending over a script for *The Golden Girls.* And what I got was this piece of insane material. The character, Chrissy, was a flight attendant—well, really a stereotype of flight attendants. And she called Stan things like Big Stan and Stick Man. I thought, "Where did this dialogue come from—*Gidget*?"

I wondered how to pull this off and make the character seem real. Chrissy was obviously a "dumb blonde," and I had played a lot of those already. So I worked on Chrissy's lines, did the audition, and soon my agent called and said I had the job. And I immediately responded, "Well, quick, make the deal before Bea finds out it's me."

A few years earlier, I had done a [1983] series with Bea called *Amanda's By the Sea*, set at a failing hotel. Really, nobody will ever successfully remake *Fawlty Towers*, but we tried, right down to similar-looking sets. Personally, I thought the show was really great, and we had such a great cast. But I never got to know Bea terribly well. She was not a person who was really all that accessible, and not just to me, but to others, too.

I think that having recently been through her divorce, Bea may have transferred some of her feelings about younger women on to me. I played her son's wife, and our characters had a love/hate relationship. So we had a lot of scenes together on *Amanda's*, and actually whatever feelings she had about me ended up working for the characters.

Still, I wondered what would happen when I walked on to the *Golden Girls* set for the first time. And sure enough, the moment Bea saw me she said, "Oh my God, is this an omen?" I think she was referring to the fact that *Amanda's* had been canceled after thirteen episodes. But as it turned out, working on *The Golden Girls* was a really pleasant experience. Betty White, Rue

> ### *"You had to bring him home? You couldn't find a drunken sailor on a street corner?"*
> —SOPHIA

McClanahan, and Estelle Getty were so darling. And of course wonderful Herbie Edelman, with whom I'd worked on an earlier sitcom called *Ladies Man*, was there, so I had a ball. Even Bea was nice. I don't remember specifically how nice, because it's been a long time. I think all the ladies had the same amount of clout. They were all divas, but they were divas together, so nobody could out-diva anyone else.

DOROTHY:

"Are you finished, or is there something else that you don't understand?"

ROSE:

"Well, actually there is. I don't understand how a Thermos keeps things both hot and cold."

THE HEART ATTACK

Written by: SUSAN HARRIS • *Directed by:* JIM DRAKE

Original airdate: NOVEMBER 23, 1985

While cleaning up from a big blow-out dinner party, Sophia begins to experience chest pains she dismisses as merely "a bubble," but that Dorothy fears may actually be signs of a heart attack. Worse yet, with a storm brewing outside, paramedics are unable to get to the house. Sophia dispenses some final words of wisdom and love to her daughter and her two best friends. But when the Girls' physician (Ronald Hunter, 1943–2013) arrives, he quickly diagnoses her pains as symptoms of a gallbladder attack brought on by overeating. Sophia celebrates her new lease on life, and recants her earlier "deathbed" confession that Dorothy is her favorite child.

◆ ◆ ◆ ◆

COMMENTARY: For the first time since the pilot, this episode takes place completely inside the Girls' house at 6151 Richmond Street. Ostensibly, the reason is that there's a storm outside; so for most of the show, the Girls are housebound, and visitors kept at bay by fallen trees. (The storm effects, the episode's director, Jim Drake, reveals, were done super low-budget, with crew members whipping branches around outside the door.)

But there's another, behind-the-scenes reason for this episode's structure as well. Earlier that year, NBC had mounted a live episode of Nell Carter's sitcom *Gimme a Break*, which had scored big-time publicity as the first live sitcom telecast since 1959. Based on that success, network chief Brandon Tartikoff devised a gimmick: to promote the late-night comedy *Saturday Night Live*, all of NBC's prime time shows would broadcast live that night as well.

Tartikoff's executives brought his idea to the showrunners of NBC's Saturday sitcom lineup:

not just *Gimme a Break*, but also *The Facts of Life*, *The Golden Girls*, and *227*. Initially planning on playing along, Susan Harris structured this episode, "The Heart Attack," as two continuous acts, each taking place in real time and almost entirely in the Girls' living room and kitchen. But then someone at the network realized: how could Fred Dryer's 10 PM detective show, *Hunter*, ever be staged live?

"And so one by one, the sitcoms, including *The Golden Girls*, backed away from the live plan," Jim Drake remembers, adding that "doing a live show would have been tough for the ladies." First of all, there was Estelle's already debilitating problem with stage fright, even without the pressure of a live nationwide audience. Plus, Jim notes, "The way each of them worked was so different. Betty would sit down at the table read on Monday with the script, and then be off book and letter-perfect for the rest of the week, and able to make any additional adjustments to the script. But Bea was still learning her lines literally up

---

DOROTHY:

"You know, Ma, you don't look good."

SOPHIA:

*"I'm short and I'm old.
What did you expect, Princess Di?"*

---

until the moment before they went out in front of the audience. That was her process." (In fact, early on during his stint on the show, the director remembers Bea requesting of Betty, "For God's sake, don't be off book so early. It makes all the rest of us feel bad!")

The storyline of Sophia's possible heart attack must have seemed to Susan Harris like the perfect way to anchor her action to the living room for an entire episode. But then, for the second time, fate dealt the Girls a behind-the-scenes blow. First Bea Arthur's mother, Rebecca, had died during production of the episode "Blanche and the Younger Man." And now, such a short time later, Betty White's mother, Tess, passed away as the girls prepared for "The Heart Attack." And so, as they played these scenes about motherly love and mortality, both Bea and Betty brought their own emotions to the screen. Here, as Rose remembers dressing her late husband, Charlie, for his funeral, we can see the real welling tears in Betty's eyes.

JIM DRAKE: From the time Betty and Bea learned that their mothers were severely ill, they had been able to play the fun aspects of each episode, but they were really already in mourning, and their tears were real. They wanted to fight them, so I said, "Do what you need to do. Don't call them up if they're not there, but at the same time, you don't have to fight them either." These episodes worked very effectively, and the show went very well in front of the audience.

SUSAN HARRIS: I am most interested when I write about death, and about what leads to that moment. It's what everybody tries to avoid thinking about, but it's been an obsession almost my entire life. Sophia's possible death was the biggest thing I could think of to present in terms of a story, and it brings out every emotion in the other characters. There is no richer place to go, and nothing you have to manufacture as a writer to get there.

A LITTLE ROMANCE

Written by: BARRY FANARO & MORT NATHAN • *Directed by:* TERRY HUGHES
Original airdate: DECEMBER 14, 1985

As Rose's relationship with Dr. Jonathan Newman (Brent Collins, 1941–88) starts to get serious, she knows it will soon be time for her beau to meet her Girls. Blanche takes the initiative to invite him to dinner, but there's just one problem: Rose has somehow neglected to mention that he's a little person. Now, Rose prepares herself to sit through a dinner peppered with faux pas. (Blanche's one-word offer of hors d'oeuvres—"Shrimp?"—is an audience favorite.)

When Jonathan tells Rose he has something important to discuss with her over dinner the next day, she agonizes over whether she is truly willing to commit to him, which would mean weathering public stares at the sight of a couple so physically different. But in the end, in a delicious twist, Jonathan is the one to dump Rose, when he realizes he just can't reconcile continuing to date someone not Jewish.

◆ ◆ ◆ ◆

COMMENTARY: Every sitcom takes a while to settle, for characters to find their voices and for audiences to get to know them and fall in love. In the series' pilot, Rose was a little too wise, Blanche a little too ditzy. But here, with episode thirteen, the series' first true classic, it's clear that everything on *The Golden Girls* has fallen into place. The jokes are fast and furious and the character lines are drawn, with hilarious and everlasting results.

BETTY WHITE: When people ask me what is my favorite episode, it's like asking what's my favorite animal—and that's anything with a leg on each corner. But this episode sticks with me maybe more than any of the others. They milked it for every short joke you could possibly have, but there was a sweetness about the episode, too.

BARRY FANARO: I always say this is my favorite episode, and Mort and I won an Emmy for it. It's funny, but to me it's also serious; it's about discrimination, and it touches on racism and sexuality. To me, Rose's dilemma is parallel to concerns about dating outside one's race or religion. So yes, we did as many jokes as possible. But underneath it all, this episode was always about making the decision and commitment to be in love with someone unlike oneself. And it was perfect Rose that she would be able to do that.

OPPOSITE:
Rose with boyfriend Dr. Jonathan Newman (Brent Collins).

Photo by NBC/NBCU PHOTO BANK *via* GETTY IMAGES.

IN A BED OF ROSE'S

Written by: SUSAN HARRIS • *Directed by:* TERRY HUGHES
Original airdate: JANUARY 11, 1986

After a month of dating, Rose finally allows her new beau Al (Richard Roat) to stay the night—as long as he agrees to be quiet during the act. And silent he is; the next morning, Sophia enters the kitchen with the news that there's a dead man in Rose's bed. Sometime during their night of passion, Al expired, bringing back haunting memories for Rose of the night her husband, Charlie, also died in the sack.

Later that day, the Girls find a phone number for Al's supposed sister—and Rose realizes she's not really a live-in sibling, but actually his wife. When guilt-ridden Rose drives up to Boca Raton to see Mrs. Beatty (Priscilla Morrill, 1927-94), the widow assumes Rose to be just the latest in a long line of philandering Al's ex-girlfriends. A few nights later, Mrs. Beatty comes over bearing reassuring findings from the coroner: Al would have had his heart attack whether in bed with Rose or not. And so, three months later, Rose reluctantly agrees to a romantic weekend away with Arnie—and they both do come home alive.

◆ ◆ ◆ ◆

COMMENTARY: For the third time in this first season, we hear about Rose's husband, Charlie, dying in bed, and Rose's growing reputation as an inadvertent man killer. Here, after getting over the death of Al, Rose goes away for another romantic weekend with Arnie, whom we met earlier in the season in episode six, "Rose the Prude," but whom we don't get to see here. But we do get to hear about their rendezvous; the ending scene, where Rose fools Dorothy and Blanche into thinking she's now killed not only Arnie but also a local sheriff with her lethal sexuality, is a favorite moment of the show's fans.

In another interesting moment, Rose refers to native St. Olafian Inga Lundqvist, who

didn't need men—to which Blanche retorts, "Who was she, some Swedish lesbian?" Interestingly enough, world-wise Blanche knows the meaning of the word here; but by next season, when Dorothy's friend Jean visits in "Isn't It Romantic?," she's surprisingly forgetful, confusing the term with the word "Lebanese."

SUSAN HARRIS: There had been a study that showed that men who are having affairs are much more apt to have a heart attack during sex. I'm sure I must have read that study before I wrote this. Or else I spurred the study.

GARTH ANCIER (*former head of current comedy at NBC*): Susan Harris wrote this great episode—

"Isn't it interesting how the sounds are the same for awful nightmares and great sex?"

—DOROTHY

---

and then the NBC Broadcasting Department told the *Golden Girls* producers that under no circumstances could they shoot it.

I did not see the problem. So I went to Broadcasting and said, "You can't stop us from making this episode. You can only stop us from airing it." Back then, as the head of current comedy, I could decide that we were making the episode, and we would pay for it from our budget if we had to. But that was a last resort. Before that would happen, I wanted to get everyone together to hammer it out.

So everyone sat down on the *Golden Girls* living room set, Susan and the *Golden Girls* people on one side and the NBC people on the other. And again, the Broadcasting people declared, "This script is just unacceptable to even think of airing." I asked them, "All of it?" And they said yes; you can't even fix this script. So I asked them to go through the script with me, which is a smart way to handle these differences, because it makes the person defend his or her decision that any particular part of it is not acceptable for the American public.

We started at the top. They said first of all: "It is unacceptable to reference a woman making noises during an orgasm." That's when Susan turned and, from behind her sunglasses, said to the guy—and I remember, because it made me laugh—"So is it NBC's official position that it's

okay for men to make noises, but not women?" "Oh no, that's not what I meant!" the guy replied, flustered. It was a session where we literally went page by page. And by the end, they had turned down every single page with some reason why "you just can't make this." But there was no good reason. And everything they objected to was adjustable anyway.

Susan didn't write many episodes over the course of the show, but when she did, it was a real treat. We proceeded to shoot the episode, with very few changes, and the Broadcasting Department was so angry with me that they sent a note to the NBC chairman Grant Tinker saying that they wanted to go on record that they'd told Garth Ancier that this show would not air, and that they would not be responsible for the four hundred thousand dollars that was going to be wasted. But of course, NBC did end up airing the episode, and it's actually a classic.

TERRY HUGHES: This episode was edgy, and came closely on the heels of other episodes that were that way, too. In this first season, the show had a run of episodes that were not only funny and heartwarming, but were about things that I hadn't seen people do before on TV. One episode after another, the show was now going like gangbusters. We hit a stride that was becoming unstoppable.

THE TRUTH WILL OUT

Written by: SUSAN BEAVERS • *Directed by:* TERRY HUGHES
Original airdate: JANUARY 18, 1986

Rose receives a visit from her daughter Kirsten (Christine Belford) and granddaughter Charlie (Bridgette Andersen, 1975–97), who is named for Rose's late husband. Rose is nervous that as executor of her will Kirsten will get a peek at her finances; and indeed Kirsten is taken aback by the numbers, accusing her mother of blowing through the family estate. But there's something this adoring daughter doesn't know: her father, Charlie, wasn't as successful an insurance salesman as she'd thought. Worse yet, from the stories Kirsten has passed on, even little Charlie has a rose-colored image of the grandfather she never met. When Rose sees that the initial white lies she concocted to bolster her husband's memory are now affecting a new generation, she finally tells her daughter the truth: Charlie Nylund was a kind, warm, caring man—but he couldn't balance a checkbook, never mind leave behind any appreciable inheritance.

♦ ♦ ♦ ♦

COMMENTARY: Unlike so many sitcoms, *The Golden Girls* for some reason didn't produce too many outtakes or bloopers. So in order to compile a "gag reel" of funny, behind-the-scenes moments, the cast and crew would sometimes resort to pranks—for example, the time the crew members substituted naughty photos in the "Men of Blanche's Boudoir" prop calendar. (See season two, episode thirty-eight, "'Twas the Nightmare Before Christmas.")

But as the show's production associate Robert Spina explains, the semi-prank that occurred during rehearsals for this episode has turned into "a clip that's aired probably as much as any clip from the actual show, because it was a great moment showing Betty White just hamming it

up." At one point during the production week, as Betty was scheduled to rehearse the scene where she has a heart-to-heart with her young granddaughter as the girl sits at the makeup vanity in Rose's bedroom, actress Bridgette Andersen was feeling sick. But Terry Hughes and his team still needed to camera block the scene—i.e., plan where cameras should be positioned based on the actors' movements. And so Doug Tobin, then the show's second stage manager, agreed to step in and read granddaughter Charlie's lines.

The rehearsal was filmed—and the outtake that resulted aired several times in the late 1980s on Dick Clark's series of *TV Censored Bloopers* specials. As Doug read Charlie's lines—sometimes giggling as he assayed the innocent

14:31:24.25

attitude of a preteen girl—Betty worked hard to pick up his cues and get her own lines out correctly. But as you can see in the clip, available on YouTube (search: *Golden Girls*—Betty White funny rehearsal), Betty's body language belies her more prankish nature. In the scene, Rose is supposed to be applying makeup to her granddaughter as they chat, and so Betty takes the opportunity to grab a big laugh. As then–assistant director Lex Passaris remembers, "Doug was 'follically challenged.' So Betty took this Soupy Sales–type powder puff, and pounded him with it, caking his whole head with pancake makeup. By the end of the scene, it looked like he was doing whiteface."

The outtake is fun to watch, but unfortunately, this whole episode has a tragic coda. Young actress Bridgette Andersen was only eleven at the time of this *Golden Girls* guest spot, with already a long list of appearances on TV and film. But sadly, she died in 1997 of a drug overdose, just a few months short of her twenty-second birthday.

In the seventh-season episode "Home Again, Rose," the character of Kirsten would return, but with Christine Belford replaced by actress Lee Garlington.

DOUG TOBIN: When we were working on this episode, I stood in to read Charlie's lines in her scene with Betty White. Looking back, I now realize something: on those run-through Thursdays, they didn't usually put tape in the cameras. So someone must have known in advance that something was going to go down here, because someone—maybe Terry Hughes or Lex Passaris—told the guys to turn on their cameras for real. I realize now that I was set up.

Betty and I started to do the scene, in Rose's bedroom, where she's talking with Charlie while at the same time giving her a lesson in makeup. Betty is absolutely as sweet as she seems on TV, and yet she has a playful and dirty side, too. So as Betty drew on me with an eye pencil, I started getting silly and messing around with my lines. Charlie is supposed to be talking about her date Robert, and I added that it was Robert Spina, our production associate: "He's the P.A.!"

Well from that moment on, Betty had a look in her eye like, "Oh yeah? Well let me show you how it's done!" And she did! As she got her own lines back on track, she clobbered me with a really loaded powder puff, completely coating the middle of my face.

The clip that's available on YouTube shows only part of the scene—but originally, we played out the whole thing, with me now covered in powder. I was only twenty-eight at the time, and this was one of my first big jobs. And at some point during the scene, I realized that maybe the producers were watching this run-through, and they might get mad at me for screwing around. So actually, after Betty hit me with the powder, I started to get more serious, which made the whole thing even more ridiculous.

Looking back at that day, I realize how naïve I was. I was a young kid, and was trying to mess with Betty White? What was I thinking? The woman could destroy me in a second! As I got serious about finishing the scene, I was hoping I hadn't pissed Betty off as well; in the moment, I wasn't sure what was happening. But looking at the clip, it's obvious she was just playing and having a good time.

ABOVE:

Betty White pranks second stage manager Doug Tobin, standing in for Bridgette Andersen for rehearsal as Rose's granddaughter, Charlie.

Photos courtesy of LEX PASSARIS, *with permission from* DISNEY ENTERPRISES, INC.

NICE AND EASY

Written by: STUART SILVERMAN • *Directed by:* TERRY HUGHES
Original airdate: FEBRUARY 1, 1986

When Blanche's twenty-year-old niece, Lucy (Hallie Todd), visits Miami ostensibly to interview at colleges, it soon becomes obvious that the girl is a chip off the old slut. First, she's barely inside the Girls' front door when she announces she's off to a date with a doctor she met on the plane. Soon, she's having a rendezvous with her university interviewer—and then the airport cop who arrests him for transporting weed.

Finally, Blanche has had enough. But unfortunately, her scolding attempt to curtail her niece's activities backfires, sending the girl and officer Ed (Ken Stovitz) off into the night. After Blanche consults with Dorothy and Rose, the threesome tracks Lucy down to Ed's smarmy *Miami Vice*-themed bachelor pad. In private, Blanche explains to the girl the difference between "alluring" and just "available"— acknowledging her own hypocrisy in giving a lecture on sexual mores. As Lucy admits to compensating for childhood insecurities, Blanche reminds her of the importance of liking and respecting herself foremost.

Meanwhile, a disgusted Dorothy finally corners the mouse she's spotted in the kitchen, only to realize she's not someone who can kill a living thing.

◆ ◆ ◆ ◆

COMMENTARY: With its jokes about *Miami Vice*, this episode winks at *The Golden Girls'* own origins. The Girls would continue to make reference to NBC's megahit cop show, including a few episodes later in "The Flu Attack," with a gag about star Don Johnson's wardrobe.

Playing Lucy is then-twenty-four-old actress Hallie Todd, who had started her career in 1984 playing Penny, the bar owner's daughter on the Showtime sitcom *Brothers*. The real-life daughter of Ann Morgan Guilbert—a.k.a. *The Dick Van Dyke Show*'s neighbor Millie Helper—Hallie went on to regular roles in several series, including as the mother of the title character in the Disney Channel sitcom *Lizzie McGuire*.

HALLIE TODD: When I got to the set, I remember everybody telling me that I shouldn't be offended if Bea Arthur didn't talk to me, because she was just really shy. But I had gone to grammar school with her son Matt. I mentioned that, and she was a total sweetheart to me the whole week, as was everyone else.

I was already such a fan of Rue McClanahan's, and so when I noticed her doing yoga backstage, I was thrilled she invited me to join her. Rue was such an actress of substance that I think she definitely wanted to create a relationship with me, and make the episode real for herself. For me, that made everything easier, too—because for one thing, I had to do an accent. I'm from Pacific Palisades, California, not the South. So I just listened to Rue, and tried to do what she was doing. I felt like I was cheating. Rue made it easy because I was able just to listen to her.

KEN STOVITZ: I had stumbled into acting, getting cast in a commercial during my senior year at UCLA. But I did the opposite of what most actors do, acting only to support another career, which for me was going to law school. I never studied acting, and when I came on to a set like *The Golden Girls*—where I think I got the job because they thought I was silly and naïve enough to look like a young, wannabe Don Johnson—it was obvious that everyone else but me knew what they were doing!

I loved the great twist, that it was really Rose that this guy was pining for. But right about at this moment, my life flashed in front of me, and I knew that as soon as I passed the bar, I had to get away from acting. I knew what I was good at—and this wasn't it. And I saw that I could probably end up as a third banana on a show, never having a great career. I'd be a thirtysomething guy with a ponytail, chasing eighteen-year-old women—a lot like this character.

"Good night, Ed. We're going to go home now. And I want you to know, we'll all sleep a lot better knowing you're . . . off-duty tonight."

—DOROTHY

THE OPERATION

Written by: WINIFRED HERVEY • *Directed by:* TERRY HUGHES

Original airdate: FEBRUARY 8, 1986

Just as she is set to dance with Blanche and Rose in a recital, Dorothy injures her foot in tap class and needs surgery. At the hospital the night before, Dorothy freaks out and heads home. Sophia convinces her to return for the operation. When she does, she discovers she has a new roommate, Bonnie (Anne Haney, 1934–2001), an old pro on the eve of her second mastectomy. Bonnie's upbeat outlook brings an epiphany for Dorothy, who admits that in comparison, she feels "Like a fool. Like a damn fool." On the day following the surgery, all three Girls emerge victorious, as Blanche and Rose visit Dorothy's bedside fresh from the recital with news: the former Tip-Tap Trio is now known as the Two Merry Widows, with a whole new routine that knocked 'em dead.

• • • •

COMMENTARY: At the end of season 1, we're really getting to know the Girls and their histories. Here, Dorothy and Blanche reveal childhood traumas, but the episode provides the most surprising insight into the character of Rose, as the ever-competitive blonde throws some tough love at Blanche, forcing her out of her stage fright and out of the house.

WINIFRED HERVEY: I loved that we got them dancing—and I remember we all said, "Damn, Betty has some good legs!" This episode was also a good way to see a new side of Dorothy. The thing about Dorothy—and the thing about Bea to some extent—was that she had this very tough exterior, but really there was a very soft and gentle person in there. So by showing Dorothy's fears about the surgery, this was a situation where that could come out. It wasn't a side of the character we got to see all the time.

RUE McCLANAHAN: Every time they'd give me a chance to dance, I was all for it. For this episode, they gave us a really cute little soft shoe to do, and we dressed up in those top hats and tails and went to the hospital to dance for Dorothy, which was a lot of fun. Betty picked up dancing very quickly, so she was easy to work with. I certainly never studied tap; that was something I had to learn to do. I was a natural, too, at least in soft shoe, and could pick things up very fast.

BETTY WHITE: Rue and I put our tap shoes on on Monday of that week, and we just kept them on. I'm not a trained tap dancer, but you just ad lib and make it up when you practice on your kitchen floor. I've been doing that all my life. All week, Rue and I were walking up and down the halls, getting used to that click of our taps. And pretty soon, you can't wear tap shoes in a hallway without playing a little bit. Rue has a great sense of fun, and we'd challenge each other to come up with new things.

THE FLU ATTACK

Written by: STAN ZIMMERMAN & JAMES BERG   •   *Directed by:* TERRY HUGHES
Original airdate: MARCH 1, 1986

As the Girls eagerly anticipate their night at the Friends of Good Health awards, Rose is beginning to feel feverish. Before long, she, Blanche, and Dorothy all have symptoms their doctor (Sharon Spelman) confirms to be the flu. And with at least a week of recovery required, Saturday night's banquet plans are now off the table.

Miserable and angry about missing the big night, the three patients squabble over heating pads and the primo spot on the couch. Then, just as they're about to reconcile, Sophia enters with news: when she called to cancel the other Girls' banquet reservations, she got the sense that one of them was set to win the night's trophy in recognition of her volunteer work. Suddenly, the Girls forget all about their flu, as their competitive natures take hold. They pull themselves together and show up—only to watch Sophia take home the prize.

• • • •

COMMENTARY: Here, as *The Golden Girls* prepares to wrap its first, already-successful season, Sophia gives an acceptance speech that underlines the series' overall theme: the value of friendship. The episode is known for one of its visuals as well, with the three sick women, Blanche, Dorothy, and Rose, arranged on the couch, clutching their ailing orifices in "See No Evil, Hear No Evil, Speak No Evil" poses.

TERRY HUGHES: This was a hard episode to do. When people have the flu, they're crabby, depressed, and slow moving. So the trick we had to pull off was playing that, but also playing against it so that we didn't turn people off. The actresses did such a great job that by the end of the week, we all had convinced ourselves that we really did have the flu, because we'd been living with the suggestion all week.

BEA ARTHUR: People often ask me how I didn't break up, with all the outrageous things the Girls did and said. But in this episode, I just broke up and broke up and broke up. There was a charity auction, and Don Johnson was supposed to emcee. This was at the height of *Miami Vice*'s popularity; all the men were doing the no-socks thing. But at the last minute, they announced onstage that Don couldn't make it, but he had sent his wardrobe. And they held up a hanger with a white jacket on it. I've never seen anything funnier in my life. I couldn't not break up. I think eventually they had to just cut away from me.

BLIND AMBITIONS

Written by: R. J. COLLEARY • Directed by: TERRY HUGHES
Original airdate: MARCH 29, 1986

Rose's visiting sister, Lily (Polly Holliday), thinks she has a handle on living without her sight. But when she panics after accidentally causing a grease fire on the stove, Dorothy and Blanche convince Rose that she needs to intervene. Lily, however, has her own plan, to ask Rose to move back with her to Chicago. After agonizing over the decision, Rose ultimately finds the strength to stop coddling Lily and instead shows some tough love, convincing her scared sister to seek professional help to get on with her new life as a blind person.

Meanwhile, the Girls plan to raise money for a new TV by holding a garage sale. But after haggling with a few customers, they soon realize they can't bear to part with any of their so-called junk.

◆ ◆ ◆ ◆

COMMENTARY: Six years after she last told her boss Mel Sharples to kiss her grits on CBS sitcom *Alice*, Polly Holliday has left Phoenix and arrived in Miami, albeit a little less independent as Lily Lindstrom, Rose's newly blind sister. Here, she gets a taste of her own sassy grits from Rose—and Betty White gets a chance to shine in a more serious, dramatic moment.

R. J. COLLEARY: I was on the writing staff of Witt/Thomas/Harris's show *Benson* during its final season, which overlapped with the first season of *The Golden Girls*. On *Benson* we worked basic sitcom hours, and on weekends only in a rare emergency. But *The Golden Girls* was so new, and had become

a hit so fast, that at this point its writers, all of whom had come from *Benson*, were pretty crazed in trying to figure out what the show would become.

Shows today don't even use freelance writers, but back then they did, if only to get a script draft down on paper that the writing staff could later go back and fix. But it's generally really hard to try to come in from the outside and write a show. And it's even harder if, as in this case, the show is still airing its first season, so there aren't many episodes to study. Still, I was happy to be asked to write a freelance script for this new show that people were seeming to like. But of course, I didn't realize what it was going to

OPPOSITE:

Rose counsels her newly blind
sister, Lily (Polly Holliday).

Photo courtesy of PHOTOFEST, *with permission
from* DISNEY ENTERPRISES, INC

become. Now, this one episode of *The Golden Girls* is the credit that my daughters and their friends, who are in their twenties, are most impressed by.

TERRY GROSSMAN: Even today, I don't think people give Betty White credit for how great an actress she is. She doesn't have just comedy chops, and it's not just her personality. I remember in this episode, watching the rehearsals, and noting how fabulous an actress

Polly Holliday is, particularly in the serious moments between Lily and Rose. At the time I worried, "Maybe Betty's not going to be able to hold her own with her." But then on Friday night, the audience came in. And once the cameras started rolling, Polly Holliday virtually disappeared. Betty's performance was so brilliant and touching, it made this other great actress seem not to exist. I remember that dramatic moment more than I do so many of the big comic moments of the show.

THE WAY WE MET

Written by: KATHY SPEER, TERRY GROSSMAN, WINIFRED HERVEY, MORT NATHAN, & BARRY FANARO
Directed by: TERRY HUGHES ◆ *Original airdate:* MAY 10, 1986

Blanche brings us back to the morning she finally kicked out her previous two room-mates, as she first meets a cat-carrying Rose while posting roommate-wanted flyers on the bulletin board in the neighborhood supermarket. Evicted by her landlord for refusing to give up her rescued aforementioned feline, Mr. Peepers, Rose prattles on about her "wild" habit of eating raw cookie dough. Blanche is about to call the whole thing off—until she witnesses her potential roommate's purity of heart, as Rose gives Mr. Peepers to a young boy (Edan Gross) grieving his own lost pet.

With one roommate selected and one to go, Blanche gives a house tour to quack psychic Madame Zelda (Shirley Prestia, 1947–2011), who scares her with visions of murder and demonic possession. Enter Dorothy Zbornak, with her mother in tow. Dorothy's fears that Sophia's stroke-induced candor has jeopardized the interview prove unfounded, as Blanche agrees for the former to move in. But soon, as new roomies Dorothy and Rose meet for the first time, there's already tension; Blanche has mistakenly promised each of them the same bedroom.

Their final memory is of their first food-shopping trip as a household. As Dorothy and Blanche consider each other's grocery selections extravagant, ridiculously honest Rose keeps correcting prices for the cashier—in the store's favor. The bickering spills over into the kitchen, and just as the threesome is about to conclude that living together just won't work, Rose pulls out her St. Olaf story about the famous Great Herring War. And as they laugh together at the image of a circus-trained herring being fired from a cannon, the Girls realize that perhaps their sensibilities will prove compatible after all.

◆ ◆ ◆ ◆

COMMENTARY: The best sitcom pilots begin with a bang, an "inciting incident" that changes the lives of the show's heroes and sets up the situation we'll be watching for, hopefully, seasons to come. In the pilot episode of *Frasier*, dad Martin moves in; on *Friends*, Rachel leaves her groom at the altar. *The Golden Girls*, too, had its own big moment, with the unexpected arrival of Sophia after the destruction of her nursing home, Shady Pines. But now, with this episode, we get so much more. In comic book terms, this episode depicts the Girls' full "origin story," the circumstances by which Blanche, Rose, and Dorothy came to be such a powerful trio.

The episode also contains a brief appearance by Dom Irrera, as a produce clerk in the Girls' grocery; Dom had appeared earlier in the season as a waiter in "The Flu Attack," and during *The Golden Girls*' original casting days, had auditioned to play the ultimately doomed character of Coco.

TERRY HUGHES: This show made for an interesting week. It probably looks like we meant to save this story of how they all met for the last show of the first season. But actually, it was because we didn't have a script. We shot a show on Friday, and we didn't have anything to start working on the following Monday. I remember that the whole gang of writers worked on this episode over the weekend, and when I came in on Monday morning and met them in the parking lot, they were all bleary-eyed, having been able to go home for only about three hours. Then, when we did the table read of the show that day, there were gales of laughter—and you should have seen the looks of relief on the writers' faces. We would end up doing more episodes that were constructed from individual vignettes and flashbacks. And it was all because this one ended up going so wonderfully.

ABOVE:
The supermarket bulletin board by which the Golden Girls first met.
Photo courtesy of the EDWARD S. STEPHENSON ARCHIVE *at the* ART DIRECTORS GUILD.

GOLDEN DIVERSITY

WHEN IT COMES to sitcoms, they don't make 'em like *The Golden Girls* anymore. Chasing the all-important Adults 18–49 Nielsen rating, today's youth-obsessed network executives would rather OD on Metamucil than try to sell advertisers on a sitcom where all four characters are age fifty plus (and then some!).

But there's another reason why you might not see a small-screen foursome that looks like Dorothy, Blanche, Rose, and Sophia today, and it's a nobler one. Now, more than ever, networks are committing to programming with racially, ethnically, and even sexually diverse casts, and from a more diverse pool of writers and producers.

The Girls, of course, were not just four older ladies, but four older white ladies at that. But even back in the less progressive eighties when the characters were born, *The Golden Girls* producers were mindful of the diversity of cultures to be found in the show's Miami setting, and worked to cast some of its secondary characters accordingly. When Dorothy's son, Michael (Scott Jacoby), turned up in town with Lorraine (Rosalind Cash, 1938–95), the woman he wanted to marry, she turned out to be not only much older, but African American. And she came complete with her mother and two elderly aunts (Virginia Capers, Lynn Hamilton, and Montrose Hagins), to whom fans today often refer as the Black Golden Girls. Sophia first cozied up to a neighbor's Japanese gardener (played by the venerable Chinese American actor Keye Luke, 1904–91), and later befriended Alvin (Joe Seneca, 1919–96), an elderly black man, on the boardwalk. Dorothy was dedicated to her prized pupil, a Cuban American kid played by the Mexican American Mario Lopez. And, further reflecting the Cuban flavor of South Florida, Rose began working for consumer advocate Enrique Mas, a man who could roll his Spanish *r*'s hilariously—a feat even more impressive when you consider that he was played by Italian American actor Chick Vennera.

"Paul Witt and Tony Thomas, and especially Susan Harris, were always cutting edge and progressive," says Chick, who had worked with the producing trio on a previous sitcom, the female-president comedy *Hail to the Chief,* and who before Enrique Mas had also played a different character, Cuban boxer Pepe, in a *Golden Girls* episode, "Fiddler on the Ropes." "*Hail to the Chief* was way before its time. With *Soap,* they were the first to show a family with a gay son. The Cuban population in Miami is really huge, so of course it makes sense they wanted to create a Cuban American character."

Later, too, three of the Girls would work at the titular hotel in *Golden Palace* alongside African American hotel manager Roland Wilson (Don Cheadle) and Mexican American chef Chuy Castillos (Cheech Marin). But behind the scenes, the world of *The Golden Girls* was less colorful. Writer Winifred Hervey was not only one of just a handful of women ever to write for the show, but during her three seasons on *The Golden Girls* was the sole person of color on its writing staff. "I don't think that really affected the job much, though," says Wini, who, after all, had just finished working with the *Girls'* show-running foursome Kathy Speer, Terry Grossman, Mort Nathan, and Barry Fanaro on another Witt/Thomas show, one with an African American lead, *Benson*.

On one occasion, the writers, all together in the writers' room, cooked up a story about the Girls hiring, and then firing, Caribbean-born maid Marguerite Brown (Paula Kelly), who they then think has put a voodoo curse on them (season three, "The Housekeeper"). Perhaps to eliminate the potential for racial insensitivity, the producers assigned the fleshing out of the story idea into a script to Wini. "I remember feeling wary about that one," she remembers. "It was a hard script to write, because it was a black woman as the housekeeper. There hadn't been that many black characters, and this one has to put a voodoo curse on them? So I came up with a solution: we should find out she's going to law school. And the producers were fine with that being how we redeemed the character. They were always very receptive to that kind of stuff, because they never wanted to offend anybody."

Wini adds that the producers were also amenable when, during dress rehearsals, she sometimes suggested that in order to better reflect Miami they should add people of color among the background actors. "The producers were totally open to it, because it was a realistic note," she remembers.

But of course, you can't please all of the people all of the time. Eventually, the *Golden Girls* producers received a letter from a peeved fan. "It said: 'I'm tired, every time the Girls go to a restaurant, of seeing all these black people in the background!'" Wini recalls with a laugh. "It was only one letter, but it was hilarious to receive it."

RIGHT:

Dorothy's extended family *(left to right)*: new daughter-in-law, Lorraine (Rosalind Cash); son, Michael (Scott Jacoby); and Lorraine's mother, Greta (Virginia Capers).

Photo by JOSEPH DEL VALLE/NBC/NBCU PHOTO BANK
via GETTY IMAGES.

• EPISODE 26 •

END OF THE CURSE

Written by: SUSAN HARRIS • *Directed by:* TERRY HUGHES

Original airdate: SEPTEMBER 27, 1986

Blanche is startled to discover that she may be pregnant. But when the doctor's diagnosis is instead the onset of menopause, she goes into a deep depression. Meanwhile, the other three ladies decide to breed minks for profit. Their efforts are thwarted, however, when the minks fail to show any interest in each other. After the other Girls drag Blanche to a psychiatrist to deal with her depression about menopause, another doctor, a handsome veterinarian (Philip Sterling, 1922–98), arrives to check on the minks—and a perked-up Blanche decides to question him on other "animal" matters in private. Rose argues that the minks are not useless just because it's turned out they are too old to breed, and Blanche wholeheartedly agrees. Then, two of the minks do start to get frisky after all. The problem is, they're both males.

◆ ◆ ◆ ◆

COMMENTARY: Gay minks! Actually, the alternative lifestyle of the minks may be the only aspect of this episode's B plot that Bea Arthur, Rue McClanahan, and Betty White found amusing. All three of them animal activists, the ladies hated doing an episode showing the Girls farming animals for fur, but all agree that it was too late in the process to refuse to do the script, lest they have nothing to shoot that upcoming Friday. "I absolutely hated that part of this episode, and to this day I am sorry that we did it," Bea explains. "But it was the first episode of the sec-

ond year, and there was nothing we could do. It was already written and scheduled."

Here playing veterinarian Dr. Barensfeld, Philip Sterling would show up again in season three episode "Three on a Couch," as Dr. Ashley, the therapist mediating the Girls' housemate disputes.

TERRY GROSSMAN: I knew Betty was an animal activist, but none of us realized Bea and Rue were, too. In the first season, Bea had told me that on *Maude*, Norman Lear had assured her that "if there's an episode that we make and

you absolutely hate it, I will not air it." I knew I couldn't make the same promise, but I did offer what I thought was the next best thing. I said, "I promise that if you hate an episode, I'll stand up for you. I'll go in to Paul Witt and Tony Thomas's office, and say, 'I'm leaving if this episode airs.'" Susan Harris had written this episode, and really she would have had to be the one to

agree to any changes. And in the end, Bea was willing to go through with the episode and just get it over with. I admired the integrity she had. She just wanted to do good work, and not present messages that were harmful.

BETTY WHITE: We all hated this episode. Bea was the one most upset. We were so glad to get through it. It was a difficult week, as I remember—and not that funny. I'm sure we all gave opinions about certain things in it, and we made the point about what happens to the animals. And anyway it was so out of character for the Girls to be raising minks—but it was too late to change.

RUE McCLANAHAN: I would have preferred having [our characters] see the light about fur, but that's how they wrote it. And I have to say it was a funny ending when the two males started copulating.

LADIES OF THE EVENING

Written by: BARRY FANARO & MORT NATHAN • *Directed by:* TERRY HUGHES
Original airdate: OCTOBER 4, 1986

BURT REYNOLDS:

"Which one's the slut?"

Blanche, Dorothy, and Rose dress up for the premiere of Burt Reynolds's new movie, but are instead arrested as Miami's most "experienced" hookers when they stop for a drink in the lobby of a South Beach hotel. Whilst in the slammer, the Girls dispense some aged wisdom to their young, sex-working cell mates; they even talk Meg (Rhonda Aldrich), coincidentally a St. Olaf native, out of "the life." When none of the three Girls is willing to relinquish her spot at the premiere to Sophia in exchange for bail, Sophia grabs the tickets, attends the event alone—and makes fast friends with Burt Reynolds, who later shows up at the house to escort her to lunch.

◆ ◆ ◆ ◆

KATHY SPEER: As we talked about Florida in the writers' room, the Burt Reynolds Dinner Theatre kept coming up. We'd write lines like: "We're going to see Mr. So-and-So at the Burt Reynolds Dinner Theatre." Burt Reynolds had been and still was a huge movie star, and I think perhaps the only reason he was willing to do our show at all was because it gave him a chance to dispel the false rumors that were circulating at the time that he had AIDS.

BARRY FANARO: Right from season one, people in Hollywood knew about *The Golden Girls*, and wanted to be a part of it. We would find out celebrities were watching. Betty would sometimes come in and say, "You know who loves the show?" In one case it was Burt Reynolds. So we asked Betty, "Do you think he would do an episode?" And she agreed to find out. Burt's appearance turned out to be our first big cameo, and it drove the writing of this episode. We knew he wanted to do only a couple of lines, and so we decided to save him for the end. We came up with the idea that the ladies would win Burt Reynolds movie premiere tickets, and then worked backward from there.

Burt was terrific, even though he was, weirdly enough, kind of nervous. We put him in a tough predicament, having to come in cold and deliver punch lines at the end of the episode, and he was afraid he was going to flub. If you listen to the episode carefully, you can hear his throat kind of catch. But the scene ended up working perfectly. From the shock of seeing him at the front door, through Sophia saying she knows him, through his question, "Which one's the slut?" and the three Girls replying in unison, "I am!" there were huge, rolling laughs that went on forever.

RUE McCLANAHAN: This one was a heck of a lot of fun to work on. For one thing, one of the little chippies in the cell with us was played by my niece, Amelia Kinkade, before she became a very successful pet psychic. Burt Reynolds had just one scene at the end, and as I recall he came in only on tape day. But certainly, we realized our show was a big deal when we got Burt to come on!

LEX PASSARIS (*associate director*): Our costume designer, Judy Evans, God bless her, had dressed all the hookers as sexy as they could be while still being in good taste. But by the time we got to the middle of shooting the dress show, the first of two times we taped the episode that night, one of the young ladies, Rue's niece, had apparently decided she needed to tart it up a little more. So where Judy had given her a flesh-colored brassiere for under her top, she had opted not to wear it. The director made sure we got a close-up of her saying her one line, and

> ## "I can't believe these dumb cops would think anyone would pay money to sleep with you!"
> —SOPHIA

suddenly there she was, with her top semi-exposed for the camera to see. We didn't have the term then, but it was a "wardrobe malfunction."

Everyone in the booth simultaneously screamed, "Oh my God!" Food, falling out of people's mouths. And of course, Judy ran into the booth and said, "It wasn't me! I gave her a brassiere!" Once everyone realized who it was, we realized, "Okay, she's just being a little ambitious." So we fixed it for the second show, the one that aired, and she still has her line, but while properly dressed.

RIGHT:

Sophia visits the Girls in jail before using their tickets to Burt Reynolds' movie premiere.

Photo by ALICE S. HALL/NBCU/NBC PHOTO BANK *via* GETTY IMAGES

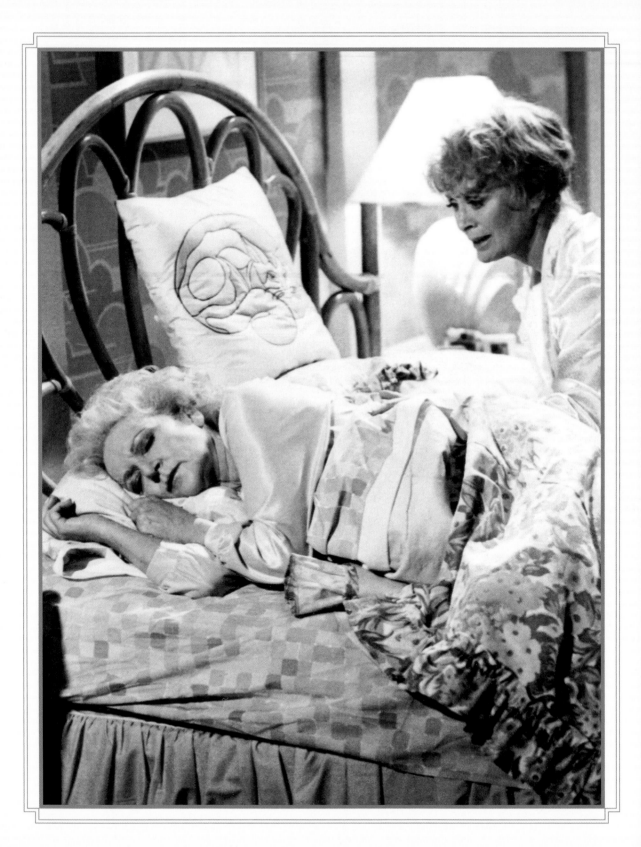

ISN'T IT ROMANTIC?

Written by: JEFFREY DUTEIL • *Directed by:* TERRY HUGHES

Original airdate: NOVEMBER 8, 1986

Dorothy gets a visit from her college friend Jean (Lois Nettleton, 1927–2008), who is mourning the loss of her partner, Pat. As only Dorothy knows, Pat was short for Patricia; Jean is a lesbian. During her stay, Jean finds she has much in common with Rose; but problems then arise when Jean admits to Dorothy that she may be falling in love with her naïve roommate. Sophia reveals she always suspected about Jean's lesbianism, but Blanche is shocked—and jealous that Jean would prefer Rose over her. The last to catch on, Rose feigns sleep as Jean awkwardly attempts to explain her feelings of affection one night at bedtime. But the next morning, Rose tells Jean that she's flattered, and the two women decide that friendship is certainly enough.

◆ ◆ ◆ ◆

COMMENTARY: This episode marks the first time the post-Coco *Golden Girls* addressed the issue of homosexuality. Its most famous joke in its most famous scene—where the concept of liking anything but men is so foreign to Blanche that she briefly confuses the words "lesbian" and "Lebanese"—was conceived as an in-joke referring to producer Tony Thomas's famous family.

Prior to this episode, Estelle Getty had not met Lois Nettleton, but they shared a mutual friend in TV director John Bowab. John had advised Lois to downplay the character as much as possible, "because if you try to compete with those four ladies, you'll come up a loser. It's not a funny role, so play it as honestly and simply as you can." Lois took her friend's advice to heart. And as John recalls, although Estelle had at first loved the idea of casting a feminine woman like Lois to play Jean,

"at the table reading, she thought Lois sounded dull. Estelle says she thought to herself, 'Gee, she's one of those actresses who's not going to do anything at the table reading.' Then, the second day of rehearsal came, and Estelle thought, 'She's *really* not doing anything. I wonder when she's going to do something!' On the third day, Estelle was convinced the producers were going to fire Lois: 'She's not doing a damn thing! She's just lying there!' And then, Estelle says, on the fourth day, she realized, 'That bitch! She's making the rest of us look like we're overacting!'" John says that from that point on, Estelle and Lois became great friends. "And Estelle ended up telling that story five thousand times, and said that she learned so much herself that day."

Loaded with first-time on-TV laughs, this episode earned a 1987 Emmy nomination for Outstanding Writing for

OPPOSITE:

Jean (Lois Nettleton) professes her true feelings to Rose.

Photo by NBC/NBCU PHOTO BANK *via* GETTY IMAGES.

a Comedy Series. For directing it, Terry Hughes took home not only the Emmy, but that year's Directors Guild of America Award as well. And after Betty White's 1986 Emmy win for Outstanding Lead Actress in a Comedy Series, Rue McClanahan took home the trophy in 1987, partly due to her performance here.

PAUL WITT: This was a great episode. We knew that people loved the show, and we didn't worry about any backlash about doing an episode with a lesbian character. The idea that these [experienced] women, among their children and friends, would never have had contact with gay men and women would have been absurd.

MORT NATHAN: Because the show was a hit, we had the license at the time to try things that other shows couldn't do. When we would talk about gay and lesbian relationships, it wasn't so much that we wanted to do a "gay" show or an "issues" show that was controversial, but more that we thought this was an area that seemed interesting, funny, and organic to what we do. We felt there would be big laughs there, areas of unmined comedy, and we could get away with it because we were who we were. We loved taking advantage of those opportunities, like having Blanche, someone with so much sex experience, turn out to be a little ignorant of terminology and not even know the word "lesbian." It was a chance to make fun of how she thought she was sexually sophisticated. The fact that people were emotionally touched by us reaffirming gay rights or any of the social issues we brought up was an additional benefit. We weren't consciously trying to make a preachy show, but we were touched later that people appreciated what we did.

RUE McCLANAHAN: After Blanche singing on the piano at the Rusty Anchor, that ["lesbian"/"Lebanese"] scene is my second favorite because the writing is so brilliant. Blanche has her areas of conservatism, and she obviously didn't know what a lesbian was; she didn't get the word. And then it's such a beautiful turnaround

from that to being jealous. Blanche wanted to be queen again, no matter what the context.

BETTY WHITE: Even someone as naïve as Rose is able to sense when something is outside her ordinary realm of experience, and so she senses that Jean is attracted to her. In the eighties, we weren't quite where we are today when it comes to gay issues, and so particularly for the time, I'm glad Rose let Jean down easy.

For the scene with Jean talking to Rose in bed, the director kept close-up on my face all the while, and when she started talking, I popped my eyes open and didn't move a muscle. That was the thing about the way the show was directed. A lot of the comedy was not from what was said but what was *not* said—the reactions.

JEFFREY DUTEIL: I had watched *The Golden Girls*' first season and was surprised that after the gay houseboy in the pilot the show hadn't featured any other gay characters. So, during the summer between the first and second seasons, I wrote this episode—"Isn't It Romantic?"—as a spec script. Shortly afterward, I saw the name Winifred Hervey, with whom I had worked on *The New Odd Couple*, in the show's credits, and sent the script to her. I was so naïve. Producers almost never agree to read spec scripts of their own shows; actually they barely have time to read anything at all.

But Wini liked my script, and forwarded it to the showrunners, who called me in to meet with them. As it turns out, *The Golden Girls* had been looking to do a gay episode, and when mine came across the transom, the timing was just right, and they bought it. And in fact, they ended up bumping it up to be the fifth episode of the season, rather than the twelfth or thirteenth as originally planned.

In the first draft I'd written, Dorothy's friend visits with her daughter, and it was the daughter who was gay. But everything seemed wrong about the story, and I was struggling to get through it. And then something happened that has never happened to me before or since. My partner, Scott, and I were in Las Vegas, and I dreamed the entire episode as I ended up writing it. I woke up in the middle of the night and scribbled it on a yellow pad. The show just laid itself out, a beginning, middle, and end. I can't explain it.

The lines that people like to quote from this episode, where Blanche confuses the words "lesbian" and "Lebanese"—"Isn't Danny Thomas one!"—came from my original script; in fact, I recently came across a copy that I'd typed out on my Selectric. This was the first episode where we ever saw Rose's bedroom. And in the scene there

---

BLANCHE:

"I've never known any personally, but isn't Danny Thomas one?"

DOROTHY:

"Not 'Lebanese,' Blanche! 'Lesbian!'"

---

between Jean and Rose, my original script was the same as what ended up airing—up until the point where Jean says, "I'm quite fond of you." I had written that when Rose—not knowing how to react—fakes snoring, Jean would just get under the covers and go to sleep too. But when I went to the episode's taping, I saw that they had added a couch to the bedroom, so that at that moment, Jean instead would take a blanket and move over to this little lounge, and sleep separately. After the episode's table read, I hadn't been invited to rewrites or to run-through rehearsals, so I don't know at what point it changed, or who called for the change; I won-

dered if it had been NBC's Standards and Practices. But someone had obviously not wanted to leave the impression that Jean and Rose were going to stay in bed together for the rest of the night. I guess this was, after all, 1986.

LOIS NETTLETON: When they were casting Jean, I think what they were probably looking for was the way I actually played her, and that is, as a very straight person. Not "straight" in the sense of not being gay, but rather as an ordinary-seeming woman. I had played a gay woman one other time in the early seventies, on *Medical Center*, and I think that character was similar to what they wanted for Jean—someone who just didn't seem stereotypically masculine in any way.

I guess this is a somewhat historic episode, but I just approached Jean not by concentrating on her sexuality but by figuring out who she is as a human being. Straight or gay, we all have so many different types of relationships with other people; what are hers? Well, from that wonderful, hilarious script, you could see Jean was sensitive, outgoing, and had a good sense of humor, at ease with herself and with life. She's suffered a loss, and I've had mine, too; all I had to do was substitute a woman for a man. And it wasn't hard to imagine falling in love with Rose. It was perfectly logical, because her character was so charming and honest and innocent—the kind of person anyone can like and feel affection for.

All week during rehearsal, I laughed when I saw Rose's wonderfully funny reaction when I tell her I love her, where her eyes pop wide open facing away from me in bed. And I'll always remember the lines in the scene where Blanche gets jealous that Jean picked Rose over her. The writing was great, and so were the women, getting laughs all over the place. In fact, after rehearsal one day I told my friend John Bowab that I was starting to get nervous that I wasn't getting any laughs. Was I approaching this the wrong way? He told me to keep doing what I was doing, because I was there to be the "straight man." And he turned out to be right. The episode worked beautifully.

DOROTHY'S PRIZED PUPIL

Written by: CHRISTOPHER LLOYD • *Directed by:* TERRY HUGHES
Original airdate: MARCH 14, 1987

Dorothy surreptitiously enters one of her students' English class papers in a writing contest, but the surprise turns out to be an unpleasant one for young Mario Sanchez (Mario Lopez), an illegal Cuban immigrant, when his first-place win draws the attention of the INS and gets him deported. Meanwhile, Rose's sudden streak of losing things leads her to become Blanche's *wiedenfluegen*—in English: slave—for an entire week when it appears she's lost a pair of her earrings. But in the end the roles are reversed, after Blanche's boyfriend Sam Burns (John Braden) stops by with an entire cache of Blanche's jewelry he's found between the cushions of his loveseat.

❖ ❖ ❖ ❖

MARIO LOPEZ: Even before *The Golden Girls*, I had already gotten to work with Bea Arthur a couple of times—the very first time I was on television, on a Norman Lear–produced show called *a.k.a. Pablo*, and on a pilot for Witt/Thomas Productions called *The Arena.* I loved her. Even as a kid, I could recognize how brilliant and funny all four of those ladies were, and of course now as an adult, I appreciate them even more.

They were class acts, the way everybody should be. I was just some kid, but they were so sweet, inviting me to lunch, which they didn't have to do. And they were always willing to help me with my lines—which meant learning from the best. Even today, people come up to me and tell me they loved the episode, and it just cracks me up. That show is timeless, and I'm happy to have been part of it.

ABOVE:
Dorothy does homework with young tutee Mario (Mario Lopez).

Photo by ALICE S. HALL/NBC/NBCU PHOTO BANK *via* GETTY IMAGES.

IT'S A MISERABLE LIFE

Written by: BARRY FANARO & MORT NATHAN   •   *Directed by:* TERRY HUGHES
Original airdate: NOVEMBER 1, 1986

The Girls pass around a petition to oppose the city's efforts to widen Richmond Street, which would require chopping down a historic tree. But the owner of the property on which the tree sits, Frieda Claxton (Nan Martin, 1927–2010), won't sign.

Ever the optimist, Rose plies the no-good neighbor with pastries, until finally she appears to agree to support their cause. But when the Girls present the petition to the city council, and Mrs. Claxton testifies about her hatred of all living things, Rose commands the misanthropic matron to drop dead—and then, right there on the spot, she does.

Rose resolves to put together a funeral for friendless Frieda. The Girls all agree to chip in, despite the high prices quoted by mortician Mr. Pfeiffer (Thom Sharp), but their expensive gesture is nearly for naught, as no one shows up to pay any respects. Then, just as they're about to give up hope, one elderly woman (Amzie Strickland, 1919–2006) approaches the casket—only to give it a good kick when she realizes it's not her good friend, but mean old Mrs. Claxton inside.

But Mrs. Claxton isn't inside the box at all; she has been accidentally cremated, her ashes given to the Girls. Rose spreads Mrs. Claxton's cremains around the base of the oak, thus ensuring that the tree is protected after all as a final resting place.

◆ ◆ ◆ ◆

COMMENTARY: Guest star Nan Martin was only fifty-nine years old at the time of this episode, but with the help of some silver hair spray, played a crotchety eighty-three. She would return at the end of the *Girls'* fourth season, in the episode "Foreign Exchange," as Philomena Bosco, the woman who, courtesy of a hospital mix-up, might possibly be Dorothy's real birth mother. She is perhaps best known for a role later in her career, as department store owner Mrs. Louder on *The Drew Carey Show*.

BEA ARTHUR: One of my favorite jokes was in this episode. The funeral director pronounces his name without the silent P: "P-feiffer." And I have to say things like "Well, Mr. P-feiffer…" "Look, Mr. P-feiffer …" "Mr. P-feiffer, we have already told you…!" It just kept going. And I remember thinking, "Oh God, who dreamed this up!"

KATHY SPEER: I want to say that this is pretty much a standard sitcom plot. The idea is to show how it affects your characters to see that when the meanest person dies, there is nobody there for him or her at the end. But in this case, the story is based not only on a previous sitcom episode we'd done, but also somewhat on real life. On *Benson*, we actually had an actor playing the meanest person die on the set. It was awful.

BETTY WHITE: The first time I read this script, I thought the mean neighbor's death was a rather shocking surprise! But then again, with all those funny people sitting around in our writers' room, who knows what could happen. It just fascinates me the things they came up with.

ABOVE:
Rose commands meanie neighbor Frieda Claxton (Nan Martin) to drop dead—and she does. OPPOSITE: Miami-Dade County Commission Chambers and the funeral home, where Mr. P-feiffer wants to sell the Girls the top-of-the-line model.

Photo by ALICE S. HALL/NBC/NBCU PHOTO BANK *via* GETTY IMAGES.
Photo courtesy of the EDWARD S. STEPHENSON ARCHIVE *at the* ART DIRECTORS GUILD.

> ## *"Now if you don't like it, Mrs. Claxton, you just sit there and shut up while we have our say. And if you don't like it, just drop dead!"*
>
> —ROSE

It was August 24, 1983, and I was pregnant with my daughter, Nora. The story of the episode was that a plumber recommended by Kraus comes to Benson's apartment, and then dies there. The problem is he was a crotchety, nasty guy, and nobody wants to throw the funeral.

We hired the actor Jack Somack, whose claim to fame had been the "Spicy Meatballs" Alka-Seltzer commercials. We rehearsed his first scene, and noticed that he was going up on his lines a little bit. But it was only Wednesday at this point, so who cares. Then for the next scene, he's supposed to be under the sink, which is where Benson finds him dead. But tragically, right before the actor went under the

sink, he actually did die. He had a heart attack, right there on set. And the eeriest part is that the way it was written Benson talks to the guy under the sink, not realizing he's dead. And had Mr. Somack gone under the sink thirty seconds earlier, he really would have been dead under the sink, and nobody would have known.

It was a terrible moment. That day had actually been my due date, but I didn't actually have the baby until September first. I know some people had been hoping that the baby would be born that day, as kind of "a life for a life." It shows how people deal with a sudden passing of a virtual stranger in their midst, which is ironically what we were trying to do in the *Benson* and *Golden Girls* episodes.

BIG DADDY'S LITTLE LADY

Written by: RUSSELL MARCUS • Directed by: DAVID STEINBERG

Original airdate: NOVEMBER 15, 1986

Blanche's father, Big Daddy (David Wayne, 1914–95), visits Miami to announce a surprise—the arrival the next day of his brand-new fiancée, the widow Spencer. Thrilled, Blanche insists on throwing the couple a wedding right there in the Girls' living room. But her joy turns to jealousy when she gets a glimpse of the bride. Assuming Margaret (Sondra Currie) to be a gold digger, Blanche makes her typical embarrassing scene, only to relent and offer her blessing when she hears Big Daddy talk about finally finding hope and love again in the aftermath of his beloved wife's death.

Meanwhile, Rose and Dorothy team up to compete in the Miami Retailers' Association's contest for writing the best song about the city. Their first two efforts, a ditty called "Miami Is Nice," and an outright melodic steal called "M-I-A-another M-I," are disappointments. But on their third try, the duo comes up with a winner in "Miami, You've Got Style"—well, a second-place winner that is. They don't take home the grand prize, but they do get the joy of gathering with Blanche and Sophia around the piano for a sing-along that has become one of the series' most beloved moments.

◆ ◆ ◆ ◆

COMMENTARY: This episode featured the return of Big Daddy—but not the return of the actor who first played him. Murray Hamilton, who had appeared just five months earlier in the series' first season, died just as this episode was conceived, and was replaced by another veteran actor, David Wayne.

This episode is noteworthy for its director as well; comedian David Steinberg had been a staple on *The Tonight Show*, and was known for his hit comedy records and TV specials of the late 1960s and early '70s. *The Golden Girls* came at the beginning of his segue into directing, although he would go on to work on such classic shows as *Designing Women*, *Newhart*, and *Curb*

Your Enthusiasm. Most recently, he has been the host of the Showtime series *Inside Comedy*, on which he interviews today's top comedic actors.

RUSSELL MARCUS: In a sitcom, once you start to get over the first-season hump of introducing and establishing the personalities of your lead characters, the next natural thing to do is to start bringing in their immediate family members. So here, the producers had the idea to bring back Big Daddy, who had already been introduced in season one. The twist here was that he'd not only have a new bride, but she'd be young and beautiful, so as to put her in competition with the vain Blanche. I thought that

Blanche's scene with her new stepmother had a great electricity to it.

For the B plot, with Dorothy and Rose writing their ode to Miami, the show's musical director, Scott Gale, wrote the melody, and I have to fully admit that it was really Mort Nathan and Barry Fanaro who wrote the lyrics to "Miami, You've Got Style." The scene and the song may have had a touch of my thoughts, courtesy of my first draft going in, but Mort and Barry are really the ones who made it funny.

DAVID STEINBERG: The hardest part of directing the show turned out to be Estelle Getty's mental block about the live audience. She dropped all of her punch lines in front of the audience, never getting her lines out right. So all the air went out of the comedy. At first, no one had told me about it, but then the other women clued me in. Estelle was talented beyond belief, and really could give an incredible performance. So what we did was steal her performance during rehearsal earlier that afternoon. I worried that if we waited to pick up

her lines after the rest of the taping, she'd be demoralized about not having gotten it right. So we taped the afternoon, without the audience and when she was feeling confident, and edited it all together later.

Bea Arthur just nailed everything. Not necessarily easy to work with, in that she didn't take one single note I gave her in all the time I was there. But it's not like a director really needed to ask for changes to her performance. All of the women were at such a high level of comedy that as a director, all you needed to do was listen to the rhythm and hope that you got it right.

SONDRA CURRIE: I had auditioned for the show two or three times, at which point they told me to hang loose, because a part would be coming soon. And I was thrilled when I got this role as Margaret. Especially because it started out as a great role that was supposed to continue on in the series.

But that's not how things worked out. When I saw the script for the first time at the Monday table read, I was thrilled. Margaret had scenes and lines all the way through the episode. But the next day, when I got the revised script, I was heartbroken. Most of what had been my dialogue was now coming out of Big Daddy's mouth. I had had long scenes with Rue, and those were gone, too.

My role became so much smaller, and it was clear the character wouldn't recur. In the episode as it aired, there are so many shots of the back of my head that my friends joked that I should have at least gotten a shampoo commercial out of the whole thing. Still, I look at it as a gift just to have been part of the show. There's an old saying that as an actor, you should always steal from the best. And with their expert timing, those quintessential comediennes would take even a line that wasn't written funny and add their double takes to make it great. So I knew to watch them and take in everything that I could. And so even though the experience was so disappointing, I wouldn't trade it.

ABOVE:
Blanche is unsettled by a visit from her father, Big Daddy (David Wayne), and his new fiancée, Margaret (Sondra Currie).

Photo by ALICE S. HALL/NBC/NBCU PHOTO BANK *via* GETTY IMAGES.

'TWAS THE NIGHTMARE BEFORE CHRISTMAS

Written by: BARRY FANARO & MORT NATHAN   ♦   *Directed by:* TERRY HUGHES
Original airdate: DECEMBER 20, 1986

After exchanging Christmas gifts, the Girls plan on heading back to their respective hometowns for the holiday. But en route to the airport, as they arrive to pick up Rose at work, they are held hostage by a gun-wielding psycho Santa (Terry Kiser). Eventually Sophia comes to the rescue, with her innate Sicilian ability to discern Santa's toy gun "from a real piece." They arrive at the airport with only minutes to spare, only to learn that all flights departing from Miami are canceled due to the weather. The Girls take shelter from a freak Miami snowstorm at a diner, whose wise proprietor Albert (Teddy Wilson, 1943–91) helps them realize that despite everything that went wrong, they do get to spend Christmas with their true family after all.

ABOVE:
Rose, Blanche, and Dorothy are held captive by a psycho Santa (Terry Kiser).
OPPOSITE: A freak Miami snowstorm (!) puts the Girls in a Christmas mood.

Photos by RON TOM/NBC/NBCU PHOTO BANK *via* GETTY IMAGES.

COMMENTARY: This episode underscores the theme of the Girls as surrogate family, which is so appealing to viewers who find that their friends are, in fact, their closest loved ones. And although it requires a suspension of disbelief that Miami could experience a snowstorm, the episode will also be forever a fan favorite for featuring perhaps the most famous prop of the series other than Sophia's purse—the naughty "Men of Blanche's Boudoir" calendar—and behind the scenes, the series' most beloved prank. Because it turned out that thanks to the men of the *Golden Girls* crew, that calendar ended up being more of a lurid page-turner than even Blanche had counted on.

MORT NATHAN: In so many of the best sitcoms, the true family is the group inhabiting the screen, not necessarily the family they're related to. And that's what *The Golden Girls* was about. They went through a journey each week to discover what America already knew: they wanted to be with each other, and were each other's family. They were who they would really want to be with at Christmas. That's why this episode works so well.

LEX PASSARIS (*associate director*): I got the heads-up that something fun was to happen, and that I should come over to the stage. It was a Thursday afternoon, when we would tape the camera run-through. And what happened next had been well planned. The camera guys were in on it, so they even knew enough, when it came time to rehearse the scene where Blanche gives out her Christmas gifts, to turn off the time code window that blocks part of the screen.

They rehearsed Blanche giving wrapped boxes to the other Girls containing the calendar. But unbeknownst to them, a whole group of the production guys—stage, lighting, props, cameramen—had stayed late the night before and made up a new prop calendar, having taken some of the most provocative pictures. You could sell these in West Hollywood. They were all in just their shorts. For one shot, the prop guys got a saddle, and one lighting grip who was a huge black man bent over with the saddle on his back, and Jimmy the prop guy, who wasn't a big guy, sat on his back with a cowboy hat. And there was whipped cream.

ROBERT SPINA (*production associate*): There are lines of dialogue as each of the ladies opens her present, so it doesn't happen all at once. They are all supposed to open it and say something like: "Oh, that's lovely." I think Betty was the one to go first, and she keeps talking as she's flipping the pages, but the look on her face is "oh my God!" And then Bea got hers, and they all just dissolved into laughter. Bea laughed so hard that she cried for nearly five minutes.

THE MEN OF
BLANCHE'S BOUDOIR

Blanche's homemade Christmas gift to the Girls: a calendar of
all her boudoir conquests. Watch out for September!

Photo courtesy of the ESTATE OF RUE McCLANAHAN, *estateofrue.com.*

**During rehearsal, the Girls react to
the crew's prank photos in the "Men of
Blanche's Boudoir" calendar.**

Photos courtesy of LEX PASSARIS, *with permission from*
DISNEY ENTERPRISES, INC.

THE SISTERS & LONG DAY'S JOURNEY INTO MARINARA

Episode 39, written by: CHRISTOPHER LLOYD ◆ *Episode 46, written by:* BARRY FANARO
& MORT NATHAN ◆ *Directed by:* TERRY HUGHES
Original airdates: JANUARY 3, 1987 & FEBRUARY 21, 1987

In "The Sisters," Dorothy has planned a big surprise for her mother's birthday party: she's flown Sophia's sister in from Sicily. But it turns out there's a reason why the two women haven't spoken since widowed Angela (Nancy Walker, 1922–92) returned to Europe. With some coaxing, the sisters tell their separate sides of the same story, all taking place during a Brooklyn Christmas party in 1955: Angela says Sophia kissed her husband, Carmine, under the mistletoe, and Sophia thinks Angela blabbed to the party that a drunken neighbor had grabbed her for a similar smooch. In the end, it's all revealed to be a misunderstanding—but only after a frustrated Dorothy reveals how much the estrangement between her mother and favorite aunt is tearing her apart.

In "Long Day's Journey Into Marinara," Angela's decision to move to Miami permanently sparks a sibling rivalry with Sophia. Meanwhile, Rose accepts a pet-sitting gig—to take care of Count Bessie, the piano-playing chicken.

◆ ◆ ◆ ◆

COMMENTARY: Whether you know her best as Rosie, the simple counterwoman obsessed with Bounty paper towels; as Mildred, the secretary on *McMillan and Wife*; or as Ida Morgenstern, *Rhoda*'s meddling mother, Nancy Walker was a TV icon. As they went nose to nose in "The Sisters" in their matching white wigs and even matching wicker purses, Sophia and Angela looked so perfectly and hilariously like long-lost sisters that the character returned only seven episodes later for a second visit, in "Long Day's Journey Into Marinara" (where the Girls famously suspect she may have plucked and fried the piano-playing poultry). As a result, Nancy competed against two fellow *Golden Girls* guests, Lois Nettleton and Herb Edelman, for 1987's Outstanding Guest Performer in a Comedy Series Emmy; they all lost.

OPPOSITE:

Rose is awed, and Blanche skeptical, at the talents of Count Bessie, the piano-playing chicken.

Photo by RON TOM/NBC/NBCU PHOTO BANK *via* GETTY IMAGES.

Appearing alongside Nancy Walker was a particular treat for Estelle Getty, although for her own reasons. Estelle's friend Michael Orland remembers her eagerly looking forward to taping the first Aunt Angela episode. "Estelle told me how for years when she lived in New York, she was Nancy Walker's stand-in for those Bounty commercials," Michael remembers. "And Nancy never gave her the time of day. She wasn't mean, but she never went out of her way to talk to Estelle. So when Nancy got booked on *The Golden Girls*, Estelle was excited, and started plotting how she was going to go up and say something to her. But then the moment Nancy walked on to the set, and now it was Nancy coming on to Estelle's show, Estelle said she no longer felt the need to bring it up. So she never did."

MORT NATHAN: Sophia is such a hilarious, larger-than-life character, and we loved the idea that she could have a sister who would be her diminutive alter ego. We checked to make sure Nancy Walker was available, and we wrote it specifically for her, because she was the only person we could think of who was such a perfect fit.

BETTY WHITE: Of all things, I still have moments where someone will stop me in the market or on the street and say, "Remember the chicken who played piano?" That chicken was so dear and so cute, and played the piano just the way she was supposed to. And actually, Bea was very upset about that. First of all, birds frighten her a little bit. Plus, she was concerned about the chicken working and being exploited.

THE ACTOR

Written by: BARRY FANARO & MORT NATHAN • *Directed by:* TERRY HUGHES
Original airdate: JANUARY 17, 1987

As Dorothy argues with Sophia over her new job at the pirate-themed fast-food joint Captain Jack's Seafood Shanty, Blanche and Rose come home with the Miami Community Players' most exciting news ever. Accustomed to putting up with "Miami's answer to Meryl Streep," Phyllis Hammerow (Janet Carroll, 1940–2012)—who Dorothy points out was so bad in *The Diary of Anne Frank* that the audience continually cried out through the second act: "She's in the attic!"—the local troupe will now have the pleasure of working with handsome TV actor Patrick Vaughn (Lloyd Bochner, 1924–2005).

From the moment of Patrick's arrival, the smitten Girls swoon, and vie for the chance to play Josie opposite Patrick's Biff, "the drifter" in this *Picnic*-esque but unspecified play. During auditions, Dorothy ad-libs an extra kiss, while Blanche unveils giant new balloon breasts that unfortunately deflate during the scene's tight embrace. Before long, Patrick announces that Phyllis has again landed the leading lady part, with all three Girls left among the group of "nonspeaking townspeople." But Patrick has a special way of consoling Blanche, then Rose, then Dorothy—by promising each of them a secret date that night, at eight, ten, and midnight respectively.

A week later, on opening night, the Girls realize they've literally all been had—and so has Phyllis. Their bickering spills out onto the stage, ultimately replacing the show's hammy plot with much juicier accusations of Patrick's real-life adultery. As the show's improvised climax, the "townspeople" rise up as one, kicking Biff / Patrick out of their town / Miami for good, earning some hard-won applause.

◆ ◆ ◆ ◆

"Don't you worry about a thing, Patrick. My backup pair can take a lot more punishment."

—BLANCHE

MORT NATHAN: This episode was a favorite of my partner Barry Fanaro's and mine at the time, because it was silly, with lots of big gags, and because Lloyd Bochner and the ladies were all such great sports. We had a feeling that the ladies would like to do a show within a show, and they were great at it, at playing fumfering versions of themselves. Just like when Lucille Ball, who of course was one of the all-time greatest entertainers, would as Lucy Ricardo be asking, "Gee, how do I get into the show?" And of course the joke was that she was funnier than anybody—and better than Ricky. It's the same thing when Bea Arthur, Rue McClanahan, and Betty White pretend here that they're not talented. We get to be in on the joke, and that's part of the fun.

BETTY WHITE: This week was fun on the set, because we all liked Lloyd Bochner a lot, both onstage and off. I also remember this episode because when it came to dating, Rose didn't go up against Blanche very often. Rose would tend to stumble into her relationships rather than actually going after them. That's why it's a surprise here that Rose's affair with the actor builds the way it does and lasts, because usually by some point a man would get wise that Rose was even less bright than she seemed.

OPPOSITE:

In her attempt to seduce visiting actor Patrick Vaughn (Lloyd Bochner), Blanche's hopes deflate along with her boobs. ABOVE: Betty, Bea, and Rue in between rehearsal takes, with Janet Carroll as Phyllis Hammerow.

Photo by GENE ARIAS/NBC/NBCU PHOTO BANK *via* GETTY IMAGES. *Photo courtesy of the* EDWARD S. STEPHENSON ARCHIVE *at the* ART DIRECTORS GUILD.

SON-IN-LAW DEAREST

Written by: HARRIETT WEISS & PATT SHEA • *Directed by:* TERRY HUGHES
Original airdate: APRIL 11, 1987

Expecting a visit from her daughter, Kate (Deena Freeman), Dorothy can't hold in the good news when Stan arrives: she thinks they may be about to become grandparents. But Kate's announcement turns out to be far less exciting: she's separated from cheating husband Dennis (Jonathan Perpich).

Having gone through a similar breakup with Stan, Dorothy coaches Kate on staying strong. But later that night, Dennis begs Kate to hear him out and take him back. Dorothy is dismayed when the two do in fact reconcile, and she seeks counsel in Sophia. She reminds Dorothy of the night of her own first anniversary with Stan, when he missed their special dinner and arrived home without a present but with a lipstick stain on his collar.

In the morning, as Kate and Dennis prepare to leave, Dorothy and Stan have a stern talk with their son-in-law on the lanai. Dennis professes love for his wife and vows never again to stray—and Dorothy intends to keep her surgeon son-in-law to that promise, or she'll break every bone in his hand.

◆ ◆ ◆ ◆

COMMENTARY: This episode, written by two women, certainly gives us an insight into the Girls' sex lives. We learn that Rose fooled around with her late husband, Charlie, every night from seven to midnight, and from five to seven each morning—and until noon on Sundays; no wonder the man died in the sack! We're even privy to one of Sophia's sexual fantasies, as she recounts her dream of being held captive on a desert island by Cesar Romero in a loincloth. (Luckily for Sophia, dreams do come true. See season six, "Girls Just Wanna Have Fun . . . Before They Die.")

Writers Patt Shea and Harriett Weiss had gotten their start on *All in the Family*, at a time

when, Patt notes, "Women were just breaking into comedy, and some of the old-timer men who worked on shows thought, 'Women can't be comedy writers.'" But when the series' star Jean Stapleton pressured the network to bring in a few females to provide an authentic voice for her character, the distaff duo got their big break.

Patt and Harriett's script brings back the character of Dorothy's daughter, Kate, with Deena Freeman and Jonathan Perpich replacing Lisa Jane Persky and Dennis Drake, who had played the roles in season one. Deena was previously best known for her recurring role in 1981–82 as April Rush, niece of Ted Knight's Henry on

ABC's *Too Close for Comfort*, and now appears on HBO's *Togetherness*.

PATT SHEA: When *The Golden Girls* started, I had thought Harriett and I would be perfect as writers for the show, because we were about the same age as the characters, and so the show would be about stuff we know.

We had just done a stint on *Cagney and Lacey* when our agent got us the opportunity to write a *Golden Girls* episode. As we started to think of stories to pitch to the producers, we knew that Dorothy had a daughter, and so Harriett told me about something that had happened in her own family, and I thought it was perfect. Harriett's daughter and son-in-law had gotten into an argument, and as Harriett took her daughter's side, she said some things about her son-in-law that she probably shouldn't have. Then, when the couple got back together, Harriett's daughter was furious with her. It was a real and funny story, and one that I'm sure happens to lots of mothers and daughters.

LUCY AND THE GIRLS

THE B PLOT of "Son-in-Law Dearest" references *I Love Lucy*, that other TV classic that keeps attracting new fans, generation after generation. But that wasn't the only link that the Girls had to *Lucy* and to its star, Lucille Ball. In the *Golden Girls'* first season, its producers had looked to Lucy to guest star in "Blind Ambitions" as Rose's sister Lily, the role that ultimately went to Polly Holliday. Although she and husband Gary Morton were big fans of the show, Lucy had declined, citing impending dental surgery. There was also a second reason, her longtime friend and assistant Tom Watson reveals, why the comedy legend had decided to pass. Having just starred as a homeless woman in the gritty CBS TV movie *Stone Pillow*, Lucy wanted her next project to be funny, to satisfy her scores of fans. "Lucy was afraid that having her name on the 'marquee' alongside those of Bea Arthur and Betty White, audiences would expect a delightful laughfest," Tom explains. And unfortunately, the role of Rose's blind sister "was anything but sidesplittingly funny."

The *Golden Girls'* producers understood, offering to find another way to work the redhead onto Richmond Street—but, admits executive producer Mort Nathan, "for whatever reason, probably scheduling, we never did." But they did stay in touch, Tom reveals. When they cooked up their *Lucy*-marathon plot line for "Son-in-Law Dearest," the show's writers sent a delighted Lucy a script to peruse in advance. And earlier that same season, as she prepared to launch her final sitcom, ABC's short-lived 1986 *Life with Lucy*, the legendary comedienne—who with her famous husband Desi Arnaz had literally invented many aspects of the multicamera sitcom format in the early 1950s—thought it might be wise to check in to see how things were being done in the eighties. And so, on the night of August 29, 1986, Lucy bestowed on the Girls the sitcom equivalent of a Papal visit. During the taping of the episode "Joust Between Friends," to air in season two, "she sat in the audience and laughed her head off," Mort remembers.

Lucy—who had been Bea Arthur's costar in the 1974 film *Mame* and friends with Betty White since 1957, when Betty filmed her sitcom *Date with the Angels* at Lucy's studio, Desilu—had a great time, Mort remembers. "It was interesting to see them all side by side. And that night, the thought crossed my mind: 'I wonder if they could have asked Lucy to be one of these ladies?' But for whatever reason, they hadn't. Who knows what might have been, or if it would have worked. I guess it just wasn't meant to be. Lucy had her place in TV history, and our ladies had theirs."

TO CATCH A NEIGHBOR

Written by: RUSSELL MARCUS • *Directed by:* TERRY HUGHES
Original airdate: MAY 2, 1987

As the Girls clean up from hosting their new next-door neighbors for dinner, two police detectives—the TV-typical old man /cute young rookie combo—arrive with upsetting news: the seemingly ordinary McDowells are actually dealers in stolen gems. After some debate, the Girls not only allow Detective Al Mullins (Joseph Campanella) and his young associate Bobby Hopkins (George Clooney) to stay for a stakeout, but even agree to a secret mission to plant a bug in the McDowells' home. Ultimately, the sting goes awry, and Bobby is shot—but ends up with four doting grandmother figures to tuck him in as he recuperates.

◆ ◆ ◆ ◆

"Detective Mullins. I am Blanche Devereaux, and these are my roommates Dorothy and Rose. They're innocent. I'm not."

—BLANCHE

COMMENTARY: Before he was *ER*'s Dr. Douglas Ross or Booker on *Roseanne,* and just as he finished a career-building stint as handyman George on *The Facts of Life,* silver fox George Clooney was a dark-haired young Miami cop.

It's apparently a gig the movie megastar looks back on fondly. At the Screen Actors Guild Awards ceremony in 2010, George stepped onstage as a presenter shortly after Betty White had accepted a Life Achievement Award, with a speech mentioning costars she'd "had."

"In 1987, I did an episode of *The Golden Girls,* and I would like to thank Betty White for her discretion," George joked. He added, "A friend of mine told me she was a bobcat in the sack."

RUSSELL MARCUS: The story idea for this episode was conceived by Tony Thomas and Paul Witt. This was to be the last regular episode of the second season, other than a wraparound show and the first attempt at an "Empty Nest" pilot, and sometimes at a point like that, as writers, you want to test the boundaries of your show a little bit. *The Golden Girls* wasn't normally the kind of show that would have a gunshot in it, but I think that at this point, Paul, Tony, and Susan Harris wanted to get serious and dramatic for a moment, to show that we could.

RUE McCLANAHAN: At this point, George Clooney was totally unknown and very young. He must have been all of twenty-five, and he was so good—and so gorgeous! I said, "This guy's got it all. He's going to have a big career."

TERRY HUGHES: I've told this story before: even a little after this period, when I'd be involved in casting a pilot, I remember people running through all the actors who were available, and then closing the door and saying, "Well, worse comes to worst, there is always George Clooney." That's where his career was at the time. I think that's a great inspirational story for people!

BARRY FANARO: I'll always remember the story about how we cast George Clooney. We got a call from his agent, who said, "You guys know George, right?" At the time, he'd been kicking around sitcoms, but hadn't worked in a while. So the agent asked us, "Would you guys consider putting George Clooney in an episode, so he can maintain his medical insurance?"

I'd never worked with George before, and he couldn't have been nicer. And now, when we see him in something, I get to joke with my kids, "If not for me and the insurance he needed, that guy would not be *the* George Clooney! So let George Clooney know it's because of Barry Fanaro he's a superstar. He couldn't have done it without us on *The Golden Girls.*"

PREVIOUS PAGE:

Sophia, Rose, and Blanche at the hospital bedside of injured young officer Bobby Hopkins (George Clooney).

Photo by RON TOM/NBC/NBCU PHOTO BANK *via* GETTY IMAGES.

A PIECE OF CAKE

Written by: KATHY SPEER, TERRY GROSSMAN, BARRY FANARO, & MORT NATHAN
Directed by: TERRY HUGHES • Original airdate: MAY 9, 1987

As the Girls plan what's actually a surprise party for Blanche, they reminisce about parties past. In one vignette, Rose surprises Dorothy with a birthday soiree—at Mr. HaHa's Hot Dog Hacienda, complete with screaming kids and one obsequious clown (Alan Blumenfeld). In a second story, Rose remembers the last cake she would ever bake in St. Olaf, as she pretends that her recently departed husband, Charlie, is throwing her a birthday party; speaking to him out loud, she breaks the news that she's selling the house and moving to Miami. And Sophia harks back to Brooklyn in April 1956, to a celebration with her husband, Sal (Sid Melton, 1917–2011), and young Dorothy (Lyn Greene), where she finds out that due to an error in her birth certificate, she is actually turning fifty instead of forty-eight.

In the final vignette, soon after moving in together, the Girls throw a surprise shindig for Blanche—who comes home already infuriated about the birthday party coworkers had thrown for her at the office. To make things worse, Sophia, who has shown up unexpectedly from Shady Pines, tips Blanche off that there are hordes of partygoers awaiting her on the lanai. Blanche is relieved when Dorothy and Rose promise to send everyone home—until she gets a glimpse of just who her guests have turned out to be. In compiling the guest list, Rose has invited an all-male cadre from Blanche's little black book, inadvertently turning the night into one of Blanche's happiest occasions.

◆ ◆ ◆ ◆

COMMENTARY: This episode introduces the two beloved recurring characters of Sophia's husband, Salvadore Petrillo (face hidden entirely under a newspaper), and their young daughter Dorothy, both seen only in flashbacks. A bit of trivia: the other birthday kids called onstage alongside Dorothy at Mr. HaHa's, Bobby Spina and Jeannie Taylor, are named for two members of the *Golden Girls* crew.

BETTY WHITE: I loved doing this episode, where Rose puts on the birthday party for Charles. It hadn't been that long since I'd lost [my husband] Allen [Ludden], and so I just let it all hang out. As

I set everything out for the party, that's as close to Betty as Rose ever came. Here, Rose wasn't just putting a party together; she was doing something that she emotionally needed to do, and she believed she was talking to him. To do something like that, I had to draw from genuine emotion. You couldn't fake that. So in my head, absolutely, I was making that party for Allen, not Charlie.

ROBERT SPINA (*production associate*): I loved all the episodes with Lyn Greene and Sid Melton, where Estelle had the opportunity to play her own age. Anything that had to do with the history of these women was something I got a kick out of, however brief the scenes. And Lyn Greene's performance was remarkable. It could have gone the wrong way and become a caricature. But Lyn got it right, and did it with respect. As a result, Bea was

absolutely on board, and I know that meant a lot to Lyn.

TERRY GROSSMAN: Sid Melton, who'd worked with Danny Thomas on *Make Room For Daddy*, auditioned for the role of Sal, and we cast him—and then Tony Thomas came in and said, "I know it's Uncle Sid, but you don't have to do this." The thing is he was good, particularly playing a shleppy old man from Brooklyn.

Estelle and Sid and Lyn Greene were great together, and the flashback scenes really worked. But when Tony would watch the run-through, he would always come over to me and say, "I'm paying hundreds of thousands of dollars for the Golden Girls. Do you see the Golden Girls?" I got what he meant. The scenes in Brooklyn were nice, but where were the ladies? Let's see the real Bea Arthur!

ABOVE:
Rose's kitchen at home in St. Olaf.
OPPOSITE: Estelle loved looking younger in flashback episodes, like here in Season 3's "Mother's Day."
Photo courtesy of the EDWARD S. STEPHENSON ARCHIVE *at the* ART DIRECTORS GUILD.
Photo by WAYNE WILLIAMS.

"*After eighty, every year without a headstone is a milestone.*"

—SOPHIA

LYN GREENE: My friend Lonny Price, the actor and director, is a friend of *The Golden Girls* producers Terry Grossman and Kathy Speer. Lonny always felt that they should see me, because I reminded him so much of Bea Arthur. Then, at one point, the show was auditioning for an actress to play Dorothy's daughter.

I immediately wanted to audition, but honestly when I got the sides and read the lines, I was disappointed because the daughter wasn't really like Dorothy, but just kind of generic. Nevertheless, when Lonny physically pushed me into the room for the audition, I decided to read the character not as the ingénue, like it was written, but as a young version of Dorothy.

I did my idea of a young Bea Arthur—and nobody moved or said anything. It was horrible. I was so eager to be like Bea, because she was my idol. One of my earliest roles in theater had been Lucy Brown in *Threepenny Opera*, the role she originated in New York. So my audition was really an homage to her, and when there was no response at all, I was crestfallen. I neither smoked nor drank at the time, but when I went out for sushi with friends that night, I belted back some sake and lit up a cigarette. Looking back, I was not as upset about not getting the part as I was about missing out on the chance to let my idol Bea Arthur know how much I admired her.

The part was supposed to be this young, effervescent girl, and I'd played her as mature, deep-voiced, and acerbic. I was convinced I'd embarrassed myself, and I hated Lonny for his terrible idea of having me audition. But then, it wasn't long after that that Lonny called and told me the producers had asked him, "Where did you find her?"

Lonny told me, "They're going to write something for you." It was a total shock! And then they came up with this idea of a flashback, showing Dorothy as a young woman. I think mostly what they wanted was the opportunity to show people that Estelle was not old. Estelle was thrilled to get the chance to look good!

As I went in to do the first episode, "A Piece of Cake," I knew I didn't want to do an imitation of Bea. But I did study many episodes on tape, to observe how she moved, how she held her hand when she delivered a line. There were things that she did, and I knew I could do one or two of those and people would recognize the connection between my young Dorothy and Bea.

I was told that Bea had watched my performance in "A Piece of Cake," and that she was pleased. For me, that was as good as it could get. I was just a guest performer, and was only about thirty-one years old, and Bea Arthur had watched me; I was happy. I do also think I caught Bea smiling as she was watching the taping of one of my scenes once.

• EPISODE 52 •

BRINGING UP BABY

Written by: MORT NATHAN & BARRY FANARO • *Directed by:* TERRY HUGHES
Original airdate: OCTOBER 3, 1987

When Rose gets a telegram stating that her uncle Hingeblotter has died and left her his baby, she and her roommates excitedly prepare for impending motherhood. But it turns out that the baby is not a baby, but Baby, Hingeblotter's prized pig. And he's also a cash cow, coming with a hundred-thousand-dollar stipend for his care.

At twenty-nine, Baby has already exceeded typical porcine life expectancy, and so the greedy Girls agree to put up with their new male roommate's belching and destructive tendencies just long enough to bring home the bacon. Sure enough, Baby soon takes ill, and Blanche, Dorothy, and Sophia take to the mall, to spend their new riches in advance.

But when a visiting veterinarian (Tom McGreevey) diagnoses that Baby is actually dying of homesickness, a guilty Rose makes arrangements to ship the pig back to Minnesota—with initially resistant Blanche, Dorothy, and Sophia now arguing for him to stay. Ultimately, days after sending Baby back and relinquishing the money, Rose gets a letter from the animal's new caretaker informing her that after just thirty-six hours with Cousin Gustav, Baby died peacefully in his new pen.

— ◆ ◆ ◆ ◆ —

COMMENTARY: The Girls had already appeared with a cat and, in season two's "Joust Between Friends," a living room full of dogs. But now, largely due to the actresses' real-life passion, the animals showing up on-screen are getting larger. The title of this episode is the same as that of the classic 1938 screwball film comedy; but for the TV version, it's the Girls taking care of a pig rather than Cary Grant and Katharine Hepburn looking after a leopard.

Also noteworthy for production purposes: with this episode, the first shot for the show's third season, *The Golden Girls* moved from the Sunset Gower Studios to the nearby indepen-

"Four grown women decide to live with a pig, and he's the one with the mental problem?"

—DOROTHY

dent Ren-Mar (now renamed Red Studios Hollywood), the onetime home of *I Love Lucy* and its stars Lucille Ball and Desi Arnaz's company, Desilu. Through the mid-1990s, the lot would be a similar mini-empire once more, as the home of a handful of Witt/Thomas sitcoms including *Empty Nest* and *Nurses*.

KATHY SPEER: I remember this episode because it was an example of how Bea could take a line that was not really a strong joke and make it huge. Dorothy didn't want to have Baby the pig around, but the moment she found out about the money involved, Bea did one of her turns and said, "Welcome, Baby!" Every time she did that, she killed me.

BETTY WHITE: I've been working with the LA Zoo for nearly fifty years, so don't think you're ever going to find an animal I *don't* love to work with! I was excited that in this episode I got to sleep with a pig—an actual pig! Everybody who ever mentions this episode to me seems to think it was a piglet, but it was actually this huge, pink, three-hundred-pound pig! He was so good, though—a really good actor.

TERRY HUGHES: As we rehearsed this show, of course we couldn't have the pig there all week. The way we staged it, the pig had to cross the lanai. So as we did our camera rehearsal, we'd say, "Enter the pig." But there was no pig there. So I'd estimate the timing for the actresses by saying, "Okay . . . pig, pig, pig, pig, pig . . . now speak!"

On the night of the taping, the pig was great at hitting his marks and crossing through the room correctly. In fact, the next week, as we were rehearsing a scene, Estelle had to cross the room, and she said to me, "I can't figure out how to get the timing to work here." So I just said to her, "Well, the pig did it." After that "the pig did it" became one of our internal catchphrases.

LEX PASSARIS (associate director): In the first few seasons, we used an establishing shot of a house in the Brentwood section of Los Angeles to represent the Girls' house in Miami. And this episode marked one of the few times we ever shot any live scenes there as well, with a cab pulling up in the driveway to drop off [an unseen] Sophia, and then a tow truck towing the Girls' Mercedes away at the end.

OPPOSITE:
Sophia tolerates a visit from the Girls' newest roommate.

Photo by ALICE S. HALL/NBC/NBCU PHOTO BANK *via* GETTY IMAGES.

STRANGE BEDFELLOWS

Written by: CHRISTOPHER LLOYD • *Directed by:* TERRY HUGHES
Original airdate: NOVEMBER 7, 1987

As the ladies wrap up a campaign party for Gil Kessler (John Schuck), candidate for city councilman, they find a forgotten folder. Blanche is elected to take the materials over to his house, only to be "caught" by paparazzi who turn their photos into a major extramarital scandal. Blanche insists that nothing happened—but when Kessler plays along with the publicity, her roommates refuse to believe her, knowing her appetite for men. Only when the candidate finally refutes the story do the other Girls realize they owe Blanche an apology. And apparently now hooked on the honesty Blanche advised, Kessler decides that he should also admit to another secret from his past that ultimately costs him the election: he used to be a she.

❖ ❖ ❖ ❖

COMMENTARY: Interestingly, although this episode touches on transgender issues, it does so only as an ending beat for a story that is actually about the hurt feelings that come from friendship betrayed. Its writer, Christopher Lloyd (*not* the *Taxi* and *Back to the Future* actor), began his writing career as an apprentice on *The Golden Girls*, then moved up the writers' ranks, eventually becoming an executive producer on the gay-sensibility-friendly hit *Frasier*, before most recently co-creating *Modern Family*.

CHRISTOPHER LLOYD: For this episode, we originally had a different ending, but then we sort of pasted this together. At some point in the story Gil had to allude to rumors about him, so that the Girls could take that to mean an affair he was having with Blanche. And originally, he had some other dark secret, although I don't remember what it was. The episode had a good issue at its center, an emotional place where Blanche's roommates didn't believe her because of her reputation. But the ending is often where all the hard work comes in in storytelling, and I think if there was a fault in the writing of *The Golden Girls*, it was that sometimes there could be a sort of slapdash ending to some of the episodes. This one even at the time seemed slightly unsatisfying.

RUE McCLANAHAN: The reason Blanche gets so upset in this episode is because her dearest friends are calling her a liar. There's no way she can prove that she's telling the truth, and it's very painful and devastating. This one was easy to do because those emotions were very clear and true the way they were written. It was also easy to have a crush on John Schuck, who played Gil Kessler. I thought that it was a delicious piece of casting, that he was once a woman, and John played that with such subtlety and humor.

It may not be politically correct how the ending suggests that because he's transgender he can't get elected, but that is still going on today.

JOHN SCHUCK: I had been a big fan of *The Golden Girls* right from the beginning. When I auditioned for the role of Gil Kessler, I thought it was a delightful and fun script. But I was a little nervous about doing the show. I had worked with Betty White on game shows, and had known her from doing some animal rescue work, but I had never before worked with Bea Arthur, and I'd heard she could be difficult.

But Bea seemed happy with the show, and made good suggestions about her character. The only time I saw Bea get a little impatient was when Estelle was having trouble remembering her big "Picture it: Sicily"–type speech. Eventually, we did have to record that again after the audience went home, with Estelle using cue cards for the lines.

But that was the only moment of dissension. Most of my stuff that week was with Rue, and we just laughed from beginning to end. It was a great week, because the script was in very good shape. Everyone was off book very quickly, and the director, Terry Hughes, was extremely supportive of all the actors.

The episode's ending, where Gil turns out to have been born female, was actually the clincher that made me really want to play the part. I had done a failed series with Sharon Gless called *Turnabout*, in which our characters went to sleep, and our spirits switched bodies. And so when I wake up, I'm the woman. In those days, it was very funny for Sharon to chomp on a cigar and do all sorts of butch stuff, but my part was harder to pull off. Audiences then would have had a hard time if I were to have become truly effeminate, and so I always had to look for psychological gestures, like pantomiming taking off an earring when I put the phone to my ear. So now, having had that experience, I knew instantly what I was going to do with Gil at the end. I wanted to find a gesture that would not be offensive to anybody, and yet would get the point across immediately. So I did a sort of Jack Benny take, with my hands on the side of my face— and it worked.

ABOVE:

Gil Kessler's campaign headquarters.

Photo courtesy of the EDWARD S. STEPHENSON ARCHIVE *at the* ART DIRECTORS GUILD.

OLD FRIENDS

Written by: KATHY SPEER & TERRY GROSSMAN   ◆   *Directed by:* TERRY HUGHES
Original airdate: SEPTEMBER 19, 1987

Sophia befriends elderly black man Alvin Newcastle (Joe Seneca, 1919–96) on a bench on the boardwalk, bonding over her veal-and-pepper sandwich. But when Sophia asks Alvin about his late wife, Edna, he suddenly becomes upset.

The next day, Dorothy thinks it best to tail her mother down to the boardwalk, where she confers with Alvin's similarly concerned daughter, Sandra (Janet MacLachlan, 1933–2010). When Dorothy then breaks the news to her mother that Alvin has Alzheimer's disease, and soon will have to go live with a doctor nephew in New York, Sophia decides to savor whatever laughs the two of them have left.

Meanwhile, believing it to be junk for donation, Blanche mistakenly gives Rose's teddy bear, Fernando, to seemingly helpful "Sunshine Cadet" Daisy (Jenny Lewis)—who then refuses to return Rose's cherished childhood memento. It turns out Daisy is a Sunshine Cadet with a dark side; when her demands are not met, she sends Blanche a message she can't refuse, in the form of a stuffed brown ear. In-person negotiations don't go much better, with Daisy threatening the bear with a pistol filled with red ink until the Girls agree to buy her a ten-speed Schwinn.

When Rose comes home and sees Daisy with a one-eared Fernando, she initially demands that Blanche pay the ransom to set things right. But by the next morning, Rose has seemingly had a change of heart. Taking Daisy by the shoulders, Rose gives the girl a heartfelt speech about accepting loss; then, just as Daisy least expects it, Rose grabs the bear and pushes the brat out the door with these words of wisdom: "Sometimes life just isn't fair, kiddo."

◆ ◆ ◆ ◆

COMMENTARY: Guest star Joe Seneca had started his career as a singer and songwriter, penning hits like "Break It to Me Gently" and "It's Gonna Work Out Fine." On-screen, he portrayed two college presidents, in Spike Lee's 1988 film *School Daze*, and as the head of the fictional, historically black Hillman College on *The Cosby Show*. Ironically, at the time he played Alzheimer's-stricken Alvin, his real-life career was just starting to sizzle. In fact, *Golden Girls* showrunners Terry Grossman and Kathy Speer remember, Joe had just come off back-to-back roles in the hit films *Crossroads* and *Silver-ado* at the time, so his casting was considered a coup for their Saturday night sitcom.

Interestingly, the episode's other main guest star may not have had a musical connection at the time—but she does now. In 2015, singer/song-writer Jenny Lewis revisited her child-star past in the music video for her single "She's Not Me," with a reprise of her character from the 1989 film *Troop Beverly Hills* as well as a re-creation of her teddy-threatening moment in the living room of "The Gilded Gals," with Zosia Mamet as a Dorothy look-alike, Vanessa Bayer impersonating Rose, and Fred Armisen as an eerily convincing Sophia.

The Girls' new studio for season three and beyond, Ren-Mar, was in what was then a seed-ier section of Hollywood, but the new digs offered more room for some fun new toys. This episode marks the first time we see the show's boardwalk set; it would return later in the series, such as in fourth-season episode "Sophia's Wedding: Part 2," as Sophia and her new husband, Max Weinstock (Jack Gilford), decide to open a stand selling pizza and knishes.

With its multiple levels, angles, and even light-ing effects suggesting lapping waves, this board-walk is the type of set for which the show's produc-tion designer, Ed Stephenson, had already become famous—or perhaps infamous. By the show's later days, writer Jamie Wooten remembers, "When we wrote our scripts, we would have to write in the stage directions 'a *small* banquet room,' 'a *small* convent.' Because Ed was from the movies, and would build these things huge and cavernous, and they were expensive. So our line producers would ask us always to stress the word 'small,' because that's how they kept him reined in."

TERRY GROSSMAN: This was the episode we submitted for Emmy consideration for *The Golden Girls*' third season— the year we lost. But I think this was a really good episode. In fact, afterward, we would get mild pressure from the network about the character

of Daisy: "You could bring her back. You estab-lished that she lives down the street." Especially because we had a show about older characters, the network was always looking for a way to get younger people in there. But we countered their suggestion by noting that we didn't need a child character, because we knew we already had chil-dren in the audience tuning in to watch Estelle.

TERRY HUGHES: I know Betty was really anx-ious about pushing the girl. She was concerned about whether the audience would accept it. She asked me: "What are people going to think?" And I told her: "They are going to cheer, because the girl is a little monster, and she's asking for it!" Rose's actions were totally justified by the episode's setup. And when that moment came, and the audience did erupt, I think Betty felt a great deal of relief.

BETTY WHITE: This episode ended up being one of my favorites. I was working with a little girl actress, a very professional little girl. She was very much the little spitfire, and had a kind of stagey mother with her. We rehearsed the scene, and by the time we got to play it in front of the audience, I thought, "I've kind of had it with this little actress." So I really grabbed that bear and pulled it in, and the audience fell apart, because I think they were feeling the same thing: get that kid's bear! The character was a monster, so actu-ally I'm sure my feelings were for the character, not for the little girl. At least I hope with all my heart that I was better than that! But I can't be sure. I'd like to say I pulled my punch, but I'll bet I gave her a pretty good shove. Because I really had to pull the bear away, shove her and slam the door quickly, and make sure the door didn't hit her. In the heat of the battle, when you're playing the scene, that's a lot to keep track of. In the end, I loved that moment, because Rose, the one you'd least expect, got the chance to stand up for herself. She didn't often get the chance to come out on top.

NEXT PAGE:
Sophia with her new friend on the board-walk, Alvin Newcastle (Joe Seneca).

Photo by ABC PHOTO ARCHIVES/ABC *via* GETTY IMAGES.

GRAB THAT DOUGH

Written by: WINIFRED HERVEY • *Directed by:* TERRY HUGHES
Original airdate: JANUARY 23, 1988

Sophia has four contestant tickets to be on the Girls' favorite game show, *Grab That Dough*. Problem is Sophia accidentally gave the show the wrong return address; she had the tickets routed through Sicily, and now the Girls have until tomorrow to get themselves out to Hollywood for the taping. On their last-minute westbound flight, the airline promptly loses their luggage. And what's worse, the officious desk clerk Nancy (Lucy Lee Flippin) has already given away their hotel rooms.

For a seventy-five-dollar bribe, Nancy lets the girls sack out in the lobby, where during the night, somebody else plays Grab That Dough by stealing all of their purses. Still, they do make the morning's game show taping, where Blanche suggests to Dorothy that they dump Rose and Sophia and team up with a couple of ringers from Milwaukee, the Kaplan brothers. Dorothy points out that splitting up doubles their chances of going home with prize money, but a suddenly-smart Rose isn't buying it. In fact, while Willard Kaplan (Charles Green) keeps forfeiting points with his itchy buzzer finger, Rose and Sophia clean up in the trivia lightning round.

But Dorothy and Blanche's green team is back on top when they win the chance to Grab That Dough in the show's signature vacuum-pressured money booth, and Dorothy gives it a go, hauling in nine hundred dollars with—as host Guy Corbin (Jim MacKrell) so indelicately puts it—her "big meat hooks." But greed then gets the better of the Girls, as they impulsively trade their winnings for what's behind curtain number three: an electric skillet and a lifetime supply of soup.

OPPOSITE:
Grab That Dough host Guy Corbin
(Jim MacKrell) helps Blanche
spin the show's big wheel.

Photo by ALICE S. HALL/NBC/NBCU
PHOTO BANK *via* GETTY IMAGES.

COMMENTARY: Two things always seem to get the Girls in trouble—greed, and their competitive natures—and both are on display in this cautionary game show tale. Still, they get to spend time in the presence of the show's host, Guy Corbin, who Rose calls "the cutest game show host on TV . . . like Gene Rayburn, Chuck Woolery, and Bob Eubanks all rolled up in one." (And after her storied marriage to *Password* host Allen Ludden, Betty White ought to know.) This episode provides viewers with a treat, in the form of one of the show's silliest stunts,

as Dorothy dons an apron and goggles, and Grabs That Dough—although, as noted below, the moment initially inspired panic in Bea Arthur.

In other trivia, when Sophia says, "Picture it: Sicily," have you ever wondered exactly where you should be picturing? Well this episode reveals the octogenarian's former address on the Italian isle: "Two miles west of Palermo, underneath the old bridge."

ABOVE:

The vacuum-sealed money booth on *Grab That Dough.*

Photo courtesy of the EDWARD S. STEPHENSON ARCHIVE at the ART DIRECTORS GUILD.

WINIFRED HERVEY: We were always looking for new combinations of the four characters, and this episode allowed us to team Dorothy and Blanche against Sophia and Rose in a way we hadn't done before. I think we all came up with the concept for "Grab That Dough" together in the writers' room—and now we had to build this big machine with the cash inside it. I remember Harry Waterson was our budget guy, and he was really wary about the cost. But we writers on *The Golden Girls* were lucky in that we were able to write what we thought would work, and our production team would make it happen.

MICHAEL HYNES (*associate designer*): When we got the heads-up about this game show episode, we had only two days to put it all together—including the money booth Bea would be in. So we did what we could in the time we had. We found this transparent cabinet, which had a floor that we removed, and we added the mechanism to blow the money around.

It really was a tight squeeze inside that thing. And Bea wouldn't let us close the door on it until we shot it. So we rehearsed with the door open. But the whole thing was a nightmare, trying to get the money to fly around in that thing, because with the door not closed tight there was no vacuum and it wouldn't work. So we didn't really know if and how the stunt was ever going to work properly until we shot it in front of the audience.

BEA ARTHUR: I loved doing silly things like this game show. We had done a game show on *Maude* called *Beat the Devil*, where Rue and I had mallets and had to hit this little devil statue on the head. My thoughts about doing little stunts like this were just like those about doing any of the other stuff that we did: if something served a purpose at the time and was funny, then I enjoyed getting to do it.

LUCY LEE FLIPPIN: To get the lines out, as this horrible person in a funny scene, I had to use all of my skills not to break up.

At one point, during the run-through, I was standing there, looking at these four famous faces, of women I'd totally admired forever—and I was so overwhelmed that I went completely blank. Luckily, I snapped out of it, and was fine in front of the audience. Besides, the atmosphere seemed very tolerant there. The ladies had been together for a while at that point, and all seemed to get along so well, to the point that they even seemed to talk to each other in their own secret language.

SOPHIA:

"I've got something in this old lady purse that's going to make you scream, holler, and jump for joy."

BLANCHE:

"Are the batteries included?"

DOROTHY'S NEW FRIEND

Written by: ROBERT BRUCE & MARTIN WEISS • *Directed by:* TERRY HUGHES
Original airdate: JANUARY 16, 1988

Dorothy feels like she's stuck in a rut, until she attends a lecture given by glamorous and sophisticated local novelist Barbara Thorndyke (Bonnie Bartlett). The two become fast friends; but on her first visit to Richmond Street, the snooty blonde elicits quite a different reaction from Rose and Blanche.

Soon Dorothy is skipping movie dates with the Girls in order to attend pretentious theater events with the imperious authoress. Over lunch one day, Dorothy confesses to Barbara that their friendship has left the other Girls feeling left out. And although Barbara flat-out states that she thinks Blanche and Rose are "limited," she invites everyone and their dates to a swank evening at the exclusive Mortimer Club. But when the night of their group date arrives—and so does Sophia's new squeeze Murray Guttman (Monty Ash, 1909–98)—Barbara calls Dorothy in to the kitchen to reveal a problem: Jewish surnames like Guttman are not welcome at the restricted Mortimer. As Barbara shrugs off the anti-Semitic policy as something out of her control, Dorothy finally sees the ugliness behind Barbara's polished patrician exterior. After dismissing the phony for good, Dorothy apologizes to Blanche and Rose, and even offers that after all the practice she's had lately, she'd be honored to partake in Rose's two-person masquerade ball costume, and dress as the horse's behind.

◆ ◆ ◆ ◆

COMMENTARY: We know Rose can come off dumb, but Blanche, too? Yes, she may be obsessed with Elvis to the point she's willing to believe tabloid tales told from beyond the grave. But the woman does work in an art museum, after all; so surely we can grant her some level of sophistication. Obviously, then, it's Barbara who isn't very astute, in confusing Blanche's somehow endearing shallowness with plain old simplemindedness.

This episode's theme—of an interloper causing friction in a beloved friendship—and even its denouement are strikingly similar to a 1972 episode of *The Mary Tyler Moore Show*, "Some of My Best Friends Are Rhoda," in which Mary Richards's new pal Joanne, played by Mary Frann, similarly discourages Mary from inviting her Jewish bestie, Rhoda Morgenstern, to join their tennis match at her club. Of course, there are only so many ideas under the sitcom sun, and the best themes bear repeating. Still, "it would have helped if we had just had *The Mary Tyler Moore Show*'s bible," jokes *Golden Girls* executive producer Terry Grossman. Adds his wife and fellow showrunner Kathy Speer, "We stole from the best."

Here in the "Mary Frann role" is Bonnie Bartlett, who appeared with her husband, William Daniels, on such shows as ABC's *Boy Meets World* and NBC's *St. Elsewhere*, for which Bonnie won two Emmy Awards in 1986 and 1987 for Outstanding Supporting Actress in a Drama Series.

ROBERT BRUCE: Obviously, Dorothy couldn't stay friendly with this outside character, and she had to get back in with Rose and Blanche. So we needed something about Barbara that would be much more reprehensible than just being snobby. That's why we ended up making her anti-Semitic, because Dorothy is clearly not going to stand for that.

When we were writing the script, I named Sophia's boyfriend after a real guy named Murray Guttman, a big construction guy in my hometown of Cincinnati. I thought it would be fun to put in somebody's real name. Nowadays, studios do a "clearance" process, where they won't let us use the name of anybody who they find to exist in the United States. But back then, all they checked for the show was Miami, and there was no Murray Guttman there. Many years later, I saw the real Murray Guttman at my father's funeral. He came up to me, and I wondered if he knew about the show, and if he did what he would say. It turns out he was really appreciative. "It's one of the better things that's happened to me—my name was on *The Golden Girls*!"

BONNIE BARTLETT: Figuring out who Barbara Thorndyke was was very easy for me—because she was just like my mother. The only thing that made me nervous was being on such a good comic show and worrying that I wasn't going to be very funny. Bea was very friendly in helping me through it, and so was Rue. Rue even told me that after getting hired on *Maude*, she had had the same wor-

ries. She didn't think of herself specifically as a comedian, and she was such a wreck the first year, worrying about getting laughs, she ended up seeing a psychiatrist. It made me feel better, because look at what a great job she always did!

I didn't want to overplay the part, and make Barbara too obviously rotten from the start. But then I was also worried I wasn't doing enough. Well, I must have been, because I sure did get a

> *"Rose, sweetheart, this Friday I can choose between rubbing elbows with Norman Mailer, or doing the hokey-pokey in a horse costume with your behind in my face."*
>
> —DOROTHY

reaction. When we came out in the beginning, the audience was all smiles. But by the end of the show when we came out to take our bows, everyone was looking at me as if they hated me. And during my last scene with Dorothy, they literally booed me. Here I was, coming off *St. Elsewhere* where I'd gotten two Emmys for playing this wonderful lady. So I was a little shaken. My husband, Bill, had come to one of the two tapings, and afterward, he said to me: "Bonnie, I don't think you should ever play a Jew hater again. Because they're going to boo you." I had to wonder why didn't I think of these things!

BLANCHE'S LITTLE GIRL

Written by: KATHY SPEER & TERRY GROSSMAN • *Directed by:* TERRY HUGHES
Original airdate: JANUARY 9, 1988

After a four-year estrangement, Blanche's daughter Rebecca is about to visit. Blanche is eager to put their disagreement, about her daughter's pursuit of a career as a Parisian fashion model, behind them—and indeed once she lays eyes on the now-plus-sized Rebecca (Shawn Schepps), the argument does seem moot. The real problem now is Rebecca's relationship with her verbally abusive boyfriend, Jeremy (Joe Regalbuto).

For two weeks, Blanche keeps her opinion of the guy to herself, afraid of losing her daughter once more. But finally, as the two prepare to elope, she begs Rebecca to reconsider. As feared, Rebecca sees her concern as more meddling, and seems doubly determined to marry the jerk—until Blanche's words sink in on the way to the airport, bringing Rebecca back to thank her mother for reminding her of her self-worth.

Meanwhile, fed up with mistreatment from her manager at Pecos Pete's Chow Wagon, Sophia rallies coworkers Mildred and Edna to strike. At a conference around the Girls' kitchen table, teenage tyrant McCracken (Scott Menville) responds to Sophia's list of demands with a decision to fire them all. But luckily, as the kid's grandmother, Edna (Meg Wyllie, 1917–2002), has one last negotiating tactic up her sleeve, blackmailing the brat by threatening to reveal the true story of how his father's car got dented.

◆ ◆ ◆ ◆

COMMENTARY: This episode marks the first time we meet Blanche's daughter Rebecca—the first of her kids we ever see, and yet the one Blanche seemingly forgot to mention earlier in the season, when in episode fifty-two, "Bringing Up Baby," she listed her four children: Skippy, Biff, Doug, and Janet. It's also the only time we'll ever see Shawn Schepps in the Rebecca role.

RUE McCLANAHAN: It was lovely doing this episode, and I felt that this was an important storyline. I travel everywhere to give speeches, all around the country, and people have come up to me in person to tell me how important this episode was to them.

SHAWN SCHEPPS: The episode was about Rebecca learning to find self-esteem despite her size, and so when I met with the producers they asked me to wear a padded "fat suit," which made me about three sizes bigger. The ironic thing was that I myself was suffering from the same kind of abuse from my boyfriend. I had been an actress since age six, and even then, my agent had told my parents to watch my weight. I had told my boyfriend how hurtful that had been, and he would use those memories against me and go on these fat rages, which was awful.

My life mirrored what was going on in the script, but I was too young to see that mirror. I just compartmentalized, going to work, doing the role, and then coming home and getting shit about being fat. But then, shortly after I did this episode, he wanted to get married, and I knew that would be the worst, so I broke up with him. Now I realize that my decision defi-nitely could have been subconsciously affected by having played out Rebecca's story.

JOE REGALBUTO: My character was such an outrageously awful guy that everyone had fun teasing me about it after we'd rehearse a scene. Joking with me—"You are *nasty*!"—was one of the ways that amazing cast made me as a guest actor feel at home.

As a guest you're there to be a foil for the regular characters, and it's fun to be able to make the most of it and be just a beast. It certainly wasn't a dull or bland part, which is why I think today, almost three decades later, I still get stopped by fans. I always think the person is going to mention *Murphy Brown*, and very often that's the case, but it's amazing how many times someone will bring up this episode. "I just saw it again last night—and wow, were you a prick!"

BLANCHE:

"We were always so much alike, and so close, just like Siamese twins."

SOPHIA:

"It's a shame when they separated you, you got both butts."

MY BROTHER, MY FATHER

Written by: MORT NATHAN & BARRY FANARO • *Directed by:* TERRY HUGHES
Original airdate: FEBRUARY 6, 1988

With Sophia's brother Angelo (Bill Dana), a priest in Sicily, about to visit the States, the old lady needs a big favor: for Dorothy and Stan (Herb Edelman) to pretend they're still a couple, living together—but without Blanche or Rose—under one roof. Dorothy accedes to Sophia's begging, realizing the ruse will last merely for an afternoon's visit. But when a brewing hurricane then forces closure of Miami's airport, trapping the group together for days, Dorothy doubts her ability to continue putting up with her "husband," Stan.

Worse yet, after Rose idiotically suggests that the two celebrate their "fortieth wedding anniversary" as her parents once had—by renewing their marriage vows—Stan warms to the idea, because reminiscing with Dorothy in her bedroom overnight has rekindled loving feelings. But just as he tries to convince her to let her uncle remarry them, it's Angelo who comes out with the bombshell revelation: he's not a priest, and never was. En route to the seminary in Palermo in 1914, he got turned on by the behind of barmaid Filomena, married her, and lived happily for seventy-two (!) years.

Meanwhile, Blanche, who is used to sleeping her way into lead roles, is upset when she and Rose land mere supporting parts, as nuns, in *The Sound of Music*—because the theater's new director is gay.

◆ ◆ ◆ ◆

COMMENTARY: Uncle Angelo mentions that in 1914 Sicily he promised their dear sainted mother on her deathbed that he would become a priest. Well, it turns out he's not the only liar in the family. Their dear sainted mother must have faked her own death, because as we see just eight episodes later, there she is in 1957 Brooklyn, elderly, crotchety—and played by Bea

Arthur, no less. It's just one more example of how, while the *Golden Girls* writers were great at creating comedy, they were not so great at continuity or building a convincing family tree.

Another example of *The Golden Girls* landing big guest stars is with Bill Dana, whose career had been intertwined with that of Tony Thomas and his family since the early 1960s.

After developing his popular comic character, Jose Jimenez, Bill brought Jose as an elevator operator to Danny Thomas's sitcom *Make Room for Daddy* and soon to his own spinoff *The Bill Dana Show*, where Jose became a bellhop in a New York hotel. After segueing into TV writing—penning the famous installment of *All in the Family*, "Sammy's Visit," in which Archie Bunker has a tête-à-tête with superstar Sammy Davis, Jr.—Bill would return to *The Golden Girls* four more times as Uncle Angelo in its later seasons, and in the episode "Valentine's Day," would play Sophia and Angelo's father, also named Angelo, as well.

what we'd later dub the Terry Hughes Curtain of Comedy. At the time, we thought it sort of bent the rules with the audience, who feel like they're at your taping so they can see everything. Now, though, it's done all the time.

Terry came over to the crowd and made a speech on the microphone. "You've been such a gracious audience. Now I want you to watch the monitors over your heads, because something very special is happening." We began the scene, with the three-shot of Bill and the two ladies, and the laugh started. We then cut around the room, to Dorothy, to Stan. Not a word had been spoken yet in the scene, but we got, I believe, a

LEX PASSARIS (associate director): Sometimes on a sitcom there's a reveal that's so good that you want to get the audience's initial reaction, so you have to find a way to hide the actors until the right moment. You often do that to cover the entrance of a surprise guest star. I remember we had done a "rolling black," a moving screen, to hide Burt Reynolds (in season two, "Ladies of the Evening").

At the top of act two, after the commercial break, there's the great visual of Uncle Angelo sitting in the middle of the couch, surrounded by Blanche and Rose, dressed as nuns. It's such a funny picture, and Terry knew we were going to get a huge laugh. So we dropped a curtain in front of the audience—

solid minute and a half of laughter. Obviously, some of that had to be cut. But it was because the situation had been set up so perfectly.

BILL DANA: From the first time I read this script, I read it in an Italian accent, because Angelo was visiting from Sicily. I was very familiar with the accent, because growing up in Quincy, Mass., I lived next door to the DiMatteo family, and all those guys *talka like dees*. I'm good with accents and languages; I would never get lost in France, or Germany, or Spain, or Italy. So with this character, his speech seemed really automatic to me. I don't remember ever having a discussion with the producers about why Sophia

ABOVE LEFT:
Betty and Rue maneuver their giant wimples backstage.
ABOVE LEFT: Sharing a laugh between scenes (*left to right*) Herb Edelman, Bill Dana, Bea Arthur, Betty White, and Rue McClanahan.

Photos by WAYNE WILLIAMS.

ANGELO:

"Is he still making you laugh like he used to?"

DOROTHY:

"Not really, but then again I haven't seen him naked lately."

spoke with a Brooklyn accent, and yet her brother *talka like dees*. It was never a consideration. We just did what we thought was funny.

Prior to my first appearance as Uncle Angelo, my wife and I had been living in Maui. But when we decided to spend more time on the mainland, I met with Tony and the gang, and ended up with a role on the show. I already knew Betty White somewhat, because we shared an agent and had worked on some animal causes together. And I had known Bea Arthur socially a little bit back in the fifties in New York, when I would watch her perform as a singer and comedienne at a nightclub called Le Ruban Bleu.

Among my original memories of coming to the *Golden Girls* set is Tony greeting me, and reminding me that I'm going to do a great job as Uncle Angelo, but that I should forget that I'm a writer. Normally, I describe myself as a writer/performer, with "writer" being the title that comes first. The words my comic character Jose Jimenez said were always about ninety percent mine. And on any other show I ever did, especially in comedy/variety shows, it was always kind of a free-for-all. Those shows' writers and producers were usually happy that way, for actors to contribute lines and bits.

But here, what Tony was telling me was that what's on the page is what goes to the stage. You were welcome to make suggestions along the way; once in a while, at a run-through, you could go to the director and say, "You know, it might be good if . . . " And he would take it to the writers. And obviously after the table read of each script, there would be changes. But there wasn't usually much of a need to change anything, because those *Golden Girls* scripts were some of the best written I'd ever seen, practically ready to go on camera from the moment we sat down to read them. There was a unique discipline to the way *The Golden Girls* seemed to be written—and although I've never worked in legit theater, I know it's the way things work on Broadway; as an actor, you can't change an "a" to an "an" or add a comma without the writer's permission. It doesn't usually work that way on TV, but it did here, and I think that was a testament to how those people knew what the hell they were doing.

I ended up doing six episodes of the show. I never knew Uncle Angelo would become a recurring character, but it's kind of a rule in TV that if something works, you keep going with it. The producers never made any kind of "multiple-show deal" with me or anything like that. My continued appearances were always just based on our friendship. I didn't know that my sixth episode would be my last, or that the show itself would be ending soon after that. I'm sure if I had known I would have had some emotional reaction, because *The Golden Girls* was a lovely place to work.

LARCENY AND OLD LACE

Story by: JEFFREY FERRO & FREDRIC WEISS ◆ *Teleplay by:* ROBERT BRUCE & MARTIN WEISS ◆ *Written by:* MORT NATHAN & BARRY FANARO
Directed by: TERRY HUGHES ◆ *Original airdate:* FEBRUARY 6, 1988

Dorothy arrives home early from the beauty parlor, only to interrupt Sophia's date with her new cigar-chomping, gambler boyfriend, Rocco (Mickey Rooney, 1920–2014). Dorothy resents the self-professed former Detroit mob boss's bad influence over her mother, and is even more mistrustful when the man asks to store some of his stuff in Sophia's bedroom—especially when one item turns out to be a satchel full of cash. Retracing the details of her day with her boyfriend, Sophia describes to the Girls what sounds like a bank robbery—and worse yet, one where she inadvertently drove the getaway car.

After Rocco readily admits to the heist, Sophia promises Dorothy she'll get him to turn himself in. But Rocco proffers other plans, to whisk Sophia away to Mexico in the middle of the night. When Sophia tells him she can't be in a relationship with a criminal, her paramour finally comes out with the truth: the closest he ever really got to hot water was as an assistant cook at the Chowder House in Bayonne, New

Jersey. And the forty-five grand in his bag represents his hard-earned life savings, with which he intended to treat Sophia like the queen he sees her to be.

Meanwhile, having secretly read Rose's diary, Blanche and Dorothy are showing little patience for their goody-two-shoes roommate, who writes of the "two pigs" with whom she lives; and Rose is upset at the invasion of her privacy. But in a late-night counseling session in Sophia's bedroom, the three reconcile, after Rose reveals that she didn't even know her roommates at the time she kept that journal—a 4-H diary about the summer she raised two actual pigs for the county fair.

◆ ◆ ◆ ◆

COMMENTARY: Guest star Mickey Rooney was a film and TV legend whose career spanned ten (!) decades. He started in vaudeville at the age of seventeen months; following his *Golden Girls* appearance, Mickey continued to appear frequently on TV and in films, all the way through two posthumous 2015 releases, including the second sequel to *Night at the Museum*.

As she ruminates about Rocco, Sophia is apparently not the only one who's confused in this episode. Take a good look at the board game the other three Girls are playing late at night in their kitchen. They're answering Trivial Pursuit–like questions, from red Monopoly Chance cards, as they navigate a board that's clearly from the game Sorry.

ROBERT BRUCE: Mickey Rooney was really good, but he was also uncontrollable. He liked to do a lot of vaudeville shtick. He liked to go for big jokes—like in the one scene where he climbs over the wall onto the lanai. What we didn't use was him grabbing his crotch.

TERRY HUGHES: Mickey didn't have the same approach to the work that the ladies had. I don't know if it was because he was having trouble remembering his lines or getting into the character as written, but he seemed to think the script was just a leaping-off point. He was a mighty force, and we had to work around him a bit.

PREVIOUS PAGE:
Dorothy and Blanche fume as they pore through Rose's diary. ABOVE:
Sophia and Rocco (Mickey Rooney) rendezvous on the lanai.

Photos by WAYNE WILLIAMS.

MOTHER'S DAY

Story by: KATHY SPEER & TERRY GROSSMAN
Teleplay by: MORT NATHAN & BARRY FANARO • *Directed by:* TERRY HUGHES
Original airdate: MAY 7, 1988

The Girls are all decked out to go to a Mother's Day brunch. But with each of them hesitating to leave the house before hearing from her kids, there's plenty of time to reminisce about holidays past. Dorothy tells of a visit with her disapproving mother-in-law Zbornak (Alice Ghostley, 1924–2007). Blanche recounts a trip to her mother's Virginia convalescent home, where she's relieved to realize that the often-forgetful eighty-nine-year-old (Helen Kleeb, 1907–2003) still remembers all her slutty teenage antics. Rose recalls a bus station stopover en route to frigid St. Olaf, where she provides an alibi for an elderly nursing home escapee (Geraldine Fitzgerald, 1913–2005). And Sophia conjures Brooklyn on Mother's Day 1957, when she, her husband, Sal (Sid Melton), and their young daughter Dorothy (Lyn Greene) convince her own mother to move in with them.

◆ ◆ ◆ ◆

COMMENTARY: A "wraparound" show featuring each Girl in a separate Mother's Day–themed vignette, this episode is noteworthy, first off, for the switch in which Bea Arthur plays Estelle Getty's mother. So in essence, Bea became her own grandmother—and as Lyn Greene remembers (next page), in the end, wasn't all that happy about it. This episode also reveals another bit of *Golden Girls* trivia. Blanche's mother may advise her here never to disclose her true age, but this vignette discloses the closely guarded number nonetheless, revealing that Blanche's near marriage to a sketchy older man happened on Christmas Day 1949, when she was seventeen.

But most interesting about "Mother's Day" is the episode's guest cast. Perhaps best known as *Designing Women*'s memory-challenged matron Bernice Clifton or as *Bewitched*'s bumbling Esmeralda, the late Alice Ghostley was a Tony winner and a TV icon. Here Alice plays Mrs. Zbornak, Dorothy's tough-as-nails mother-in-law who secretly shares her daughter-in-law's frustration with Stan, that perennial yutz.

Playing Blanche's mother, Elizabeth, is character actress Helen Kleeb, best known as Miss Mamie Baldwin on CBS's long-running drama *The Waltons*. And then there's the legendary stage and screen actress Geraldine Fitzgerald—who received an Outstanding Guest Actress Emmy nomination for her work in this episode—and who would return in season five, in episode 109, "Not Another Monday."

MORT NATHAN: We always liked the idea of Estelle playing Sophia younger, which always worked well, so we decided to experiment with the idea of Bea playing Estelle's mother. We asked Bea if she wanted to try it, and she was up for anything. We liked the idea, too, that there's a genetic pattern in the family, where some women are really tall like Bea, and some really small like Estelle. It made us laugh in the writers' room.

LYN GREENE: When I read the script for this episode, I didn't feel that the writing was as strong as it usually was for *The Golden Girls*. Then, on the set, I noticed that the writers seemed to be suffering from "producer laugh"—that's when writers and producers laugh loudly at their own material, particularly when it's not funny, as if they're trying to convince themselves it is. That always sounds really stupid to actors, and I kept expecting Bea to call them on it. But to my surprise, she didn't.

Bea was playing Sophia's mother this time, meaning she was the one who had to get into the old-age makeup. It took forever, it wasn't flattering to her, and I don't think she enjoyed it. But frankly, the biggest problem was that Estelle and Sid Melton kept going up on their lines, and I never knew when to make my entrance. Walking into the scene that night was like entering an aphasia ward. Not only did the two of them never get their lines right, but what they did say was different with every try, meaning I had no idea when to wheel Bea into the scene.

I was in awe: I was pushing Bea Arthur in a wheelchair! And of course I didn't want to do it wrong. The first chance I got, I guessed at my cue and wheeled her in, and nothing played well to the audience. I didn't really have anything to do with the lack of response, but I felt personally responsible. Doing that scene was like hitting an iceberg. If there were jokes, nobody would notice them, because oceans of silence

went by as you waited for the next person in the scene with something to say.

Then, the second time I wheeled Bea in, I accidentally pushed her into the door. As the takes went on, the scene got less and less funny—and yet more and more funny because of how badly things were going. At this point, Bea was not subtle about her displeasure. She said in her loud voice, and of course the audience could hear, "It's not going to get any better the next time!"

It was a mess, and not a pleasant evening. And it was certainly not the scene I wanted to do, at long last, with Bea Arthur! As I looked down at an unhappy Bea, my idol, in my wheelchair, I was convinced some of the stink of this evening was going to end up on me. And I remember thinking that this was a sad way for me to have said goodbye to the show.

I was convinced they were never going to be able to salvage that vignette for the episode, but actually, when I saw it on the air, it came together much better than I had thought possible. And over three years later, they did ask me back on the show for one last episode, "Dateline: Miami." In fact, so much time had passed that they called me and asked if I was still young enough to play Dorothy as a young woman. I was just glad that all was forgiven.

OPPOSITE:
Sal Petrillo (Sid Melton) at right, facing three generations of females: his mother-in-law (Bea Arthur), Sophia, and daughter Dorothy (Lyn Greene). ABOVE: Sophia and Sal's home in 1957 Brooklyn.

Photo by WAYNE WILLIAMS. *Photo courtesy of the* EDWARD S. STEPHENSON ARCHIVE *at the* ART DIRECTORS GUILD.

THE DAYS AND NIGHTS OF SOPHIA PETRILLO

Written by: KATHY SPEER & TERRY GROSSMAN ◆ *Directed by:* TERRY HUGHES

Original airdate: OCTOBER 22, 1988

While Dorothy, Blanche, and Rose have a lazy rainy day at home, Sophia sets out on her daily ritual: to take a round-trip on the bus to buy a nectarine. The three Girls snack, tell stories, and at one point fret over how poor Sophia no longer has anything constructive to do with her life. But little do they know, the old lady is actually out running circles around them. Sophia leads a senior citizens' band to raise funds for a clinic. She volunteers as a Sunshine Lady at the local hospital, where she cheers up old Mrs. Leonard (Ellen Albertini Dow, 1913–2015) and gives her daily nectarine to a terminally ill young patient, Sam (Don "Kokko" Burnaby). Sophia returns home to find the Girls still in their pajamas from the previous night. As the three lie about the hard work they've done during the day, they ask Sophia what she has been doing that has kept her out so late. "What I do every day," she replies. "I bought a nectarine."

◆ ◆ ◆ ◆

OPPOSITE:

Sophia's volunteer station at the hospital.

Photo courtesy of the EDWARD S. STEPHENSON ARCHIVE *at the* ART DIRECTORS GUILD.

COMMENTARY: For as brilliant as Estelle Getty was in portraying Sophia Petrillo, and as perfectly as she landed the character's many jokes, the actress was also often consumed with stage fright and plagued by problems remembering her lines. Sometimes, the show's writers say, they would try to use Sophia sparingly, so as not to burden Estelle. On other occasions, particularly later in the series after director Terry Hughes had departed, it became necessary to allow the actress to redo her scenes after the audience had been released, reading her lines from cue cards. Still other times, the show's editors would assemble some of Sophia's longer speeches in postproduction, from bits of several different takes.

Estelle "was the only actress who ever asked for fewer words," says Marc Cherry, who worked on the show in its final three seasons. "And if you would write something long that you loved for her, they would say, 'Oh, she'll break your heart.' Because come tape night, we would have to stay late and 'pick up' that speech after the audience went home. And it was excruciating for her."

Writer Richard Vaczy, too, remembers that although he and his fellow writers loved providing Sophia with her colorful stories, they eventually had no choice but to phase them out over time. "When we'd read the script on Monday, and there'd be a big Sicily story in there for Estelle, it would make us laugh," Richard remembers. "Because after the reading, Estelle would start setting up excuses, or rationalizing why it was going to be difficult for her to do [during the taping] on Friday."

"God bless her, Estelle had never really done anything like *The Golden Girls* before. That's why she had a great deal of trouble," explains Kathy Speer. Watching a feed from the stage on a writers' room monitor, "we used to throw pencils at the screen, because of all the material that we'd written for her, and then had to cut back." Estelle became famous for sneak-

ing her lines into spots on the set, scribbling on the kitchen tablecloth, inside the cabinets, and even on the salt-and-pepper shakers—and if someone were to move one of her special props, she was prone to panic. But overall, producers opted for patience with the relative newcomer, not only because Estelle was beloved, but also because, as Kathy notes, "it worked. Estelle was petrified on most Friday nights. But with those eyes, the way she looked at everybody like a deer in the headlights—it sounds crazy, but it worked perfectly for the character."

Hidden within this episode in a brief exchange is a landmark moment in network television. At this point in 1988, the AIDS epidemic had been growing steadily for seven years, and yet almost no one on a scripted network show had even mentioned the dreaded virus. *The*

Golden Girls wouldn't tackle the subject directly until a year later (see season five, "72 Hours"); but here, although not specifically by name, the show does allude to the disease and its deadly toll, as Sophia provides encouragement for the young hospital patient she has befriended while volunteering.

ELLEN ALBERTINI DOW: This episode was my first on *The Golden Girls*—and the experience nearly broke my heart. When the show had first started, friends would ask me, "Why didn't you audition for it?" And I answered them that at the time I was still a teacher. Now, just a few years later, here I was, on the show!

I was thrilled when I got the call to audition, and when I got the call that I'd gotten the part I was ecstatic and told everyone I knew. But then,

ABOVE:
Sophia comes home with her customary nectarine. OPPOSITE: The produce section where Sophia picked out nectarines—and Estelle picked out her lines.

Photo by NBCU PHOTO BANK
via GETTY IMAGES. *Photo courtesy of the*
EDWARD S. STEPHENSON ARCHIVE
at the ART DIRECTORS GUILD.

I got another call, that they'd changed the script and written out the character I was supposed to play, Mrs. Leonard. Well, I cried and cried and cried. That's why I remember this episode so well, this many years later. Because I vowed never again would I tell anybody I'd gotten a part until I'd actually filmed it. But then luckily, my agent called again, and guess what—they'd decided to put the part back in. It was a roller coaster I went through to get this part.

My husband, Gene Dow, who was a great actor and director, came to watch my rehearsals, and he gave me a little bit of direction. He said that on my way out, as I'm wheeling away the cart with the flowers, I should look at the flowers with excitement. Because even though Sophia is just using me to get out of delivering them, Mrs. Leonard is so lonely and is thrilled to think that someone has sent her all this. When the episode aired, I saw how Gene's idea really helped make the scene, and I was delighted.

NINA FEINBERG WASS (*producer*): Estelle was paralyzed with stage fright. What should have been the most joyful experience for her, being on *The Golden Girls*, she was often crippled by. She was a little cowed by the fact that the other ladies never went up—which is almost freakish—and were always so spot-on. She would have periods that were almost a remission from it, and feel sort of liberated. But still, it was a weird chemical thing—Estelle would be so afraid she'd say she felt like she was out of her body, and she didn't know what she was saying—but she'd still nail the joke.

As a sort of security blanket, Estelle would hide copies of her lines somewhere on the set. My first taping was of this episode—I had just joined the show as a production coordinator—

and we were doing one of the scenes in the supermarket. The producers and I weren't down on the floor with the actors, but upstairs in a booth, watching a feed. I remember saying to Mort Nathan, "Should Estelle really be staring at a banana? Is that odd?" And he said, "Oh my God, she's written her lines on the fruit." He sent me down to the stage to take the banana away.

And that's how I met Estelle for the first time: I went down and said, "Hello, Estelle. I'm Nina, and I need to move your banana." Well, Estelle took my arm and said, "You may *not* move my banana!" So I said, "Okay, I'll tell you what. You tell me where I can move the banana, and I'll move it an inch in that direction, and you can pick your head up a little bit when you're delivering the line." So we negotiated where to move it—a little bit more here, a little bit higher over there—and found a place more comfortable for her.

MICHAEL HYNES (*associate designer*): Everything in the vicinity of the kitchen table was graffitied by Estelle. Her writing was everywhere. We'd clean off what we could, but a lot of it we couldn't. And the thing I could never understand was, if she can remember where she scribbled them this week, why can't she just remember the lines? But she just couldn't.

YES, WE HAVE NO HAVANAS

Written by: BARRY FANARO & MORT NATHAN ◆ Directed by: TERRY HUGHES
Original airdate: OCTOBER 8, 1988

After five dates with Blanche, Fidel Santiago (Henry Darrow) finally meets the rest of the Girls. But soon, Blanche is concerned that her new beau may be seeing someone else. And that night, after dinner, Dorothy, Rose, and Blanche do indeed catch Fidel canoodling on the boardwalk with another woman: Sophia.

Fidel avows his attraction to both women, and leaves it to them to decide how to proceed. And although Blanche swears she'll never share a man, soon she and Sophia are doing just that. But the custody arrangement does not go down smoothly, and eventually breaks down all together when the Latin lover double-books the Girls for a date to see Ruth Buzzi at the Burt Reynolds Dinner Theatre. But before either of them can call him to straighten things out, the phone rings with news. Cut to Fidel's wake, populated entirely by middle-aged women in black. There, Sophia interrupts the priest to deliver her own form of eulogy, wherein she faults Fidel for his philandering, and yet thanks him for reawakening her appreciation for physical affection.

Meanwhile, when Dorothy begins teaching an adult education night class, she's quite surprised at the sight of one of her students: Rose. It turns out, having contracted mononucleosis during a stint at the kissing booth at St. Olaf's Founders' Day fair, teenage Rose slept day and night for the next six months, right through her class's graduation. Now, Rose is excelling in all subjects except history, a failing she blames on her high school teacher Mr. Fritz Shtickelmayer, who was part of a Nazi plot to misinform America's youth. After Rose indeed flunks her history exam, Dorothy breaks the news that she won't be able to get her diploma. That is, until Rose cracks open the textbook, and points out both old Mr. Shtickelmayer, a.k.a. Adolf Hitler, and Eva Braun, the St. Olaf PE teacher who it was rumored was once his main squeeze.

◆ ◆ ◆ ◆

COMMENTARY: When *The Golden Girls'* producers first conceived the role of Fidel Santiago, their first choice to play him was Cesar Romero. At the time eighty-one years old, Romero had built a career out of playing the romantic Latin lover, and his casting would be considered a coup. When Romero turned out to be unavailable (although he would later turn up in season six, as Sophia's boyfriend Tony in "Girls Just Wanna Have Fun… Before They Die"), producers turned to much younger actor Henry Darrow, outfitting the then fifty-five-year-old with a white wig. And as the show's director, Terry Hughes, explains below, Henry—at that point best known as heroic Manolito Montoya from his four seasons on NBC's Western *The High Chaparral*—turned out to be just the right man to fit into Fidel's white linen suit.

MORT NATHAN: My writing partner, Barry, and I were talking about funny permutations we could come up with within romantic storylines for the Girls. And we came upon the idea: what if the eighty-year-old woman and the fifty-year-old woman were after the same guy? Cary Grant was still alive, and there were then, as there are today, older, dashing men like him who were with younger women. So we thought our storyline, with an older man being interested in both a younger woman and a woman his own age, was the perfect combination of preposterous and believable at the same time.

It was Barry who liked the idea of it being a Latin lover at the center of the love triangle. Barry and I were members of the Grand Havana Room, a cigar club in Beverly Hills. At the time, we were both very into Cuban cigars. So we made the guy Cuban just because it was in our heads at the time.

TERRY HUGHES: When I was living in England, we got our first color television in about 1965, and at that time *High*

PREVIOUS PAGE:
Blanche finds out her Latin lover, Fidel (Henry Darrow), has been two-timing her with Sophia.
ABOVE: Fidel's funeral chapel.

Photo by ALICE S. HALL/NBCU PHOTO BANK *via* GETTY IMAGES. *Photo courtesy of the* EDWARD S. STEPHENSON ARCHIVE *at the* ART DIRECTORS GUILD.

Chaparral was airing. Henry Darrow was one of the leads, and I remember he was really good. When his name came up during our *Golden Girls* casting meeting, everyone remembered him. And I realized he had the exact kind of urbane air and suave Latin charm that we wanted.

RICK COPP (writer): I remember Estelle having real trouble with the lines in this episode. Because often when that happened, or a scene wasn't playing as well as they wanted, the producers would send me down into the audience to laugh, because my laugh is somewhat loud and obnoxious.

HENRY DARROW: My experience on *The Golden Girls* was really enjoyable. I had fun doing my scenes with Rue and with Estelle, and the episode has such a funny moment with Dorothy at the end, as she announces at Fidel's funeral that she's the only woman there who hadn't slept with him. And one of the other women says, "I guess even he had his standards." Poor Dorothy always got slammed.

On my first day on the set, I met all the ladies. Rue and I knew people in common from the Pasadena Playhouse (where one of my classmates was the fabulous Ruth Buzzi, who's mentioned in an in-joke in this episode). Betty was blonde and had an uplifting personality, and in that way reminded me of my mother. Bea Arthur had just had a facial peel a few days before, and as she was recovering her face was still reddish, and I noticed her keeping more to herself.

With Estelle Getty, I was amazed how she could be so cranky in scenes as Sophia, but then would be so warm with me between takes. But as I first met her, the first thing she did was blurt out, "By the way, did you know they tried to get Cesar Romero for your part?" I wasn't offended, because it's the nature of this business that often you're second or third choice. But Bea Arthur overheard, and came over to apologize for the remark.

On that first morning, Bea actually hadn't really acknowledged me, even when, at the craft services table as we were getting coffee, I said, "Good morning." Her apology about Estelle's comment was the only thing she said to me that day. On the second day again, I said "Good morning," and still, nothing. Then, later that second day, Bea was watching a rehearsal of a scene with Estelle, Rue, and me. At one point, I ad-libbed something, and it broke Bea up with laughter. So then, on the third day, when I came in in the morning, Bea was the one who came over to me. She said, "Good morning. Would you like some coffee or something?" We hit it off after that. And of course Bea, like all the other ladies, was really wonderful and professional to work with.

BLANCHE:

"Now, if you'll excuse me, I'm going to go take a long, hot steamy bath, with just enough water to barely cover my perky bosoms."

SOPHIA:

"You're only gonna sit in an inch of water?"

SOPHIA'S WEDDING

(PARTS 1 & 2)

Written by: BARRY FANARO & MORT NATHAN ◆ *Directed by:* TERRY HUGHES
Original airdate: NOVEMBER 19 & 26, 1988

When Sophia's lifelong friend Esther Weinstock (Fritzi Burr, 1924–2003) passes away, Sophia refuses to attend the funeral out of resentment for Esther's husband, Max (Jack Gilford, 1908–90). As the story goes, Max ruined the pizza-and-knish business he and Sophia's late husband, Salvadore, had founded by gambling away a week's receipts. But after Dorothy nudges Sophia into going to the funeral, they learn that it was Sal who was the gambler, and Max who bravely covered for him to save Sophia's marriage. Sophia sees Max in a new light—and later, even gets caught in bed with him. The two decide to marry.

Meanwhile, Rose's application to start an unauthorized chapter of the Elvis Presley Hunka-Hunka-Burnin'-Love Fan Club has been approved. But as membership begins to sag, Blanche realizes that what the club really needs is an Elvis impersonator.

When Dorothy refuses to give her blessing to Sophia and Max's union, Sophia locks herself in the bathroom on her wedding day. It is only Dorothy's subsequent change of heart, after realizing that she is selfishly guarding the memory of her late father, that convinces her mother to proceed. But there's just one problem: Rose has confused her mailing lists, and now all of Sophia and Max's wedding guests are Elvis impersonators.

In part two, Dorothy has secretly resumed smoking, while Sophia and Max realize they have no place to live together. The newlyweds move back into Sophia's old

OPPOSITE:
Newlyweds Sophia and Max
Weinstock (Jack Gilford) come
home to Richmond Street.

Photo by CHRIS HASTON/NBCU PHOTO
BANK *via* GETTY IMAGES.

room, but after three weeks with a man in the house, the living arrangements are getting too close for comfort. After a day of apartment hunting, Sophia and Max stop by the boardwalk, where they're inspired to sink their savings into renting a concession stand where they can re-create their old pizza-and-knish business. But right after their grand opening, Sophia and Max catch cold, and are unable to man the stand for the weekend's big beach festival. And so, guilted into filling in, the Girls spend a long afternoon making pizzas and luring in customers.

That night, as everyone sits at home celebrating the day's boost in sales, Dorothy answers a disturbing phone call, informing her that the stand has burned to the ground. As they stand in front of the smoldering remains, Dorothy confesses to having sneaked a cigarette, which she must not have properly extinguished. But just as she pleads for Sophia's forgiveness, a fireman stops by to explain the true cause: a faulty coil in the pizza oven.

Blanche happily proclaims that with their insurance payout Sophia and Max can rebuild, but neither member of the couple is excited to do so. It turns out neither had enjoyed re-creating the past venture in the absence of their departed former spouses. So they sit down for a heart-to-heart, in which each admits that their love, although real, will never measure up to their feelings from their former marriages. They decide to separate—Catholic Sophia doesn't want to divorce—with Max returning to Brooklyn, and Sophia staying in Miami with the women she has come to consider family.

◆ ◆ ◆ ◆

COMMENTARY: This episode introduces Raye Birk's gay caterer character, who proved popular enough to be brought back two seasons later as Dorothy nearly remarries Stan in "There Goes the Bride," and then once again on *Golden Palace*. The actor may otherwise be most recognizable to fans of *Star Trek: The Next Generation* as Wrenn.

These two particular half hours are also remembered for the scene where Dorothy comes across the disturbing visual of her mother and Max postcoitally in bed together—and for Sophia's response about what's going on in her bedroom: "Afterglow."

And notably only in retrospect, "Sophia's Wedding: Part 1" features an early and rare act-ing appearance by one of today's hippest writer/directors. No, you're not seeing things. Yes, that *is* Quentin Tarantino as an Elvis impersonator—back row, center—just before the takeoff of his big-screen career.

JAMIE WOOTEN (writer): One of my top three favorite jokes in all of *The Golden Girls* was in "Sophia's Wedding"—when Dorothy attempts to regain her composure after finding Sophia and Max in bed together. She says to him, "When did you get in?" And then there's a beat before he says, "Oh, into Miami!"

MORT NATHAN: In the eighties, wedding episodes were very popular. The network always wanted weddings, and we loved the simultaneous absurdity and reality of an eighty-two-year-old woman in a white wedding gown. We liked getting to explore the emotional area of a daughter having to give a blessing to her mother, for a man replacing her father. As far as Quentin Tarantino goes, I read an article about him when he first became a phenomenon as the director of *Pulp Fiction*. He was talking about how he got started in the business and broke in as an actor, and he said that one of the early things he did was *The Golden Girls*. So I went back and took out some stills of this episode, and there he was. I had no idea he was one of the Elvises.

LEX PASSARIS (*associate director*): Typically, we'd have extras, like all the guys who played the Elvises, on the stage only on Friday, which was our tape day. But because of the complexity of this two-part episode, and the "Blue Hawaii" number at the end, we decided to have them in on Thursday as well. I had no idea who Quentin Tarantino was back then, but the funny thing is I remember him because he never broke character from being Elvis on set for the whole two days.

QUENTIN TARANTINO: This was the first acting gig I ever got paid for—and I didn't even have to audition for it. All these Elvis impersonators, and actors who could play Elvis, just sent in their head shots.

I was nobody at this time, and this was a huge gig for me—because the whole Elvis bit ended up on one of the best-of *Golden Girls* episodes, and the show continued to play all the time. So I ended up making a lot of money over the course of about five years, from being in constant rotation.

My *Golden Girls* gig has become a thing to talk about on talk shows—and actually, I would be embarrassed by it more often if the rights to the clips weren't so expensive. All these talk shows always want to show the scene, but it's too costly for them. So whenever they do show it on something, I have respect. I think, "Ooh, you actually spent some money to dig this out!"

BARRY FANARO: I remember the bit about the mix-up between the Elvis fan club membership and the wedding guests tickling Bea to no end. I can hear her laugh in my ear to this day, from the first time we read it at the table read. That was pure Bea, just enjoying the hell out of something. As a writer, I lived for that. Bea wasn't an easy laugh, and we writers worked hard to please the ladies, because we respected them so much. We knew that working with them, we were going to comedy college.

RAYE BIRK: When I first heard about the role of the caterer from my agents, they passed along the breakdown they had received, which said something like "forty-two-year-old caterer, gay, in four scenes." I didn't have any problem with that, because I'd played lots of gay characters in the theater. I got the sides, and I liked the character and thought he was funny, because he had another dimension to him. I thought he was sweet and sentimental, and that made me feel better that his hallmark wasn't just that he was gay. They were trying to do something with the character.

Certainly there were laugh lines about the fact that he's gay. In one scene, Blanche turns to me and has a line: "You're ready to fly right outta here, aren't you?" It had been in the script from the beginning, and was very successful all throughout the process. The writers loved it, and it ended up paying off big with the audience—a huge laugh.

The show went through a lot of changes and rewrites in the course of five days, and at one point we lost some of the elements of the character that I really liked. He originally had a lot of lines where he talked about 1940s movie stars, and I thought those had been terrific because they showed an emotional side to the character. I was upset, and went to the producers and writers and said, "I don't think I want to do this role, because you're reducing it to something that's just a stereotype. I have gay friends, and I'd feel bad doing this clichéd version of a character. No judgment about you guys, but maybe you need to have another actor to do this." And to their credit, they had a conference and restored most of the dialogue.

ABOVE:

Max and Esther Weinstock's home in Brooklyn.

Photo courtesy of the EDWARD S. STEPHENSON ARCHIVE *at the* ART DIRECTORS GUILD.

SCARED STRAIGHT

Written by: CHRISTOPHER LLOYD • Directed by: TERRY HUGHES
Original airdate: DECEMBER 10, 1988

When Blanche's baby brother, Clayton Hollingsworth (Monte Markham), arrives for a visit, the Girls find themselves face-to-face with a male version of the Southern belle: charming, good-looking, and on the prowl—for men. Yes, Clayton is gay—a fact he confesses to Rose after he ditches the woman with whom his sister had set him up on an uncomfortable blind date. Rose encourages Clayton to come out to his sister, and he initially agrees. But when he comes home to a querulous Blanche, he instead blurts out that he and Rose slept together. Blanche hates the thought of her brother dating Rose, and harasses Rose until Clayton finally is forced to reveal the truth. Blanche initially refuses to believe it, but eventually comes around to accepting that she and her brother may just have the same excellent taste in men.

◆ ◆ ◆ ◆

COMMENTARY: There was briefly a gay houseboy, there was a lesbian college friend, and there was a gay caterer. But this episode marks the first time someone in one of the Girls' families has turned out to be Family. Storywise, the episode is very similar to a landmark 1972 episode of *The Mary Tyler Moore Show*. In "My Brother's Keeper," directed by Jay Sandrich, the gay brother of nosy landlady Phyllis Lindstrom (Cloris Leachman) pretends to date Rhoda (Valerie Harper) rather than coming out to his sister. That episode ends differently: in a clever twist, Phyllis is not devastated to hear that her brother is gay, because that is at least preferable to him dating "that awful Rhoda."

It makes sense that the two shows would do similar episodes because after all, playing gay and coming out for laughs is a time-honored tradition. "Scared Straight" writer Christopher Lloyd, whose father, David, wrote for *Mary Tyler Moore*, remembers hearing how the late Robert Moore, the actor playing Phyllis's brother Ben Sutherland, had been worried on the night of that episode's filming that the audience was not going to respond to his gay character. "And his lover said something to him along the lines of, 'Honey, you've got nothing to worry about. They've been laughing at fags since Aristophanes. You're gonna kill 'em.' He went out there and of course the audience ate it up."

CHRISTOPHER LLOYD: We frequently rolled in relatives to upset the stasis of the household and be a jumping-off point for stories. A gay relative seemed like a natural idea for the show, and perfect for Blanche. Dorothy is from Brooklyn, so it would have shocked her less, but Blanche is not only the most sexual of the characters, but you could say she is the most fiercely heterosexual. Plus, she's from the South and

"The man's as gay as a picnic basket!"

—SOPHIA

rather traditional. And of course, we could play on the idea of Blanche and her brother both liking guys, which we knew would be a fun avenue to go down. We got to have our cake and eat it too in this show: we could do our gay jokes, and then have a nice, tidy, lovely ending where Blanche embraces her brother and everyone is happy. These are women who grew up in an era when they were a little bit discriminated against, when women were second-class citizens. And now they are being re-discriminated against because they're women in their sixties, who are a little bit outcast in society. So they can speak a message of tolerance, from a place where they know what they are talking about.

RICK COPP: During the time I was a writer on *The Golden Girls*, I didn't really talk about being gay, but people knew. I remember being very happy during the week of this episode with Blanche's brother. Clayton was a good portrayal of a gay character—and there were so few on TV at that point anyway that I would have thought that anything remotely positive was a win.

RUE McCLANAHAN: I semi-enjoyed doing this episode. What I mean is, it wasn't my favorite, because it was very hard to play. I'm not homophobic and Blanche was, somewhat—certainly when it came to her brother. I'm just glad she came around.

MONTE MARKHAM: When I got the script for "Scared Straight," I thought it was well written and funny as hell. I'd known Betty White and Paul Witt since the late sixties, so doing the show would be like old home week. And I never thought twice about playing gay or being typecast. If I were to do that, then I'd be in the wrong business.

We went through several rewrites, and I actually thought the first draft had had funnier lines. Sometimes they fix these things to death. In the first draft, when Rose finally figures out that Clayton is gay, she had a line, "Are you . . . light in the loafers?" She was obviously quoting things she'd heard that she took too literally and didn't really understand. And I remember that during a break after the first act, someone in the audience asked the warm-up comic, "Is Monte Markham gay?" The warm-up answered no, and the same guy said, "But he's playing a gay character!" And I remember the warm-up guy answering back, "If he were playing a murderer, would you think he is one?"

I've answered every piece of fan mail I've ever gotten about *The Golden Girls*. People really respond to the dignity of Clayton's character, and I'd like to say the role was groundbreaking. The word actually reminds me of the only time I ever went to a political fund-raiser, and Billy Crystal was on the dais, back when he was on *Soap*. Someone introduced him as playing a "groundbreaking gay character." (I remember he looked over at me and gave his funny smile, shrugged modestly, and said, "It's a living.") I'd like to think of Clayton as historic like that.

OPPOSITE:
Clayton (Monte Markham) unloads his secret on naïve Rose.

Photo by NBCU PHOTO BANK *via* GETTY IMAGES.

LOVE ME TENDER

Written by: RICHARD VACZY & TRACY GAMBLE • *Directed by:* TERRY HUGHES
Original airdate: FEBRUARY 6, 1989

As Dorothy awaits the arrival of her blind date, she finds out some disturbing news: it's not with Sophia's friend's attractive doctor nephew, but instead a matchup from a computer dating service Sophia saw advertised on the bus. And although tiny, unassuming Eddie (John Fiedler, 1925–2005) initially appears to be a physical mismatch for tall Dorothy, she soon appears to have fallen completely under his spell.

A week later, Dorothy reveals to Rose the secret behind this new relationship: Eddie is the greatest lover she's ever had. Disapproving, Sophia notes that while casual sex may be fine for some people, she knows her *pussycat* will eventually yearn for something more. And so Dorothy agrees to break up with Eddie, but finds it's tough to quit him—as it turns out to be as well for Blanche, Rose, and even Sophia, as all four women fall prey to the irresistible charm that Eddie explains has always been his curse.

Meanwhile, Rose conscripts Blanche to help out with the "Be a Pal" program, which matches mother figures with wayward young girls. At first Rose is happy to befriend Marla (Shana S. Washington), while Blanche warms to Jackie (Stefanie Ridel), who not only knows enough to flatter her beauty, but shares her appreciation of a shirtless Mel Gibson. But the Pal program takes an ugly turn when the little darlings make the Girls the fall guys for their shoplifting, attempting to extort a bribe from Blanche before they'll agree to tell a judge the truth.

◆ ◆ ◆ ◆

COMMENTARY: Like several other *Golden Girls* episodes, this one features a B story that bears a strong resemblance to a plot from *The Mary Tyler Moore Show*—and in this case, it's even one that had starred Betty White. In the 1975 *MTM* episode "Mary's Delinquent," Mary Richards and Betty's Sue Ann Nivens also take charge of a pair of troubled teens, with Sue Ann getting so carried away that she shows up at the WJM newsroom sporting a matching blonde version of her "little sister" Celestine's afro.

Guest star John Fiedler was best known for his recurring role on the original CBS *Bob Newhart Show* and for voicing the character of

Piglet in the *Winnie the Pooh* movie and TV series. But for those who worked on *The Golden Girls*, this episode is actually most notable for its behind-the-scenes story, and for a few jokes that the audience never got to see.

RICHARD VACZY: For a long time, *The Golden Girls* had been making fun of how Bea looked: they compared her often to a man, and to various beasts. So by the time Tracy [Gamble] and I joined the show in season four, we thought for our first *Golden Girls* script, "Wouldn't it be nice to do a show where Dorothy is truly attracted to—and attractive to—a man, and has her first purely sexual relationship?" It wouldn't be about dating, but the guy would find her incredibly beautiful and attractive. And when we wrote it, we thought the script came out well.

The problem with it first arose with casting, which I wasn't involved with at this point on the show. Instead of bringing in a good-looking George Hamilton type, the casting people chose a little bald guy. When Bea saw him at the table reading that first morning, she was immediately upset. But then it got worse, as we got into the script. The executive producers had rewritten some lines. One of the new jokes said that Dorothy looked like Buddy Ebsen. When we got to that page, Bea broke down crying, right there at the table read, saying, "You've been calling me a man for seventy episodes now!"

By two o'clock that afternoon, she had threatened to quit the show. And I was pretty much packing up my office and preparing to be fired. The irony was, it hadn't been our fault. It wasn't our line! It was our first script, and we had been trying to do something nice for her. Eventually, the next season, Tracy and I wound up writing another episode for Bea, "Love Under the Big Top," where we did bring in a good-looking guy, Dick Van Dyke. And that episode did make her happy.

TERRY GROSSMAN: Bea was having a big problem with this episode. But I reminded her we can't tear the show apart on Thursday and try to have something completely new to shoot the next day, and we can't shut down production. I told her, "This will work. Will it be one of the episodes you're proudest of? I don't think so, but the audience will love it."

That next night, when we shot it, the audience response was fabulous. The show got great laughs. Immediately afterward, Bea came up to me, and acknowledged it had worked. Then she said, "But it still stinks."

DOROTHY:

"Ma, I cannot believe you sent my picture in to a total stranger?"

SOPHIA:

"I didn't send in your picture. I sent in the picture that came with my wallet."

BLIND DATE

Written by: CHRISTOPHER LLOYD ◆ *Directed by:* TERRY HUGHES
Original airdate: JANUARY 28, 1989

Ditched once again by her unseen boyfriend Tom Gallagher, Blanche is delighted nonetheless to meet a handsome man on the next bar stool. In fact, John Quinn (Edward Winter, 1937–2001) has been stood up, too. Blanche slips John a napkin bearing her phone number and leaves, satisfied with her flirting—but failing to notice John navigating his way out of the bar with the help of a long white cane.

A week later, after dating John every night, Blanche cancels on him in favor of scoundrel Tom. Blanche admits her insecurity about dating a man with whom she can't rely on her looks, first to her puzzled roommates and later that night to John. But when John then describes the vision he has of her in his mind, the portrait he paints is so flattering that Blanche can't help but want him back. They make a plan to connect again the next week—just as Blanche's young, blonde replacement takes a seat at John's table.

Meanwhile, ultracompetitive Rose coaches a football team of eight-year-olds and enlists Dorothy as her second in command. But the schoolteacher turns out to be a stickler for the rules, and the Girls quarrel over qualifying their star player Billy (Kristopher Kent Hill) for the big game. In the end, it's Sophia who leads the team to victory when Dorothy and Rose catch the flu.

◆ ◆ ◆ ◆

BLANCHE:

"Girls, quick, I need some advice."

SOPHIA:

"Wear half as much makeup and twice as much underwear."

COMMENTARY: With this episode, *The Golden Girls* takes the opportunity to create a positive portrayal of disability with the character of John Quinn, a blind man with dignity and a sense of humor. The show's writers were obviously taken with Blanche and her newfound sensitivity—because two seasons later, they would test it again, as Blanche dates a man who uses a wheelchair in the very similar episode "Stand by Your Man."

TERRY HUGHES: Ed Winter was a lovely guy, with whom I worked many times. It was a very tricky thing he had to do, to play blind and yet not give it away in the first scene with Blanche. Ed did a lot of research, and talked to many people for this role. He was very good, and came very prepared.

CHRISTOPHER LLOYD: I had come up with this story because I was looking for ways to turn Blanche's character on her head a little bit. What would it be like for a woman who bases her power on her sexuality to date a guy to whom looks mean nothing? And then, how do you break up a relationship or even a friendship with someone who has a disability or is a minority, without it seeming like that is the reason for your doing it?

For the B plot, we'd always liked finding ways to show Rose getting really competitive. It's such a contrast to the other more innocent parts of her character. Admittedly it's strange that these older women would be coaching a kids' team. We could have shown her getting competitive by playing tennis with Dorothy, but it wouldn't have been as funny as showing Betty surrounded by little kids who come up to her waist, and yet berating them like she's Vince Lombardi.

THE IMPOTENCE OF BEING ERNEST

Story by: KEVIN ABBOTT • *Teleplay by:* RICK COPP & DAVID A. GOODMAN
Directed by: STEVE ZUCKERMAN • *Original airdate:* FEBRUARY 4, 1989

Rose's new man, Ernie Faber (Richard Herd), is a nice guy, and as a corporate lawyer, a good catch to boot. But soon, Rose becomes depressed about her new relationship, perplexed as to why he hasn't made a single move to get her into the sack. When Ernie whisks her off to a resort for a romantic weekend, he admits his problem: erectile dysfunction. And so, on Blanche's advice, Rose practices patience. But ironically, just as she professes to Ernie that sex isn't all-important, their dinner conversation inadvertently turns dirty, and an "excited" Ernie calls for the check. Unfortunately, once cured, Ernie renews his hopes of reconciling with his ex-wife. Rose is hurt, but relieved; when finally potent, Ernie was the worst lover she ever had.

Meanwhile, after Sophia receives an envelope from her cousin Vito in Sicily, containing only a single black feather, she reveals to Dorothy the details of the Venuccio vendetta from generations past. With the feather signifying that Sonny, the last Venuccio, is somewhere in Miami, Sophia vows that it's up to her to carry out vengeance on behalf of her family. Later, Dorothy reads in the newspaper that the body of a man has washed up on the beach, with a tan bamboo purse found at the scene. And Sophia even admits she probably left her now-missing purse right next to Sonny's body—right after she finished making love to him one afternoon. Because it turns out, the evil eye and kiss of death she gave Sonny on his doorstep ended up being quite the effective turn-ons for such a Sicilian.

❖ ❖ ❖ ❖

COMMENTARY: Although *The Golden Girls* usually seems so contemporary, it's important to remember that the show existed in the days before cell phones—hence that all-important yellow wall model in the kitchen—and before the Internet. (Which is just as well; Dorothy was happy to have an actual, printed newspaper with which to hit Rose over the head once in a while.) This episode predated yet another invention that would revolutionize the lives of a certain generation: Viagra. In 1989, there was no little blue pill to fix what was ailing Ernie. Instead, he was lucky to experience the magical, libido-restoring powers of a buxom blonde from St. Olaf.

KEVIN ABBOTT: As a freelance writer, I met with Paul Witt and Tony Thomas to pitch *Golden Girls* episodes, and of my two stories, they chose this one for me to write. But I got only as far as writing and submitting an outline when, the very next day, the writers' strike of 1988 began. During those five months, I was not permitted to write any scripts, including this one I'd sold. And the day after the strike ended, I accepted a job offer from *Growing Pains*—as it turns out, just hours before an offer also came in to join *The Golden Girls*, but by then it was too late. Soon afterward, I got a call that the producers wanted to go ahead and have someone write the episode based on my outline. Rick Copp and David Goodman kept the vendetta B story mostly unchanged, and altered the main impotence story a fair amount. They took it and ran with it, and did a great job.

DAVID A. GOODMAN: I was really glad that even though Rick and I didn't come up with these two stories, we got to develop them in our own way. "The Impotence of Being Ernest" was my title—and it's the last time I came up with a good title, in my whole career. Many of the individual jokes that went to the table read on Monday were from our original script, which is pretty rare. There had been one scene, though, that we hadn't quite cracked, and that was the scene with Rose and Ernie in the restaurant, where as they talk he gets sexually excited. Chris Lloyd rewrote that scene, and did a great job making it really funny. But other than that, the episode was ours.

RICK COPP: David and I named the character Ernie

just so we could use the title. Sitcom scripts are always punched up by the show's writing staff, but in this case so much of our original script stayed intact. I was really proud of one of my lines where, as Blanche is about to suggest a cure for impotence, Dorothy tells her, "Blanche, dessert toppings are not the answer!" But the best joke in this episode came from Tracy Gamble. I'll never forget it. Dorothy is talking about how when Stan went through the same problem, they tried eating aphrodisiacs. "I fed that man so many oysters, when he passed a kidney stone, I had it appraised."

RICHARD HERD: Impotence was something they didn't really talk about much on TV, but everybody, especially people my age, knew what it was. And for anyone who saw Tyrone Power in *The Sun Also Rises*, it was nothing new. I didn't give the subject matter much thought, because I was more focused on how impressive the script was. First of all, I particularly loved the title! And it was such strong writing, with the bittersweet ending where you think Ernie's going to propose to Rose, but instead he tells her he's going back to his wife. That got lots of "awwws" from the audience, because although the relationship had just been created within that one episode, they still felt so bad for Rose.

TWO RODE TOGETHER

Written by: MARTIN WEISS & ROBERT BRUCE
Directed by: TERRY HUGHES • *Original airdate:* FEBRUARY 18, 1989

After the funeral for Sophia's friend Edith Flannery, Dorothy becomes acutely aware of how little together time she and her mother may have left. So she decides to take Sophia away for a weekend of quality time. But once at Disney World, the two women turn out to have differing definitions of fun; while Sophia wants nothing more than to try out the park's roller coaster, Space Mountain, Dorothy would rather reminisce than ride. Finally, Sophia has had enough of sifting through family snapshots, and attempts an escape, only to be foiled by a sudden thunderstorm.

Twenty-four hours later, Sophia does flee to the hotel bar. When Dorothy finds her there, Sophia explains that quality time can't be forced, but has to come naturally in life's little moments. And so, as the rain lets up on the day of their departure, Dorothy has just enough time for one last surprise: some spontaneous fun with Sophia as they scream together on Space Mountain.

Meanwhile, inspired by the fable of Toonder the Magnificent Tiger that Rose picked up in St. Olaf, Blanche whips up some illustrations of the feline magician, and proposes that the two of them team up to turn the tale into a children's storybook. The collaboration starts out strong—until wordsmith Rose has the nerve to criticize Blanche's artwork. In the end, their artistic differences are moot. Rose learns that the tale of Toonder was not created by her parents, as she'd thought, but indeed has already been published by St. Olaf's most famous fabulist, Hans Christian Lockerhoeven.

◆ ◆ ◆ ◆

COMMENTARY: In this episode, Dorothy worries about Sophia's mortality—and as well she should. After all, how old is the woman, really? Here, she says Sophia is eighty-two. But considering that some of Sophia's Sicily stories take place just after the turn of the twentieth century, perhaps she has shaved a few years off her age.

Or maybe it's just the writing. After all, there's a similar inconsistency to the age of Dorothy herself. In this episode, she unearths her baby photo from 1932. In season three's "Nothing to Fear, But Fear Itself" we learn that Dorothy was conceived in 1931, and in season seven's "Hey, Look Me Over," she has already turned sixty by the fall of 1991. This would all make sense, pointing to a fall 1931 birth. But a few episodes from now, in "Till Death Do We Volley," we'll learn she was in the high school class of 1946—meaning that barring the skipping of any grades Dorothy was born in 1928. (To confuse things further, Bea Arthur herself was born far earlier, in 1922.)

Furthermore, none of Dorothy's estimated birth dates really matches the ages of her children, Kate and Michael. Throughout the series, we hear about how Dorothy and Stan conceived their first child while on a high school date, and in the fifth-season episode "An Illegitimate Concern," we learn that a pregnant Dorothy married Stan on June 1, 1949. But when her elder child, Kate, shows up in Miami in 1985, in the series' fourth episode, "Guess Who's Coming to the Wedding?," she seems younger than her mid-thirties.

As the show's producer Paul Witt admits, issues like this arose because, unlike on some series, like his own previous *Soap*, "on *The Golden Girls* we didn't have a formal 'show bible.'" Without access to such a holy reference document, which would contain the official biographies and histories of a show's characters, the writers were allowed leeway to make up backstories as needed—often conflicting with what had been earlier established. "Some of our characters were planned, and some were accidents of creative convenience," Paul explains. For example, he notes, "Did we know exactly how many children each character had? I'm not sure we ever did." Only in the show's latter seasons did its writers become more conscientious about such fine details—particularly with the hiring of Marc Cherry and Jamie Wooten: "We became the guys holding the bible, because we had already been fans and had seen everything," Marc explains. "So I was correcting backstory: No, that's not what Rose's uncle in St. Olaf is named!"

This episode's B plot was at least partly inspired by Rue McClanahan's real-life artistic talents. As producers undoubtedly noticed, and as Rue's longtime friend Michael J. LaRue explains, during the weekly table reads of each episode, the actress used to doodle her artwork all over the covers of her scripts.

BEA ARTHUR: This is an episode I fondly remember. Sophia sitting in the bar asking the piano player she calls Sam to play her favorite song—and then he plays "It's a Small World." That barrage of photos and memories Dorothy had planned for Sophia—it was so ludicrous! Had I been Sophia, I would have been out of there five minutes later!

BARRY FANARO: I got the idea for this episode from something my wife's grandmother said to me. She told me before she died she wanted to go to Disneyland and get on Space Mountain. She was about ninety years old at the time—and they did take her.

ROBERT BRUCE: My one disappointment about this episode is the moment at the very end. [My writing partner] Marty [Weiss] and I had wanted a real shot of Bea and Estelle getting into one of the cars on Space Mountain, figuring because the show was produced by Touchstone, which is part of Disney, why can't we take them to Disneyland? But for some reason we didn't. We showed the lights of the ride, with Bea and Estelle's lines in voice-over.

But overall, this was my favorite episode Marty and I wrote. The idea had come from the show's executive producers, but it suited us well to write it. We always tended to write Dorothy stories, because we had more sarcastic things to say. And our B stories, then, tended to be about Rose and Blanche. As writers, we didn't go much to the stage, particularly in the early years, when there was a stricter line of demarcation. During the week, we would be in the writers' room.

But this particular week, I was there for a run-through, and was standing at the craft services table when Bea came over to me. You wouldn't think it based on the characters she's played and her size, but she was actually very shy. I could see that she was almost reticent. She asked me, "Robert, do you think I'm doing a good job?" Well, how do you answer her?! Of course I told her, "You're doing a great job! Why do you ask?" She told me that the relationship that Dorothy had with Sophia was a lot like the relationship she'd had with her own mother, and so this episode meant a lot to her. It was touching to hear that from her. And so consequently, I like this episode the best.

YOU GOTTA HAVE HOPE

Written by: BARRY FANARO & MORT NATHAN
Directed by: TERRY HUGHES • *Original airdate:* FEBRUARY 25, 1989

Things don't start off well when Dorothy is placed in charge of the variety show for the Ladies' Auxiliary. Ticket sales are slow, and other than the adorable trio Sophia is representing as an agent, the Donatello Triplets (the Del Rubio Triplets), all of the available acts stink. (Including Sophia's other new client, her absentminded new boyfriend, Seymour [Douglas Seale, 1913–99], a.k.a. magician the Great Alfonso.)

After the show's emcee drops out, Rose comes up with a cheery plan to get Bob Hope to host— because after all, he is her father. She explains that before being adopted by Gunter and Alma Lindstrom, she had spent her first eight years in the St. Olaf Orphanage, dreaming that Bob was her real dad. And throughout her life, in times of trouble, Rose had turned to the legendary actor/comedian, writing him a letter or just going to one of his movies. Because Bob has never let Rose down, she knows in her heart he'll agree to show up for the Girls' charity show.

After Rose gets the members of the Ladies' Auxiliary all excited about Bob, the Girls have to make good on her premature promise. So they crash the men's locker room—in male golfer drag, no less—of the local country club, hoping to grab a word with Bob as he plays in a local tournament. But they're too late; they've just missed him.

The night of the show, as expected the Donatellos rock. But disastrously, Rose has forgotten to take Bob Hope's name off the program, and so she prepares to announce the error and offer the audience a refund. But then, a miracle happens. The Great Alfonso has put in a call to his old vaudeville partner, and after Sophia enters the magician's magic cabinet, abracadabra! None other than Mr. Bob Hope steps out. As Bob does his stand-up routine for the crowd, Rose vows never again to get carried away with silly fantasies. But she can't help muttering her gratitude to the man onstage: "Thanks, Dad."

◆ ◆ ◆ ◆

COMMENTARY: Rose, Blanche, and Dorothy turned out to be fans of the kitschy Del Rubio Triplets and their version of the Pointer Sisters' "Neutron Dance," and they weren't alone. This episode's coauthor, Mort Nathan, explains that he and Barry Fanaro had seen the three identical guitar-strumming ladies putting their own strange, unique spin on the pop tunes of the day, and decided to write them in to *The Golden Girls.* Because after all, like the Girls, here were three older ladies with a hip cult following. "In addition to mainstream stunt casting," Mort explains, "we would also try to go with some more esoteric choices."

Bob Hope (1903–2003), who makes a splashy cameo appearance here, had a career in movies, television, and onstage that spanned some seven decades. Throughout conflicts from World War II to the 1991 war in the Persian Gulf, the British-born, American-bred actor produced and hosted a traveling show for the USO, bringing Hollywood's top talents to entertain our servicemen abroad. And perhaps he truly was

Rose's biological father, because it seems as if longevity must run in the family.

Here, in their attempt to beseech Bob personally to emcee their event, the Girls crash a local country club's locker room—in male caddy getups that make them look, in Dorothy's words, "like Sam Snead with a hormone problem." As Dorothy and Blanche comfort their crying friend, they elicit stares from two men who approach, fresh from the shower. "That does it. We've got to get that antique dealer off the membership committee," vows one homophobic duffer (Patrick Stack) to the other. Those are some pretty strong words, coming from two gents parading around in towels.

BARRY FANARO: We got to work with some huge guest stars who were all incredibly nice because they were fans of the show. For this episode, we first had the idea that Rose would have been an orphan, and knew that often kids without parents fantasize about being the

children of famous people. We pitched Betty the whole idea, and told her: "We're going to need a celebrity, old enough to play your father." As we explained, the whole storyline really did hinge upon if we could get somebody.

BETTY WHITE: Susan Harris called me and said, "I know you're friends with Bob Hope. Would you take exception to calling him and asking him to do the show?" Well, I'm not good at that. I'll show off, but when it comes down to actually confronting somebody, I'm no good. But I did call Bob, and he couldn't have been sweeter. He said, "Sure, I'd love to." Well, I felt like such a hero when I could go back and say, "Yes, we've got Bob Hope!"

MORT NATHAN: We asked Bob Hope how he wanted to be paid, which was whatever the minimum was at the time. I asked his manager, do you want us to donate it to charity? So the manager said, "That's not all Bob wants. Bob wants jokes." He informed us that Bob was performing at the Bob Hope Desert Classic golf tournament, which the president was going to be attending. "You guys are joke writers—so write him ten Ronald Reagan jokes, and he'll do your show." So we did, and Bob used some of them.

RICK COPP: This episode marked a personal victory for me. The four showrunners Kathy, Terry, Mort, and Barry—whom we all called the Beatles—had asked all

ABOVE:
The stage for the Girls' variety show benefit.

Photo courtesy of the EDWARD S. STEPHENSON ARCHIVE *at the* ART DIRECTORS GUILD.

the writers to come up with jokes for Bob Hope. And I was so excited because I had a joke in the episode that he delivered, and it made the cut. Ronald Reagan was just leaving office, and the joke was, "Nancy is upset about them moving back to California. She's afraid Ron won't have as much free time to spend with her anymore." Stupid joke, but it made it!

BEA ARTHUR: I had worked with Bob Hope once on a variety show, and he had always been very complimentary to me. When he came to the set for this episode, he gave me the full set of "Road" movies that he had made with Bing Crosby. He was charming and seemed so thrilled to be working with us.

ROBERT BRUCE: For me, Bob Hope was the most memorable guest we ever had on the show. I remember walking on the Ren-Mar lot when all of a sudden we saw this Chrysler—Bob's longtime sponsor—heading toward us with this little head behind the wheel. Everybody scrambled: "Bob Hope's driving—get out of the way!" After all, the man was in his late eighties at the time.

Bob went to his dressing room, and I asked the other writers, "Has anybody gone over to visit the guy?" They all said they didn't want to bother him. But I had brought in one of his books, and I thought, "What the hell. I'm going to go over and ask him to sign it." When I entered his dressing room, there was no entourage. Just an old man sitting there, very un–Bob Hope looking, pale and with virtually no hair.

At the dress rehearsal, Bob didn't really seem to get what he was supposed to do. He knew that the story was that Rose thought he was her father, and he would come out and do his Bob Hope bit. And amazingly, when he stepped out of the magician's box, he had makeup on, and he had a tan, and I guess they'd shoe polished his hair in—and all of a sudden, this little old man had turned into the spry Bob Hope. He'd pulled himself together, and it was amazing to see the difference. But in that dress rehearsal show, instead of the Reagan jokes you see in the episode, he was doing jokes like "You know, the thing about these Golden Girls is . . . " He kept referring to them as the Golden Girls, within the show. We obviously couldn't do that. By the second show, he got it. He had some new material, and he was good.

ABOVE:

Sophia finds the perfect act in the Donatello Triplets (the Del Rubio Triplets).

Photo by ABC PHOTO ARCHIVES/ABC *via* GETTY IMAGES.

TILL DEATH DO WE VOLLEY

Written by: RICHARD VACZY & TRACY GAMBLE
Directed by: TERRY HUGHES ◆ *Original airdate:* MARCH 18, 1989

Dorothy's former tennis teammate Trudy McMann (Anne Francis, 1930–2011) comes to Miami for their high school reunion, reviving their old rivalry. But the visit turns tragic when Trudy suddenly dies on the tennis court, leading Dorothy to blame herself.

That night at the reunion—inexplicably being held in the Girls' living room—Dorothy dreads relaying the news of Trudy's demise. But then, just after she musters the courage and makes her big announcement, voilà! In marches a very-much-alive Trudy, gloating over having pulled her best practical joke of all time.

After facing her friends' horrified reaction, Trudy barges in to Dorothy's bedroom to apologize for her cruel trick—and finds her husband, Jack (Robert King), nestled in bed with her supposedly grieving friend. Trudy is outraged, and Dorothy vindicated; throwing off the covers, Dorothy reveals that she and Jack are fully clothed underneath. Dorothy is Sicilian, after all—and earlier, when she realized she'd been duped, she had set out to exact the perfect revenge. And once achieved, all is forgiven, with Dorothy proclaiming her long-lost frenemy has "made this one hell of a reunion."

◆ ◆ ◆ ◆

COMMENTARY: The late Anne Francis had been a sex symbol since her days as the sexy title character in the 1965–66 ABC detective series *Honey West*. Here, Anne traded in Honey's pet ocelot for a tennis racket, but in faking her death-by-heart-attack on the tennis court, proved she still had the moves.

A child actress on the stage, Anne had gone on to land roles in noteworthy fifties films *Bad Day at Black Rock* and *Blackboard Jungle* in 1955, and camp classic *Forbidden Planet* in 1956. In 1960 she famously played a confused mannequin-come-to-life, shopping for a gold thimble in the *Twilight Zone* episode "The After Hours."

And yes, for some reason, Brooklynite Dorothy's high school reunion—or possibly just the league champs of 1946 reunion, because it's not clear—is being held in the Girls' Miami living room. Just go with it.

ANNE FRANCIS: When I got sent this script for *The Golden Girls*, I thought it was a fun role. They were all strong actresses, and I liked doing comedy very much, so I felt very comfortable. Working toe-to-toe with Bea was fun, too. I noticed during the shoot how Bea loves to be in bare feet. I did a TV movie with her around that same time, too, called *My First Love*, where

again I played an old friend from school days. We shot on location, and I noticed Bea was running around on downtown streets barefoot as well, which I thought was relatively dangerous. But she really doesn't like to wear shoes.

DAVID A. GOODMAN: When my writing partner, Rick Copp, and I joined the show in the fourth season, we quickly learned not to do something the writers had come to call "Dorothy bashing." Obviously, it's the *character* of Rose who is stupid, of Sophia who's senile, of Blanche who's a slut—and those are the types of jokes you'd write for those characters. But in the first couple of years, there were lots of jokes about how big and ugly Dorothy was. Bea started to feel very insecure about it, and so the writers had to take those jokes out of their scripts. As a young writer, that was a very good lesson to learn.

But in this episode, something interesting happened. There was a line where, in being competitive with Trudy, Dorothy reminds her about their upcoming tennis match: "I think you forget, Trudy, we have to wear tennis dresses." The joke there being that you should be worried, Trudy, because you know what you look like in a tennis dress. The problem was Anne Francis was gorgeous, so the joke didn't work at all. It made no sense, and never got a laugh at run-throughs or rehearsals. But Bea really liked the joke, because it essentially implied that it was now the other woman who would look less attractive. And when the writers suggested cutting the line, Bea would say, "No, no, I can make it work!" It was clear that it was very much a mission for her. I remember her really emphasizing the words, "*Tennis. Dresses.*" And the look on her face afterward would be like: "Are people not hearing me?!" It really was a fascinating moment to watch.

ABOVE:
These bleachers provided the perfect vantage point for witnessing someone faking a heart attack.

Photo courtesy of the EDWARD S. STEPHENSON ARCHIVE *at the* ART DIRECTORS GUILD.

HIGH ANXIETY

Written by: MARTIN WEISS & ROBERT BRUCE
Directed by: TERRY HUGHES • *Original airdate:* MARCH 25, 1989

After Sophia accidentally knocks Rose's bottle of pills into the sink, the Girls realize that Rose is unable to live without the pain killers she has been taking—for thirty years! Rose resents the Girls' implication that she may be addicted, and hands the bottle to Dorothy for safekeeping. But then, in the middle of the night, Rose awakens all her roommates as she breaks a vase while rummaging through the kitchen cabinets in need of a fix. Even after admitting she has a problem, Rose is too embarrassed to consider getting help.

Rose initially persuades them to help her quit cold turkey, keeping her comfortable through the night. They play spirited rounds of the world's stupidest game, Googenspritzer, which is much like Monopoly, except using St. Olaf's geography; they wolf down some Bundt cake. Finally, at sunup, Rose is encouraged that she made it through the night. But soon, of course, she does fall off the wagon, taking another pill. So Rose makes the call to a rehab center herself, and one month later, she's back home, prepared to live her life drug-free, one day at a time.

Meanwhile, after striking up a conversation with a man at the Little Slice of Sicily pizzeria at the mall, Sophia comes home with an offer from the chain's owner to appear in its new TV commercial. While scouting locations, director Sy Ferber (Jay Thomas) comes to the house, meets Dorothy, and comes up with an even better idea: for the mother/daughter duo to appear together in the spots for the family restaurant chain.

When the cameras roll, Sophia is a natural, but Dorothy is unnaturally stiff. Worse yet, upset by the spot's grammar, the English teacher starts rewriting her lines. So Sy makes a change of his own, recasting Dorothy as a nonspeaking pizza server. But ultimately, it's Sophia who spoils the deal, after tasting the product she derides as "slime on a shingle." Declaring that Sicilians are unable to do two things— lie about pizza, and file a tax return—she storms off, sacrificing the big payday.

• • • •

COMMENTARY: With this episode, *The Golden Girls* shines some light on a problem that is still prevalent today, dependence on opioids and benzodiazepines originally prescribed legitimately as pain-killers. It's strange, though, that at this point, four seasons in, no one among Rose's pals and confidantes has noticed that the woman is addicted to her pills. Luckily, she's able to kick the habit quickly; and even though she professes the twelve-step motto of "one day at a time," Rose is apparently able to control her cravings so permanently that we never hear about her problem again.

Dorothy's fixation on the grammatical errors in her pizza commercial lines was gleaned from real life; as writer Gail Parent reveals, both Bea Arthur and Estelle Getty were perfectionists about proper speech. "Sometimes a line might have a grammatical error in it, especially if we had thought it might be funnier that way. But in Bea's and Estelle's heads, it would then seem hard to say," Gail explains. "Luckily, there's always another way to do the line."

ROBERT BRUCE: Marty and I had written this same addiction episode for *The Ellen Burstyn Show* in 1986. The show was so short-lived on ABC I don't think anybody ever saw the episode. I don't even remember if it aired. In fact, the funny thing was the character we wrote the storyline for was Ellen's mother, played by Elaine Stritch. And after the table read, she came up to us and said, "You've got me sounding like one of the goddamn Golden Girls here!"

We thought it was a shame to let a funny episode go to waste. So we thought, why not do the episode again on *The Golden Girls*? I think in the back of our heads we were even hoping we'd get some award for spreading an antidrug message. Of course, the way Rose suddenly has a drug problem, and then just as suddenly gets over it, the episode ended up not being very realistic.

JAY THOMAS: At this point, I'd done a lot of sitcoms, and I always work the same way; in rehearsals, I might throw out an ad-libbed line.

Not to rewrite the script, but if I thought of something, I might try it. But ironically, on *The Golden Girls*, as I was rehearsing one of the pizzeria scenes with Bea and Estelle, I transposed two words, but completely by accident. It had truly been a mistake—but it got a laugh. So of course, I was happy, and made a mental note: "Oh, that got a laugh!" But it seemed like I'd thrown a line, and I could see the muscles in Bea Arthur's cheek begin to grind.

It was only the first day of rehearsal, so I really thought nothing of it. But then Estelle Getty came over to me later and said, "Boy, you're a brave one!" She told me Bea doesn't like ad-libs, and I'd better be careful. I already knew Betty White a little bit and loved her, and from

> ## "There are two things a Sicilian won't do: lie about pizza, and file a tax return!"
> —SOPHIA

that moment on, I ended up making friends with Estelle that week, too. We would hang out between scenes.

So then the night of the taping comes, and I knew I wanted to do the line the transposed way again. The producers could end up cutting it, of course, but if a line gets a laugh, I've never known a show that wouldn't let you at least try it. And sure enough, when I said the line, it got a pretty decent-sized laugh. And I tell you, those muscles in Bea's cheek really started grinding, and she got a derisive look on her face. Between takes, Estelle said to me, "You are either really stupid, or really brave."

But I could see I'd really pissed Bea off.

LITTLE SISTER

Written by: CHRISTOPHER LLOYD
Directed by: TERRY HUGHES • *Original airdate:* APRIL 1, 1989

On the eve of a visit, Rose confesses to the Girls that she and her little sister, Holly (Inga Swenson), have never gotten along. From Rose's description of the woman, Blanche and Dorothy are prepared to meet a green-eyed monster, but instead are delighted as the outgoing Holly invites them to dinner, and the movies, and to other outings—but each time, neglecting to inform Rose of their whereabouts, and once, even giving her false directions to lunch. Rose insists that Holly's neglect is deliberate, born just like in their childhood out of envy and spite, but her friends refuse to believe her.

Only Sophia is willing to give credence to Rose's claims that not only did Blanche's boyfriend, prominent mortician Gary Tucker (Jerry Hardin), come on to her, but he also had a make-out session on the couch with Holly. But when horny Gary finally does get caught with Holly, literally with his pants down, it's time for Rose and her sister to have a talk. Holly admits to being jealous of Rose's ability to have and keep friends. So Rose sends her sister packing, but with the hopes that someday they might be able to become not just siblings, but friends themselves.

Meanwhile, after Sophia agrees to dog sit for the vacationing Westons, she notices only days later that the pooch has gotten loose. Panicked, Sophia goes out and buys a doggie double—but then is in double-trouble when the real Dreyfuss returns. With the pet shop closed for the weekend, Sophia is stuck with two identical pooches, inevitably unable to tell them apart. Luckily, it's dog-loving Rose to the rescue, resorting to the characteristically simple tactic of calling the dog by name.

◆ ◆ ◆ ◆

"No, Dorothy, she plays the flout. It's a Scandinavian instrument that looks like a tuba except it's got hair on the bottom."

—ROSE

COMMENTARY: Nebraska native Inga Swenson is best known to TV audiences for playing the high-strung German cook Gretchen Kraus on Witt/Thomas/Harris' earlier sitcom hit, *Benson*. Prolific stage, TV, and film actor Jerry Hardin must have had great chemistry with Rue McClanahan, because this episode marks his second *Golden Girls* appearance, both times in Blanche storylines. In the show's first season, in "Adult Education," he's the sleazy professor who tries to coerce Blanche into bed; here, he's the sleazy boyfriend who hits on Blanche's friend and houseguest.

Finally, after making his first crossover cameo earlier in the season in "Bang the Drum, Stanley," one of the series' most beloved recurring characters reappears here. Playing *Empty Nest* neighbor Dr. Harry Weston's dog, Dreyfuss, animal actor Bear was, according to his trainer, Joel Silverman, a mix of purebred St. Bernard (mother) and Golden Retriever (father). Ironically, echoing the theme of the episode's A plot, Bear appears here with his faster, cross-eyed brother Julio, his occasional *Empty Nest* stand-in with whom he did not get along.

CHRISTOPHER LLOYD: At this point it was already getting harder and harder to find ways to put the Girls in conflict with each other. I'm sure the idea for this episode started with us needing a Rose story, and then saying, "Is there a relative of hers we haven't seen?" So we came up with her younger sister, and this *All About*

Eve–like situation, where there would be conflict with the sister, but an even greater conflict with her roommates, who won't believe or trust Rose's instincts.

INGA SWENSON: As I had learned doing *Benson*, when you're a nuclear family on a sitcom like those four ladies were, you have a lot of work to do, learning a new script every week—if not every night, because the writers change it every day. So you don't have time for socializing or chatting with strangers on the set. Doing *The Golden Girls*, I had the same expectations—as the guest star, I didn't expect anyone to hang out with me. In fact, the hair and makeup people were so busy with the four stars that I ended up doing all of that for myself.

But one great thing was that that week, there were the two dogs on the set. With animal actors, you can't really go up and pet them or interact much, because only the trainer is allowed. But because Betty White is such an animal person, I ended up having a nice conversation with her about dogs.

JERRY HARDIN: Sometimes guest stars can be made to feel like outsiders, but I never felt that on *The Golden Girls*. Rue was wonderful to work with, and Betty too. Bea was more reserved, and didn't chitchat a lot. But Estelle did, joking around while we were waiting for setups between scenes. And I found her to be the funniest of the ladies in real life.

SOPHIA'S CHOICE

Written by: RICHARD VACZY & TRACY GAMBLE
Directed by: TERRY HUGHES ◆ *Original airdate:* APRIL 15, 1989

After receiving a big bonus check at work, Blanche decides to have her breasts enlarged. After consulting Dr. Myron Rosenzweig, she brings home a stack of post-op photos as samples of the work done by "the Picasso of plastic surgeons."

Meanwhile, Sophia returns from attempting to visit her friend Lillian (Ellen Albertini Dow, 1913-2015) at Shady Pines, only to find out that the woman has been transferred to an even worse facility, Sunny Pastures. So Sophia decides to "adopt" Lillian, vowing to visit her frequently. But when she and Rose later pay one such visit, Sophia has a surprise: she's decided to bust Lillian out and take her home.

But it turns out that even if Sunny Pastures does offer subpar services, there's a reason why Lillian needed nursing-home care. The woman is forgetful and frightened, and tending to her is exhausting. Vowing to force Sunny Pastures to do its job properly, Dorothy and Sophia meet with its overworked administrator (Ron Orbach) to lodge their complaints—and are surprised when he doesn't put up an argument. The entire U.S. eldercare system, he complains, is broken and underfunded.

Just as Dorothy and Sophia return home depressed, Rose enters with what she thinks is good news: she has found a better, more caring nursing home for Lillian. Just one small problem: Lillian's social security benefits will come up $150 per month short. Dorothy despairs, but Blanche has a noble idea, to spend the money she had earmarked for her breasts on helping Lillian instead.

OPPOSITE:

Sophia and Rose debate about busting Lillian (Ellen Albertini Dow) out of Sunny Pastures.

Photo by CHRIS HASTON/NBCU PHOTO BANK *via* GETTY IMAGES.

COMMENTARY: This episode is an example of what *The Golden Girls* did so well, bringing attention to a social issue like the high cost of eldercare. Playing Sunny Pastures chief Dan Cummings, actor Ron Orbach is the cousin of the late Jerry Orbach, who would appear in the show's fifth-season episode "Cheaters," playing Dorothy's married lover Glen O'Brien. And one final story note: at one point here, Blanche says that there were no nursing homes in the South, at least when she was growing up. But they must have cropped up in her adult years, because in the season-three episode "Mother's Day," we see her visiting with her own elderly mother in such a facility.

RICHARD VACZY: For my writing partner, Tracy, and me, this episode saved our asses. We were new to the show, and had written a few scripts that hadn't gone over well. This was our third try, and we knew if it didn't work, we would be out. At the table read that Monday morning, we were really nervous. Now I look back at this as the moment where we came into our own as writers on *The Golden Girls*, because we hooked in to something that was organic to the show, to the struggles associated with aging. I'm really proud of this episode, especially because it had a relative lack of jokiness and was somewhat moving.

My grandmother had died of Alzheimer's in 1988. For this episode, I drew on my memories of visiting her, and wanting so much to get her out of there, but knowing I couldn't. But we wanted to see what would happen for someone like Sophia to act on the impulse to help her friend, and do something she probably knew she shouldn't.

For the B plot, the story about Blanche considering a boob job was perfect because we were otherwise dealing with such serious story matter it was a relief to balance it with something really frivolous. And I love the moment when Dorothy is leaving the living room, which is covered with photos of breasts. And she remarks that no matter where you go, it's like they follow you everywhere.

ELLEN ALBERTINI DOW: When I got this part, I was really excited, because it was at the beginning of my TV career, and this was a major role. At that time, I knew no one with Alzheimer's disease. I do now, because I had a very dear friend die of it. So at that time, I didn't find it depressing to play someone with the disease; now I probably would. But then, to me, it was just another way of playing a character.

Working with the director Terry Hughes was wonderful. I did have some funny lines, like when I insulted Blanche about her bosom. But at other moments, Terry would let me know if I was in danger of getting too sad. "Now that's enough, Ellen."

The episode went great, and with all the laughter and applause, I felt higher than a kite. After the taping, Rue McClanahan came over to me and told me I had been the best guest they'd had. She asked me if I was alone, and I told her I was married. She said, "I'm so glad. In this business, you have to have someone to go home to." I'll always remember her for that, for showing me warmth that you don't get often as a guest.

FOREIGN EXCHANGE

Written by: SANDY & HARRIET B. HELBERG
Directed by: TERRY HUGHES • *Original airdate:* MAY 6, 1989

Sophia's friends Philomena and Dominic Bosco (Nan Martin, 1927–2010, and Vito Scotti, 1918–96) visit from Sicily, bearing a surprise: they believe they are Dorothy's true parents. Their hospital mix-up theory, arising from the results of their daughter Gina's (Flo DiRe) premarital blood test, makes sense: the two women were born within minutes of each other in the same Brooklyn facility, and Dorothy certainly bears more resemblance to tall Philomena than she does to short Sophia. When Gina then comes to the door, it's even more eerie; she's a junior version of Sophia.

When the Boscos start doting on Dorothy, Sophia has finally had enough, vowing to take a blood test of her own. At the hospital, Sophia calms her daughter's fears, reminding her of the emotional bond they share with a remarkably on-point reminiscence about Dorothy's first day of school. Moments later, when the test results come back, Sophia rips up the readout without even a glance. Luckily, back at home the Boscos have come to the same conclusion, and so they depart with their devoted Gina on a boat back to Italy.

Meanwhile, Blanche convinces Rose to join her in taking lessons in "dirty dancing," as popularized by the hit film. But to everyone's shock, Blanche stinks at this latest craze, while Rose turns out to be a natural.

◆ ◆ ◆ ◆

COMMENTARY: This episode is especially memorable for two fan-favorite visuals, of Dorothy and Sophia each matched with more size-appropriate possible relations, and of Blanche and Rose in the living room, locked in their dirty dancing embrace. It's also noteworthy because of its behind-the-scenes relationship to another sitcom; writers Sandy and Harriet Helberg are the real-life parents of *The Big Bang Theory* star Simon Helberg, a.k.a. Wolowitz.

FLO DIRE: When my agent told me about the audition to play Gina, I thought back to a story I'd heard about Estelle's audition for the role of Sophia. And later, when I was on the set with Estelle, she told me it was true. Estelle had red

with my line, "I'm-a Gina!" It worked. They all laughed. Then, I did something I'd watched Estelle do and loved: I turned and stared at them like they were crazy. I really think making that entrance was why I ended up getting the part.

Once I was on the set, though, I thought I should dress like a fancy actress, so I showed up the first day in slacks and high heels. Estelle was so sweet to me, taking me under her wing from that moment on. She told me she'd put her best friend up for my part—but she didn't have any animosity that I was the one who had gotten it. Instead, she advised me to go back to the look that the producers had liked. In heels, I was too much taller than she was. So from the next day on, I went back to a cardigan and flats. "You don't want to rattle them," I remember Estelle telling me. "You want to remind them what it was they liked about you."

hair at the time, but she sprayed it gray, and showed up dressed as a little old lady, to the point where they didn't recognize her. But they loved the look.

I decided to use the same tactic. I copied everything I'd noticed about Estelle. I knew that the joke in the show would happen so fast, of Gina being just like Sophia when she comes to the door, that there had to be a very strong physical resemblance. I'm also very short, so that worked. And like Estelle had done, I went shopping at antiques stores and found a wonderful cardigan, glasses with a chain like Sophia's, and even a purse much like the one she always carried on her arm.

Then, when I showed up for the audition, I asked the casting director if we could do something different. Rather than her escorting me into the audition room, I asked her to go in ahead of me, and just tell the producers that I would knock at the door. Then, when they shouted out to come in, I would walk in in character, and start out

SANDY and HARRIET HELBERG: When we were first starting out as writers we were able to get in to the door at *The Golden Girls* through one of the four showrunners, Barry Fanaro, who was a friend from performing in the Groundlings in Los Angeles. And so our meeting at *The Golden Girls* became the first one we ever had.

At that time, there was a big breaking story that had happened somewhere in California, about babies having been switched. It had even made the cover of the *L.A. Times*. We were watching the coverage one night on Maury Povich's show, *A Current Affair*, and we thought, "What if this happened to Dorothy and Sophia?" That became the A plot we used.

A second one of our A story pitches, about Blanche and Rose trying dirty dancing, would become our B plot. We were relieved that everything worked really well together—especially when we learned that the episode we were writing would be the show's one hundredth.

ABOVE:

Sophia meets Gina (Flo DiRe), who certainly seems like she's her natural-born daughter. OPPOSITE: The ladies celebrate the show's 100th episode milestone.

Photo by JOSEPH DEL VALLE/NBCU PHOTO BANK *via* GETTY IMAGES. Photo by CHRIS HASTON/NBCU PHOTO BANK *via* GETTY IMAGES.

THE
MAKING
OF THE
100TH
EPISODE

1

At the script's table read early in the week, producers first hear the script read aloud by the Girls and their guest stars, including Vito Scotti and Nan Martin (*back left*).

2

The Girls in their places at the table read.

3

Later in the week, Estelle rehearses with Bea, who preferred to remain on book until the very end.

4

Multiple monitors keep track of each camera during the *Girls'* taping.

5 & 6

Betty and Rue, pictured here with director Terry Hughes (*left*) and assistant director Lex Passaris, preferred to be off book during rehearsals.

3

4

7

8

11

12

15

16

7

On tape night, producers Tony Thomas and Paul Witt look on as Bea and Rue consult the script between takes.

8

Producer Tony Thomas and creator/producer Susan Harris consult with the Girls.

9

Director Terry Hughes (*left*) onstage between scenes.

10

Blanche and Rose about to dirty dance across the living room, while script supervisor Robert Spina (*right*) follows along on the page.

11 & 12

Dance practice.

13, 14 & 15

In between the night's two tapings, the Girls, in their white bathrobes to keep their costumes clean, play with the producers' daughter, Nora Grossman, during their dinner break.

16

After the two tapings are complete, a cake to celebrate the 100th episode occasion.

Photos by KARI HENDLER PHOTOGRAPHY.

VALENTINE'S DAY

Written by: KATHY SPEER, TERRY GROSSMAN, BARRY FANARO,
& MORT NATHAN • *Directed by:* TERRY HUGHES
Original airdate: FEBRUARY 11, 1989

When Dorothy, Rose, and then Blanche's dates cancel on Valentine's Day, they join Sophia—whom they don't believe when she claims to have a date with Julio Iglesias—around the table, eating chocolates and reminiscing about Valentines past. Sophia claims to have witnessed the St. Valentine's Day Massacre while stopped in a Chicago auto garage with her father, Angelo (Bill Dana), and husband, Sal (Sid Melton), on a cross-country trip. Rose takes the heat for the time she mistakenly booked the three Girls at a mountaintop nudist resort. Blanche reminisces about the time she inadvertently coached a gay man (Tom Isbell) on how to propose to his boyfriend. And Dorothy blushes even remembering the time the Girls made a spectacle of themselves buying condoms to bring on a cruise, enduring an embarrassing PA-system price check by the store's clerk (Pat McCormick, 1927–2005). Finally, the doorbell rings: it's dates Edgar, Raymond, and Steve (Michael J. London, Joe Faust, and John Rice), who with Sophia's help were just pulling a romantic Valentine's Day surprise. Dinner and dancing await all but Sophia, who holds out for Julio and his private serenade of "Begin the Beguine."

◆ ◆ ◆ ◆

COMMENTARY: In *Golden Girls* parlance, a "wraparound" show is made up of four independent vignettes, tied together by a frame story that usually involves someone saying, "Remember the time when . . . ?" They are a standard writer's trick; the vignettes can be divided among the staff and cranked out more quickly than a more involved single storyline. But for viewers . . . they sometimes stink.

But not this one. "Valentine's Day," written by the show's four executive producers, is a comedy treasure trove, containing not one but two of the most beloved moments in the entire series. In the first, the Girls accidentally book a package at a clothing-optional resort. But just when they steel up their nerve to join the natives au naturel, they arrive in the dining room, only to notice that they're the only ones who are naked. "Ladies," a waiter says derisively. "We always dress for dinner."

In the second famous moment, *The Golden Girls* became one of the first sitcoms to promote

safe sex, with an infamous and hilarious vignette in which the Girls somewhat embarrassedly purchase condoms. True to form, it is Blanche who reminds the Girls as they pick up sundries for an upcoming romantic cruise to the Bahamas that to be safe and socially responsible, they ought to buy some "protection."

In yet a third fun vignette, Blanche makes her annual visit to the bar where George proposed to her over champagne, still following the tradition now that he's gone. As she explains her request for two glasses to the waiter, a man at the bar overhears and remarks on the romance of it all. When he mentions that he is at the bar because he himself is about to pop the question, Blanche realizes that they two were meant to meet, so that she could coach him to propose the same beautiful way that George had with her. It may have been meant merely as a punch line, but this small moment depicting a same-sex proposal, sandwiched among other stories in the episode, presaged the current gay marriage issue by decades.

Meanwhile, Sophia's somewhat fabricated tale of witnessing the St. Valentine's Massacre in 1929 leaves viewers with plenty to ponder. First, there's the way that looks tend to run in Sophia's family; the previous season, in the episode titled "Mother's Day," Bea Arthur also played her mother, and here, Bill Dana, who has a recurring role as Sophia's brother, Angelo, now plays father to them both. And then there is the age issue. Continuity was never *The Golden Girls*' forte, but as the episodes unfurl in the late eighties, it is often said that Sophia is an octogenarian. In season-two episode "A Piece of Cake," we even learn that she turned fifty in April of 1956. Maybe we viewers might be able to buy that Sophia could have crossed paths with Capone's crew in Chicago. But we're also expected to believe that at the time of the St. Valentine's Day Massacre, Sophia, as played by sixty-something Estelle Getty, is not yet twenty-three.

As if all that weren't enough, this episode contains

ABOVE:
The nudist resort's dining room, where "we always dress for dinner."

Photo courtesy of the EDWARD S. STEPHENSON ARCHIVE at the ART DIRECTORS GUILD.

TOP:

The Chicago auto garage where Sophia claims she and her family witnessed the 1929 St. Valentine's Day Massacre. BOTTOM: The drugstore where the Girls shop for "Condoms! Condoms! Condoms!"

Photo courtesy of the EDWARD S. STEPHENSON ARCHIVE at the ART DIRECTORS GUILD.

one of the show's most beloved guest star cameos. From the very beginning we've known that the Girls are heavy into Julio Iglesias; in the show's pilot, Dorothy uses tickets to his concert in an attempt to lure a depressed Blanche out of her bedroom. Now, three and a half years later, it's Sophia who lands him, as a Valentine's Day date no less. Having lunched with Burt Reynolds and now about to dine with Julio at Wolfie's, that old lady definitely gets the hottest dates.

RUE McCLANAHAN: The nudist camp part of this episode was so much fun, figuring out how we were going to come downstairs nude—so we each came down behind a great big cardboard heart. When we shot it, you could see us bare from the shoulders up—but of course we were all really wearing something that went from the underarms down.

MORT NATHAN: We flat-out stole the idea for the condom scene from Woody Allen's *Take the Money and Run*, a movie that I saw as a kid and thought was hilarious. I remember the joke I loved—Woody Allen asking for a "price check on an orgasm." Ours had different situations and joke constructions, but it was an homage to that specifically. The reason we went down that road is because we thought we could really top it, like with the line about Rose accidentally picking up the extra-sensitive condoms in black.

KATHY SPEER: The network often would ask us to write in some guest stars, and to do some stunt casting during sweeps months. In this case, they called and asked me, "How about Clint Eastwood?" I asked them, "Do you know Clint Eastwood?" No. I asked, "Can you get Clint Eastwood?" No again. "So why are you calling and asking me?!"

The ladies had met Julio Iglesias at the Royal Variety Performance for the Queen

and Queen Mother the year before, and struck up a friendship that resulted in him coming on the show. And he was a great choice for the end, to be Sophia's date.

NINA FEINBERG WASS (*producer*): Julio Iglesias was supposed to come in at the tag and serenade Sophia. But when he arrived, he said he didn't want to sing. I assumed he didn't feel like he was in good voice. I was concerned that Paul and Tony would be upset, but Estelle bailed me out. She said, "Honey, I'll take care of it." Estelle had always had her own issues with stage fright, and so she was so compassionate for someone feeling apprehensive that she was able to take care of him in that moment. And so she took his arm, and she sings to him—and that's the way you see it in the episode.

ABOVE:
Sophia joins Julio Iglesias for a round of "Begin the Beguine."

Photo courtesy of PHOTOFEST *with permission from* DISNEY ENTERPRISES, INC.

The producers and cast of *The Golden Girls'* first four seasons, by which point the show had already won two Emmys for Outstanding Comedy Series, and acting awards for each of its four leading ladies. Back row (*left to right*): Director Terry Hughes, executive producers Paul Witt, Barry Fanaro, Susan Harris, Tony Thomas, Terry Grossman, Mort Nathan, and Kathy Speer.

Photo by ABC PHOTO ARCHIVES/ABC *via* GETTY IMAGES.

SICK AND TIRED

(PARTS 1 & 2)

Written by: SUSAN HARRIS • *Directed by:* TERRY HUGHES
Original airdate: SEPTEMBER 23 & 30, 1989

For five months Dorothy has assumed she had the flu. With her lethargy getting continually worse, she doesn't know which doctor to turn to next.

After being assured she's fine by Drs. Raymond and Schlesinger, Dorothy sees Dr. Stevens (Jeffrey Tambor), who dismisses her symptoms as signs of loneliness and depression. Still, he recommends that if Dorothy really wants to pursue the diagnosis of a physical illness, she should consult his mentor, a neurologist in New York.

So Dorothy heads north, with Rose. Dorothy views Dr. Budd (Michael McGuire) as her last chance at treatment, but sadly, during her appointment, the man is even more blunt in his opinion that she is not truly sick. He advises his wearied patient to "take a cruise, go to a hypnotist [or] change your hair color." Back at their hotel later that evening, frustrated Dorothy cries on Rose's shoulder. And Sophia, too, worries at the prospect of outliving her daughter.

Meanwhile, inspired after reading *Lady Chatterley's Lover*, Blanche decides to fulfill the destiny of greatness her mother once foresaw for her by becoming a romance novelist. But unfortunately, the moment she sets out to begin work on her masterpiece, she comes down with a case of writer's block.

In part two, Dorothy consults her friend and neighbor, *Empty Nest*'s friendly pediatrician, Dr. Harry Weston (Richard Mulligan, 1932–2000). The first doctor to believe Dorothy's assertions of sickness, Harry refers her to his hospital's virologist Dr. Michael Chang (Keone Young). And when Dr. Chang diagnoses Dorothy with an actual disease, an emerging and perhaps viral illness called chronic fatigue syndrome, a thrilled Sophia can't help but exude compliments about Chinese food and culture. But unfortunately, with the syndrome so newly identified, the doctor can't offer Dorothy any conclusive prognosis; for now, she'll just have to live with her symptoms.

In celebration of having an actual diagnosis, Dorothy takes the Girls to dinner, ordering expensive champagne. When she spies Dr. Budd, she pulls up a chair to his table and eloquently confronts the man who had refused to acknowledge her illness and dismissed her due to her gender; at that point, even the man's wife (Bibi Besch, 1940–96) is on her side as she has the last word.

Meanwhile, still trying to join the pantheon of great Southern writers, Blanche stays up for seventy-two straight hours, becoming crazy eyed and delirious. And sadly, it wasn't worth it; as Rose soon discovers when she's given a sneak peek, sleep-deprived Blanche's "masterpiece" is actually a work of total gibberish.

◆ ◆ ◆ ◆

Someday, Dr. Budd, you're going to be on the other side of the table. And as angry as I am, and as angry as I always will be, I still wish you a better doctor than you were to me.

—DOROTHY

COMMENTARY: Season five brought a new regime to power in the *Golden Girls* writers' room; gone were "the Beatles" as showrunners, and in were Marc Sotkin, a head writer with experience on such shows as *Laverne & Shirley* and *It's a Living*, and a whole cadre of his new hires. With these two installments, the show's creator, Susan Harris, also returned temporarily, to pen episodes shedding light on a disease with which she herself had been suffering: chronic fatigue syndrome. As Dorothy voices Susan's own real-life frustrations with physicians' reluctance to recognize the ailment, the storyline is intended as a challenge to the medical community.

Meanwhile, the episode sets up what will become yet another inconsistency in the Girls' backstories. Here, Sophia is horrified to hear how Blanche had opted to go out for a pedicure while her husband lay comatose and dying. But a year later, in season-six episode "Mrs. George Devereaux," Blanche would recount to her late husband, in a dream, how she was at home when she received the phone call informing her that he'd been killed instantly in a car accident.

At the time of this appearance, Jeffrey Tambor was already an established TV character actor, and had played a regular role as the title characters' nemesis on the 1979 *Three's Company* spinoff *The Ropers*. In 1992, he was cast in the career-making role of sidekick Hank Kingsley on Garry Shandling's landmark HBO comedy *The Larry Sanders Show*. In 2003, he began another defining role in *Arrested Development*, playing the patriarch of the screwed-up Bluth clan. Jeffrey debuted in the fall of 2014 in his latest series, Amazon Prime's *Transparent*, as transgender dad Maura Pfefferman, a role for which he won the 2015 Golden Globe and Emmy Best Actor awards.

BEA ARTHUR: I didn't particularly think of this episode as being controversial at all—and don't forget, I had gone through the abortion thing with *Maude*. So after that, everything else seemed low-key. I remember I wasn't so concerned with making this episode funny as much as I was in making it real for myself.

SUSAN HARRIS: I really wanted to write this story, because it was my story. I was sick. I had chronic fatigue syndrome, which is probably viral, although they still don't know a whole lot about it. That's probably the reason why I didn't write so many *Golden Girls* episodes, because my life at that time had been consumed with going from doctor to doctor, all over the country. My experience with the medical profession during those years was something I know many people had faced, especially women. And if I, with my resources, was having the trouble I was having with doctors, I could only

BLANCHE:

"Oh, Girls, I have writers' block!
It is the worst feeling in the world!"

SOPHIA:

"Try ten days without a
bowel movement sometime."

imagine what women without those resources or without that strength were going through.

Dorothy was the character who spoke the most like I felt, so it was natural for the story to be centered on her. She was the strongest, and could articulate what was going on with her, and at the end, articulate to the doctor how let down she felt. Of course, you have to take license with the show; we couldn't have Dorothy chronically tired and sick for the rest of the series. So these two episodes were just a statement we made, and you have to just assume Dorothy gradually got better and is okay. And in a lot of cases, people did get better and were okay. After all, there are people who have chronic fatigue syndrome who climb mountains. There are all kinds of levels, and Dorothy was apparently at the mountain-climbing one.

After this episode aired, the response was enormous. Women who had thought they were crazy, and felt so alone, now felt validated. The disease predominantly affects women, five to one. And these women were just so grateful that there was someone out there like Dorothy who was saying the same things they were. That last monologue of Dorothy's,

where she tells off the doctor in the restaurant, was very personal for me. I had to restrain myself and watch my language, because I was a whole lot angrier than she was. And Bea delivered that monologue fabulously.

JEFFREY TAMBOR: I was happy to play this part, because my scenes were with Bea, and the storyline was something that I knew was very close to Susan Harris's life. Guesting [on a sitcom] is really hard. You really have to have it together. One of the best things to come out of this was that one of the *Golden Girls* writers I met during this week, Mitch Hurwitz, would later become my mentor, as the creator of *Arrested Development*.

THE
ACCURATE CONCEPTION

Written by: GAIL PARENT ◆ *Directed by:* TERRY HUGHES
Original airdate: OCTOBER 14, 1989

Blanche is thrilled to be bonding with her visiting daughter Rebecca (Debra Engle)—that is, until the unmarried young woman announces that she intends to be artificially inseminated via a sperm bank. Upset and uptight, Blanche sets herself out a midnight feast, where she's joined by the other Girls and their own grossed-out opinions about the then-innovative procedure. Blanche just can't understand why her attractive daughter would resort to such a solution—particularly by paying for it. Sadly, her hard line on the subject threatens to sever her relationship with both her daughter and her future grandchild.

Rebecca tries one last time to reach out to her mother, bringing her on a tour of a local sperm bank to show her the process is legit. Out of curiosity about this new-fangled life choice, the other Girls tag along. But when Dr. Manning (James Staley) explains the procedure, a mortified Blanche storms out.

When the Girls catch up with her at home on the lanai, they advise stubborn Blanche to show some support and respect for her adult daughter, who's about to leave for the airport. When Blanche finally musters an apology, Rebecca dismisses her cab so that she and her mother can ride to the airport together and brainstorm baby names.

◆ ◆ ◆ ◆

COMMENTARY: We've seen Southern Blanche be conservative before, but this reaction still seems strange; she's objecting to a procedure that could produce a beloved grandchild. But it's important to remember that while today both artificial insemination and in vitro fertilization are commonplace, back in 1989 the technology was still in its infancy.

This episode touches on a larger issue as well, the decision to embark on a life of single parenthood. Here, Dorothy answers the question that may be on viewers' minds when she reassures Blanche that a single parent can do just as good a job at raising a child. Obviously, then-vice president Dan Quayle was not watching that week. (And why would he? After all, the show regularly took potshots at him!) Because three years later, during the 1992 presidential election, Quayle would turn an episode of *Murphy Brown*, in which the title character played by Candice Bergen opted for single motherhood, into his rallying cry about the erosion of family values.

BEA ARTHUR: In this episode, Rue had the best line that's ever been written: "Sperm used to be free. It was all over the place!"

RUE McCLANAHAN: Debra Engle was fun to work with. But I had to put all that "eeew" stuff on, because I don't feel that way about artificial insemination at all. Even back then, even if it was controversial, it wasn't controversial with me. So I just had to act all that. I just knew instinctively that Blanche would not want to go along with her daughter's plan. I think in her case, her conservatism, just like everything else about her, has to do with her being Southern.

GAIL PARENT: There was one line in this episode that we ended up using for the next three years, when we were trying to decide on a place where the Girls could go where we would get laughs. It came from the fun way Estelle delivered Sophia's line, "Oh boy, we're going to a sperm bank!" From then on, that became our code phrase for putting the Girls in some situation. Should they go to a hospital? And somebody would say, "Oh boy, we're going to a sperm bank!" Which meant the situation probably had the comedic germ we were looking for.

DEBRA ENGLE: I grew up in Chicago, but at the audition to play Rebecca, they instructed me to do a Southern accent, because of Blanche's family's background. I did a really mild one. When you do an audition for a guest part like this one, you don't get the whole script, just your lines, what they call the sides. So when I heard I got the part, I didn't really have any great expectations about it, because I didn't realize just how funny this episode would end up being.

The topic of artificial insemination was pretty risqué back then. When we taped the show, the audience just went insane. I had done a lot of sitcoms before *The Golden Girls*, and I would do a lot afterward. But I don't think I've ever done anything where the audience responded like they did here. This was a topic people hadn't heard about on TV before at that time—never mind to have those four ladies discussing it! I remember after we finished the taping that night, the producers said the episode had the biggest "laugh spread" [amount of filmed time spent on laughter] they'd ever had. And the writers were all running around really excited, because obviously the audience had liked a lot of the sperm jokes!

ABOVE:
Oh boy, we're going to a sperm bank waiting room and doctor's office!

Photos courtesy of the EDWARD S. STEPHENSON ARCHIVE *at the* ART DIRECTORS GUILD.

LOVE UNDER THE BIG TOP

Written by: RICHARD VACZY & TRACY GAMBLE • *Directed by:* TERRY HUGHES
Original airdate: OCTOBER 28, 1989

Dorothy prepares for another date with Ken Whittingham (Dick Van Dyke), a handsome, wealthy lawyer. But Dorothy is most attracted to Ken's sensitive and giving side; the man gives up his weekends in order to dress as a clown and entertain sick kids.

When Ken calls and mentions he has something to discuss with Dorothy, the Girls naturally assume the man is ready to pop the question. It turns out Ken has made a major life decision, all right—to quit practicing law and become a full-time clown. But at dinner that night with her beau's new carnie friends, Dorothy finds that she doesn't fit in with the other clowns' wives. And worse yet, when Ken asks her to join him in traveling with the circus, she fears she'll have to break up with him.

Meanwhile, Rose and Blanche come home from a day at sea upset about the dolphin they saw tangled in a tuna fisherman's net. At Rose's urging, they join the Friends of Sea Mammals and set off for a protest on a pier. And when some rough fishermen arrive and manhandle Rose, Blanche comes to her friend's defense with a well-placed right hook.

Arrested for trespassing, the Girls and their Friends of Sea Mammals mates await arraignment in the courtroom. But just as Dorothy makes a show of bragging to the judge (Mel Stewart, 1929–2002) about her lawyer boyfriend coming to the rescue, Ken clomps in in full clown regalia, complete with red wig and nose. His impassioned defense prevails, and in the end, the charges are dropped—but so is Ken. Dorothy has realized that she must not love the man, because if she did, clown or not, she would have been willing to follow him anywhere.

◆ ◆ ◆ ◆

COMMENTARY: This episode is noteworthy for several reasons—not the least of which the revelation that Blanche has a rich interior monologue in which she addresses herself as Water Lily. But the episode's main attraction is its guest star, the legendary Dick Van Dyke. The *Golden Girls* producers had reached out to the multitalented actor repeatedly over the years, including offering him the guest star role in season-three episode "Charlie's Buddy," which eventually went to Milo O'Shea.

Dick Van Dyke had started his Broadway career in 1959, and the following year won a Tony Award for originating the starring role of Albert Peterson in the classic musical *Bye Bye Birdie*. His singing and dancing performances in musical films of the sixties like *Mary Poppins* and *Chitty Chitty Bang Bang* continue to enthrall new generations. And in 1961, he began starring in the self-titled CBS show that would earn him three Emmy Awards, run for five seasons, and set a new standard for situation comedy. In 1993, he landed another long-running TV role in the detective drama *Diagnosis Murder*. Today, at ninetysomething, he continues to act on TV and in film, with an appearance in the 2014 big-screen sequel *Night at the Museum: Secret of the Tomb*.

Playing the exasperated judge must have come easily to Mel Stewart, who was best known for playing Louise Jefferson's exasperated brother-in-law, Henry, in nine episodes of the landmark seventies sitcom *All in the Family*. A veteran of TV and film, he also appeared from 1983 to 1987 on CBS's hour-long spy comedy *Scarecrow and Mrs. King*.

TRACY GAMBLE: When we came up with the B plot, we knew that the actresses were all involved in animal activism. I had spent a lot of time in Hawaii and San Diego, and so I was aware of protests over dolphin deaths. It seemed like a good subplot for the Girls. The only thing was tuna fishermen tend to be in the Pacific, not the Atlantic. So we kind of hoped nobody would notice that.

RICK COPP: I remember that this episode was hilarious all week long, and we hardly had to change anything. And just having Dick Van Dyke there made it a special week. He was such a lovely guy, and I remember Bea was on cloud nine all week, because not only did she have a story about a love interest, but she got to play off of Dick Van Dyke.

RUE McCLANAHAN: We very rarely got to do any animal rights stories, and this one had us marching on the pier carrying a sign saying, "Don't buy tuna." And I get to sock a guy in the jaw. Boy, I liked that.

OPPOSITE:
Dorothy's new boyfriend, Ken (Dick Van Dyke), is a real clown.

Photo by ABC PHOTO ARCHIVES/ABC *via* GETTY IMAGES.

NOT ANOTHER MONDAY

Written by: GAIL PARENT • *Directed by:* TERRY HUGHES
Original airdate: NOVEMBER 11, 1989

Days after attending the funeral of their mutual friend Lydia, Sophia and her friend Martha Lamont (Geraldine Fitzgerald, 1913–2005) meet at a swanky restaurant, where the once-mourning Martha seems to be displaying renewed vigor. But it turns out Martha's euphoria arises from a dark place. Plagued with health problems, the elderly woman plans to commit suicide, and asks Sophia to come to her home to help.

Unable to sleep that night, Sophia confesses the situation to the rest of the Girls; and while Rose objects to Martha's plan on moral grounds, Dorothy is more concerned for her mother's emotional well-being after witnessing the death of a friend. But Sophia decides what's most important is to be there for Martha in her time of need.

The next night, Sophia arrives at Martha's apartment to find that the woman has already organized her affairs. Martha presses a new ten-carat ring into Sophia's hand as a thank-you; but as the woman prepares to take her pills, Sophia exhorts her to focus on the positive parts of life. It soon becomes clear that Martha's biggest problem may be not her physical ailments, but loneliness. As Sophia cries she notices tears on her friend's face, too, which she presents to her as evidence that she's not yet really ready to die.

Meanwhile, the other Girls are excited to babysit their neighbors' newborn—who soon develops a fever. So Dorothy enlists the Girls' neighbor, pediatrician Harry Weston (Richard Mulligan), to make a house call. But the true tonic turns out to be something that always worked for Rose back in St. Olaf: a serenade of the Chordettes' 1954 hit song "Mr. Sandman." While Sophia may think the Girls' version really stinks, it works in putting the kid to sleep. Baby Frank's fever eventually breaks, just as his parents return. As the other Girls leave the kitchen to answer the doorbell, Sophia steals a moment alone with the infant, telling him, as she has just successfully convinced Martha, that despite its twists and turns, life is a worthwhile adventure.

◆ ◆ ◆ ◆

COMMENTARY: In addressing assisted suicide, this episode touches on another controversial topic—and does it as only *The Golden Girls* could. Only a show with a feisty eightysomething protagonist like Sophia could deliver such a heartfelt lesson about life and yet throw in well-crafted punch lines at the same time.

Playing Martha, Irish-born Geraldine Fitzgerald was a renowned actress from Hollywood's Golden Age. She received a Best Supporting Actress Oscar nomination for her work in 1939's *Wuthering Heights*, and that same year, starred opposite Bette Davis in *Dark Victory*. From the 1950s on, she found more work on stage and in television, appearing on such series as *Alfred Hitchcock Presents*, *Naked City*, *St. Elsewhere*, *Trapper John, M.D.*, and *Cagney & Lacey*. In 1982, she became one of the first women to receive a Tony Award nomination for directing, for the play *Mass Appeal*. Among her later films, she appeared opposite Rodney Dangerfield in 1983's *Easy Money*, and as the grandmother to Dudley Moore's drunken title character in both 1981's *Arthur* and its 1988 sequel. After Geraldine's work on *The Golden Girls*, she played only one more part, in the 1991 CBS TV movie *Bump in the Night*.

GAIL PARENT: We wanted to tackle controversial topics, because that was an important part of the show. There are not too many shows where you'd be able to portray comedy and tragedy at the same time like you could on *The Golden Girls*.

I was so honored we were able to talk about rough concepts like assisted suicide and euthanasia. I remember when I first pitched the story, some of the other writers said, "How are we going to do that?" But my first novel, *Sheila Levine Is Dead and Living in New York*, was structured as a long suicide note, so clearly I must love approaching black humor in that way.

TERRY HUGHES: The topic of assisted suicide was definitely a heavy one to tackle, but *The Golden Girls* had earned the right to go there.

The episode's B plot, with the Girls singing "Mr. Sandman," wow was that funny. Especially when Bea came in with her low bass: "Yessss . . . ?" I remember that when the women first did the song at the table read, everybody fell apart with laughter. It was really the perfect counterbalance to the poignancy of the main plot, and that's what the show always did so well.

ABOVE:
The Girls bust a move to
"Mr. Sandman."

Photo by ABC PHOTO ARCHIVES/ABC
via GETTY IMAGES.

DANCING IN THE DARK

Written by: PHILIP JAYSON LASKER   •   *Directed by:* TERRY HUGHES
Original airdate: NOVEMBER 4, 1989

While Blanche suffers through a dating drought, Rose has begun seeing her ballroom dancing partner, Miles Webber (Harold Gould), a college professor. On the dance floor, the two are perfectly compatible. But after attending a party at Miles's apartment, Rose begins to fear that she isn't smart enough to keep up with her new boyfriend's brainy comrades. So she convinces Blanche to step in and attend a concert with Miles in her stead. Luckily, Miles does nothing all through the date but pine for Rose.

The Girls all head down to the ballroom, where Blanche ends her slump by meeting an ear, nose, and throat doctor "who's been looking for love in all the wrong places"; Sophia continues to make a dime a dance; and Dorothy melts into the arms of a fellow Glenn Miller fan during "Moonlight Serenade." And most importantly, Rose confesses her fear of intellectual inferiority to Miles, who reassures her he finds her stories refreshing. "Life is a ballroom, Rose," he tells her. "If you hear something you like, don't analyze it. Just dance to it."

❖ ❖ ❖ ❖

COMMENTARY: Over the course of *The Golden Girls*' seven seasons, quite a few actors appeared multiple times, as multiple characters—but none so famously as Harold Gould. After his memorable appearance in season-one episode "Rose, the Prude" as Rose's boyfriend and cruise ship companion Arnie Peterson, Harold returns here as her new man, Miles Webber. Ultimately, Miles would cross the Girls' threshold again and again, becoming the only steady love interest any of them ever had during the run of the show. The frequently recurring character became an audience favorite, as evidenced by the fact that when Rose, Blanche, and Sophia migrated over to the sequel series *Golden Palace*, it was a no-brainer that Miles should show up there, too.

PHILIP JAYSON LASKER: The audience related to these four women so personally, as friends. And people liked seeing Rose with somebody to make her happy. One of the things we always liked addressing with the Rose character was the intelligence factor. And here, by making Miles a college professor, we could explore how one's self-image affects a relationship, and whether love requires intellectual compatibility. We didn't know at this time that Miles would end up becoming a recurring

character. But he and Betty, despite us saying their characters were so different, worked so well together as a couple.

BETTY WHITE: It was a surprise to me that Miles and Rose would continue seeing each other, because as a big smart professor, he was far too intellectual for her. I don't know what he saw in her. She was such a sexpot and was so gorgeously built . . . and maybe it was a nice switch for him that with all the intellectuals he knew with Rose he could just relax and enjoy her innocence.

When you get into a scene on *The Golden Girls*, you're playing with the big kids. And it was lovely doing scenes with Harold— not only was he up to the task, but I felt I was trying to hold my own with *him*. The

one worry I would have was that I always had to make sure my lipstick was all powdered down, because I didn't want to get it on his nice white moustache.

HAROLD GOULD: I had done a lot of situation comedies before, sometimes with people who were green, who didn't know where the phrasing was, or didn't know timing. But you knew coming on to this set that the ladies were great at all of that. Their confidence was comforting, and that made the whole experience more relaxed and informal. Betty in particular was a great person to be in a scene with. We'd often work out bits of business that we'd come up with together. And when we'd be outside the door, waiting for our cue to enter and we'd look at each other, you could see she was having fun.

ABOVE:
The ballroom where Rose and Miles find their romantic rhythm.

Photo courtesy of the EDWARD S. STEPHENSON ARCHIVE *at the* ART DIRECTORS GUILD.

CLINTON AVENUE MEMOIRS

Written by: RICHARD VACZY & TRACY GAMBLE ◆ *Directed by:* TERRY HUGHES
Original airdate: FEBRUARY 3, 1990

When Sophia forgets her upcoming wedding anniversary, Dorothy fears that her mother's memory may be fading. Later, as the two women reminisce over a family photo album, Sophia mentions a carving her late husband made on the backside of her Brooklyn pantry door: SAL LOVES SOPHIA. But Dorothy notes that the pantry door was actually where her father tracked his three kids' height measurements.

So Sophia decides to jog her memory with a trip back to the old homestead, and she and Dorothy head north, ringing the bell of the brownstone apartment where now Mr. Hernandez (David Correia) and his family reside. Once inside, Sophia touches the unchanged wallpaper, catches the familiar view out the bay window, and then heads for the kitchen to prove to her daughter that the carving she remembers is for real. But she's dismayed to discover Dorothy was right; even now, through layers of paint, the height marks are visible on the pantry door.

Dorothy consoles her mother with a memory of her brother, Phil, as a newborn; in a flashback, we see Sophia (Flo DiRe) and Sal (Kyle T. Heffner) fussing over their son's bassinet in the kitchen as a jealous young Dorothy (Jandi Swanson) enters. But the reminiscence does little to soothe Sophia. For one last shot at remembering, she heads for the apartment's bedroom. Pulling out his photo from her all-purpose purse, she asks her dead husband for guidance—and gets it, from a spectral Sal (Sid Melton) himself. Sal urges his beloved wife to work hard, even in old age, to keep up her spunk and sense of joie de vivre. And soon, Sophia is her old self once more. Because on the bedroom closet door, there indeed is the famous carving: just as she had remembered, but in the wrong place.

Meanwhile, Blanche declares her burning need for an appointment with Robert, Miami's most talented hairstylist, but can't afford his three-hundred-dollar fee. And so Rose helps her out with a job, hiring her to assist with the senior health care survey she's conducting for Enrique Mas. But Blanche, accustomed to putting in a grueling twelve-hour week at the museum, turns out to be the world's laziest employee.

◆ ◆ ◆ ◆

COMMENTARY: By this point, in the *Girls'* fifth season, we've already met Sid Melton's Sal, and two different Dorothys, in both Bea Arthur and Lyn Greene. But up until now, there has only been one Sophia.

However "Clinton Avenue Memoirs" brings us a different kind of flashback, to an earlier time in the characters' lives—and so it requires a whole new set of actors. Here, there's yet another, even younger Dorothy. And if this new, young Sophia looks familiar, it's because a season prior, in the episode "Foreign Exchange," actress Flo DiRe was Gina Bosco, a young Sicilian look-alike who may or not be Sophia's natural-born daughter.

BEA ARTHUR: I still laugh when I remember the scene where Dorothy takes Sophia back to the apartment in Brooklyn. When we ring the doorbell, and when the guy comes to the door, and I put my hand over her mouth because I know she's about to say something about Puerto Ricans. I like the scene where he keeps saying to us, "Don't take anything."

FLO DIRE: After my first appearance on the show, I was so happy that the producers remembered me and wanted me back—and this time, to play Sophia herself! I had studied Estelle Getty's mannerisms carefully, the way she would twist her head and stare at someone who'd said something she didn't like. I did that as I said my line to the actor playing Sophia's husband about the birth of their new baby: "Caesarean!" One of the writers watching the scene loved the delivery and cackled so loudly that we had to wait for her before we could go on. So I knew I was doing something right.

RICHARD VACZY: I have to admit I didn't like the show's St. Olaf stories. Early on they were okay, because they would take us to this offbeat

world. But as the show went on, they got so out there and ludicrous, where we would sit in the writers' room and try to top the last St. Olaf story in terms of weirdness. Instead, what I loved about the show was when it stayed in reality. This episode is an example I'm proud of, where Sophia went home to reclaim her memories. Tracy and I always tried to exploit the real things that face people at that point in their lives.

TRACY GAMBLE: Every now and then we liked to do an episode where we addressed the fact that Sophia was much older than the others. We also always liked to do flashback episodes, because we got to work with Sid Melton, whom Tony Thomas called Uncle Sid. Estelle always enjoyed the flashbacks, too. She got an Emmy nomination for this episode, and even before that, I remember that she liked it and thanked us for it—whereas usually, her reaction was usually more along the lines of panicking, "Oh my God, look how many lines I have!"

ABOVE:
Sal's carved declaration of love for Sophia, on their Brooklyn bedroom door.

Photo courtesy of the EDWARD S. STEPHENSON ARCHIVE *at the* ART DIRECTORS GUILD.

AN ILLEGITIMATE CONCERN

Written by: MARC CHERRY & JAMIE WOOTEN • *Directed by:* TERRY HUGHES
Original airdate: FEBRUARY 12, 1990

A mysterious young man shows up at the house looking for Blanche's late husband, George, and is soon seen skulking around the Girls' local supermarket and staked out down the street. Convinced the man is obsessed with her, Blanche confronts young David (Mark Moses), and is shocked when he claims to be George's illegitimate son.

Meanwhile, Sophia persuades Dorothy to enter the Shady Pines mother/daughter beauty pageant so she can finally beat her archfrenemy, Gladys Goldfine. They roll in a piano and practice their talent: a duet of "I Got You Babe" dressed as Sonny and Cher. Later, they return from the pageant as runners-up, but feeling victorious; they beat Gladys, who sang "Try to Remember"—but couldn't.

♦ ♦ ♦ ♦

COMMENTARY: This episode contains one of the series' most famous gags, a visual so perfect it will stay with you forever: Bea Arthur and Estelle Getty, as Dorothy and Sophia, impersonating Sonny and Cher brilliantly. Much of the credit for making this storyline work must go to the show's costume designer, Judy Evans Steele, whose work in transforming the two actresses into the famous 1970s husband-and-wife singing duo Bea calls "incredible."

JAMIE WOOTEN: We wanted to think of a story where something that happened to George could affect Blanche's life today. Once we had that, the story became kind of obvious to us, and we couldn't believe they hadn't come up with it yet. We had ten stories ready to pitch, and once they heard this one, number three on our pitch list, they said, "That's it." We never even got to the rest. But the interesting thing is, although we pitched it with a mother/daughter pageant as the B story, the Sonny and Cher part was not in it. Marc and I later came up with that on our own, and we didn't ask them if we could do it; we just put it in. We ran the risk that they could have gotten it and said, "What the hell is this Sonny and Cher thing!"

BEA ARTHUR: I had never done a Cher impersonation before, but of course I had seen her, so I picked up the hair flip and the tongue thing that I did in this episode. I actually was very upset that we didn't get to do more than we did with it, because I loved it. I loved seeing Estelle with that little furry jacket and the moustache on.

TERRY HUGHES: Once Bea entered in the Cher costume, the audience reaction was so loud that she had to stand there and vamp, just picking at her hair while waiting for the laugh to die down.

LIKE THE BEEP BEEP BEEP OF THE TOM TOM

Written by: PHILIP JAYSON LASKER ◆ *Directed by:* TERRY HUGHES
Original airdate: FEBRUARY 10, 1990

When Blanche's cardiac test results show a slow pulse, Dr. Stein (Peter Michael Goetz) encourages her to check into the hospital for installation of a pacemaker. Mere days later, Blanche is already physically on the mend, but emotionally scarred by this reminder of the loss of her youth and worse yet, someday beauty. On her first postsurgery outing with Simon (Robert Culp, 1930–2010), Blanche ends the evening early, afraid to finish the date with her usual exertions. Even as the Girls counsel her to resume her normal life, Blanche makes the pronouncement that she has officially given up sex.

For the next two weeks, Blanche copes with celibacy by sucking down a constant supply of popsicles. But dealing with Simon will prove much trickier. Finally, as they return from one sexless dinner date too many, Blanche confesses to him her fears about physical intimacy. So before he agrees to leave, Simon demands a kiss. And when that doesn't kill Blanche, she leads him back into the bedroom. When the other Girls get back from their movie, they head down the hallway to check on their friend, and are reassured by Blanche's happy purring that life is back to normal.

Meanwhile, as part of her work for consumer advocate Enrique Mas, Rose brings home a bag full of ridiculous weight-loss products, like slacks that hook up to the vacuum cleaner and an electric upper-arm-flab stimulator. Rose manages to prove that the gimmicky gadgets don't work—and in the process, gains four pounds.

◆ ◆ ◆ ◆

COMMENTARY: Contrary to common belief, microwave ovens do not affect the operation of today's pacemakers, which have built-in protections from the types of interference caused by common household appliances. That's why, as writer Philip Jayson Lasker explains, after complaints from microwave manufacturers, several lines of dialogue referencing the Girls' need to give away their microwave were cut from the syndicated version of the episode, and also do not appear on the show's season-five DVD box set. But the full scene is available on YouTube, under the search term "GoldenGirls cut scene NOT ON DVD." There, in its full context, Sophia's response, which remained in the episode, to Blanche's depressed complaint about the meaningless of life—"Who's for popcorn?"—finally makes sense.

PHILIP JAYSON LASKER: The genesis of this episode was that my wife had recently received a

pacemaker. What was great about *The Golden Girls* was that because of the women's ages, it was one of the few places where you could incorporate that kind of story. A big segment of our audience had probably dealt with something like pacemaker surgery, or was afraid to deal with it, so I was proud of the reassurance we were able to deliver.

PREVIOUS PAGE:
Blanche hesitates in having sex
with Simon (Robert Culp).
ABOVE: Bye-bye, microwave?

Photo by ABC PHOTO ARCHIVES/ABC
via GETTY IMAGES. *Photo courtesy of the*
EDWARD S. STEPHENSON ARCHIVE
at the ART DIRECTORS GUILD.

72 HOURS

Written by: RICHARD VACZY & TRACY GAMBLE • *Directed by:* TERRY HUGHES
Original airdate: FEBRUARY 17, 1990

Rose receives a letter from the hospital where she had her gallbladder removed warning that during her transfusion she might have been exposed to blood containing HIV antibodies. As the ladies accompany her to the hospital for an AIDS test, Blanche comforts a very frightened Rose by explaining that she too had the test and knows what her friend is going through. But after checking out fine physically, Rose is surprised to learn that she must wait three days for the test results.

Unable to sleep, Rose begins to become hysterical, leading the ladies to realize how traumatic waiting for results can be. They discuss times when they've had to wait and were afraid, then vow to help Rose through whatever comes along—even though, as Sophia points out, it's scary when the disease is so close to home. The seventy-two hours finally over, the girls all breathe a sigh of relief as Rose finds out that she's fine.

◆ ◆ ◆ ◆

COMMENTARY: Again capitalizing on its license to tackle hot social issues, *The Golden Girls* was among the first sitcoms to mention HIV and AIDS at all, and further to suggest that the epidemic was a problem for everyone, not just the gay community.

RICHARD VACZY: Tracy and I really loved the idea of showing what must that time be like between knowing something might be wrong and finding out what it is. And with the theater backgrounds of everyone on the show and the people they knew with HIV and AIDS, we thought everyone would appreciate and therefore love it. We guessed wrong. It turned out to be the darkest week I ever experienced on that stage, because the material hit so close to home.

BETTY WHITE: Not only were people understandably afraid of AIDS, but a lot of people wouldn't even admit it existed. So this was a daring episode to do, and the writers went straight for it. It's interesting that they picked Rose for that situation. Blanche was such a busy lady, but if it had been her story it would have taken on a whole other color. But with Rose being Miss Not-Always-With-It, it came as a real surprise.

DAVID A. GOODMAN: When Richard and Tracy were pitching the idea for this episode, I have to admit I didn't really get it. Rose is going to have an AIDS test? I didn't see how that could work. Now, of course, having had a career on *Family Guy* making AIDS jokes, I can't really point a finger.

There was a running joke in the episode where Sophia would follow Rose around, washing everything she touched. Estelle, who was already a big AIDS activist, was not happy. She didn't like the jokes, and so she really tanked them at the table read. In general, I remember that table read being very scary, because it didn't score. And *The Golden Girls* was a show where otherwise, table reads had always gone very well.

RICK COPP: I was only twenty-four when I was hired on the show, a "baby writer." I was semi-closeted—and I think part of the reason is that I was petrified about AIDS. This episode happened only a few years after Rock Hudson had died, and Elizabeth Taylor was among only a few people who were making a big effort to get the word out about the disease. There wasn't a lot of information out there like there is now.

PETER D. BEYT (editor): It was while I was working on *The Golden Girls* when we found out my partner, Dean, was HIV positive. Estelle Getty was the first person I told. Her nephew was HIV positive, so she and I now had a connection. This was a new, scary world we both had to face. News stories would show the hospital room no one would go into, except in full hazmat suits. For six months, a family member—who works in infectious diseases—wouldn't let me go near his children, because they didn't yet know how HIV spread. It was a lot to go through. And when I would get to work, and be carrying all this baggage, Rue and Betty and Estelle, and occasionally Bea, were friends I could talk to.

Later on, I would start directing *Golden Girls* episodes. But when I was an editor, I would sit with the footage every Monday after tape night, and of course watch everything very closely and carefully. And I often felt like the episodes were really relevant to my life. In "Old Boyfriends," Dorothy has a moment where she tells the dying woman, Sarah, "The only time you're wasting is the time you and Marvin should be spending together." That really hit home with me, and was one of the things

ABOVE:

A relieved Rose gets her AIDS test results from the doctor (Tony Carreiro).

Photo by ABC PHOTO ARCHIVES/ABC *via* GETTY IMAGES.

that inspired me to take a year off to care for Dean. In a later episode, "Home Again, Rose," which I directed, the Girls can't get in to see Rose after her heart attack because they're not immediate family; well, I'd just had the same experience with Dean, after he'd had a seizure in a restaurant.

But it was really "72 Hours" that for me showed what TV can do, and how far a sitcom can reach. I hadn't gone to the taping of the episode, but I was set to edit it. I hadn't read the script, and I had no idea what it was about, or what was coming. This was in early 1990, a time when there was still so much shame about the disease. Having grown up in Louisiana, I already was feeling shame about being gay. My partner was dying, and now I was ashamed about that, too, and feeling on some level like I deserved this.

So here I was, editing away, watching the episode for the first time. And I got to the point where there's an argument between Rose and Blanche. I looked up at the screen in time for Blanche to say, "AIDS is not a bad person's disease, Rose. It is not God punishing people for their sins!"

My heart stopped. All of a sudden, unexpectedly, here was this woman on a sitcom I was cutting, talking about what I was feeling. I always admired Rue as a star and a friend anyway, but now a character I'd come to know so well was saying what I needed to hear. I broke down, of course. I had to stop working. And then I pulled myself together—and from that point, right in the middle of my partner's battle, I no longer thought I was a bad person. The show changed me in that moment of desperation. And my God, did the world ever need that to be said!

TRACY GAMBLE: This episode was based on a true story that had happened to my mother. She got notified that if you had had a transfusion in this certain period of time, you had to get checked. She and my dad were scared to death. It ended up fine, and she knew that the odds were against there being anything wrong. But it was hell to sweat out those seventy-two hours until she got the results.

My writing partner, Richard Vaczy, and I thought it would be a good storyline for Rose, partly because the audience might view her—and she views herself—as the last person who might have to worry about HIV. After all, she's just a Goody-Two-Shoes from Minnesota. We also liked how with the four characters, everyone could have a different opinion about the subject, which would be a good way to raise issues we wanted to raise while still being entertaining. So, Rose had the common reaction of thinking, "I've never been bad—why did this happen to me?" She then lashes out and says to Blanche, "You must have gone to bed with hundreds of men. All I had was one innocent operation!" When Blanche responds, "Hey, wait a minute; are you saying this should be me and not you?" it raises questions of what is "good" and what is "bad," and what does it matter, anyway? As Blanche reminds her that AIDS is not a bad person's disease, she's saying that just because I'm promiscuous, that doesn't mean I'm a bad person.

Before we started writing, Richard and I talked to HIV experts at UCLA and asked what information they'd like us to put across. At that time, there was a cottage industry of testing centers where people could walk in, and then would call up days later for the results. And while it was good that people were getting tested, the UCLA people stressed that there needs to be counseling for people when they get their results, whether positive or negative. So we were happy that this episode became an opportunity to get the message out there that either way, people need support—which is what we have the doctor say to Rose when he says that she's fine. In Rose's case, she has the built-in support system of Dorothy, Blanche, and Sophia. They are the ones to help her make it through the three-day waiting period and all of the denial and panic. And they do it by letting her know that no matter what Rose's test results might be, she is going to be okay because she is loved.

SISTERS AND OTHER STRANGERS

Written by: MARC CHERRY & JAMIE WOOTEN • *Directed by:* TERRY HUGHES
Original airdate: MARCH 3, 1990

Blanche gets a call from her estranged sister Charmaine (Barbara Babcock), who is coming to town for a bookstore signing of her novel, *Vixen: Story of a Woman*. As Charmaine and Blanche reminisce, they're shocked to see that maturity has brought them the possibility of friendship; they get along so well that when Charmaine asks for Big Daddy's pocket watch, Blanche promises to bring it to the signing. But before that can happen, Blanche tears through the roman à clef and decides it's a cheap, sensationalistic retelling of her own romantic life. She makes a scene at the signing, and later refuses her sister's calls. Only when Charmaine comes back to the house and barges into Blanche's bedroom looking for the watch do the two reconcile as they realize the true reason they never got along: they're too much alike—to the point that even their tawdry escapades seem similar.

Meanwhile, Stan's cousin Magda (Marian Mercer, 1935–2011), a recent émigrée from Czechoslovakia, visits Miami; and when she can't stand Stan's cheap ways, she stays with the Girls instead. Magda loves Slurpees, but is otherwise very critical of America and longs for simpler Communist days. At the bookstore, Dorothy suggests two tomes for her to read to understand the importance of freedom: Thomas Paine's *Common Sense* and Vanna White's autobiography. Ultimately, it's the latter that does the trick, convincing Magda to return to her homeland in order to be part of its new, free future.

◆ ◆ ◆ ◆

COMMENTARY: When the Berlin Wall fell in November 1989, the oppressed peoples formerly behind the Iron Curtain gained the potential for a new freedom—and *The Golden Girls* writers gained a new storyline. This episode, written just weeks after this major shift in world politics, addressed the differences between the dueling ideologies of communism and capitalism the way only this witty sitcom could: with both intellectual debate and jokes about 7-Eleven and *Wheel of Fortune*.

Playing Stan's cousin Magda, blonde musical comedy actress Marian Mercer had won a Tony Award for her performance in 1968's *Promises, Promises*. In 1980, she appeared in the classic film comedy *9 to 5*, and was soon cast in the role for which she is perhaps best known, as Nancy, the maître d' in the rooftop restaurant at the center of the Witt/Thomas/Harris sitcom *It's a Living*.

JAMIE WOOTEN: This episode was another example of how Marc Cherry and I came up with ideas for the show because we had been such big fans as viewers. We knew from earlier episodes that Blanche had a sister, Charmaine, whom she did not like. And I'm from North Carolina, so I loved the idea of a Southern sister you already don't trust. Then we added to that by figuring: what makes it worse? Having her come to town to bite you on the ass with her new book! I still have the prop

book that we used in the episode, in fact. The prop people made the cover for *Vixen: Story of a Woman*, and we put it as a book jacket over a copy of the Mary Wilson memoir *Dreamgirl: My Life as a Supreme*. Which is pretty gay. And after all, only gay men could come up with an arcane word like "vixen" in the first place.

BARBARA BABCOCK: Sometimes you can have a very good actor playing opposite you, but it's almost like making music, in that if the other person's rhythm is different, it might not work. Perhaps partly because Rue and I were both using Southern accents, I found we were both right in sync. Early in my career, I'd played a lot of small TV roles where I became known for doing accents, and I'd done Southern in a few Tennessee Williams plays. You can slide a lot of insinuation into a Southern accent, moving your voice through the word and adding all kinds of innuendoes.

I don't have a sister, so the sibling rivalry between Blanche and Charmaine was something I had to imagine. But it wasn't hard, because I found that Rue and I worked very well together. When Blanche and Charmaine both look up and check themselves out in the mirror over Blanche's bed, that was something Rue and I cooked up during the week, during rehearsal. It added a nice, silent endnote that underscored their relationship.

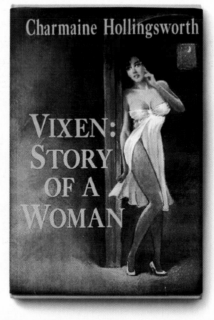

Charmaine Hollingsworth

VIXEN: STORY OF A WOMAN

CHEATERS

Written by: TOM WHEDON • *Directed by:* TERRY HUGHES
Original airdate: MARCH 24, 1990

After Dorothy gets a phone message from Glen O'Brien (Jerry Orbach, 1935–2004), the married man with whom she'd had an affair four years earlier, she stays home waiting for another call. Glen does phone again, mentioning something important to discuss, and leading a nervous Dorothy to his apartment doorstep.

Newly divorced, Glen proposes rekindling their romance, kissing Dorothy and leading her to the bedroom. The next thing you know, Dorothy's taking him home to meet Mom and the rest of the Girls. But even before they walk through the door, a bribe of cannoli in hand for Sophia, the man asks Dorothy to marry him.

Blanche and Rose profess their joy, and Dorothy can't believe her own happiness. But the next day at his apartment, their bliss is interrupted by a call from Glen's ex-wife, Bernice. When Glen lies to her and claims he's alone, Dorothy's eyes are opened to Glen's true motives, to score a wife to take care of him.

Meanwhile, at the mall, Blanche and Sophia fall prey to a scam artist (Sam McMurray), who pretends to find a wallet full of cash, and his accomplice, a "nun" (Nancy Lenehan). Tricked out of two thousand dollars, the two Girls admit the embarrassing affair to Enrique Mas's newest protégée, Rose, who informs them they've been victims of a con called the Pigeon Drop, and urges them to contact the police. Blanche does ultimately speak to a Sergeant Delfino, who asks her not only to come to the station to make an identification from a lineup of nuns, but also to have dinner with him that Saturday night.

OPPOSITE:

Dorothy rekindles her romance with a very different-looking Glen O'Brien (Jerry Orbach).

Photo by ABC PHOTO ARCHIVES/ABC *via* GETTY IMAGES.

TOM WHEDON: In the show's first season, Dorothy had had an affair with Glen O'Brien (then played by Alex Rocco), only to find out he was married. I wanted to put her into that situation again. It was about Dorothy being a woman, not a big ugly woman like some of the Girls' insults too frequently implied. There's a moment at the end of the first act, where Dorothy and Glen are about to go into his bedroom, and she says to him, "The last thing my mother said to me was that she wanted me to keep my feet on the floor." And he says, "My mother wanted me to be a priest." To which Dorothy replies, "I guess it's a bad day for mothers," and walks with him into the bedroom. Bea was so happy with the episode, and told me that closing line for the act was her favorite line ever on the show.

SAM MCMURRAY: I had worked with Witt/Thomas before, including on the first episode of *Empty Nest* after the pilot. My mother was an actress and was friends with Bea, and I'd worked not only with Rue, but even with Estelle, when she guest starred on a series I did in New York called *Baker's Dozen*. But really, when I got the call asking if I'd do this episode, the main reason I said yes was Jerry Orbach. I didn't know him, but I wanted to. So I had a lot of fun doing the episode—even though I thought it was really odd. After all, I play a con man—who gets away with it!

NANCY LENEHAN: It was thrilling getting to work with people like Bea Arthur and Jerry Orbach. But I also remember this episode because my character was supposed to confuse everybody with her scam—but the whole thing just ended up confusing me. I would do take after take, and I kept double-talking myself until I was so confused. I couldn't get it straight, and I swear by the end I had my eyes crossing. Finally, Rue had me put the lines on her chest so that I could just read them.

THE MANGIACAVALLO CURSE
MAKES A LOUSY WEDDING PRESENT

Written by: PHILIP JAYSON LASKER • *Directed by:* TERRY HUGHES
Original airdate: MARCH 31, 1990

Dorothy's goddaughter Jenny (Tanya Louise) is about to marry the grandson of Giuseppe Mangiacavallo (Howard Duff, 1913-90), the man who had been arranged to marry teenaged Sophia in Sicily but stood her up at the altar as he fled to America—and so naturally, young Sophia put a curse on him and all future generations of his family.

Meanwhile, the other Girls are having problems of their own: after lending dateless Dorothy one of her men, Blanche tries to steal Doug (Stuart Nisbet) back. And with Miles out of town, Rose will be solo, too—which presents a problem, because ever since Rose's own nuptials with her late husband, Charlie, weddings have made her uncontrollably horny. So, as Dorothy and Blanche have a showdown in a ladies' room stall, Rose flirts with a waiter (Jonathan Schmock), and then leaves on Doug's arm—before ultimately coming to her senses and catching a flight to meet up with Miles.

Finally, just as the man who once jilted Sophia asks her to dance, the curse kicks in, as the bride and groom quarrel on the dance floor. Giuseppe asks Sophia to undo her malediction; and as he recounts his own teenage fears of being trapped in marriage and in his tiny village, he gives Sophia closure by revealing that leaving her behind had been the hardest thing he ever had to do. At the same time, Dorothy intercepts Jenny in the ladies' room and encourages her to go talk with her new husband, Joey (Myles Berkowitz). And by the time Sophia and Giuseppe open the doors of the bridal suite, it's abundantly clear the couple has reconciled.

◆ ◆ ◆ ◆

COMMENTARY: This episode expertly weaves its two main stories, Sophia's Mangiacavallo curse and Dorothy and Blanche's rivalry, with yet a third storyline, or "runner," about Rose's suddenly raging sex drive. As writer and theater lover Tom Whedon explains, it was he who came up with "Mangiaca-vallo" (Italian for "horse eater"), stealing it from the surname of the male lead in Tennessee Williams's Tony-winning 1951 play *The Rose Tattoo*.

Howard Duff, here playing Mangiacavallo, started his career in radio, as Dashiell Hammett's famous private eye in *The Adventures of Sam*

Spade from 1946-50. Recognized today from his role as Dustin Hoffman's attorney in 1979's *Kramer vs. Kramer*, Howard built his career in film noir and Westerns of the '40s and '50s, often appearing opposite his wife Ida Lupino. By the eighties, Howard had found another niche in TV's primetime soaps such as *Flamingo Road*, *Dallas*, and *Knots Landing*.

Playing the waiter, actor and writer Jonathan Schmock is probably best known for another restaurant role, as the snooty maître d' in the 1986 film *Ferris Bueller's Day Off*. This episode marked his first *Golden Girls* appearance, but he would soon pop up in three more in the show's final two seasons: as a robber in "Melodrama," a theater director in "Even Grandmas Get the Blues," and a cop in "The Monkey Show," and would later pen the Christmas episode of its spinoff, *Golden Palace*.

PHILIP JAYSON LASKER: Tom Whedon came up with the name "Mangiacavallo," which made me laugh. The rest of the title, "Makes a Lousy Wedding Present," was the type of thing I would typically come up with at three in the morning. I obviously like to come up with odd titles, like "Like the Beep Beep Beep of the Tom Tom" [a play on a lyric from Cole Porter's "Night and Day"]. I remember one time, right after we finished a table read for an episode—it could have been this one—Bea muttered aloud to herself, "Do you bring in someone to come up with these lousy titles?" I was sitting right across from her, and I said, "Bea, that's my title." This is where Bea's brutal honesty came in, and I loved her for it. She said, "I'm sorry I hurt your feelings, but . . . it's a lousy title."

BEA ARTHUR: Growing up, I idolized Ida Lupino. That's who I wanted to be: a little blonde floozy who gets involved with bad people in roadhouse movies. Howard Duff, her former husband, had been a very famous radio detective. He was always very sexy, and very interesting. But when he came on *The Golden Girls*, I was disappointed that he wasn't young and gorgeous anymore. The part here wasn't even something heroic, and I caught myself wondering, "Why is he doing this?" Then I remembered how my mother would say the same things about Bette Davis, and I would get so angry with her.

◆ EPISODE 129 ◆

BLANCHE DELIVERS

Written by: GAIL PARENT & JIM VALLELY ◆ *Directed by:* MATTHEW DIAMOND
Original airdate: SEPTEMBER 22, 1990

As Rose announces her intention to revive her long-forgotten figure skating career in the U.S. National Senior Sports Classic, Blanche prepares for a visit from her now-pregnant single daughter (Debra Engle). Rebecca's latest surprise is that she'd like to have the baby in Miami—and not in a hospital, but in a birthing center.

Luckily for Blanche, when the Girls visit said center, run by a vegetarian midwife (Leila Kenzle), Rebecca is scared off by all the screaming that accompanies the unanesthetized version of the miracle of birth. But when Blanche, still embarrassed by the stigma of artificial insemination, presses her luck by attempting to convince her daughter not to deliver in her hometown, Rebecca vows to leave in the morning for Atlanta, alone.

However that night, in the beginning of labor, Rebecca comes to Dorothy and Sophia for help. Rose screws up the one little job with which she's tasked, calling the wrong "coach"—her ice-skating instructor Mr. Ninervini (John O'Leary)—to the hospital instead of the woman from Lamaze. The delivering doctor (Ken Lerner) orders everyone out, but Blanche insists on staying to support her daughter. And in the end, it's Blanche's compliments about her daughter's bravery that give Rebecca the strength to make that one last push, bringing a new little girl into the world.

OPPOSITE:
Rose, Blanche, and Dorothy coach
Blanche's single daughter Rebecca
(Debra Engle) through childbirth.

Photo by NBCU PHOTO BANK
via GETTY IMAGES.

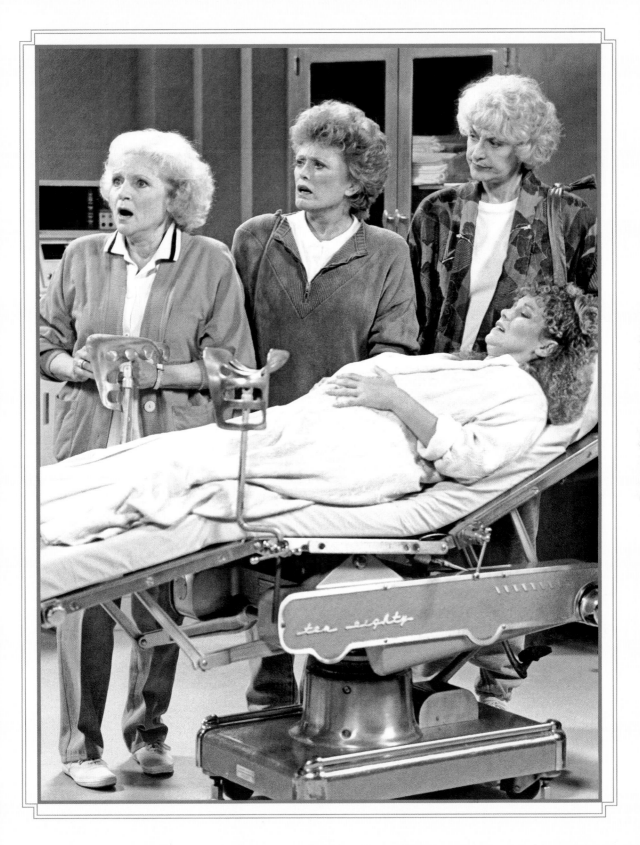

COMMENTARY: This episode features the return of Blanche's daughter Rebecca, whose artificial insemination storyline in the episode "The Accurate Conception" had proven to be an audience favorite. Both Rebecca's storyline and the show's B plot, about Rose's push for ice-skating accolades in order to please the long-gone Lindstroms, touch on the theme of parental expectations; as Dorothy advises Rose: "It doesn't matter what your parents want. You're never going to make them happy."

GAIL PARENT: On many sitcoms, the writers would plan out story arcs for the characters, and that would give them six shows laid out at a time. But on *The Golden Girls*, we never sat down to do that. We would revisit stuff later, though, and here we realized that because Rebecca had been inseminated about a year earlier, it was about time that we could have her give birth. The first episode with the sperm bank had gotten a great audience response, so we thought, "What would be the next step? How are they going to deal with the birth?" Because no matter how much you search for the "big topics" in writing a show, the most meaningful shows are usually the ones about birth, death, or marriage. That's it.

JIM VALLELY: I am proud to say that Gail Parent and I were the first to write a vagina reference into the show. Throughout the episode, Sophia keeps telling

Dorothy how hard it had been to give birth to her. She says Dorothy's birth weight was thirty-two pounds, three ounces. She says it took days. Finally, as they wait in the hospital for Rebecca to give birth, Dorothy has had enough. She says, "Ma, you're hurting my feelings." To which Sophia replies, "Not as much as you hurt my oonie." It was the first time we'd said anything like that. Sophia's response may seem tame now, but back then, it was pushing the line. As a writer, you always want to be one of the people who are moving that line. And I think *The Golden Girls* moved a lot more lines than most people realized.

DEBRA ENGLE: Right after my first episode [season five, "The Accurate Conception"] the producers had told me that they wanted to use me again. But this ended up being a difficult episode for me to do. Not necessarily physically, because they had an extra off camera who did a really great birthing scream for me (although because she had been chewing gum, Bea had wanted to have her replaced). But not long before, I'd had a late-term miscarriage, and so pretending to have a baby on camera was emotionally hard. Especially when they brought in the real baby for me to hold—played by twins, who were screaming in the background. Later, when I came back to do another episode, I had had my daughter. I brought her with me, and all the Girls were very sweet to her.

ABOVE:
Rebecca briefly considers having her baby in this New Age-meets-Victorian birthing center.

Photo courtesy of the EDWARD S. STEPHENSON ARCHIVE *at the* ART DIRECTORS GUILD.

ONCE IN ST. OLAF

Written by: HAROLD APTER ◆ *Directed by:* MATTHEW DIAMOND
Original airdate: SEPTEMBER 29, 1990

Sophia is scheduled to undergo surgery for the hernia she seems to have incurred while moving a wicker couch out of the garage at Dorothy's request. On the day of Sophia's operation, Rose, ordinarily a candy striper, works the hospital admissions desk, where she meets Brother Martin (Don Ameche, 1908–92), a fellow native of St. Olaf. Instantly sensing their connec-

tion, the monk asks Rose if she knew an Ingrid Kirklevaner, a nineteen-year-old chatterbox who worked in the kitchen of his silent monastic order. In fact, not only does Rose know of her, but she also knows the tragic story of Ingrid's death in childbirth. Rose herself was that baby—and as the holy man then explains, he himself is her father.

After at first avoiding the issue, Rose finally confronts Brother Martin, who is convinced that their reunion is a sign he has God's forgiveness. He seeks the same absolution from his long-lost daughter—and gets it, as Rose realizes how grateful she is to have ended up with good parents in the Lindstroms, and a life that included a loving husband and children.

Meanwhile, after getting a call that someone has misplaced Sophia, Dorothy rushes to the hospital to find her. After a farcical search of each floor, the Girls prepare for the grim task of checking the one place they haven't looked: the morgue. But as they get on the elevator, there Sophia is, having been left there on a gurney, hallucinating that she's in Heaven. Dorothy delivers a tearful apology, which guilts her mother into coming clean: her hernia was caused not by moving furniture, but by a prank she and her fellow seniors pulled on Gladys Goldfine, lifting her VW onto a lawn.

◆ ◆ ◆ ◆

COMMENTARY: When we first met Alma Lindstrom (Jeanette Nolan) in the show's first season, Rose gave no indication that the woman was not her natural mother. Nor was there any hint when blind sister, Lily, visited that she was not Rose's sibling by blood. It was only in the season-four episode "You Gotta Have Hope" that Rose had finally revealed details of her eight earliest years in St. Olaf's orphanage. From then on, the writers went with that version of her origins, and were inspired to create this storyline about Rose meeting her long-lost birth father.

Playing Brother Martin is film legend Don Ameche, who in 1939 played the part with which he would be most closely associated, as the inventor of the telephone in *The Story of* *Alexander Graham Bell*. His career had heated up again late in life, courtesy of a pair of big-screen roles in 1983's *Trading Places* and 1985's *Cocoon*, for which he won the Oscar for Best Supporting Actor at the age of 78.

BETTY WHITE: This was an interesting week. Working with a star of Don Ameche's magnitude was wonderful. But we were all really worried about Don, because he was having a difficult time with his lines. We wanted to protect him as much as you can, but in the end there's nothing you can do to help. You just have to sweat it out and dig your nails into your palms as you hope he'll get through it.

PREVIOUS PAGE:
It's hard to believe no one could spot Sophia in this two-walled elevator. ABOVE: By apparent divine design, Rose meets her birth father, Brother Martin (Don Ameche).

Photo courtesy of the EDWARD S. STEPHENSON ARCHIVE *at the* ART DIRECTORS GUILD. *Photo by* ABC PHOTO ARCHIVES/ABC *via* GETTY IMAGES.

WHAM, BAM, THANK YOU, MAMMY

Written by: JAMIE WOOTEN & MARC CHERRY
Directed by: MATTHEW DIAMOND ◆ *Original airdate:* OCTOBER 20, 1990

As the Girls help Blanche prepare her late father's possessions for auction, Blanche gets a call from Viola Watkins (Ruby Dee, 1922–2014), her former "mammy" who then disappeared without a word when Blanche was just ten. Having read in the Atlanta newspaper about the sale, Mammy Watkins arrives with a request for an antique music box she had once given the family—actually, in particular to Big Daddy, her longtime lover.

Blanche is horrified, and even considers burning the letters the woman leaves with her as proof of the affair. The next night, persistent Viola comes over to explain that Curtis—tellingly, he wasn't "Big Daddy" to her—was the only man she'd ever loved; in another time and place other than the Jim Crow South, they would have been married. But it turns out, the affair isn't the main thing bothering Blanche; it's the abandonment she felt when Mammy suddenly disappeared from her life. That's when Mammy reveals something remarkable; not only did she continue to ask Big Daddy about Blanche, but she even sneaked into the back of Blanche and George's wedding and hid among the help, so that she could watch the bride dance to the "Tennessee Waltz" with her father. And so finally, Blanche agrees to give Mammy what she came for—only for the women to realize the music box among Big Daddy's possessions is not the right one. This one is walnut, and plays the theme from *Bonanza*—clearly a gift from yet another woman.

Meanwhile, Sophia surreptitiously hires matchmaker Mrs. Contini (Peggy Rea, 1921–2011) to find a date for Dorothy. Not knowing that Jack (Richard McKenzie, 1932–2002) is an ex-convict, Dorothy initially has a great time on their night out—until he spills the beans about the source of the blind date. Furious, Dorothy decides not to speak to her mother—until Rose reminds her that Sophia was merely trying to ensure that her daughter wouldn't be lonely.

◆ ◆ ◆ ◆

But as Jamie Wooten reveals, the role had originally been conceived not for Ruby Dee but for another African American icon, Esther Rolle (1920–98). The then sixty-nine-year-old actress was beloved by TV audiences from her days as Bea Arthur's most worthy foil on *Maude*, and then later, when her character Florida Evans was spun off on to her own ground-breaking Norman Lear sit-com, *Good Times*.

JAMIE WOOTEN: Marc Cherry and I wrote this part origi-nally for Esther Rolle, because we were such fans of *Maude*. We wanted to be the ones to bring Esther Rolle and Bea Arthur back together—and she was going to do it, too. But then, she had a terrible, near-fatal car accident on the way to Las Vegas and was in the hospital for weeks. Marc and I were devastated that she couldn't do it. The part then went to Ruby Dee, whose deliv-ery I found a little bit slow. But I think really, I wasn't satisfied with the performance mostly because I was so resentful that it hadn't worked out to be Esther Rolle.

COMMENTARY: In this episode, Mammy Wat-kins sure does stir up a maelstrom—and it's not just the one about the music box. The woman who raised Blanche up until age ten now repri-mands her by her full name, Blanche Marie Hollingsworth. But later, in the seventh-season premiere episode, "Hey, Look Me Over," it would be revealed that Blanche's middle name is actu-ally Elizabeth. That would make sense; it was the first name of Hollingsworth matriarch Big Mommy. And, in a poetic cosmic sense, the mid-dle name of Elizabeth would make the initials of Blanche's married name spell B.E.D. Perhaps, in some great Southern tradition, Blanche has more than one middle moniker. So is she Blanche Marie Elizabeth or Blanche Elizabeth Marie?

Playing the bearer of such vital information was the venerable actress Ruby Dee. Having appeared for five decades on Broadway, where she originated the role of Ruth Younger in Lorraine Hansberry's 1959 landmark play, *A Raisin in the Sun*, Ruby was theater royalty. She and the late actor Ossie Davis were both also civil rights trailblazers, and were one of Hollywood's longest-married power couples until his death in 2005.

MARC CHERRY: I was a big fan of the older actress Beah Richards, but when I suggested her for this role, Paul Witt didn't think she was attractive enough. I was fascinated by that, because I thought, "The character is a very old woman. How attractive does she have to be?" So they got Ruby Dee, and of course had to put her in a gray wig because she looked fantastic, and was around the same age as the other women. And as great an actress as she was, there were a couple of moments in the episode where I think you can see Ruby struggling to maintain the age of the character.

FEELINGS

Written by: DON SEIGEL & JERRY PERZIGIAN
Directed by: MATTHEW DIAMOND ◆ *Original airdate:* OCTOBER 27, 1990

Dorothy is excited to teach an English class for an entire semester at St. Sebastian's high school. But not everyone is so thrilled, especially star football player Kevin Kelly (Christopher Daniel Barnes), whom Dorothy is flunking, making him ineligible to play in the weekend's game. Nor is the boy's coach, Nick Odlivak (Robert Costanzo), supportive of Dorothy's emphasis on education. Stressing how much the team needs Kevin, Odlivak first tries to sweet-talk Dorothy into relenting about the boy's grade. When that doesn't work, he calls in the big guns, sending the school's dean, Father O'Mara (Frank Hamilton, 1924–91), to beseech the teacher via veiled threats.

Dorothy offers Kevin private tutoring, but he rudely refuses. But karma catches up with the kid, who does play in the game but is then blindsided in a tackle, destroying his knee. And so later that day, Dorothy shows up at the hospital, not just to sign Kevin's cast but to begin educating her captive student with a reading of Dickens's *A Tale of Two Cities*.

Meanwhile, Rose returns home from a dentist's appointment with the uneasy feeling that Dr. Lou Norgan (George Wyner) may have been fondling her breasts while she was under anesthesia. At Blanche's urging, Rose confronts the pervy DDS at her next appointment—but he manages to convince her that she had hallucinated the incident. Then, just as he gets to work on her crown, horny Norgan aims his light at her apparently irresistible breasts and lets out an audible "wowie wow wow wow." This time, Rose isn't having any excuses, fending the man off with his own air gun as she vows to report him to the state dental board.

◆ ◆ ◆ ◆

COMMENTARY: This episode touches on two different scenarios involving workplace ethics, with Dorothy and Rose each challenged to stand up for her beliefs. And all of the challengers happen to be played by recognizable character actors whose careers have spanned decades.

Playing Coach Odlivak is Robert Costanzo, who has made a specialty out of playing Italian American characters like the father of Matt LeBlanc's Joey Tribbiani on *Friends* and who also appeared on Witt/Thomas's shows *Soap*, *It's a Living*, and *Empty Nest*.

In October 1990, Christopher Daniel Barnes was just seventeen years old like his character in this episode, but had already appeared as a series regular in both the 1986–87 ABC series *Starman* and the 1988–89 NBC sitcom *Day by Day*. In film, Christopher had played a landmark role as the voice of Prince Eric in Disney's 1989 animated *The Little Mermaid*; but his face may be best known as that of the new Greg Brady, in the 1995 *Brady Bunch Movie* and its 1996 sequel.

And prolific character actor George Wyner, who plays Dr. Lou Norgan, has been appearing on TV since the early 1970s, often as doctors, lawyers, and cops. His best known of these many roles is his five-season run as Irwin Bernstein on NBC's hit police drama *Hill Street Blues* from 1982 to 1987. And among his many film roles, George says he's most often recognized from his appearance in Chevy Chase's 1985 detective comedy *Fletch* or as Colonel Sandurz, the clumsy henchman in Mel Brooks's 1987 sci-fi spoof *Spaceballs*.

DON SEIGEL: The main story, with the coach threatening Dorothy for flunking the star athlete, came from my own experience. I never thought I was going to be a writer; I had thought I was going to be a baseball player. My high school coach in Niles, Illinois was the real Nick Odlivak, for whom I named this character. He had himself been a star athlete who had played football for the legendary coach "Bear" Bryant at the University of Kentucky. Odlivak coached high school football and baseball for decades, and everyone was afraid of him. He would do anything to win the state championship. I was a terrible student in math and science, but he would intervene with my teachers. One time, he threatened my algebra teacher: "You pass him, or I'll kick your ass!" It was so extreme. I was really embarrassed. But it worked—because somehow, despite my grades, I went downstate to play in the championships.

For the B plot, we combined stories that had been in the news, of dentists allegedly fondling their patients, with a character from my real life. My next-door neighbor at that time was a gynecologist who was always making "pussy" jokes. It was unseemly behavior you wouldn't expect of a doctor. It got me thinking: "Why do we trust doctors, really? They're human beings. What makes a woman take off her clothes in a doctor's office, when she wouldn't do it for a guy on a third date?"

JAMIE WOOTEN: You may notice that after a while, and particularly in seasons six and seven, there are a lot of weird names for the guest characters, many beginning with the letter *n*. That's because it became so difficult to get character names approved by NBC's legal department, who simply would not allow us to use anyone's name on the air if there was a living person with that name anywhere in the greater Miami area. [The showrunner] Marc Sotkin got sick of having character names not being approved, and of wasting his staff's time coming up with and submitting potential names to NBC. So he simply started changing the first letter of the last names to the letter "N." So if we wrote "Lou Morgan," he would send it in as "Lou Norgan." And of course it would be approved, because who is named Lou Norgan? The names became more and more ludicrous, but it was a game that NBC had started.

GEORGE WYNER: When you're a guest star, the best thing to do is just simply to observe and do your thing. You don't intrude into their world unless you're invited in. Well in my case on *The Golden Girls*, I was prepared to walk quietly onto the set. But Betty White was remarkable, greeting me with open arms. She literally ran over to me. I actually turned to see if there was someone behind me, but no, she was greeting *me*. She started talking about how much she loved something I'd done. She had a way of making a guest feel comfortable in her home, which is very important. When Betty White hugs you and says these wonderful things, all of a sudden you just exhale and realize you can go have some fun.

HOW DO YOU SOLVE A PROBLEM LIKE SOPHIA?

Written by: MARC CHERRY & JAMIE WOOTEN
Directed by: MATTHEW DIAMOND • *Original airdate:* NOVEMBER 10, 1990

When her best friend—albeit one we've never heard of before—Sister Agnes dies, Sophia hears God's voice at the funeral, calling her to the habit. It's apparently a vocation she had always wanted—that is, until age seventeen, when her future husband first put his hand in her blouse. Sophia somehow manages to pass her preliminary postulant's examination, and lands a spot in the convent. But when she can't give up her worldly wise-ass ways, Mother Superior (Kathleen Freeman, 1919–2001) wants her out. It's up to Dorothy to break the news, pointing out that Sophia does plenty of good works in her secular life.

Meanwhile, without permission, Blanche borrows Rose's car in order to execute what she considers a "meet cute": rear-ending prospective dates. Unfortunately this time, Blanche's victim, Mr. Arthur Nivingston (Paul Willson), sues Rose for his supposed whiplash, and so the two Girls concoct a plan to catch him on camera, getting physical in Blanche's bedroom.

◆ ◆ ◆ ◆

COMMENTARY: Kathleen Freeman, who plays Mother Superior in this episode, was a veteran character actress who might be best-known to modern TV audiences as Peg Bundy's mother on *Married with Children*, and who found one of her biggest successes just before her death in 2001, receiving a Tony nomination for her role in the Broadway version of *The Full Monty*. And if her subordinate Sister Anne looks at all familiar to you but you can't quite place her, try picturing her minus the habit and plus a hairdo that's even taller. Yes, that's none other than Lynne Stewart—Miss Yvonne from *Pee-Wee's Playhouse*!

Paul Willson, who here plays Blanche's accident "victim," appeared in the beloved cult film comedy *Office Space*, and spent four seasons on Fox's *The Garry Shandling Show*. But Paul is best known for his years as a barfly, also named Paul, on NBC's landmark sitcom *Cheers*.

JAMIE WOOTEN: Marc and I were looking for a mother/daughter story, and we thought the show hadn't yet dealt much with Dorothy and Sophia's

Catholicism. We said let's do something church oriented—Sophia? Nun? How can we make that work? It turned out to be an easy sell. The second the producers heard that pitch, they said, "Write it."

MARC CHERRY: With Kathleen Freeman, I felt like I was working with a piece of TV history. But there were so many of those on *The Golden Girls*, you got kind of jaded. One of my favorite things about doing this episode was researching it, because we met with a woman who had been married and had a family, and then became a nun at age fifty-five. She said one of the things the church did was psychological testing, so that Rorschach inkblot test in the episode is actually based on truth.

I had a joke in this episode that got rewritten—and I had loved it. In one scene, Sophia is praying, asking God what he wants from her, and what is her purpose in life. I had written that when

Dorothy enters her room, she would be behind Sophia, and would announce, "The nuns want you out." Then Sophia would reply to God, "I didn't think your voice would be that low."

The show actually nearly got sued over this episode. There had been a joke where the Mother Superior asks Sophia why she found a copy of *Dianetics* in her room. And Sophia says, "*Dianetics*? I thought it said 'Diuretics!'" The Church of Scientology threatened to sue, and Paul and Tony realized it was cheaper to remove the reference than to fight it in court.

LYNNE STEWART: It was so much fun playing a nun—and actually, every once in a while in an interview someone will recognize me from this episode, despite the habit. And that habit was much more comfortable than being dressed up in Miss Yvonne drag, with the high heels and corset and huge wig, which made me unrecognizable in a different way.

TOP:
Sophia spruces up her spare chambers with an icon of her own. BOTTOM: The convent
Mother Superior would like Sophia to leave . . . yesterday.

Photos courtesy of the EDWARD S. STEPHENSON ARCHIVE *at the* ART DIRECTORS GUILD.

MRS. GEORGE DEVEREAUX

Written by: RICHARD VACZY & TRACY GAMBLE
Directed by: MATTHEW DIAMOND • *Original airdate:* NOVEMBER 17, 1990

In "Mrs. George Devereaux," things get weird at 6151 Richmond. First, Blanche lands a secret admirer, who sends her a florist shop's worth of roses. Stranger yet, the bounty is even greater for Dorothy, who has her choice of two different famous men: Sonny Bono (1935–98) and 1970s TV heartthrob Lyle Waggoner.

After accepting a lunch date with her admirer, Blanche is stunned to learn that the attention has been coming from her supposedly dead husband, George (George Grizzard, 1928–2007), who turns out to be alive and well. After following an upset Blanche home, George explains that he staged his death nine years ago in order to evade embezzlement charges for a crime his business partner had committed. But now, not only is George back, but he also has a proposal, asking Blanche to be his wife once more.

Furious with the man, Blanche refuses his phone calls, and even sets a date with her old standby, Mel Bushman. But Rose intervenes, pointing out that most widows, like her, would do anything for a second chance with their beloved mates. And so Blanche has a talk with George, confessing to having seen other men—many, many men—in the past nine years.

Meanwhile, the two actors escalate their attempts to woo the lady Zbornak, with Sophia cheering on Team Sonny, and Rose on Team Lyle. Eventually, Dorothy picks Sonny—and Blanche wakes up, revealing that the whole episode has been another instance of her haunting, recurring dream. But this time, she tells the Girls, it was a good dream, because it ended differently: she got to hug George one last time.

◆ ◆ ◆ ◆

COMMENTARY: This episode is remembered for its campy cameos, which offset a very touching A story for Blanche. George Grizzard returns as George Devereaux, having previously played the character's twin brother, Jamie, in the fifth-season installment "That Old Feeling."

As they insult each other in their competition for Dorothy's hand, the episode's two other guest stars, Sonny Bono and Lyle Waggoner, good-naturedly play on their own images as seventies TV icons. Teamed with his wife, Cher, Sonny Bono had been a musical sensation in the

sixties, writing and performing hit singles like "I Got You Babe" and "The Beat Goes On." The two then cemented their status as pop culture icons as they starred in their own musical variety shows throughout the seventies. At the time of this episode, Sonny Bono was serving as the mayor of Palm Springs, California, an office he would hold until 1992. In 1994, he was elected to Congress, representing the state's Forty-Fourth District until his death in a skiing accident in 1998, at age sixty-two.

Tall, dark, and handsome Lyle Waggoner is beloved from two of his great TV roles, as a featured player from 1967 to 1974 on *The Carol Burnett Show*, and from 1975 to 1979 as Major Steve Trevor on *Wonder Woman*.

TRACY GAMBLE: This is my favorite episode that Richard Vaczy and I ever wrote. We dictated it, and it came in exactly right, at forty-five pages, perfect and balanced. At this point, we'd been on the writing staff longer than anybody else, but we still rarely got to do Blanche episodes; the show always seemed to need Dorothy or Rose episodes. We wanted to do something meaty and substantive for Blanche, and to show how, beneath all her sexual bravado, her husband, George, had been the only man she ever loved. And so Richard suggested, "What if George had staged his death?" We didn't want to undermine the series, though. So we decided to turn it into a dream, but we had to fool the audience. We came up with a setup I was really proud of: in the cheesecake scene, Blanche tells the women and the audience that she has a recurring dream.

BLANCHE:

"Come on, Dorothy. How much trouble can I get into in a public place?"

DOROTHY:

"How soon we forget the Greyhound terminal incident."

RICHARD VACZY: This was also my favorite episode that Tracy and I wrote. I acknowledge that dream episodes are usually cliché, but I think here the dream provides a framework for a funny Dorothy story and a Blanche story that was emotional and meaningful.

All through the week, as we negotiated with guest stars, we kept swapping names in and out: at one point, one of the guys was going to be Telly Savalas. But in the end, Sonny Bono and Lyle Waggoner were great to work with. And

because it was a dream, we were able to step outside reality. It was a tough balancing act, because the audience doesn't know it's a dream until the end. We could go a little crazy, but we also made sure to ground it in some sort of reality by saying that the guys were playing locally at the Burt Reynolds Dinner Theatre, which made it make at least a little sense.

MATTHEW DIAMOND: I found this to be a stunning episode, with an amazing concept. I salute the writers, and the actresses for playing it one hundred percent straight. It's such a sweet story, and it's written with a very light touch. Blanche isn't blown away or scared by George's return, but instead just thinks it's wonderful.

In the middle of Sonny and Lyle competing for Dorothy and all the other madness going on, the writers planted a line where Blanche says she's been having a recurring dream. It sounds like a throwaway line at the time—until the end, when you realize how well constructed the episode has been all along.

LYLE WAGGONER: When I think about this episode I get nostalgic, because Sonny Bono was there. What an interesting man he was—businessman, entrepreneur, politician. I had known him for a long time, because I had guest starred on *Sonny and Cher* a few times, which was shot on the stage right next to where I was working on *The Carol Burnett Show*.

Doing *The Golden Girls* was a different experience for me, coming from *Carol Burnett*. Both were three-camera shows in front of a live audience, but on *The Golden Girls*, they had to, but didn't like to, stop and do pickups if you made a mistake. On *Carol*, if we'd make a mistake, we'd usually just leave it in, because the audience got such a kick out of it. And I loved working with the ladies. I knew Betty, and had worked with Rue a few times on the road, and Bea on *Maude*. But I had never met Estelle, who was so cute, and so much fun. It was such a happy set, with them all making each other laugh. After all, they all had such great comedy instincts.

GIRLS JUST WANNA HAVE FUN ...BEFORE THEY DIE

Written by: GAIL PARENT & JIM VALLELY • *Directed by:* MATTHEW DIAMOND
Original airdate: NOVEMBER 24, 1990

Sophia has the hots for Tony Delvecchio (Cesar Romero, 1907–94), so she enlists Blanche's help in making her irresistible for their upcoming date. The date does go well—so well, in fact, that in a postcoital moment in bed, Sophia gets caught up in the moment and lets slip the "L word." Unfortunately, Tony's response is a little lacking: all he can manage is "I care for you." Furious, Sophia storms home, where Blanche offers advice not to divulge her feelings. But ultimately, Sophia decides to avoid playing games and instead confronts Tony, who confesses that he hasn't expressed affection for a woman since his wife died. He finally does say "I do love you," and they kiss, settling in for a pleasant evening of looking at old family photos.

In the episode's B plot, Rose receives a letter from the St. Olaf Department of Water and Coffee decreeing that in order to alleviate the town's current drought, all native St. Olafians must abstain from sex. As ridiculous as the request seems, Blanche advises her to use the situation to her advantage; the way Blanche sees it, holding out on her boyfriend Miles (Harold Gould) without explanation will help Rose score more of the control in their relationship. So Rose uses her homespun ingenuity to find ways to hold Miles's libido at bay—for example, taking him out for an evening of lesbian poetry. But when Miles ultimately breaks up with her, Rose realizes she too needs to ignore Blanche's bad advice and just tell him the whole ridiculous truth.

FOLLOWING PAGE:
Together, Marc Cherry and Jamie Wooten and the show's costume designer took their 84-year-old character and made her look like a 65-year-old drag queen.

Photo by ABC PHOTO ARCHIVES/ABC *via* GETTY IMAGES.

> *"I want to present Blanche Devereaux's latest creation. I took an eighty-four-year-old woman and made her look like a sixty-five-year-old drag queen."*
>
> —BLANCHE

COMMENTARY: This episode offers a rare glimpse into Sophia's sex life, showing her in bed with a man without that visual itself being the joke. Of course that man was Cesar Romero, otherwise known for his lavender suit and his propensity to wear waaay too much makeup. *The Golden Girls* producers had placed the actor on their casting wish list at least as early as season four. And, stripped of all the Joker's accoutrements, it turns out that his portrayal of Tony is rather endearingly shy and romantic.

Cesar Romero began his film career in the early 1930s, playing a Latin lover in musicals and romantic comedies and a tough hombre in Westerns. He appeared in the original *The Thin Man* film in 1934, and in multiple movies with Shirley Temple. His film career continued with such titles as 1960's *Ocean's Eleven* and the 1985 comedy/Western *Lust in the Dust*, starring Divine. From 1985 to 1988 he played billionaire industrialist Peter Stavros, love interest of Jane Wyman's Angela Channing, on CBS's prime time soap *Falcon Crest*. But it's of course from one TV role, as the Joker on ABC's campy 1966–68 *Batman* series, that Cesar Romero will always be remembered.

The episode also features the return of Harold Gould as Miles—something that might not have happened if other TV fortunes had gone differently. After his appearance in the latter half of season five, in the episode "Twice in a Lifetime" in February 1990, Harold began headlining the new NBC show *Singer and Sons*. The network, however, ordered just four episodes to sample the delicatessen-set sitcom—and then aired them in a deadly time slot, on four Saturday nights in June (ironically, following *The Golden Girls* and

ABOVE:
Sophia says a few words too many in bed with Tony Delvecchio (Cesar Romero).

Photo by ABC PHOTO ARCHIVES/ABC *via* GETTY IMAGES.

preempting reruns of the *Girls*' spinoff *Empty Nest*). With the summer show's quick cancellation, Harold was available once again to portray Miles, and most *Golden Girls* fans were none the wiser that he'd ever been gone.

MATTHEW DIAMOND: When Sophia comes back from her date, she tells Dorothy why she confessed her love to Tony: "I just wanted to hear someone say 'I love you' to me one more time." I thought that was wonderful, one of the great things about *The Golden Girls*. So few shows served an older generation in this kind of a complex fashion. Frequently, it's the curmudgeonly grandfather who lives downstairs, a character who's one-dimensional.

MARC CHERRY: Jim Vallely's original joke about Sophia's makeover was that Blanche took an eighty-four-year-old woman and "made her look like a sixty-five-year-old gay man," but the censor wouldn't let us say it. He thought that we were saying that all gay men are drag queens or wear dresses. Immediately, our showrunner Marc Sotkin turned to Jamie and me and said, "You're gay. Get on the phone with this guy." It was a fascinating moment for me, because I never thought of Jamie or myself as "the gay writers," but in that moment they suddenly needed a spokesman, and looked to us right away. It stunned me to realize that when they look at me they first see "gay guy," but I didn't mind. So I got on the phone and said to the censor, "I'm gay, but I am not offended by this joke." And the censor, who was not gay, was so protective that despite my arguing and arguing, we had to turn "gay man" into "drag queen"—which is still funny, in a different way.

ABOVE:
The restaurant where Blanche meets her "secret admirer," aka her dead husband George.

Photo courtesy of the EDWARD S. STEPHENSON ARCHIVE *at the* ART DIRECTORS GUILD.

EBBTIDE'S REVENGE

Written by: MARC SOTKIN • *Directed by:* MATTHEW DIAMOND

Original airdate: DECEMBER 15, 1990

As Dorothy prepares to give the eulogy for her cross-dressing brother, Phil, Sophia is intent on continuing her twenty-six-year feud with Phil's widow, Angela (Brenda Vaccaro), who is coming to Miami for the funeral. With neither of them able to understand the reason for Sophia's anger, Dorothy convinces Angela to stay for a few days to try to mend fences with her mother-in-law. But Sophia isn't budging; she insists on staying mad at Angela, as she claims, over a bounced dowry check.

Furious at the thought that Sophia had become distant with her and Phil over a forty-seven-dollar dispute, Angela writes a check to make amends. But perhaps Rose's days at the grief center truly did teach her something, because surprisingly, it is the naïve supposed nitwit who recognizes what is truly going on here: Sophia is mad at Angela because she never stopped Phil from dressing as a woman. When Rose reassures her—via a St. Olaf story, no less!—that there was no shame in loving Phil, Sophia admits that every time she saw her son, she wondered what she had done wrong. With Angela's added affirmation that her son was indeed a good man, Sophia finally lets her true feelings show. In one of the show's few downbeat ending lines, Sophia finally mourns as she cries out, "My baby is gone."

◆ ◆ ◆ ◆

ROSE:
*The point is, it was shame that kept Aunt Katrina from loving
Slow Ingmar. And it ruined her life. Don't let that happen to you, Sophia. Let go of
the shame. So what if he was different! It's okay that you loved him.*

SOPHIA:
*I did love him. He was my son, my little boy. But every time I saw him,
I always wondered what I did, what I said, when was the day that I did
whatever I did to make him the way he was?*

COMMENTARY: Isn't it interesting: a mere four seasons earlier, the unabashedly heterosexual Blanche Devereaux hadn't even known the word for "lesbian." (See season two, episode thirty, "Isn't It Romantic?") But now, as she attempts to correct Sophia, Blanche shows she is up-to-date on the difference in connotation between "gay" and "queer." One might cynically conclude that as with so many other inconsistent *Golden* details, Blanche's vocabulary varies in order to serve each individual episode's storyline. But perhaps Blanche really has learned something about the LGBT community, just one of the many benefits of having an out gay brother—whom, it turns out, she'll confront again in just two more episodes. (See episode 142, "Sisters of the Bride.")

It was writer Tom Whedon who suggested that unseen in his casket Phil should be said to be wearing a woman's teddy. "Over the years, the show had had all these cross-dressing jokes about Phil," he explains. "So I figured this was the one last cross-dressing joke we could do."

Here, playing Angela, is Brenda Vaccaro, who started her career in such classic films as *Midnight Cowboy* in 1969, 1971's *Going Home*, and *Airport '77*. She had previously been nominated for an Oscar and had won an Emmy before receiving her third Emmy nomination (of four, to date) for her work in this episode, as Outstanding Guest Performer in a Comedy Series.

JERRY PERZIGIAN: I had heard that earlier, before my time on the show, the producers had started getting phone calls from Cher, who would say, "I love *The Golden Girls*. I watch video tapes of it while I'm on my treadmill!"

ABOVE:
At her son Phil's funeral, Sophia can't bear to sit next to her estranged daughter-in-law, Angela (Brenda Vaccaro), who for years she's insultingly called "Big Sally."

Photo by ABC PHOTO ARCHIVES/ABC *via* GETTY IMAGES.

and that she wanted to be on an episode. So several times, they created roles for her, and each time, she would decline at the last minute. This character, Angela, was one of the roles they created for her, and I think the last time they tried.

MARC SOTKIN: By the time of this episode, we had pretty much used up the unseen character Phil comedically. He had served his purpose, and I was sort of tired of the cross-dressing jokes. What I found more interesting was if this guy is indeed a cross-dresser, how did that happen? Everybody can make jokes about having a cross-dresser in the family, but I'll bet it messes up the dynamic in some way. His wife obviously had found some way to live with it, and to love him and raise a family with him, and I wanted to explore how she did that.

Emotionally it turned out to be a tough week. We were talking about someone's son dying, and actors don't just turn the emotions off just because they're done rehearsing. It was particularly hard for Estelle. On that Tuesday night, she actually called me and said she didn't want

to do the episode. It took quite a while on the phone before I realized what was bothering her: early in the week, when we rehearsed them going to the church, Sophia originally went up to Phil's casket. But Estelle really had a problem with looking at her dead son and making jokes. It didn't feel honest to her—and she was absolutely right. So we changed it, and it became a better piece, and got nominated for a Writers Guild Award.

BRENDA VACCARO: I was transfixed by how brilliant Bea was, in the eulogy Dorothy gives in this episode for her brother, Phil. I couldn't take my eyes off of her. That speech, about understanding and loving one's family, was one of the most amazing things that Bea ever got to do on the show. She was such an amazing talent, and there will never be another like her. I think the reason why she could be so funny was because she was free. Bea said it the way it was, and nobody scared her about the truth. And in the end, the truth is what you have to have, and who you have to be.

ABOVE LEFT:
The cemetery where Phil is buried.
ABOVE RIGHT: Phil's funeral chapel.

Photo courtesy of the EDWARD S. STEPHENSON
ARCHIVE *at the* ART DIRECTORS GUILD.

SISTERS OF THE BRIDE

Written by: MARC CHERRY & JAMIE WOOTEN
Directed by: MATTHEW DIAMOND • *Original airdate:* JANUARY 12, 1991

Blanche's brother Clayton (Monte Markham) arrives from Atlanta with a big surprise: his fiancé, Doug (Michael Ayr). Although Blanche claims to have accepted her brother's sexual orientation, seeing him with his male lover takes her aback. When Clay overhears her obsessing about what people might say, he assures her that his and Doug's commitment to each other is all that matters, and reveals that to celebrate, they plan to marry.

The other ladies invite the men to the Volunteer Vanguard Awards banquet that they are producing, but in Blanche's eyes the event becomes their "coming-out" party. She attends anyway, in support of her friends, but annoyingly tries to interrupt Clay from introducing his fiancé around. When it becomes obvious that Blanche has yet to truly accept her brother's life, Clay gives her an ultimatum: come to terms with it, or stay out of it. Ultimately, wise Sophia counsels Blanche that everyone wants someone to be with as they grow older, with Clayton being no exception. And so, after Doug assures her that he loves her brother, Blanche finally welcomes her future brother-in-law to the family.

◆ ◆ ◆ ◆

COMMENTARY: Like earlier episode "Valentine's Day," "Sisters of the Bride" matter-of-factly presents a gay marriage more than two decades before it became a nationwide legal reality in 2015. While this episode treads some of the same ground as did Clayton's first episode, "Scared Straight," the reappearance of the character ups the ante for Blanche, illustrating how complex the act of "acceptance" can be. Blanche ended that first episode accepting the fact that her brother was different; yet old habits and fears resurface when now she is presented with an actual flesh-and-blood man who sleeps with her brother.

MARC SOTKIN: When Marc Cherry and Jamie Wooten first came in to pitch freelance stories to us, every show they pitched ended with "... and he's gay." Blanche meets a man and falls in love with him "... and he's gay." Dorothy's old teacher comes to visit "... and he's gay." But when they started working full-time on staff, they were so funny and always came up with good stories. They proved they actually could come up with other concepts. So this ended up being the first gay-themed show that they did get the okay to write. After all, they were good at coming up with gay stories, and if you can't do them on *The Golden Girls* then you can't do them.

MATTHEW DIAMOND: In the conversation where Clayton announces he's marrying Doug, Dorothy has to clarify for Rose that it's the two

men who are going to wed. And literally, the way the line is written in the script for Rose, it's just: "Oh. Oh. Oh." That may look like it's written badly, but it's actually written brilliantly, because the writers knew exactly what they were doing giving that line to Betty. She said "oh" three different ways, suggesting three different meanings. And each one of those "oh"s makes you laugh out loud. Betty always hit things like that out of the park.

MARC CHERRY: This episode had just two sentences that could be seen as political, and the line is mine when Sophia says, "Everyone just wants someone to grow old with. Doesn't Clayton deserve that, too?" To me, that was as thought provoking as I wanted to go, and as much as the episode needed.

We were so happy to write something with a gay character, because at the time it was still pretty rare to write gay stuff on TV. After it aired, a magnificent thing happened. We got a call from a gay couple who had gotten married who had said the episode's jokes had made them smile. Jamie [Wooten] and I went to their home, and they showed us a photo album of their wedding. We found out after that that one of the men was HIV-positive, and it was only about three or four years later that he passed away. I like to remember all the joy that the episode brought to them, because now they had something to relate to, like so many straight couples can when they watch TV.

JAMIE WOOTEN: The show used to get tons of letters and fan mail, and they would bring some of the interesting ones into the writers' room. After this episode aired, I was surprised we got so much hate mail. Boy, I needed to grow up fast with that stuff; I was so naïve. I saved one letter in my scrapbook, because I wanted to remember that what you do on TV can affect people, and you never know how people are going to react.

Here's the letter. On the front, it says: "The Worst Show Faggots."

"Golden girls will never be watched in our home again. It made us truly believe in abortion. Faggots are embarssemt [sic] to the world. What's funny about 2 males acting like <u>Queers</u>. Queers should be gassed and no one should suffer their shame. Those actors should be out of work. Loinest [sic] garbage yet. Faggots disease the world. So do you."

My favorite part of the whole postcard? The "America the Beautiful" stamp.

But to put it in perspective, we got far more letters about Bea's hair than any other topic, episode or controversy ever. In general, they hated it. And they would give us very specific ways how to fix it, which I thought was hilarious—and touching that they really cared. I don't think they ever let Bea know.

THERE GOES THE BRIDE
(PARTS 1 & 2)

Part 1: Teleplay by: MITCHELL HURWITZ ✦ *Part 1: Story by:* GAIL PARENT,
JIM VALLELY, & MITCHELL HURWITZ ✦ *Part 2: Written by:* GAIL PARENT
& JIM VALLELY ✦ *Directed by:* MATTHEW DIAMOND
Original airdates: FEBRUARY 2 & 9, 1991

In the first half of this two-part episode, Dorothy begins dating her ex-husband, Stan (Herb Edelman), finding that he's a changed man, a caring friend and solicitous lover. Sophia doesn't take well to the news that Dorothy might be in love with the yutz again, faking chest pains; but that doesn't stop Dorothy from going to dinner with him, where the newly wealthy Stan has a surprise hidden in her baked potato: a scalding hot engagement ring.

After Dorothy accepts, Blanche throws her a bridal shower out on the lanai—but Sophia announces her intention not to attend. Assessing the problem, Blanche urges Dorothy to set up an old-fashioned sit-down between Stan and Sophia, where he can formally ask for her daughter's hand in marriage. But the plan backfires when Sophia not only refuses her blessing, but also tells Dorothy that if she makes the mistake of remarrying a man neither of them can trust, she'll be cut out of her mother's life forever.

Meanwhile, with Miles away in Europe, Rose innocently asks his friend Ray to be her escort to the Children's Hospital fundraiser, but the man's jealous ex-wife Myra tracks them to a seafood restaurant and attacks Rose with a lobster. When Myra starts calling the house with threats, Rose reports the situation to the police—only for the responding officer to be confused for the stripper at Dorothy's shower.

In part two, Rose is truly scared after her brakes mysteriously fail, and installs a new doorbell with the sounds of angry dogs barking. Eventually, Myra (Meg Wyllie) does indeed come to the door, but only to tell Rose she's giving up fighting for Ray, and is instead checking in to a lovely retirement home called Shady Pines.

Meanwhile, Dorothy's nuptials are three days away, and Blanche begins the process of interviewing new roommates. After turning down a dozen applicants whom she deems too threateningly young and pretty, Blanche is relieved to meet Truby Steele (Debbie Reynolds), a spitfire who just buried her third rich, elderly husband.

The day before the wedding, as Dorothy and her wedding planner (Raye Birk) rehearse her march down the aisle, a confused Sophia enters and accidentally tips her hand about her plan to object during the ceremony. And so the next morning, as workers tie flowers to chairs on the lanai, Blanche and Rose intervene with the old lady, convincing her that Dorothy is a grown woman who should be allowed to make her own decisions.

Truby moves in, just in time to join Blanche, Dorothy, and Rose in a gab session about marriage as the bride puts on her makeup. Even Sophia comes around, entering the bedroom in her best blue suit, ready to offer her blessing. Dorothy is good to go, veil on her head, when Stan introduces her to his best man, real-life attorney Marvin Mitchelson (1928–2004)—who asks Dorothy to sign a prenuptial agreement. Infuriated that Stan doesn't trust her after their original thirty-eight years together, Dorothy throws out her groom, and announces to her guests that there won't be a wedding.

That night in the kitchen, the now five Golden Girls realize there's no longer any room for Truby on Richmond Street. But luckily, she'll be able to stay a few more days; because rather than letting two plane tickets to Aruba go to waste, Dorothy has resigned herself to her worst nightmare: taking her mother on her honeymoon.

❖ ❖ ❖ ❖

COMMENTARY: When it looks like Dorothy is about to remarry Stan, the Girls bring in new roommate Truby, played by Debbie Reynolds. Which presents the viewer with a problem: we don't want Dorothy to leave, but why can't Princess Leia's mom stay a while?

Guest star Debbie Reynolds is a Hollywood legend who starred in the classic musical *Singin' in the Rain* when she was just nineteen and went on to perform in MGM musicals over the next dozen years. Among her many film roles, she's known for 1957's *Tammy and the Bachelor*—for which her recording of the title song, "Tammy" hit number one on the Billboard charts—and 1964's *The Unsinkable Molly Brown*, for which

she was nominated for the Academy Award for Best Actress. Her later high-profile roles include the title character in Albert Brooks's film *Mother* in 1996, the mother of Kevin Kline in 1997's *In and Out*, and the recurring role of Bobbi Adler, the mother of Debra Messing on NBC's landmark sitcom *Will and Grace*.

MARC SOTKIN: As we were writing the sixth season, we knew it was possible that Bea might decide to leave the show. So we debated: do we start bringing aboard a "guest star of the week" to see if anybody else might be a good fit to replace her? Debbie Reynolds was the first test of that idea—and really the last test of it too. Because

ABOVE:
Blanche finds out she has a lot
in common with ill-fated housemate
Truby (Debbie Reynolds).

Photo by ABC PHOTO ARCHIVES/ABC
via GETTY IMAGES.

although Debbie was great, we knew that it really wouldn't matter who would come in to replace Bea. The chemistry just would never be as good.

DEBBIE REYNOLDS: The producers had said at the time that because Bea Arthur was looking to leave the show to go do some theater there was a possibility my character, Truby, might stay. I told them yes, I'd be interested in that. I think the other actresses were a little confused and concerned that I was coming on: what was I coming on for? I wasn't involved in any of the conversations about Bea possibly leaving, and I don't know what that was about. I do think they might have brought me on partly to make the actresses mind the bosses.

Doing the show with those brilliant ladies was a great joy. I was happy to get to work with them for the time I did. I would have worked with them anytime, anywhere. But in the end, Bea must have changed her mind, and she stayed with the show.

Even today, I have people come up to me and ask, "Why didn't you stay?" I tell them that the show was so wonderful and funny without me that although I would have loved to have stayed I wasn't needed.

MILES TO GO

Written by: DON SEIGEL & JERRY PERZIGIAN
Directed by: MATTHEW DIAMOND • *Original airdate:* JANUARY 19, 1991

As dinner winds down at Miles's place, Sophia turns on the news just in time to catch a report about the demise of mobster Mickey "the Cheeseman" Moran. Shortly afterward, Miles is brimming with exciting yet confusing news. The man heretofore known as Miles Webber, college professor, is actually Chicago accountant Nicholas Carbone; the Cheeseman was his biggest client—that is, until Carbone agreed to turn state's evidence against the mafia kingpin. Later, when the Cheeseman escaped police custody, the informant had no choice but to enter the Witness Protection Program, bringing him to Miami and to Rose's life.

The naïve Minnesotan is understandably overwhelmed. But the next night, as she sees that Miles / Nick is still the same guy as ever, Rose agrees to accompany him on a three-month trip back to Chicago. Before she can pack her bags, a radio report reveals that the Cheeseman has actually faked his death. Now, a frantic Miles explains, in order for them to remain together, Rose will have to join him in witness protection, assuming a new identity. When she realizes that would mean severing ties with her family, and of course the Girls, Rose has to make the tough choice to part ways with her beloved for the foreseeable future.

Meanwhile, Sophia is ecstatic when Gladys Goldfine invites her to a Tony Bennett concert—but is then infuriated when Gladys rescinds the ticket in order to bring a date. As angry Sicilians are wont to do, Sophia puts a curse on her former friend, but relents when Gladys (Mary Gillis) comes over with an apology and the two tickets—to see Tony Martin.

◆ ◆ ◆ ◆

COMMENTARY: This episode adds a twist to the ongoing love story of Rose and Miles, setting up an obstacle that the couple would overcome just a few weeks later, in the episode "Witness." And although we find out here that "Miles" is not a real English professor, the man has definitely done his homework, as he decides to cook dinner in commemoration of the 117th anniversary of the birth of the American poet Robert Frost. (And although this episode aired in January 1991, the setting on Frost's birthday means that the action therein begins on March 26 of that year.)

In keeping with this literary theme, Miles punctuates his sad parting with Rose by suggesting she read the poem on page seventy-three of his poetry book. It's one of the rare times that *The Golden Girls* ends not with a comic "button," or final joke, but a bittersweet emotional moment. Miles must be reading an abridged text, however, because when Rose recites the final stanza of Frost's 1913 "Reluctance," she leaves out the middle two lines:

> Ah, when to the heart of man
> Was it ever less than a treason
> To go with the drift of things,
> To yield with a grace to reason,
> And bow and accept the end
> Of a love or a season?

In other noteworthy news, in this episode we finally meet Sophia's much-talked-about friend Gladys Goldfine, a woman in her eighties even though the actress Mary Gillis was at the time only fifty years old. A longtime character actress on TV and in film, Mary boasts a long resume that includes a regular role on Susan Harris's short-lived 1991 soap opera spoof *Good and Evil*, and a recent recurring run in 2011–12 as *Glee* teacher Mrs. Hagberg.

tion to any TV work, and I had to always try to mix in theater and film work at the same time. I always thought the Miles character could come to an end someday, so when I heard about the witness protection program, I thought, "Oh well, bye-bye!"

DON SEIGEL: Sometimes, a writer will just say something offhandedly funny in the writers' room. And if everybody laughs, it's in. So the witness protection program thing became a storyline, even though it's way over the top. *The Golden Girls* writers' room in those later years was really a political place, and there were factions: one faction liked harder and more surreal jokes, and I think that's what prevailed here.

RICHARD VACZY: [My former writing partner] Tracy Gamble is such a good writer—but I have to say the whole witness protection program thing was his idea. Afterward, I took him behind closed doors and said, "What have you done! Do you know what these crazy bastards are going to do with that!" If you think Bea Arthur reacts well, you should have seen my reaction when many of the other writers in the room had responded, "Hey, yeah, that's great!" Are you kidding me! The one good thing was that late in the series we were looking for stories, and doing this gave us a chance to bring Harold Gould back a few more times. But I still felt bad that we gave Harold all this ridiculous witness protection stuff to do.

TRACY GAMBLE: I certainly was "pro" on the subject matter, and the story arc was great, culminating in a hilarious episode [season six, "Witness"] written by a young Mitchell Hurwitz, wherein Miles is "hiding out" à la Harrison Ford in *Witness*, in an Amish community.

HAROLD GOULD: I thought the witness protection storyline was a little extreme, but at the same time I was okay with it, because I was doing a lot of other things. Every year, I would try to do a play in addi-

OPPOSITE:
Rose with Samuel Plankmaker, a.k.a. Miles Webber, a.k.a. Nicholas Carbone (Harold Gould) in "Witness."

Photo by ABC PHOTO ARCHIVES/ABC *via* GETTY IMAGES.

BETTY WHITE: Actually, I found this story fascinating because—dumb me—I hadn't known there was such a thing as witness protection, where the person took on a whole other identity!

MELODRAMA

Written by: ROBERT SPINA   ◆   Directed by: MATTHEW DIAMOND
Original airdate: FEBRUARY 16, 1991

After Blanche's date cancels, she rings up her steady backup, Mel Bushman (Alan King, 1927–2004), but becomes concerned when she can't reach him. Scared that the Zipper King may have met his maker, Blanche brings the Girls to his apartment, where weeks' worth of newspapers are piled on the doorstep. Fortunately, it turns out Mel has merely been away on a long vacation. But, realizing she's taken him for granted for years, Blanche rushes into Mel's arms and declares her love.

However, it turns out now that commitment is on the table, the couple's magic is gone. Mel longs for the days when he was merely Blanche's standby, ready with takeout, a shoulder to cry on, and the rallying call of "Bushman awaits!" As Blanche agrees that she rushed their relationship, the two agree to revert to being what would one day come to be called "friends with benefits."

Meanwhile, bored with her job as a TV consumer advocate's assistant, Rose applies for an open slot at the station as a weekend news reporter. As her audition, she's assigned to cover the Thirteenth Annual Miami Pet Dog Expo. But on the big day, just as Rose goes on camera, armed robbers burst into the convention hall, demanding wallets and jewelry. Still, courageous Rose keeps rolling—but misses the opportunity to impress when she remains focused solely on the adorable doggies, ignoring the robbery completely.

◆ ◆ ◆ ◆

COMMENTARY: "Bushman awaits!"—and for quite a while, we'd waited to see him. Blanche's long-standing standby date had often been mentioned throughout the series; now, in season six, the man Blanche has described as "Fred Flintstone with a better car" finally appears in the flesh.

Alan King began his career performing in the "Borscht Belt" club circuit of New York's Catskill Mountains. From television's earliest days, the comedian appeared on myriad variety and game shows, filling in last-minute for cancelled guests on *The Ed Sullivan Show* and eventually becoming a regular guest host on *The Tonight Show with Johnny Carson*. He hosted the Oscars telecast in 1972, and as part of his position as the Abbot of the New York Friars' Club, he would go on to preside over that organization's series of televised celebrity roasts throughout the 1990s. Prior to this role on *The Golden Girls*, Alan had appeared on TV almost exclusively as himself; but after this

turn as Mel Bushman, he took on several additional small-screen acting roles—always as seemingly Jewish characters, a few of them rabbis, and on *Murphy Brown*, as God.

ROBERT SPINA: As the show's script coordinator, I eventually got the chance to pitch stories to the producers, thanks largely to Terry Hughes, and I started by picking up on some of the show's loose threads, which can make for really satisfying episodes. For the first episode I got to write, "If At Last You Do Succeed," earlier in season six, I had picked up the Stan storyline again and given it a new beat by having him become a financial success at last in the novelty business. For this episode, I remembered the name of Blanche's long-standing date, Mel Bushman. He was seemingly always there for her—but what would happen if he didn't show?

A number of people were very generous to me in saying that I had captured Alan King's rhythm. But there's something about a comic who writes his own material; he believes his voice is unique, and doesn't like when some-

one else tries to capture it. It scares him, almost like how some native peoples don't like to have their photographs taken because they say it captures a piece of their souls. Alan fought the material for a bit during rehearsal. But just as had happened when, before this, I'd worked with Jackie Mason on the pilot for [short-lived sitcom] *Chicken Soup*, he would change two words, and then feel like he'd made things right. And I was proud that Mel's speech—"Bushman awaits!"—ended up surviving almost intact from my very first draft.

RUE McCLANAHAN: I thought casting Alan King as Mel Bushman was a stroke of genius. That was hilarious. Mel had always been her standby when she didn't have a man. There could never be anything serious there, but I think Blanche was in desperation here, panicking about not having a man in her life. If she just could have seen Mel Bushman a little more clearly, she would have realized that not having a man in her life would be better than having him in any serious way.

ABOVE:
Worrisome newspapers accumulate on Mel's front porch.

Photo courtesy of the EDWARD S. STEPHENSON ARCHIVE *at the* ART DIRECTORS GUILD.

WITNESS

Written by: MITCHELL HURWITZ • *Directed by:* ZANE BUZBY

Original airdate: MARCH 9, 1991

In Miles's absence, Rose begins getting serious with her new boyfriend, Karl (Barney Martin, 1923–2005). Seemingly sizing up his competition, Karl has questions about Miles that Rose is unable to answer. And it turns out, Miles is not completely out of the picture after all; one night, just after Rose bids good night to her new beau, Miles (Harold Gould) bursts through the door from the lanai, dressed in his new Witness Protection Program disguise as Amish farmer Samuel Plankmaker.

But far from being happy about her boyfriend's return, Rose is now more confused than ever. A jealous Miles realizes that Rose is seeing someone new; but his bigger problem is that Rose has unknowingly blabbed his whereabouts to Karl, a.k.a. mob hit man Mickey "the Cheeseman" Moran.

"Karl" returns to the Girls' living room with his gun, and as he debates how to dispose of not only Miles but also the Girls as witnesses, blind old Sophia, missing her glasses, ignores his warning and answers the door. It's next-door neighbor and police officer Barbara Weston (Kristy McNichol), who has tracked down the glasses, their thief being her own dog, Dreyfuss. Barbara pulls out her own gun and apprehends the Cheeseman, thus freeing Miles from his life of fear and enabling his reunion with Rose.

Meanwhile, as Blanche prepares to present her family tree at the banquet celebrating her initiation into the Daughters of the Old South, she's dismayed at what Dorothy finds among her paperwork. It turns out that in 1860, Blanche's great-granddaddy Walter Roquet married a woman from just a ways outside Georgia—namely, Buffalo, New York. Dorothy enjoys teasing Blanche about her fractional Yankee heritage, adding, "Did I mention her last name was Feldman?"

Blanche sets out simply to lie to the club's membership committee about her one-eighth Northern roots. But at the ceremony, she opts for a new strategy instead, sounding a call for tolerance and acceptance. Blackballed nonetheless, the newly Jewish Blanche makes a last-ditch entreaty, launching into her own rendition of Shylock's speech from Shakespeare's *The Merchant of Venice*: "Hath not a Yankee eyes? Hath not a Yankee hands?" But even as she makes her plea, Blanche realizes that perhaps it's the many diverse elements within her heritage that make her special, and uniquely American, more than would membership in any antiquated society.

◆ ◆ ◆ ◆

COMMENTARY: In this episode, Kristy McNichol appears as Barbara Weston, her character from *Golden Girls* spinoff *Empty Nest*. (Two later *Golden Girls* episodes also feature Dinah Manoff—Marty from the movie *Grease*—playing her *Nest* role of Barbara's sister, Carol.)

This episode is noteworthy for two additional reasons. First, along with earlier season 6 episode "Zborn Again," it marks the first solo episodic writing assignment for Mitchell Hurwitz, who was originally being groomed by Witt/Thomas as an executive before proving his true talent lay more on the creative side.

Mitch went on to write for a variety of sitcoms before creating the cult hit *Arrested Development*, for which he has won three Emmy Awards to date.

The episode also was the first installment of *The Golden Girls* to be directed by a woman. Zane Buzby had appeared in the film comedies *Oh, God!*, *Up in Smoke*, *Americathon*, and *This Is Spinal Tap*, and had written for the sitcom *Fernwood 2 Night* before moving behind the camera. She helmed the 1986 feature film *Last Resort* and episodes of eighties series like *Married with Children*, *Newhart*, and *My Two Dads* before landing a regular directing gig on

OPPOSITE:
The banquet hall for the Daughters of the Old South.

Photo courtesy of the EDWARD S. STEPHENSON ARCHIVE *at the* ART DIRECTORS GUILD.

Witt/Thomas's sitcom *Blossom*. At this point in *The Golden Girls*' sixth season, the show's producers had begun auditioning new directors to replace the departing Terry Hughes, and were able to bring Zane on board during a fortuitously timed *Blossom* hiatus. Afterward, unfortunately, with her commitment to the Mayim Bialik comedy, Zane was unable ever to schedule a return to the *Girls*. But her presence on the set was still a welcomed change, and something for which Bea Arthur expressed her appreciation.

MITCHELL HURWITZ: Typically, crossovers between the Witt/Thomas shows meant that the *Golden Girls* actors would go to support *Empty Nest* or *Nurses* but not the reverse, because it's not like *The Golden Girls* needed the cachet of having an *Empty Nest* actor show up. But here, this crossover really arose from a need in the story. We had painted ourselves into a corner: now the guy's got a gun, and how do we end this? Well, if you believe the logic of the shows, the Girls have a cop next door. So we had Barbara, the *Empty Nest* neighbor, pulling her own gun on the Cheeseman. It solved the problem, but I was really afraid it was never going to look good on a three-walled sitcom set. Luckily, the show was very forgiving of moments like that.

ZANE BUZBY: Tony Thomas came to me and asked me if I'd like to do *The Golden Girls*. Well of course I'd like to do *The Golden Girls*! I remember that he told me, speaking about the cast, "Zane, you're going to love this, because these are four horses who can really run the race." And boy was he right. Usually, when you direct a show that's been on forever, it's already such a well-oiled machine that you just get it done in the way that they're used to. But with this cast, once they could see that I was funny, directing the episode became a wonderful creative experience as well.

The women were amazing, Bea Arthur in particular. She

was a talent from another solar system, so fast and facile with comedy that you could literally just shoot her performance at the table read. Even though it was the first time she had ever read the script aloud, it was as if she had rehearsed it all week. And the cast had a great dynamic between them. True, Bea was a bit impatient if everyone else wasn't at performance level in the first five minutes, because she was so fast. And Betty White was right there with her. Estelle Getty was fabulous but liked to work things through and to run her lines. So Rue McClanahan took her under her wing, and gently reviewed her blocking with her. The ladies were always so supportive of each other.

Many years after *The Golden Girls*, I went to see Bea Arthur's one-woman show in Hollywood, and afterward I went backstage. Bea told me she wished I had done more episodes of the show, because "it was great having a dame at the helm." I loved that she used that word.

WHAT A DIFFERENCE A DATE MAKES

Written by: MARC CHERRY & JAMIE WOOTEN • Directed by: LEX PASSARIS
Original airdate: MARCH 23, 1991

When Dorothy gets a call from John Neretti (Hal Linden), the guy who humiliated her by standing her up for her senior prom, she agrees to see him in order to give him a piece of her mind. But not only is Dorothy unable to follow through on her planned revenge, but she soon finds herself falling for him.

John asks Dorothy for a second date during his visit, but that Friday happens to be prom night at the school where Dorothy teaches. Committed to chaperoning the dance, Dorothy agrees to invite John as her date, but reminds him that this time, he'd better show up. That's when John reveals that he did actually show up that night forty years ago, but, objecting to his attire, Sophia slammed the door in his face.

Later, at home, Dorothy confronts her mother, who admits that that fateful night, she had indeed told John to come back when he was suitably dressed—but the boy never did. Furious, Dorothy accuses her mother of sabotaging her young life, robbing her of self-esteem, and ultimately leading her into an unhappy marriage with Stan. But as she and John come home from their long-delayed prom date, he reveals that he's always wanted to thank Mrs. Petrillo, whose dressing down ended up turning his own life around. Sophia, he points out, had merely been trying to protect her daughter, as she lectured him that her little girl deserved better than a hoodlum with attitude. And so Dorothy forgives Sophia, the two of them settling into the couch to dish the details of this prom night—because at any age, it's still comforting to confide in one's mother.

Meanwhile, Blanche diets in preparation for her annual anniversary ritual of fitting into her wedding dress. After a rough few days of shakes and "sensible" five-ounce meals, she struts into the living room, triumphantly wearing her wedding ensemble. As requested, Rose snaps a shot of Blanche in the bright-red number—and then takes another one as Blanche walks away, unaware that she's burst through the gown's back zipper.

◆ ◆ ◆ ◆

COMMENTARY: Never mind her mother's meddling—doesn't Dorothy notice that now her father is interloping on her date? If the medieval restaurant waiter Don the Fool looks familiar, it's because he's played by Sid Melton, who had already been established as Sal Petrillo, Dorothy's dad. As the show's then-script coordinator Robert Spina explains, "Witt/Thomas was very much like a family. Everyone on the show used to call Sid Melton 'Uncle Sid,' because Tony Thomas did. So *The Golden Girls* producers went out of their way, at least once a season, to work Sid into an episode."

MARC CHERRY: Jamie and I had come up with the idea that it would turn out to have been Sophia's fault that Dorothy got stood up for the prom. But the script had some problems. First, we'd written that for their first date, John would take Dorothy to a place with a karaoke machine. It would be while they were onstage together that Dorothy would find out that Sophia had been the cause of her heartbreak regarding the prom—and so she would end up being really pissed off while she and John were singing. But right after we handed in our script, *Cheers* did a karaoke episode. And as I suspected might happen, Marc Sotkin said we'd have to change ours.

MARC SOTKIN: One of the thrills of working on *The Golden Girls* was getting to work with people you grew up watching. Cesar Romero. Debbie Reynolds. George Burns on *Golden Palace*. I was a big *Barney Miller* fan, and so it was great getting to work with Hal Linden. He was a great guest star, and just as importantly, it was a relatively easy week on the set because Bea was happy; she was kissing Hal Linden.

ABOVE:
After *Cheers* did its karaoke episode, John Neretti brought Dorothy to this medieval-themed restaurant. LEFT: Blanche, triumphant in her red wedding dress. FOLLOWING PAGES: Dorothy and John Neretti (Hal Linden) deal with an overzealous and yet strangely familiar waiter (Sid Melton).

Photo courtesy of the EDWARD S. STEPHENSON ARCHIVE at the ART DIRECTORS GUILD. Photos by ABC PHOTO ARCHIVES/ABC via GETTY IMAGES.

HENNY PENNY— STRAIGHT, NO CHASER

Written by: TOM WHEDON • *Directed by:* JUDY PIOLI
Original airdate: MAY 4, 1991

As Dorothy stages a grade school production of *Henny Penny* as part of a program to encourage kids to read, the Girls become last-minute replacements for kiddie cast members quarantined with measles. Where can we find an adult, Dorothy's director Frank Nann (George Hearn) wonders, with the childlike innocence to play the title role? Enter Rose Nylund; and soon Blanche is (type)cast as Goosey Loosey, Dorothy becomes Turkey Lurkey, and Nann himself essays the villainous role of Foxy Loxy. Perhaps a public appearance like this is just what Blanche needs—because, due to a malicious ex who works for the newspaper, an erroneous obit has convinced Miami that she died—at the advanced age of sixty-eight, no less.

◆ ◆ ◆ ◆

COMMENTARY: Theater lovers take notice: Foxy Loxy's meat-eating grin might look familiar—and so might all the feathery costumes. George Hearn played the butchering barber *Sweeney Todd* on Broadway in 1979–80, and originated the role of Albin in the original 1983 production of *La Cage aux Folles*.

This episode is also notable for a behind-the-scenes fact: for this series about four females this episode was one of only two to have been directed by a woman. Multihyphenate Judy Pioli had started her career as an improv performer and actress, and then became a writer/producer for such comedies as *Laverne & Shirley* and *Charles in Charge* before moving on to directing. Judy's former *Laverne & Shirley* colleague Marc Sotkin, now the *Golden Girls* showrunner, recommended her for the job of helming this 1991

episode—a noteworthy gig, considering that even now, nearly thirty years later, female sitcom directors are still rare birds.

TOM WHEDON: I had worked on another Witt/Thomas show, *It's a Living*, and in 1987 I'd written an episode where one of the waitresses on the show, Dot, was directing a production of *Little Red Riding Hood*—and when her cast of kids got sick, all her adult coworkers had to step in and perform. The *Golden Girls* producers wanted a musical episode. Because I'd done the musical episode on *It's a Living*, they asked me to do it.

The difficulty in doing that is that you don't want to repeat yourself, and so I had to figure out how to do the *Golden Girls* musical in a new way. I chose *Henny Penny* as the theme for the musical within the episode because I figured out that you could tell that whole story as songs. And the songs in the *Henny Penny* show that the Girls perform are original, for which I wrote the lyrics.

PHILIP JAYSON LASKER: I thought it was wonderful that we could do something like this. *The Golden Girls* was really flexible in terms of

what it could hold. You could get serious and deal with real issues, or you could have Rue McClanahan in a chicken suit. Not many comedies could accommodate all of that. That's one of the things that made the show fun for the writers.

JUDY PIOLI ASKINS: When I give notes to an actor, I typically walk up and whisper in his or her ear, "Why don't we try this?" On my first day, I noticed there was a little bit of business that Bea did one way in rehearsal, and then differently later in the run-through. I walked up to her and said softly, "Bea, I think the reason it didn't work as well that time was . . ." Well, as soon as I'd gotten three words out, Bea said, "You've got to speak up. I can't hear you!" I learned there didn't need to be any whispering on that set, which made things so much easier. And Bea and I really connected, because I'm six feet tall. We admired

each other's clothing, and compared notes: where did you get those shoes?

On tape night, the producers and director would give the actors notes and changes to the script at dinnertime, between the dress show, which we filmed, and the taping of the air show. I found Betty really cute how she handled the notes. She'd pull up a chair right in front of the producers' table, and sit with her notebook and pencil in her lap. Once, when we were toward the end of the stage where we had the set for the theater, Betty came up and put her arm in mine, and said, "You poor thing! The week you come to direct, we've got chicken outfits and dance numbers!" So I asked her: "Betty, do you know what show I've been directing for two and a half seasons? *Perfect Strangers!*" And we just laughed, because that show had chicken suits every week—metaphorically, if not literally.

RUE McCLANAHAN: There were about five episodes where we all dressed in costumes—this one, plus once we were cats, once we were nuns, once we were pregnant in a fantasy sequence, and once we were all dressed as male members of a country club. That was a real boon having Judy Evans as our costume designer; she was so artistic. I always got the producers to make me up a little photograph of each show with us in costume, and I put them up on the wall so that I'd have Betty and me in those getups, side by side. I just thought it was funny, both of us dressed as those things, like here I'm a goose and she's Chicken Little. And I thought Bea looked amazing as Turkey Lurkey.

ABOVE:
The Girls put on a play, with Dorothy's director friend Frank Nann (George Hearn) as Foxy Loxy.

Photo by ABC PHOTO ARCHIVES/ABC *via* GETTY IMAGES.

◆ EPISODE 156 ◆

WHERE'S CHARLIE?

Written by: GAIL PARENT & JIM VALLELY   ◆   *Directed by:* LEX PASSARIS
Original airdate: OCTOBER 19, 1991

Rose is initially thrilled to receive a ring—albeit of the non-engagement variety—from Miles to solidify their relationship. But after peering at the configuration of canta- loupe in a fruit salad in the fridge, the naïve St. Olafian becomes convinced it's a sign: her late husband, Charlie, is apparently as disapproving of her commitment to Miles as he was of cubed melon. A naughty Sophia makes things way worse by pretending to channel Charlie's spirit and ordering Rose to return the ring. To Sophia's surprise, Rose does; and it's up to Dorothy to force her meddling mother to confess to her particularly cruel joke—after all, Shady Pines, she informs her mother, is under new management: Germans—so that Rose and Miles can reconcile.

Meanwhile, Blanche begins coaching her latest amour, Stevie, in softball; and in an homage to the 1988 film *Bull Durham*, she provides him with one of her black camisoles to wear under his uniform for inspiration. Unfortunately, the plan tempo- rarily backfires, as, while on their date at the batting cages, Stevie alerts Blanche he's been recruited by a team in Tokyo. Ultimately, the softball star opts to stay in the US of A with Blanche—while sporting a newfound look: a blue satin dress, heels, string of pearls, and matching earrings. Blanche breaks up with Stevie—not because of the drag, she insists, but because he had been prepared to leave her. But as she kicks him out the door, she admits the truth to her trusted Girls: "It *was* the dress."

COMMENTARY: When sitcoms resort to ripping off the plots of recent hit movies, it's often a sign that the show's writers are running out of ideas. Take, for example, an ill-conceived episode of *Alice* during that show's sixth season in 1981, where the three waitresses, inspired by the plot of *9 to 5*, tie up their boss, Mel, in the storeroom of his eponymous diner.

Because this episode pops up so late in the *Girls* run, it, too, might seem born of writerly desperation. But Blanche Devereaux—and more specifically, Rue McClanahan—makes it work. Guest star Tim Thomerson was an inspired casting choice; not only was he tall enough to step into *Bull Durham* star Tim Robbins's baseball uniform, but he had also already shown an ability to play both hypermacho and effeminate, as the "transmute" character Gene/Jean on NBC's short-lived 1977–78 space-travel spoof *Quark*.

RUE McCLANAHAN: I liked doing this takeoff on *Bull Durham*, because I found the comedy in it very funny. They dressed me the way Susan Sarandon had been dressed in the movie, with her off-the-shoulder sweater. The problem is I had never been any good at softball. So all week, I practiced hitting with our stage manager Kent Zbornak—because I was going to have to tape this scene, and make it look like I hit what could be a home run. I was going to have to swing convincingly, and really whack that thing. And it turns out I did hit the damn thing, on the very first take. I didn't hit it very hard;

I think it would have been only a base hit. But that was a real victory for me.

TIM THOMERSON: I've had a lot of people come up to me and say, "Hey man, were you that guy in the dress on *The Golden Girls*?" And I think that's pretty cool, because it was a really funny episode.

Most baseball players are typically macho guys, so I thought that when this guy Stevie puts the dress on, it would be that much funnier if he still keeps that straight guy manliness, swaggering his way through the door. He's still walking like he's in the batting cages, and not swishing it up. But there was one more feminine gesture I decided to do, and even my wife, who's in casting, pointed it out: clutching my chest with a sigh. I felt like that really sold it.

The interesting thing for me about the table read of this episode was that in this first performance of that week's show, nobody was really that funny yet. I did notice that the women were all such pros, and they had this routine down so perfectly. They just rehearsed, and worked hard all week, and then by the end of course all four of them were hilarious.

I had most of my scenes with Rue McClanahan. I rehearsed, working out the beats with her, and of course she was terrific. Then came time for the tape night. As I waited backstage to make my entrance at the end, suited up in a gown and earrings and those fucking heels—I don't know how women do it!—I walked past Betty, who was sitting there, knitting. She did a perfect take, glancing up at me, and said, "You're the ugliest woman I've ever seen!"

That helped loosen me up. But what really did it was when I entered the scene: I ring the doorbell, and Bea answers the door. Bea was kind of a tough person to make laugh. But the moment she opened the door and got a look at me, she would lose it, every time. Bea didn't break that often, so I knew it meant that the gag was working. And then of course it was infectious, and I'd start laughing too. It took maybe four takes to get it right, but it was great, because our laughing really loosened up the audience, too. And then that frees you up as an actor, because now you've broken that fourth wall, and everybody's in on the gag together.

"Blanche, you really know how to mold a man. He comes in Steve, and goes out Eydie!"

—DOROTHY

BEAUTY AND THE BEAST

Written by: MARC CHERRY & JAMIE WOOTEN ◆ *Directed by:* LEX PASSARIS
Original airdate: OCTOBER 5, 1991

Having sprained both ankles, Sophia is temporarily wheelchair bound, prompting Dorothy to hire a nurse. And while Sophia is initially horrified to recognize Mildred DeFarge (Edie McClurg) from their prior acquaintance at Shady Pines, she soon warms to the woman's pampering, and to her bullying of the other Girls on Sophia's behalf. When Dorothy and Rose attempt to fire Nurse DeFarge, Sophia suffers a conveniently timed leg cramp, and the nurse refuses to leave until her charge is literally back on her feet. Only when Sophia gets caught not just out of her chair but dancing around the living room does the truth come out, and Nurse DeFarge decamp to aid some other patient in need.

Meanwhile, Blanche coaxes her visiting granddaughter Melissa (Alisan Porter) into forgoing fun like the circus in order to compete in the Little Miss Miami pageant. Becoming a monstrous stage grandmother, Blanche doesn't notice that Melissa is miserable until the young girl freezes during her talent competition performance of "Put on a Happy Face." In the end, Blanche recognizes shadows of her strained relationship with Melissa's mother, Janet, and apologizes to the girl—but only after bringing the number home herself onstage, complete with high kicks and fabulous feather boa flourishes.

◆ ◆ ◆ ◆

COMMENTARY: She was *The Hogan Family*'s perky neighbor Mrs. Poole, and *Ferris Bueller*'s bubbleheaded school secretary. Now, Edie McClurg turns up for a fun guest spot as imposing Nurse DeFarge—named for the villainous knitter in Charles Dickens's *A Tale of Two Cities*. Although scary to Sophia at first, she soon muscles in on the other Girls' turf, upsetting especially Dorothy as she gains permission to call her patient Ma.

Watch this episode closely for a true *Golden Girls* blooper that made it onto the screen. In the scene where Nurse DeFarge and Sophia barge into the living room and wrest control of the remote, that's probably real annoyance on the Girls' faces—and in Betty's case, real pain. As Edie explains on the next page , she accidentally pushed a wheelchair right over Betty's foot—and if you watch Betty closely, you'll see that's the take the producers opted to use.

MARC CHERRY: We had Rose, Blanche, and Dorothy about to watch *The Nun's Story*, because that's one of my favorite movies. But ever since, I've felt bad that when Nurse DeFarge says,

"She leaves the convent in the end," I'm ruining the movie for people.

There were two funny stories I remember from the production of this episode. The first one was that Estelle just couldn't handle the wheelchair. She had the worst time with it, and couldn't maneuver it very fast. She had an entrance where she was supposed to come in and say her line, but we ended up waiting too long for her to get there to say it. So we ended up having one of the stage-hands push her in, and here comes this old woman,

flying into the room, clearly not of her own power. Luckily, once she hit the carpet, the chair slowed itself down. But if you look closely at it, it looks ridiculous, and that made all of the writers laugh.

The second story is that one of our producers, Tracy Gamble, had two lovely daughters, Bridget and Carrie, and he had always wanted to get them on the show as extras. So here was the chance, as we had this Little Miss Miami pageant. The producers put Tracy's daughters in cute little costumes, and put them in the scene. But then the joke of the scene is how Blanche insults all the other contestants: "Ugly!" "No charisma!" "There's a gym teacher waiting to happen!" We all had to laugh, because Tracy finally got his daughters on TV, only for them to be dissed by Rue McClanahan.

JAMIE WOOTEN: Marc and I were devoted fans of *The Hogan Family*. We even wrote a spec script of the show when we were starting out. That's one of the reasons we begged them to hire Edie McClurg—and when they did, there was no audition. They just called to offer the job, which *The Golden Girls* hardly ever did. And we weren't disappointed, because Edie was great. But there was that awkward moment where she ran over Betty's foot with the wheelchair, and it got tense onstage. That part *was* disappointing, because we wanted everyone to be friends and it was not to be.

EDIE McCLURG: *The Golden Girls* was an iconic show, and I loved watching it. I always thought, "I'd like to be on that show." And then I was very surprised when I finally got to do it! Those women were just icons to me.

I always had loved Betty White so much—we'd done quite a few benefits together—and so doing the show with her I was pleased as punch. It was so much fun to watch those four great women working. And especially at their ages. Standing backstage on rehearsal days, I would love to eavesdrop on them gossiping amongst themselves. I wouldn't stand next to them, but I would put my ear out, just wanting to hear how they talked to one another. I could tell that Bea was very down, because one of her dogs was very ill.

The rehearsal days were on the set, but without the camera. Bea was sour. She didn't speak to me, and she didn't smile. She wouldn't even look at me. But Betty and Rue were as sweet as could be, and Estelle too, so I thought, "This is going to be okay."

Then, on the third day, it was camera-blocking day. When I came in to the set, Bea turned around and was just as nice as could be. She was smiling at me for the first time in three days, and it was

such a difference she actually frightened me. When I remarked to Betty how all of a sudden Bea had changed, Betty pointed out that this was the first day that we were on camera, with a feed going up to the producers' office so they could see what they needed to rewrite or change. This was the first time they were watching us.

Estelle was so tiny that when they tried to put her in a regular wheelchair, she couldn't control it at all. So they got a kids' wheelchair, and she fit in it just fine. On the set, there wasn't much room between the couch, where three of the women would sit, and the big square coffee table. During rehearsal, they would move the

table farther from the couch, so I could fit through, pushing Estelle in the wheelchair.

But on the night of the taping, as I was ready to make my entrance I noticed—they haven't moved the table! I thought, "What am I supposed to do? There's a live audience!" So I tried to fit in between there—and ended up running right over Betty's foot. It really hurt her, but she improvised by picking up her foot and panto-miming saying "Ow!" really big, so that they could still use the take. After that, they moved the table, but I was mortified. I hadn't had that much to do in the episode, and this had been one of my important scenes.

MOTHER LOAD

Written by: DON SEIGEL & JERRY PERZIGIAN ◆ Directed by: LEX PASSARIS
Original airdate: OCTOBER 26, 1991

When Rose mistakenly takes home her coworker Jerry Kennedy's (Peter Graves, 1926–2010) date book, it's a boon for Blanche, who scores a date with the handsome anchorman. The rendezvous is romantic—that is until Jerry's mother, Millicent (Meg Wyllie, 1917–2002), tails Blanche home in order to scare her off. Ultimately, at Blanche's urging, Jerry stands up to overbearing mama in the Girls' living room, asserting his right to love whichever woman he chooses; unfortunately for Blanche, that woman is someone named Christina.

Meanwhile, Dorothy's ex-husband, Stan (Herb Edelman), asks her to join him in a session with his psychiatrist, in order to help him move on with his life. But the moment the two sit down in the office of Dr. Richard Halperin (Steve Landesberg, 1936–2010), Stan professes his love for his "mama bear"—who turns out to be Sophia, a stand-in for his own departed mother with whom he had been unable to make peace.

Lured to their next session with the promise of going to Disney World, Sophia initially scoffs at the thought of loving the yutz who knocked up her daughter, sponged off her husband, and cheated throughout thirty-eight years of marriage. But when she remembers the happy moment at the hospital, glimpsing her grandson Michael for the first time through the nursery window, she musters enough loving memories to give the man what he needs. A jubilant Stan announces a Chinese feast to celebrate—for two; Dorothy is not invited.

◆ ◆ ◆ ◆

COMMENTARY: For an ex-husband, that Stanley Zbornak sure does find ways to weasel back into Dorothy's life—and the *Golden Girls* writers sure do find ways time and again to bring audience favorite Herb Edelman back into the house on Richmond Street.

But Herb isn't the only beloved actor visiting the Girls this week. Playing Blanche's latest paramour, Jerry Kennedy, is silver-haired guest star Peter Graves, instantly recognizable from his role as elite forces leader Jim Phelps on CBS's 1966–73 *Mission: Impossible* series and again in its 1988–90 reprise. His early career comprised appearances in Western and sci-fi films of the fifties and sixties, but much like Leslie Nielsen, who would appear in the *Golden Girls* series

finale, Peter began a new phase of his career when he proved his skills in comedy in the 1980 film *Airplane!* and its 1982 sequel. Having begun his career as a radio announcer in his native Minneapolis, the actor put his mellifluous tones to good use—not just by playing this Miami anchorman, but also in hosting A&E's long-running series *Biography* from 1987 to 2002.

By this point, Meg Wyllie was a member of *The Golden Girls'* reliable stable of recurring players, having first played an aged stewardess in the season-three episode "Nothing to Fear, But Fear Itself." In actuality only nine years older than her TV son, Peter Graves, Meg had a long-standing career on the small screen, the most noteworthy moment of which may be her role in the 1966 *Star Trek* pilot as the series' first villain, the Talosian Keeper. In her final TV role, she recurred in the mid-nineties as Aunt Lolly to Helen Hunt's character, Jamie Buchman, on NBC's sitcom *Mad About You.*

The episode's third guest star, Steve Landesberg, remains best known for his role as Sergeant Arthur Dietrich on ABC's long-running cop comedy *Barney Miller.* Immediately after this first appearance, Dr. Halperin would appear again in the

two-parter "The Monkey Show"—and in fact those episodes' most memorable prop, a stuffed monkey head atop a traffic cone, is already visible here in his office.

DON SEIGEL: The main story here is a story about Stan, whom I loved writing. He was a lot of fun—an idiot and a bullshitter, but he loved Dorothy. This story gave us an interesting look at the relationship, too, between Stan and Sophia, where we get to uncover the true, loving feelings they have for each other. I was in therapy while working on *The Golden Girls*—I'm a big advocate of it—and so I always wanted to do a show based in a therapist's office. I was happy with how these scenes came out, with Steve Landesberg as the doctor. We didn't write many lines for him, and although he was so funny, he played the part straight, as the foil for Dorothy, Stan, and Sophia.

The B plot was about Blanche dating the mama's boy, played by Peter Graves, and I think the two stories really worked well together. They were both about mother issues—but sometimes, when your A plot and B plot are mining the same theme that can be the kiss of death. I was relieved here to see that somehow they gel.

THE MONKEY SHOW

(PARTS 1 & 2)

Written by: MARC SOTKIN & MITCHELL HURWITZ ◆ *Directed by:* LEX PASSARIS
Original airdate: NOVEMBER 9, 1991

In order to help Stan (Herb Edelman) move on with his life, Dorothy accompanies the yutz to appointments with his psychiatrist, Dr. Halperin (Steve Landesberg). The doctor's strange methods include encouraging Stan to transfer his feelings for his ex-wife to a fake monkey; but with Stan now more attached to his new stuffed friend, Fifi, Dorothy is thrilled to hear the doctor's next recommendation: that she and her ex now spend at least two years without further contact.

At the same time, the Girls get a visit from Dorothy's formerly haughty sister, Gloria (Dena Dietrich), who recently lost all her money in junk bonds. At Sophia's behest, Dorothy not only agrees not to gloat at her widowed sister's misfortune, but even fixes her up with some dates while she's in town. Unfortunately, the strangers in Dorothy's little black book turn out not to be to Gloria's liking—but as everyone sees in the first episode's cliffhanger, a familiar face like Stan is. "Good news," Stan tells her as he and Gloria are caught with the covers pulled up to their chins. "I'm off the monkey."

Meanwhile, for days nobody had believed Sophia that there was a hurricane a'comin'. But now the storm is here in full force, almost preventing Dr. Halperin and his date, the Girls' neighbor Carol Weston (Dinah Manoff), from making an emergency house call to see Stan. The doctor diagnoses a "codependence transference," and things at least inside the house calm down—until Gloria lets it slip that it was Sophia who pushed her into the liaison with Stan. Dorothy fights with her mother, and Sophia heads out to wander around in the wrath of Hurricane Gil.

Things are also not going very well down at the local TV station, where Rose has drafted Blanche into helping organize an eight-hour telethon to save the McKinley Lighthouse. But with trees and power lines downed by the storm, no one else can reach the station in time for the broadcast. So Blanche and Rose take to the airwaves to perform the longest two-woman show in TV history. But in the end, all their vamping is for naught; Rose receives a bulletin to read on the air, noting that the McKinley Lighthouse has been destroyed by the waves.

When policemen come to enforce a mandatory evacuation of Richmond Street, bringing residents to the TV station for shelter, Sophia is nowhere to be found—but Gloria can be found, in bed with Stan again. Sophia, meanwhile, has made it to the apartment of her big brother, Angelo (Bill Dana), who advises her to make things right with Dorothy as they, too, head for shelter. But by that time, at the TV station with Stan, Dorothy is already working out her own feelings, admitting to having been jealous when she saw the man with her sister. The two exes agree that they're best together when they're not together, and yet still in each other's lives, as co-parents, co-grandparents, and begrudging friends.

◆ ◆ ◆ ◆

COMMENTARY: This two-part episode comprised one hour's worth of a hurricane theme night that blew through all three of NBC's Saturday night sitcoms—the others being fellow Witt/Thomas productions *Empty Nest* and *Nurses*. Since all three shows were set in Miami, NBC's Warren Littlefield had requested a November sweeps stunt where characters could cross over from show to show. So, that night, *Nest*'s Dinah Manoff checked in on the *Girls*, while Sophia visited *Nest* neighbors the Westons, and Rose showed up at *Nurses'* Community Medical Center. The stunt worked; the high winds produced monster ratings (and inspired NBC to create another crossover Saturday, "Moon Over Miami," for later that season, marking the leap-year full moon on February 29, 1992).

ABOVE:

The offices of R. Halperin, MD.

Photo courtesy of the EDWARD S. STEPHENSON ARCHIVE at the ART DIRECTORS GUILD.

The two cops who report to the house should know the address well; they're played by Jonathan Schmock, a comedic character actor who had small roles in three other *Golden Girls* episodes, and Matthew Saks, Bea Arthur's real-life son. In another nepotistic bit of casting, the telethon impressionist, Davey Cricket, is played by one of the show's writers, Don Seigel, who was known in the *Golden Girls* writers' room for his uncanny insect noise. "He'd actually done it on *The Gong Show*, and so I said, 'Let's put it in the episode!'" Mitch Hurwitz remembers.

Ironically, the lighthouse telethon would be no sweat for Betty White, who started her career at Los Angeles TV station KLAC in 1949, soon hosting up to five and a half hours per day of the live variety show *Hollywood on Television*. And in another irony, Gloria is now housebound in Miami due to bad weather—and yet, actress Dena Dietrich is best known to many fans as Mother Nature from the popular series of TV ads for Chiffon margarine that ran from 1971 to 1979. Is it just a coincidence that right after Gloria gets confronted by her sister, there's a hurricane a'comin?

PAUL WITT: This wasn't NBC's first stunt night, but it was the first one where there was this kind of continuity. A stunt night had previously been that "all three shows will

deal with Halloween." But here, the night had three of our company's shows, *The Golden Girls*, *Empty Nest*, and *Nurses*, all set in the same city, so we could have a continuing storyline.

KEVIN ABBOTT: Mitch Hurwitz wrote one of my favorite lines in this episode, for the cheesecake scene. Dorothy is talking about rough times with her ex-husband: "Stan and I went through a period where we had no marital relations at all. I totally cut off his sex." And Rose naively asks, "You mean, it grows back?"

I remember the laugh that followed. The director had a camera on each of the ladies, and he'd just switch from one to the other, capturing their separate reactions. They'd cut to Dorothy rolling her eyes, then Rose shrugging. Then Sophia, then Blanche. And with each new reaction, the audience would keep on laughing. It went on for about thirty seconds, an unbelievably rolling laugh that they had to trim way down when the show went to air. That's why *The Golden Girls* was such a fun show to work on. There was really great writing, but then we also had in the cast these complete professionals who would take what you gave them and amplify it.

MITCHELL HURWITZ: There was a point where the show started to get a little more high-concept, and this episode is an example. I was really into behaviorism at the time, having studied some of that in college. Dorothy's line about the experiments with baby monkeys was something I had studied. The idea was that monkeys will transfer their affections to something soft and warm—so we thought, "What if Stan had to do that, but he couldn't get a person, so he had a soft monkey, too?" It may have started with real science, but after that we made it up. In fact I remember that it was

---

"While Blanche is doing that, why don't I head on over to the piano? I'd like to sing you a song that I used to sing as a child. It's an old Minnesotan farm song entitled "I Never Thought I'd Grow a Hair There."

—ROSE

Tracy Gamble's joke that instead of getting rid of the monkey, Stan might end up with a smaller and smaller one, until he can keep it on his key chain.

DENA DIETRICH: I had worked with Danny Thomas on a show, *The Practice*, in the 1970s. So in the first season when *The Golden Girls* was casting for Dorothy's sister, Tony Thomas brought me in to audition—but I didn't get it. Then, years went by, and they wanted to bring the character Gloria back again. I guess they looked at me then and said well she is tall and looks like Bea. I had even done the same part of Lucy Brown, which Bea had played in *Threepenny Opera*.

Practically every week, someone comes up to me and quotes a line from the episode. Inevitably, it's a particular one of Estelle's lines, which seems to be the one people love the most. "There's a hurricane a'comin'!" Everyone expects me to know all the lines

from the episode. Of course, now that I've heard that one five thousand times, I do. It blows me away when I hear from a fan about *The Golden Girls* or Mother Nature. Even though the ads went off the air long ago, Nick at Nite showed them for years, so people would write to me about those, too. That may trail off because I think they've stopped airing. But God knows *The Golden Girls* will go on forever.

DATELINE: MIAMI

Written by: JAMIE WOOTEN & MARC CHERRY • *Directed by:* PETER D. BEYT
Original airdate: NOVEMBER 2, 1991

As Dorothy leaves for a Saturday night date at L'Auberge—a restaurant Rose claims jerks love—the other Girls reminisce about their own terrible dates of days past. Rose recalls her own not-so-romantic dinner at L'Auberge with John, a.k.a. Alan, a.k.a. Peter (Pat Harrington Jr., 1929-2016), who has apparently worked his way through all the women in Miami—and judging by the reaction of their waiter (Nick Ullett), some of the men. But what's even worse than finding out your blind date is a liar and philanderer? When the evening ends with his arrest, and the revelation that he's also known as Schlomo Ziegler, the Freeway Flasher.

Blanche recounts her own rotten rendezvous with the man who may present the biggest challenge to her skills in seduction: teetotaling, virginal Bob (Fred Willard), who is four months out of the priesthood. But actually, this New Year's Eve seems truly worse for Rose, who is forced to fend off Bob's lecherous brother Arnie (Lenny Wolpe). In crying over his supposedly dead wife, Elsie—who turns out to be merely away at a fat farm in Sarasota—Arnie tries to get his kisses, and more, well before midnight. Rose kicks him to the curb, but, remaining in the living room, ruins Blanche's chances with the ex-priest with her guilt-inducing protestations about how sex should always be with someone you love. Now alone at the stroke of midnight, resourceful Blanche, in need of a kiss to start her year right, looks to her roommate. But she strikes out there, too, as Rose reflexively warns her, "Don't even think about it."

Saved for last, Sophia's date story turns out not to be about a jerk from her own past, but about *the* jerk from Dorothy's, one Stanley Zbornak. Picture it: Brooklyn, 1948. Sophia attempts to bribe her friend's son Myron (Jesse Dabson) to date her daughter, but it's too late; young Dorothy (Lyn Greene) announces that she's expecting, courtesy of young Stan (Richard Tanner), who even in flashback Sophia has already christened the Yutz.

◆ ◆ ◆ ◆

COMMENTARY: In *The Golden Girls'* second season, it had been Rose who showed instinctual kindness on learning that Dorothy's friend Jean was a lesbian, falling in love with her. Two years later, it was Rose who became the confidante for Blanche's gay brother, Clayton, offering a supportive shoulder. And yet here, Rose seems surprisingly ill at ease with two separate same-sex situations, both nervously rebuffing Blanche's move at midnight, and even appearing to opt out of a commiserating hug from a gay waiter. If these truly are slights on Rose's part, they hardly seem like intentional statements as to her character, but more like the show's writers needing comic "buttons" to cap off the two vignettes.

What this episode lacks in Zbornak-icity, it makes up for in suitors for the remaining three Girls, with quite a few prominent male stars in guest roles. Pat Harrington had been a prolific comic actor and voice performer, and had logged a long list of appearances on late-night shows *Tonight Starring Jack Paar* and *The Steve Allen Show*, as well as roles on sitcoms such as *Make Room for Daddy*, before landing the role in 1975 for which he would become best known, as meddling superintendent Dwayne Schneider on Norman Lear's CBS sitcom *One Day at a Time*.

Appearing here in the same vignette with Harrington is Nick Ullett, who came to the United States from his native England in 1964 and worked mostly in New York theater. After appearing in the hit 1986 film *Down and Out in Beverly Hills*, he played several sitcom guest roles, including in Witt/Thomas's *Blossom*. Shortly after his work on *The Golden Girls*, from 1992 to 1994, Nick appeared on the CBS soap *As the World Turns*.

Playing the innocent ex-priest is Fred Willard, whose clean-cut exterior and midwestern accent belie a wicked wit in every character he plays. From *Sirota's Court* and *Fernwood 2 Night* in the late 1970s through later roles on *Roseanne* and *Everybody Loves Raymond*, he has spent decades as a beloved comic actor on TV and in such films as *Anchorman*, *Harold and Kumar Go to White Castle*, *This Is Spinal Tap*, *Waiting for Guffman*, and *Best in Show*.

And finally, playing brother Arnie to Fred's Bob is Lenny Wolpe, a New York stage actor who had made only a few TV appearances before being cast on *The Golden Girls*. In the years since, he has continuously appeared in guest-star spots on the small screen. More recently, he's appeared on Broadway in such recent shows as *Wicked*, *The Drowsy Chaperone*, and *Bullets Over Broadway*.

MARC CHERRY: The main reason for this being a wraparound episode was that Bea Arthur had a medical problem for which she was off the show for a month, getting an operation. So they pretaped her few scenes for the beginning and end of the show. And because Estelle had to be made up separately for the current and flashback scenes, we pretaped Estelle, too. Betty was sick that night—you can kind of hear a little soreness in her voice—so we were a little concerned. But when an episode is built on a series of vignettes like this, it's easier to write.

When Jamie [Wooten] and I had first gone in to pitch stories to *The Golden Girls*, we had pitched an idea about Blanche dating a priest—and the writers kind of made fun of us because they didn't like how we told it. That ended up becoming the Blanche vignette here, with Fred Willard. We felt that it was one of those stories that couldn't sustain a whole episode, but it could make for one perfectly funny scene as Lenny Wolpe's character tries to make it with Rose, and Blanche finds out her guy is an ex-priest, and a virgin.

Marc Sotkin had done a version of this episode on his previous series *It's a Living*, where it's just an excuse to show bad dates, and he called it "The Jerk Show." But ultimately, we showed more than just bad dates, and Jamie and I were really happy and proud that we got to construct an important moment in the Girls' long-established history: showing how Sophia learned that Dorothy was pregnant.

PETER D. BEYT: I didn't have a problem with the fact that Rose's date has slept with both women and men, because I'd been with both men and women before myself. The part I didn't really like was where, after it was revealed what a dog the guy was, the waiter still said, "Call me." Why if you have any self-respect would you want him to call? Then, as the guy is being taken away by the cops, the waiter asks Rose for a hug—and she has a little bit of a grossed-out reaction. That again wasn't my favorite thing. I remember Nina [Feinberg Wass] and I wanted to edit the scene to end it earlier, because you really didn't need that final beat anyway. It would have be fine to end on seeing Rose's surprised expression as the guy is carried off.

LENNY WOLPE: There were a lot of guest stars in this episode, because there were so many vignettes being shot. I was really awed by how good

Lynnie Greene was, playing the young Dorothy in a flashback scene. It was uncanny how she captured the essence of a young Bea Arthur; they could have made that a spinoff. With all those different storylines going on, it was kind of a complicated shoot—and yet, it was also kind of an easy week, because everybody was in a great mood.

My first job when I'd gotten to California had been a few episodes on *Empty Nest*, also for Witt/Thomas/Harris, which shot on the soundstage next door. Witt/Thomas was a very small company, so we'd see all of the *Golden Girls* people wandering around. And so I had a very fond feeling coming back to the lot to do this episode. By then, I'd also done a few episodes of *L.A. Law*, playing a character with Tourette's Syndrome. At that time, the illness wasn't very much in the public eye, and those episodes had brought it more to the forefront, and taken away some of the shame

ABOVE:

Blanche attempts to seduce virginal ex-priest Bob (Fred Willard).

Photo by ABC PHOTO ARCHIVES/ABC *via* GETTY IMAGES.

and the mystery. Well, it turned out, when I met Estelle Getty on *The Golden Girls*, she told me she had a family member with Tourette's. We spent so much time together, talking about it, with her telling me she was grateful for my character. We made a real connection, and she was wonderful, sharing stories with me.

I was cast in this episode as a cad, which was really against type for me. That's probably why I was hired, because they probably wanted someone where initially you wouldn't expect that kind of behavior. For me, it was a real treat—and I got to kiss Betty White, which was the high point of my career. She is probably the nicest person I've ever worked with, making you feel so welcome. And she was also a really good sport. She was nursing a horrible cold all week, to the point where she could barely talk. But she was so gracious about it. And as we rehearsed, every time we got to the kiss, she would say, "Lenny, you can, but I just don't want you to get sick!" I started to think, "Jeez, I wonder what's going to happen on Friday, on tape night!" Well I don't know where Betty went before Friday, but by that night she sounded great, much healthier. We smooched—and I did not catch her cold.

NICK ULLETT: I remember this episode particularly well, because it ended up being very important to me. At that point in 1991, I was battling non-Hodgkin lymphoma, which had caused me to leave the Broadway show *Me and My Girl*. I had undergone chemotherapy for more than a year, and then had a six-month remission. But just as this episode was happening, the cancer came galloping back.

I had had a lot of hair, but with a new round of really vicious amounts of chemo, it started to disappear once again. So I went to the woman, Judy Crown, who had done the hair on my wife Jenny O'Hara's show, *My Sister Sam*, and bought a wig that made me look like a weathercaster. And my *Golden Girls* audition was the first time I went out on wearing it.

My part in the show was a fun one. In my scene, Pat's character and Rose are on their date,

and first one woman comes up and tells him off, and Rose is a little disturbed, but he passes her off as his sister. Then a second young woman who is clearly pregnant comes in and berates him. And because comedy comes in threes, I was the third beat, where, as the waiter, I come up and suddenly go really hissy on him. "You *disgust* me! After the way you've treated me, I should scratch your eyes out! Call me." Basically, that was the joke.

I remember the director reminding me that when I first appear, I should make sure not to come off at all swishy. It's supposed to come as a surprise, out of nowhere. Of course, I think the way it was shot, there's not really time for any setup, where the audience at home could really notice who the waiter is before I go into it. I had a gay actor friend who tutored me on how to play a gay character, because I'd never done it before— which is surprising, because oftentimes in television in particular, it was like a shorthand: if you wanted someone to seem gay, or precious, or an academic, just give him an English accent. Let's face it, all English people are gay in any case.

When I was hired for this episode, no one knew about my cancer. From rehearsals through the tape night, I wore the wig at all times—until we took our bows at the curtain call. I don't know why I took it off; I was just fed up with the thing. I hadn't wanted to go through the entire experience pretending I didn't have cancer. But at the same time, I hadn't wanted everyone pitying me, "Poor old fool!" So I did the work, and then I made the statement.

Rue McClanahan in particular was really terrific about it. About six weeks after I did *The Golden Girls*, I performed a one-man show I'd been doing earlier, about coming to America, having adventures, and getting cancer. My new treatments were going to be expensive, and my accountant suggested that I do the show as a benefit. Rue was very supportive, and got a lot of people to come. We sold out five nights at the little theater upstairs at the Pasadena Playhouse. And then I went off and had a bone marrow transplant—and I'm still here.

RO$E LOVE$ MILE$

Written by: JERRY PERZIGIAN & DON SEIGEL AND RICHARD VACZY & TRACY GAMBLE
• Directed by: LEX PASSARIS • Original airdate: NOVEMBER 16, 1991

As Dorothy departs for a three-day Caribbean cruise with Lee, a doctor boyfriend we've never heard of before, she leaves Blanche in charge of Sophia. After going over a checklist of instructions regarding the old lady's care and feeding, Blanche thinks she can handle the assignment—until Sophia informs her otherwise. "Fasten your seat belt, Slutpuppy. This ain't gonna be no cakewalk!"

Later, while rooting through Dorothy's things, Sophia finds the list she herself wrote in 1920, titled "Things I Want to Accomplish Before I Die." Number three on the list was a vow to make amends with her first husband, Guido Spirelli—and so, while Blanche thinks Sophia is in her bedroom, spilling her feelings into a letter, Sophia sneaks off to Sicily to deliver the message in person.

Desperate to deduce the old lady's potential whereabouts, Blanche consults Sophia's brother, Angelo (Bill Dana), who suspects Sophia is just playing a trick, and is indeed still somewhere in Miami. But as we see moments later, after a plane, a train, a boat, and a burro, Sophia arrives at a Sicilian tavern, and offers her onetime suitor Guido (Phil Leeds, 1916–98) her heartfelt apology, in English. His sole response? "Ah, fuhgettaboutit."

Meanwhile, after a date at a sleazy buffet, Rose realizes her boyfriend Miles (Harold Gould) has turned into a terrible tightwad. And so Blanche convinces her friend to cheat on her parsimonious partner by enjoying an expensive dinner on a double date with rich Texans Mort and Barry (John P. Connolly and Harvey Vernon, 1927–96). But wouldn't you know it, who happens to show up at the fancy restaurant but Miles, making his customary purchase of discounted day-old éclairs.

Cuckolded by cuisine, Miles storms out. But a few days later, he makes it up to Rose by taking her to dine at the same establishment. There, the man finally admits what's really going on: with his retirement looming, and his health still excellent, Miles fears running out of money as he lives long into old age.

◆ ◆ ◆ ◆

COMMENTARY: This episode contains one of the series' standout visuals, of first Sophia and later Blanche riding a donkey through the hills of Sicily. In reality, of course, the scenes were shot locally, in the Santa Monica Mountains around Los Angeles. "It was a sunny, hot day, and I was on a donkey on that looong path," Rue remembers. "They thought it would look like Sicily, and I think it did."

DON SEIGEL: I liked writing Miles, because I thought it was interesting to see what kinds of men these women dated. But I thought that up until this point, the character was bland. I've always thought cheapness is a funny trait; Jack Benny sure went a long way with it! My writing partner, Jerry, didn't think the jokes about Miles checking the prices on the menu would work, and it's true the laughs there weren't as big as I'd thought they'd be—maybe because most people actually do that. But I was happy because making Miles cheap gave Betty something to play off of. Whether Rose empathizes with him or gets frustrated, now she can show feelings about him.

BILL DANA: This episode contains one of the biggest laughs I ever got. Uncle Angelo had built up a whole fantasy about being with Blanche, and when he realizes it's not going to happen, he says to her, "You mean I shaved my shoulders for nothing!" Well, the laugh that got was like walking against a hurricane. The blast that came out of the audience! Rue and I stayed in the scene with our eyes locked, for what must have been ten or fifteen seconds, during the longest laugh any of us ever remembered. You don't hear nearly how long it was in the finished episode, because they had to edit most of it out.

ROOM SEVEN

Written by: JERRY PERZIGIAN & DON SEIGEL AND RICHARD VACZY & TRACY GAMBLE
• *Directed by:* PETER D. BEYT • *Original airdate:* NOVEMBER 23, 1991

When Blanche learns that Grandview, her grandmother Hollingsworth's plantation, is set to be demolished, she enlists the Girls for a road trip to Atlanta for one last glimpse of the house that was the setting for her fondest childhood memories. But once there, a distraught Blanche is unable to say goodbye to the bedroom she believes houses her grandmother's spirit, and handcuffs herself to a radiator in protest mere minutes before the scheduled implosion. Meanwhile, after a near-death experience while choking on a piece of candy, and a brief reunion with her late husband, Sal (Sid Melton), in Heaven, Sophia decides to live life to the fullest—which apparently includes executing daredevil stunts like jumping off Grandview's roof regardless of her advanced age.

◆ ◆ ◆ ◆

COMMENTARY: Although Sophia's storyline goes over the top and off the roof, it provides for a touching moment with her late husband, Sal—an appearance that would be Sid Melton's last on the show. The episode also provides a powerful emotional storyline for Blanche, and fills in some of the Hollingsworth family history we began to hear the previous season in the episode "Witness."

RUE McCLANAHAN: Here was Blanche's family's home, the house where she'd grown up, and it had meant so much to Big Daddy. And now a wrecking crew was about to tear it down, against her wishes. Because the circumstances were so painful for Blanche, I found this episode to be painful to play.

TRACY GAMBLE: Blanche was the most colorful character, and so all the *Golden Girls* writers wanted to do a Blanche episode. We competed for them, and Richard and I waited three years to write one. "Big events" like this B story about

Sophia jumping off the roof after a near-death experience tended to come up in the writers' room, and we felt we could get away with it because the core of the episode was about Blanche going back to the place where she'd had happy memories as a young girl with her grandmother. So as over-the-top as the Sophia story was, the episode was grounded in reality. And the voice of young Blanche we hear echoing through the house is actually my daughter Bridget, who is now in her twenties.

RICHARD VACZY: In general, I liked the concept of this episode, about a character being about to lose a favorite place that she loves, and that's why I hooked into it. Granted, it did wind up getting a little bit out there. That wasn't the plan from the beginning. But we were getting late into the run of the show. Honestly, year after year, we'd start to notice that jokes we'd been doing for years just wouldn't get the same reaction from the audience anymore. It was like a drug. The audience needed more and more of the drug to get the same effect.

MITCHELL HURWITZ: I was working mostly on [Witt/Thomas/Harris NBC sitcom] *Nurses* at the time, and I came over to the *Golden Girls* set after a *Nurses* rewrite session. When I saw what was happening in this episode, I remember thinking, "An eighty-five-year-old woman jumping off a roof into a haystack? I think we've crossed a line with this one."

PETER D. BEYT: For a director, "Room Seven" was full of technical challenges. For one thing, there was a scene where Sophia jumps off the roof—which was not an easy task to make happen. It wasn't a real person jumping, of course, and so we had to keep testing how it would look by throwing the dummy we'd made, and then adjusting its weight just right, so that it looked like it was Sophia, sailing by the window feet first. *The Golden Girls* was not usually a stunt-heavy show, so rigging that dummy took us a whole afternoon.

But the biggest technical challenge—and something I'll always remember about this episode—happened with Blanche, and the handcuffs. I was really shy and closeted when I was on the show. We were rehearsing the scene where Blanche cuffs herself to the radiator in her grandmother's abandoned house, and everything was going really well. It was during one of the first days during the week, where we rehearsed with just minimal crew. Rue was always very technical, as far as wanting to have a command of all the props she'd be using. To save time, we set it up that Blanche would have a pair of handcuffs in her purse, which she'd show the audience—but then she'd pocket

them out of sight, and use a pair of cuffs already attached to the radiator. She'd slap that second set of cuffs on her wrist, and then she'd be really attached to the thing.

I called for us to run the scene one more time. Everything worked, and so we broke for lunch. Our prop master, Bob, had the key to let Rue out of the handcuffs, but when he tried to do so—oh my God, the key is broken! Then the big stage lights started to shut off one by one, each with a *boom*. And there was Rue, really handcuffed to a three-hundred-pound radiator, starting to get a little panicky, and claustrophobic, and pissed off.

Everyone was in shock over what to do. I just rolled my eyes, looked up at the sky, and realized: okay, I have no choice. I reached into my pocket and pulled out my keys, went over to

Rue, and freed her—with a handcuff key I just happened to have on my key ring. As Rue was expressing her relief, a few of the crew guys realized what had happened, and started to tease me. "Now what do you have going on *there*!"

Rue was having none of that. "Now you stop that right now!" she yelled at them. "There is nothing wrong with this boy having a healthy interest in sex!" It was just like Blanche would have said—and after all, Blanche, too, would have had a key. I guess that's why I so identified with Blanche. Rue shut them all down, and I never heard from anybody about it again. But now, everyone knew some of my personal business.

THE POPE'S RING

Written by: KEVIN ABBOTT ◆ *Directed by:* LEX PASSARIS
Original airdate: DECEMBER 14, 1991

As Pope John Paul II says an outdoor Mass on a visit to Miami, Sophia schemes her way into a front pew so she can request a blessing for her ailing friend Agnes O'Rourke. Later that day, she comes home with something even better than a Papal intercession: the Pontiff's ring, which slid off his finger as security whisked him away. Horrified, Dorothy makes her mother promise to return the jewel, a symbol of His Holiness's authority on earth; but unfortunately, the ring then goes missing.

Sophia seems suspiciously convinced that the bauble will turn up in a day or two—not so coincidentally, the same time frame in which she hopes the Pope might pop by the hospital to see Agnes. Later, she's disappointed when it's merely a priestly emissary (Steven Gilborn, 1936-2009) who shows up at their door, but she puts in her request regarding Agnes nonetheless.

Meanwhile, Blanche competes with Dorothy over who can give Rose the better birthday gift. Blanche's is definitely the most unusual: she's hired a private eye to follow Miles (Harold Gould) and ensure his fidelity. Although Rose is initially hesitant to accept the strange present, Blanche reminds her that Miles is, after all, the man who through the Witness Protection Program had lied about his job, his past, and even his name.

But later, when Miles gets frisky on the lanai, Rose confesses about the gift, and draws the detective (Fred McCarren, 1951-2006) out of hiding in the bushes. Infuriated, Miles presses Rose to promise she'll never again doubt his word; but when Blanche reads the investigator's report, the Girls learn that Miles is scheduled for a secret surgical procedure. So the next day, Rose rushes to the hospital—and finds that Miles is merely undergoing cosmetic surgery on the bags under his eyes. Feeling foolish, Rose and Miles promise to trust each other—just as a commotion in the hallway signals the arrival of Sophia's miracle: the Pope (Eugene Greytak, 1925-2010) has dropped by to bless the patients of St. Ignatius, including Agnes, on his way to the airport.

◆ ◆ ◆ ◆

COMMENTARY: If the priest who comes to the house looks familiar, it's because the actor, Steven Gilborn, went on to play quite a different kind of father—to Ellen DeGeneres, on her ABC sitcom *Ellen*. This was the final role for Fred McCarren, who had been in the infamous 1980 film musical *Xanadu*, and also, notably, was a series regular on Bea Arthur's 1983 *Fawlty Towers*–esque sitcom flop, *Amanda's*.

And Gene Greytak certainly made the most of his uncanny resemblance to John Paul II, impersonating the Polish Pope also in films like *Hot Shots!*, *Sister Act*, and *Naked Gun 33 1/3*. But could any of his appearances top this episode's tag, where the Pope plays poker with Sophia in the Girls' kitchen, going so far as to wager his mitre?

KEVIN ABBOTT: Originally, I had conceived the story that Sophia had a competition with a Polish friend over whether Italians or Poles make the better Catholics. When she got tickets to the Pope's Mass, she wanted to call the woman, just to rub it in her face—but her friend's phone number had been disconnected, and now Sophia was worried. All through the episode, Sophia kept talking about how miracles are possible. And at the end, the two storylines come together, because Sophia found her friend's new phone number

and address on a piece of paper on the kitchen table, appearing as if by an act of God. When Blanche explained that she had had the private detective from Rose's B story track down her friend as a favor, Sophia exclaimed, "Wait, you did something totally unselfish? It's a miracle!" I thought it all worked very well. But it was one of those cases where the showrunner, Marc Sotkin, didn't like the ending, and so in changing that, the writers ended up unraveling much of the story, including Sophia's motivation for seeing the Pope in the first place.

For the B story, I had originally pitched Rose just following Miles around, suspicious, but someone in the writers' room came up with the idea of the detective, which was very funny. And the reason for Miles's evasion changed slightly too. I had recently read in *Newsweek* that a trend among older men was to get pec and calf implants. These were guys who always worked out and were in good shape, but now with age their bodies were starting to sag. I thought it was one of the funniest things I'd ever heard, and so that's the reason I gave for Miles having surgery: pec implants. Rose even had a line where she asked him, "So you got a boob job?!" But Marc Sotkin couldn't believe this was a real trend, and I couldn't find the *Newsweek* article to prove it to him. So we changed the pec implants to another form of cosmetic surgery, but I didn't think it ended up being as funny.

ROBERT SPINA *(production associate)*: Thanks to this episode, Lex Passaris, [associate director] Tom Carpenter, and I have a backstage photo of us—with the Pope! When John Paul II died, I sent that picture out to the guys, with a [caption]: "Just good times with the Pope."

OLD BOYFRIENDS

Written by: MARC CHERRY & JAMIE WOOTEN • *Directed by:* PETER D. BEYT
Original airdate: JANUARY 4, 1992

Sophia shops for a man in a senior citizens' personals column and meets amiable Marvin (Louis Guss, 1918–2008). The problem is—supposedly because his eyesight is too poor for him to drive—the lovebirds are escorted everywhere by Marvin's "sister," Sarah (Betty Garrett, 1919–2011). When Sophia tries to get Marvin alone, the touching truth comes out: Sarah is actually Marvin's dying wife, and she is trying to find a replacement who will care for him after she goes.

Meanwhile, another native of St. Olaf, Thor Anderson (Ken Berry), shows up on Richmond Street to rekindle a romance with Rose. The only problem is Rose can't remember Thor from Adam. Over dinner, Blanche tries to help, pumping Thor for clues. Then, as her besotted suitor literally skips off to the bathroom, Rose does recall one tidbit of history: she had merely used Thor, to make her future husband, Charlie Nylund, jealous. Ironically, it's only after a mortified Rose finally confesses to Thor that it all does finally come rushing back to her, as he kisses her good-bye—because Thor was a remarkably bad kisser then, and still is.

◆ ◆ ◆ ◆

COMMENTARY: Sophia's choice, about whether to step in for Sarah to love and care for Marvin, makes for a beautiful story, but the truly fun part is the casting: guest star Betty Garrett was an accomplished film actress, a six-decade Broadway veteran, and TV star. Betty started her career in musicals both on the stage and in film, appearing in the big-screen versions of *On the Town* in 1949 and *My Sister Eileen* in 1955. Her career sidetracked for years by the Hollywood blacklist, she came back strong on TV in the seventies, playing both landlady Edna Babish on *Laverne & Shirley* and recurring neighbor Irene Lorenzo on *All in the Family.*

Character actor Louis Guss, who had played Don Giuseppe Zaluchi in *The Godfather* and who had landed another of his greatest roles at age 69, playing Cher's uncle Raymond Cappomaggi in the 1987 film *Moonstruck,* made the perfect Marvin—although he wasn't the original choice for the role. Partway through the production week, he replaced another

OPPOSITE:
Rose tries to remember the still-besotted Thor (Ken Berry).

Photo by ABC PHOTO ARCHIVES/ABC *via* GETTY IMAGES.

> ## *"And by the way, Dorothy's not my daughter, she's my lesbian lover. See, Marvin? How do you like it? Not a pretty picture, is it!"*
>
> —SOPHIA

veteran character actor, Milton Selzer (1918-2006), who had been let go when he had been unable to retain his lines.

And in another big piece of casting, this episode features Ken Berry, a TV staple since his recurring roles in the early '60s on *The Ann Sothern Show* and *Dr. Kildare*. From 1965-67, he starred in ABC's Western spoof *F Troop*, which he followed with a leading role in *Mayberry R.F.D.* from 1968-71. Ken's appearances over a decade-long span on *The Carol Burnett Show* ultimately led to his casting in his most recognizable role, that of the besotted son Vinton on *Mama's Family*, which ran from 1983-90.

MARC CHERRY: The idea for this story came from Jamie and me, and the episode had one of the biggest laughs that we ever wrote—actually, that Jamie wrote. When Dorothy walks over and opens the door, and Sarah and Marvin are standing there with a flower, Dorothy says, "Oh thank you, but we already know Jesus," and then closes the door and walks back.

When Bea got up off the couch, opened the door, said her line, slammed the door, and walked away, the audience would start a laugh that went on and on. And Bea wasn't going to stop walking until they rang the doorbell again—but they weren't going to ring the doorbell again until the laughter stopped. So Bea went and sat down on the sofa, and waited until finally the audience stopped laughing. The commotion went on for so long that Bea had to do the bit three times.

RUE McCLANAHAN: I had had a crush on Ken Berry since the late fifties, when I saw him in a revue in Hollywood. What a dancer! So when I had first gotten the chance to work with him, on the series *Apple Pie*, I was thrilled. He guest starred as a salesman named Fred, who was trying to make enough money in 1931 selling encyclopedias to move to Hollywood and make it in movies as a dancer. I got to do a soft shoe with Ken in *Apple Pie*. The episode never ended up being broadcast, but I still have it on tape.

KEN BERRY: I was a big fan of *The Golden Girls*, and was happy to appear on the show. Those four ladies were surefire; they knew just what to do with the material. That week, I remember telling one of the writers how well written the show was. And in fact, I'm not sure what I really

brought to this episode. Sometimes when a show is that well-crafted, you just have to say your lines and get out of the way.

BETTY GARRETT: Almost every actor wanted to be on *The Golden Girls*, and I was very happy with the part of Sarah, because the storyline was very sweet and was a departure for me on TV. I had the reputation of being a comedian, and I liked the fact that this story was quite serious and dramatic. In fact, I don't remember having any jokes, and I really didn't mind. I had one long monologue, and I'll always be grateful to Bea for what she said to me. In between shots, she looked at me and said, "You're such a good actress." I just treasured that. Because I had done a lot of serious parts, but when you get the reputation of just being a funny girl, you don't get that compliment often.

GOODBYE, MR. GORDON

Written by: GAIL PARENT & JIM VALLELY ◆ *Directed by:* LEX PASSARIS
Original airdate: JANUARY 11, 1992

As Dorothy prepares for a visit from her eleventh-grade English teacher, Mr. Gordon (James Callahan, 1930–2007), Sophia remembers the huge crush her daughter had on the man, recalling how she used to help him grade papers, do his laundry, and even rotate his tires. Once Mr. Gordon arrives, Dorothy turns into a giggly seventeen-year-old all over again. During lunch, when he mentions having trouble organizing his thoughts for an article he's writing, she enthusiastically volunteers to help.

Meanwhile, Rose has been promoted to associate producer of the *Wake Up, Miami* show and is looking for two women to join the panel discussion she has created. Blanche jumps at the chance for TV exposure, and volunteers, as does Dorothy. But they're both shocked, as the cameras roll, to learn that the segment, "Women Who Live Together," is about lesbians.

After several days of being mad at Rose, Blanche eventually forgives her—especially when she realizes she's stumbled upon a new method for picking up curious men. In the meantime, Dorothy invests days' worth of work on Mr. Gordon's article—only to have him turn around and have it published under his own name. Disillusioned and hurt, Dorothy tells him off and asks him to leave. As she complains to her mother that her teenage fantasy of Mr. Gordon is now tarnished, Sophia waxes poetic, reminding her that "keeping fantasies alive is a part of life."

◆ ◆ ◆ ◆

COMMENTARY: It's a question, often whispered: "They're single, over thirty, and they live together? Are they gay?" These days, it's something one wonders about any longtime, same-sex roommates. And with this episode, it's a question *The Golden Girls* gets to enjoy cleverly playing with as well.

Back in the season-two episode "Isn't It Romantic?," Blanche didn't even know the meaning of the word "lesbian"—but she sure does now. Take a close look at Kent Zbornak, playing the guy in the *Wake Up, Miami* audience who asks Dorothy and Blanche the first question, about gender roles in their supposed lesbian relationship; four episodes later, in "Journey to the Center of Attention," the *Golden Girls* stage manager will turn up again at the Rusty Anchor, as the patron Blanche nearly strangles with the microphone cord.

> ## *"Rose, we can't kill you here because there are cameras."*
>
> —DOROTHY

Playing one member of the talk show's "other" lesbian couple is Catherine Dunn, a member of the show's production staff. And playing Mr. Gordon is James Callahan, who had been a regular on such series as *The Governor and J. J.* and *The Runaways*, but remains best known as Walter Powell, the family patriarch on the 1984–90 sitcom *Charles in Charge*.

JIM VALLELY: We had fun writing the jokes in this episode, like the questions that Sophia stands up and asks to embarrass Blanche and Dorothy from the audience. But I had a big fight with one of our producers, Nina Wass, about this one. I had begged her please, please when the camera cuts to Dorothy on the talk show, put a chyron underneath the shot that says: DOROTHY, A LESBIAN. Nina promised she would, but then somewhere along the way, someone didn't. I never knew why.

ABOVE:

The set of *Wake Up, Miami.*

Photo courtesy of the EDWARD S. STEPHENSON ARCHIVE at the ART DIRECTORS GUILD.

THE COMMITMENTS

Written by: TRACY GAMBLE & RICHARD VACZY • Directed by: LEX PASSARIS
Original airdate: JANUARY 25, 1992

When Dorothy wins tickets to *Beatlemania* in a radio giveaway, she asks Blanche to take over her previously scheduled blind date. To Blanche's surprise, Jerry (Ken Howard) turns out to be handsome—but initially a dud, as he fails to open her car door and worse, asks her to pay half the dinner check.

The next day, Jerry shows up to apologize for his behavior, which the recent widower had cribbed from a guide to modern dating. And so the two give courtship another try—with even weirder results: after five dates, gentlemanly Jerry has failed to put on any moves. Blanche frets that the day may have finally come when she has lost her sex appeal. Nevertheless, feeling a love for Jerry she hasn't known since the death of her husband, George, she sets out to seduce the man by luring him to a sleazy motel, complete with vibrating bed, mirrored ceiling, and retractable trapeze. But the plan backfires, when an uncomfortable Jerry makes a hasty exit.

Later that night, Blanche offers Jerry her apology, and he explains his reticence; he had married his high school sweetheart, and as he reenters the dating world, he finds himself to be just plain old-fashioned. He extols the virtues of tender caresses and of waiting for that first long, passionate big kiss—and then he plants one on Blanche, leaving her with a blissed-out smile.

Meanwhile, having had way too good a time at the concert, Dorothy brings Don (Terry Kiser), the band's version of George Harrison, home to bed. But immediately, she begins trying make over her new faux Beatle boyfriend. As his "muse"—or, as Sophia points out, his Yoko Ono—she convinces him to quit the band in order to pursue his own music career. But Don's solo debut turns out to be a bust; the man, it turns out, has no talent.

◆ ◆ ◆ ◆

RICHARD VACZY: This episode is the last one Tracy Gamble and I wrote, and it had initially been scheduled for closer to the end of the series. But when another script needed work, the shows got reordered, and this one moved up. I was disappointed, because it had a beautiful moment of growth for Blanche that it would have been nice to end with.

The thing that had intrigued us about the story was that with Blanche, here was a woman who as a beautiful young girl had been able to go anywhere she wanted, have any meal, get on any airplane. But all of a sudden, her looks—the thing she relies upon most—are not working with this man. I loved the idea of introducing the old-world sensibility that Ken Howard's character had, as opposed to where the show had been going at that point—for example, Sophia and Cesar Romero in bed together. This went completely the other way, reverting to something more romantic and traditional. For all the episodes we did, I liked getting the chance to introduce a moral message into at least some of them. Not judging promiscuity, but showing the value of slowing down and enjoying the moment.

Not only did Rue love Blanche's storyline and the episode's ending, but Bea loved what she got to do as well. It was one of those somewhat unusual shows where Bea's story was just pure fun, and Bea had a great time the whole week doing it. The idea came about because I have a friend who's a huge Beatles fan, who took me to see a *Beatlemania* show in Long Beach. At the show, he said, "You know, what if Dorothy went after one of these guys?" At the time, I said to him, "What are you, high?" But then I started throwing the idea around in my mind. My friend didn't get credit for the idea, and he probably should have. So Andy Stone, here's your credit.

BEA ARTHUR: This episode was so so much fun, as was working with that wonderful actor Terry Kiser. I loved how far out of reality the Beatlemania storyline went. It was funny funny funny.

KEVIN ABBOTT (*writer/coproducer*): This script contains one of my favorite *Golden Girls* moments. At the end, Rose asks Blanche how Jerry's kiss made her feel, and as the last line of the show, she responds simply, "Like a lady." I remember that at the table read for the episode, Rue got to that line, closed the script, and started to tear up. She said out loud, "I love this!" Blanche was so often called a slut, and this was instead a nice moment for the character. And it was interesting to see how it really affected Rue. She really embraced that moment.

RUE McCLANAHAN: The ending said that Blanche was not a slut – and I'd been telling people that all along!

KEN HOWARD: The opportunity to guest star on *The Golden Girls* came out of the blue, just as my wife, Linda, and I were planning our wedding. It was a busy time, but I was excited to do the show because I was a fan. I knew Bea Arthur a little through Broadway circles, and Betty White through animal charities. And I'd just worked with Rue McClanahan on a TV movie, *The Man in the Brown Suit*, which had filmed on location in Spain in the summer of 1988. We'd had a lot of opportunity on the set to chat, and so I was happy when I heard I'd be working with Rue again.

Working on *The Golden Girls* was a wonderful experience, although it goes by so fast. I enjoyed watching those women work. That week, I even developed an impression of Bea— the trick was to let all the air out of my lungs before I would talk.

Afterward, Linda had the idea to send each of the ladies flowers. And they were all so touched—but the way Bea expressed it, she got mad at me. She said, "You mustn't spend your money that way, and don't you ever do that again. Do you hear me!" It was so her. Her way of saying thank you was to say, "That's excessive, and don't ever do it again!"

QUESTIONS AND ANSWERS

Written by: DON SEIGEL & JERRY PERZIGIAN ◆ *Directed by:* LEX PASSARIS
Original airdate: FEBRUARY 8, 1992

Dorothy is excited when *Jeopardy!*—her all-time favorite show—announces contestant tryouts in Miami. And after she and Blanche—who doesn't care about the
show but has a crush on its host, Alex Trebek—show up to take the written test,
Dorothy is indeed selected to proceed to a live audition.

As Dorothy studies long into the night, Sophia advises her to dial down the
intensity and instead just get some sleep. Moments later, when Dorothy does doze
off, she dreams of a nightmare scenario where she's on the show, up against not
only her lascivious *Empty Nest* neighbor Charlie Dietz (David Leisure) but her own
roommate—and the show's reigning champ—Rose. Worse yet are the first-round
categories, which seem suspiciously tailored to Dorothy's opponents: Cows, Babes,
Chickens, More Babes, Chicken Babes, and Baby Chickens. And so while Rose and
Charlie seem like ringers, Dorothy fails to score.

In the much more challenging Double Jeopardy round, however, a cocky Dorothy cleans up. But when the dream proceeds right to Final Jeopardy and its question: "American Hero Buried in Grant's Tomb," Alex declares, to Dorothy's dreamstate horror, that Rose is right: it's Cary, rather than Ulysses S. And when spoilsport Dorothy demands a ruling from the show's producers, Merv Griffin (1925–2007) himself not only sides with Rose, but also revokes Dorothy's parting gifts.

The next day, in the actual audition, Dorothy's up against much tougher competition in a NASA engineer and a neurosurgeon. And though she actually manages to win, her unsportsmanlike demeanor costs her dearly. As the show's casting agent (Derek McGrath) explains, "We don't think anyone would root for you."

Meanwhile, to perk up Rose's spirits after a tough week of volunteering, Dorothy and Blanche surprise her with a rescue dog from the local shelter. Rose recruits Jake to help out at the hospital as a therapy dog, and he soon takes a shine to the elderly Hubbards. The canine companion works miracles with Grace Hubbard (Camila Ashland) in her final days. And when Rose witnesses how much Jake has also come to mean to her husband (Bill Erwin, 1914–2010), she generously gives the dog to the new widower so he can continue to provide comfort.

◆ ◆ ◆ ◆

COMMENTARY: This episode marks at least the second time that the writers of *The Golden Girls* and *Cheers* found themselves on the same wavelength. It's actually a common phenomenon in comedy writing. As the *Girls'* showrunner Marc Sotkin explains, "Lightning never hits the planet in only one place."

This time, the *Golden Girls* didn't back down. A season earlier, the *Golden Girls* writers had changed parts of the episode "What a Difference a Date Makes" after an installment of *Cheers* featured a similar bit about a karaoke machine. Now, this episode comes even closer to something that had already happened to the habitués of the Boston bar; two years earlier, in the 1990 episode "What Is . . . Cliff Clavin?" *Cheers'* resident mailman and know-it-all (John Ratzenberger) also had appeared on *Jeopardy!* and had even

been similarly presented with seemingly tailor-made categories.

Interestingly, this episode has a second link to *Cheers*, via its casting; here playing *Jeopardy!*'s casting director, Derek McGrath had previously been best-known as *Cheers'* recurring homicidal maniac Andy Schroeder (aka "Andy Andy"). Playing Mr. Hubbard is Bill Erwin, who was cast as seemingly very old men for decades, most memorably in the 1980 film *Somewhere in Time* and in a 1993 episode of *Seinfeld*. Mrs. Hubbard is played by Camila Ashland, who had previously been known for her role as Minnie du Val on the cult '60s soap, *Dark Shadows*.

Guest star David Leisure appears here as Charlie Dietz in a crossover from *The Golden Girls'* spinoff, *Empty Nest*. He had previously appeared in one other *Golden Girls* episode— sort of. The final episode of

OPPOSITE:

The animal actor playing Jake receives his training on the set of Mrs. Hubbard's hospital room.

Photo courtesy of the EDWARD S. STEPHENSON ARCHIVE *at the* ART DIRECTORS GUILD.

the *Girls*' second season, "Empty Nests," had been intended as an embedded pilot for another series, but that spinoff was never to be; David costarred as Rita Moreno and Paul Dooley's annoying neighbor, this time named Oliver (after Paul Witt and Susan Harris's real-life son).

And finally, this episode features cameos from not just one but two TV giants associated with the game show *Jeopardy!* The show's host Alex Trebek appears here, as he had on *Cheers*; but the *Girls* up the ante with an appearance by the game show's executive producer Merv Griffin (1925–2007), himself a small-screen legend.

JERRY PERZIGIAN: I was always jealous of writers who could take an incident from their own lives and make a sitcom episode out of it. Never in my life was I writing "the truth." Instead of "What do I care about?" it was always, "We have a half hour of airtime to fill this Saturday, and what can I pretend to care about?"

But this one time, on *The Golden Girls*, we were up against the wall looking for a story, and I told this story about how, when I first moved to Hollywood, I didn't have a job and was painting houses and moving furniture. My writing partner said, "Let's go on a game show," and so we did go to audition for the show *Knockout*, hosted by Arte Johnson.

My partner flunked the written test, but I passed. The second thing was an interview, and I passed. Then a run-through for the producer and Arte Johnson, not on the set but in a rehearsal hall with a wooden podium and hotel bell. The producer told us, "To get on the show, you must get the answers right, make the host laugh, and charm the old ladies in the audience." And so that's exactly what I did.

By the end, there were about twenty people left. At that point the producer said, "Lisa, the production assistant, will be passing out an information sheet that will tell you to report on Monday. Those of you who are going to be here Monday, thank you very much, and those of you who are not, we're very sorry." And then everybody got the sheet but me.

It didn't sink in what had happened. So I went up to the producer and said, "I don't want to make any trouble for Lisa, but she forgot to give me the sheet." To which he replied, "No, she didn't forget." Still not getting it, I said, "But you don't understand. I don't know where to report on Monday." And so finally, he spelled it out: "She did not make a mistake. You're not on the show." I couldn't believe it. I pointed out to him: "But I got the answers right. I made them laugh. How am I not on the show?"

The producer looked me in the eye and asked, "Do you really want to know? On any game

---

---

show, any guest celebrity is not the star. You the contestant are the celebrity, the person the audience has to root for and like. And we don't think people would root for you."

It ended up being the only time in my life where I didn't have to make up anything. Because we had our game show producer say that to Dorothy, word for fucking word.

ALEX TREBEK: It pays to be a friend of Betty White's. I think that's why they invited me to be on *The Golden Girls*, and it's why later I got to be a guest star on *Hot in Cleveland*, too. I did watch *The Golden Girls* at the time, so I was thrilled to be asked to appear. I didn't get to have much to do with Rue or Estelle on the set. But not only did I get to work with Betty, but also Bea was a lot of fun, and we got along well.

JOURNEY TO THE CENTER OF ATTENTION

Written by: MARC CHERRY & JAMIE WOOTEN • *Directed by:* LEX PASSARIS

Original airdate: FEBRUARY 22, 1992

Blanche coerces a lonely Dorothy into joining her for a night of excitement and nickel beer at her favorite bar hangout. Once there, Blanche is soon dethroned as the queen of the Rusty Anchor when the patrons take an instant liking to Dorothy, whose singing makes her the new center of attention. To regain her stature, Blanche plans to beat Dorothy at her own game, with a sexy number sung atop the bar's piano. But her rendition of "I Wanna Be Loved by You" goes clumsily and hilariously wrong, sending Blanche running in tears for the ladies' room. Dorothy follows after her, and the two Girls admit to times when they are jealous of each other. And although neither is willing to give up her night of adoration at the Rusty Anchor, they come to an amicable settlement: they'll split up the nights of the week.

Meanwhile, after she and Rose have a grand time at Doug Kirkpatrick's Irish wake, Sophia decides to throw her own memorial to keep the party going. But after absent-minded Rose neglects to inform the congregants in the Girls' living room that Sophia's not actually deceased, the honoree inadvertently gives Myrtle (Jane Dulo, 1917–94), Eva (Ann Nelson, 1916–92), and her other dearest friends the shock of their lives.

◆ ◆ ◆ ◆

COMMENTARY: *The Golden Girls* had found a few earlier excuses to get Bea Arthur singing: she belted "Miami, You've Got Style" as the Girls entered a song-writing contest, impersonated Cher on "I've Got You Babe," and added a basso profundo "Yessss . . . ?" to the Girls' cribside lullaby of "Mr. Sandman." But this episode gives us Bea performing two classic tunes—"Hardhearted Hannah" and "What'll I Do"—leaving the patrons of the Rusty Anchor, undoubtedly the gayest dockside straight bar in all of Miami, calling out for an encore.

"Journey to the Center of Attention" provides a second treat with Rue's musical number, as she attempts to writhe sexily on the bar's piano like an older Michelle Pfeiffer in *The Fabulous Baker Boys*. But unlike Michelle, when Blanche kicks up her heel, she loses a shoe. When she plays with the microphone cord, she nearly strangles a customer. And when she slides up to the pianist, she falls right on her eighty-eights. It's one of the series' best bits of physical comedy.

RUE McCLANAHAN: I loved the choice of song for Blanche to do atop the piano, "I Wanna Be Loved by You." Marilyn Monroe had done it, and Blanche wanted to be Marilyn Monroe, after all. I also liked the song because it is something that can easily fall apart, and be made fun of. If you sing it too slowly and seriously, it doesn't work. It's supposed to be an upbeat number—"boop boop be doop!" But Blanche decided to sing it sexy. And then it just goes to hell in a handbasket.

I like doing physical comedy, and I like to sing. And I knew that the bit on the piano would have to be choreographed precisely for it to look that sloppy and in the moment. I had recently co-written the book for a musical farce at the Golden Theater in Burbank called *Oedipus, Shmoedipus, As Long As You Love Your Mother*, and worked with a choreographer named Gregory Scott Young. So I asked him to come in to *The Golden Girls* and help me work out Blanche's moves for that scene. I told him I wanted Blanche to just make a shambles of the song, and he came up with some very funny stuff, like the shoe flying off. We did it by the numbers, and I learned it meticulously. And then I had to do it like it was happening spontaneously and surprising Blanche. I was so relieved when I got through it without mishap and had to do it only once at each taping of the show. But I can't think of anything I enjoyed doing more as Blanche.

MARC CHERRY: This was the most glorious episode to work on, because we got to choose the material the ladies would sing. For Bea, we wanted something ballsy and classic, and that led us to pick "Hardhearted Hannah." And for her second number, Bea asked, "Give me something that's pretty." So we ended up with "What'll I Do."

For Blanche's bit where she gets the microphone cord wrapped around a guy's neck, she rehearsed with our producer Kent Zbornak all week long. So when it came time to do it with someone else, because it would be tricky timing, someone suggested,

"Don't trust an extra—we've got to use Kent." So when you see this episode, and see the guy being choked by the mic cord, that's our beloved Kent Zbornak, for whom Dorothy was named.

For the B plot of the episode, I remember writing Sophia's wake scene at one o'clock in the morning in my condo, when I was really tired and just throwing down some jokes. And then the scene ended up being shot very much like I wrote it, which almost never happened. Sophia's friend Myrtle [Jane Dulo] comes into the house, and to lighten the mood and change the subject, Blanche says Myrtle will do some of her impressions. Myrtle, grieving Sophia, says, "Oh God, oh God!" and Blanche guesses, "Jimmy Swaggart, right?" And Myrtle says, "What happened? I didn't even know she was sick!" And Blanche guesses, "Claus von Bülow?" Typically, my writing style is that I tend to write a gentler kind of comedy, coming from characters' attitudes. But the great thing about *The Golden Girls* for me was that I started learning how to write hard jokes.

At this point during the final season, we had been going through a stretch where we were a little short on Rose stories, and I remember counting that Rose had only thirteen lines in this episode. Other actors would have complained, but Betty never did. We did give Betty the moment at the Rusty Anchor where, after Blanche throws down the mic, Rose devilishly picks it up, and Betty played that so beautifully.

But the thing I remember most about the taping of the episode is that when it came time to do the scene where Dorothy comforts Blanche in the ladies' room, it was at the end of the night and we were running late. Rue felt that we didn't do enough takes, and was upset because she didn't feel she had given her best possible performance. And on top of that, this episode was going to be her Emmy submission. And so she made her case to the producers, and they ended up reshooting that scene again the next week— one of the very few times that ever happened.

OPPOSITE:

One of the series' most beloved locations, Blanche's favorite dockside bar, the Rusty Anchor.

Photo courtesy of the EDWARD S. STEPHENSON ARCHIVE *at the* ART DIRECTORS GUILD.

HOME AGAIN, ROSE
(PARTS 1 & 2)

Written by: GAIL PARENT (PART 1), JIM VALLELY (PART 2)
Directed by: PETER D. BEYT • *Original airdate:* APRIL 25, 1992 & MAY 2, 1992

In her never-ending quest for fresh men, Blanche convinces the Girls to crash the reunion of the East Miami High Class of '52. The scheme initially goes well—especially for Sophia, who finds a dance partner in an attendee who mistakes her for Spanish 101 teacher Mrs. Gonzales, and Dorothy, who as "Cindy Lou Peeples" gets to live out her lifelong dream of being prom queen. Rose, upset that she had to miss her own recent reunion in St. Olaf because she hadn't been feeling well, is happy to play along, too—even though she's hardly convincing as Korean exchange student Kim Fung Toy. So perhaps it's partly due to the stress from telling such an outrageous lie that Rose eventually collapses to the floor, just as the foursome is exposed as impostors.

Later, at the hospital, the Girls pace the waiting room anxiously, with Blanche going as far as to promise God she won't have sex anymore—unless the man "really, really needs it." Just then, a doctor emerges to let them know that Rose's heart attack was mild; at her bedside, they all vow to change their lives for the better. Sophia considers law school, Dorothy decides to go out more—and Rose makes her friends swear that like her they too will sign up to have their heads cryogenically frozen upon their deaths. After humoring their friend's strange request, the Girls go home relieved; but when they return to the hospital the next morning, they learn that Rose has gone into cardiac arrest, and is being prepped for surgery.

In part two, as Rose undergoes a triple bypass, the Girls grapple with the fact that they may lose their ditzy roommate forever—and worse yet, the hospital staff won't permit them, as non-family members, to see her. When Rose's blood relative, her daughter Kirsten (Lee Garlington) does arrive, she lashes out, blaming the Girls' fun lifestyle together for her mother's cardiac problems. But in the end, as Kirsten hears that the Girls are willing to go as far as mortgaging Blanche's house in order to pay for physical therapy, she relents and allows a recovering Rose to return to her true home.

◆ ◆ ◆ ◆

COMMENTARY: Although it may seem odd for the show's writers to give Rose a heart attack just weeks before concluding the series for good, these two episodes perfectly underscored for the penultimate time the *Golden Girls* theme: the power of the surrogate family. Kirsten, who has witnessed some strange goings-on on Richmond Street, may at first not understand, but she is soon won over—first by Rose's request to care for the Girls after she's gone, and then by the Girls' "extra insurance policy," as Dorothy puts it. As Kirsten hears about their pact to take care of each other in times of trouble, we viewers, too, are moved by the love to be found among this very special foursome.

The episodes contain some moments noteworthy for other reasons as well—particularly, in part two, the now-famous dream visual of Rose, Dorothy, and Blanche as mere heads, sitting atop ice-ringed platters on their kitchen table. These episodes also mark the first and only time we'll meet Blanche's oft-referenced daughter Janet (Jessica Lundy). Two of the names from the reunion are of special note as well; prom king and queen Danny Farrell and Cindy Lou Peeples are named for two of Marc Cherry's fellow cast mates from his days in the choral group the Young Americans. In fact, Cindy Lou's seems to be a go-to name for Cherry, popping up again in 2006 in an episode of his series *Desperate Housewives*.

JIM VALLELY: In my second year on the show, which was season six, the producers teamed Gail Parent and me together, because she was so great with story, and I was known for jokes. At this point in the series, we'd started to experiment a little bit with jokes that were a little more out there. And so we came up with the frozen heads scene. I couldn't believe

we did it. Of course, the ladies hated it; they were all so uncomfortable.

GAIL PARENT: I was married to a man who was really into cryogenics and wanted to be frozen, so that's where that idea came from. Even funnier, I read up on it and found out that for a certain amount of money you could get your whole body frozen—but for a little less, you could have done just your head. The moment I read that I thought, "This is great!"

RICHARD VACZY: Shortly before this episode, my hometown of Sayville, Long Island, had experienced a series of arson fires that had burned down half of Main Street. So to help the town rebuild, we auctioned off a walk-on part on *The Golden Girls*, with airfare and hotel. And in the end, the man who played the prom king paid twenty-four thousand dollars for that experience.

LEE GARLINGTON: Along with Tom Hanks and Oprah Winfrey, Betty White is one of our national treasures. She's always been so sweet, and funny, and refined. And to this day, if and when I run into her, she'll say something like, "My daughter!" because of this episode.

JESSICA LUNDY: There's so much stunt casting in sitcoms now, where guest stars on the most popular shows are already really well known. But one of the wonderful things about *The Golden Girls* was that because the show had four top-notch, well-known stars, for the guest roles the producers could cast anyone they wanted. They didn't need to bring in "names."

When this episode aired, it was still at a time where if, as an actor, you appeared on a top-ten network show, everyone would see you. In fact, years later, when I went on an audition for a role in a pilot, one of the first things the pilot's producer said was, "That's the lipstick you wore on *The Golden Girls*!" And she was right.

PETER D. BEYT: The famous scene in the second episode, where the Girls are nothing but cryogenically preserved heads on their kitchen table— "We're heads! We're heads!"—did present a big challenge for filming. Not for the prop guys, who designed a table with cutouts for the ladies to stick their heads through, and molded gelatin to look like fake ice. The bigger problem was Bea was claustrophobic. So she immediately let us know she didn't want to be in some little box, or crouched under a table with her head sticking out.

I had done some effects work before, so I had an idea. We raised the table, so that we could put Bea, Rue, and Betty in office chairs, and then roll them right into place. Then, I had to also put platforms behind the table, to bring Estelle up to the proper relative height. Finally, I cheated the perspective with the cameras, so that the cabinets and the rest of the kitchen look in the right heights and proportions. So the scene looks like it was shot with the regular kitchen table, but underneath it, Bea is sitting in an office chair, completely upright. The other women even tucked in their knees, to give Bea more legroom. She still had a brief moment of angst and panic, but nothing big. And we got the shot, for a scene that so many people remember.

NINA FEINBERG WASS (*producer***):** The scene with the Girls' heads cryogenically frozen was hilarious, and one of my favorites of all time. But when the writers were originally working on it, they were stuck on one particular joke for what seemed like forever. As Rose, Blanche, and Dorothy's heads are all frozen on the table, Sophia walks in. We'd stuffed Estelle's bra and put lipstick on her, and her body looked amazing. The setup is Dorothy asking something like, "Ma, where did you get that body of a twenty-five-year-old woman?" The writers were pitching punch lines for hours, until finally Jim Vallely said that the joke should be Sophia replying, "You didn't tip the guy?" It was genius.

OPPOSITE:
The crew sets up a complicated shot depicting Blanche, Rose, and Dorothy as frozen heads.

Photo courtesy of the EDWARD S. STEPHENSON ARCHIVE *at the* ART DIRECTORS GUILD.

ONE FLEW OUT OF THE CUCKOO'S NEST

(PARTS 1 & 2)

Written by: DON SEIGEL, JERRY PERZIGIAN, & MITCHELL HURWITZ
Directed by: LEX PASSARIS • *Original airdate:* MAY 9, 1992

Busy with a rendezvous of her own, Blanche persuades typically dateless Dorothy to entertain her visiting uncle, Lucas (Leslie Nielsen, 1926–2010). On their "date," the duo cooks up a scheme to get revenge on Blanche, by pretending to fall madly in love. But soon, it becomes clear that their phony love is all too real, and Lucas pops the question in earnest.

In part two, as the date approaches for Dorothy and Lucas's wedding, the other Girls prepare for life to change forever. Sophia initially plans to leave with Dorothy, while Rose opts to move in with her own daughter. Even Stan (Herb Edelman) recognizes this moment as the end of an era, as he commandeers the wedding limo so as to get a chance to wish his ex-wife well. In the end, both Rose and Sophia decide to stay on with Blanche in Miami, and bid a tearful goodbye—three times!—to newlywed Dorothy Petrillo Zbornak Hollingsworth as she embarks on her new life in Atlanta.

◆ ◆ ◆ ◆

COMMENTARY: Series finales are a tricky business. Whereas a show's pilot has to create a new world, to show the audience that through some incident happening right now, a can't-miss party is just starting, a finale has to accomplish the opposite, to let us know the party's over. For a hit series, it can be difficult to let your devoted fans down easy; the best sitcom finales (e.g., *The Mary Tyler Moore Show*) are the ones that show

that due to a change in circumstances, the old gang may be breaking apart, but their love will last forever. And that's exactly what this last episode of *The Golden Girls* accomplishes so beautifully.

Dorothy may be moving to Atlanta with Lucas, but as her repeated hugs and proclamations attest, her Girls will always be in her heart.

With his deep, stentorian voice, guest star Leslie Nielsen had started his career playing

OPPOSITE:

Bridesmaids Blanche and Rose, and mother-of-the-bride Sophia, flank Dorothy and Lucas Hollingsworth (Leslie Nielsen) on their wedding day.

Photo by ABC PHOTO ARCHIVES/ABC *via* GETTY IMAGES.

serious authority figures, such as the captain in 1972's *The Poseidon Adventure*. But that all changed in 1980, when he got to unleash his silly side in the megahit film spoof *Airplane!* From then on, Leslie was a hot commodity in comedy, appearing as the title character in Mel Brooks's *Dracula: Dead and Loving It*, several of the *Scary Movie* sequels, and in three *Naked Gun* films based on his own short-lived 1982 cop parody series *Police Squad!* A man famous for his love of the fart machine and joy buzzer gags, Leslie continued to appear in comedy after comedy right up until his death in 2010 at age eighty-four.

RUE McCLANAHAN: It was painful doing the finale. I just didn't want the show to end. At the end of the episode, when Dorothy leaves, and says goodbye—and then comes right back in, and we all scream and hug some more, and this goes on until she does leave for good—that was painful. Those were real tears.

LEX PASSARIS: The weekend before we shot the *Golden Girls* finale, the Museum of Television and Radio in Los Angeles [now the Paley Center for Media] hosted a *Mary Tyler Moore Show* marathon, including that show's final episode.

[*MTM* director] Jay Sandrich was there, and afterward, I went up to him, and said, "You did the *Golden Girls* pilot, and I'm doing the finale. Do you have any advice?"

The Mary Tyler Moore Show finale had that famous group hug scene, where they sang "It's a Long Way to Tipperary." Jay asked me, "Do you have your Tipperary scene?" When I responded yes, he advised me to just block it minimally, but otherwise not to rehearse it with the actors. I went back to the office and mentioned this to Paul Witt and Tony Thomas, and got their blessing to approach it that way.

As it turns out, we were running short on time that week anyway. We normally had five days to make a show, but this last week we had only four, due to a mix-up in schedule for a ceremony where Paul, Tony, and Susan Harris were getting an award. On top of that, this was one of the rare times when we had an exterior shoot, near Highland Avenue and Fifth Street, for the scene in the limo where Stan surprises Dorothy and gives his blessing. Plus, producers had decided that the standard church set that had always been used on Witt/Thomas shows from *Soap* onward wouldn't work, so we had a new one built; not only did the new set not arrive until the last minute, but it turned out to be difficult and time-consuming to shoot in.

When we finally got to the final scene on our last rehearsal afternoon, and started running through it, Leslie Nielsen said his line, "Ready, Freddie?" and then exited—and the ladies were about to start in to their goodbye lines. I stopped them. I told Bea the basics of which doors she should use for each of her entrances and exits, but then said let's move on. I had explained it all so fast that Estelle went over to Betty and Rue and asked, "What did he say?" I requested that the two of them just steer Estelle in the right direction, and once I told them I was acting on Jay's advice, they got right away what was happening.

Even at the table read of this episode on that Monday, Bea couldn't get through that final dialogue without crying. And so the tears you see in the episode from all the ladies are the real thing, with these actresses saying their own real farewells for the first time. The producers had made very lucrative offers for Bea and all the ladies to continue, and I know the decision to leave had been hard for Bea. You could see it in her eyes on that last day. But I absolutely respect her decision, and I think she was right. She felt that after seven seasons the show had done everything it could do with the character of Dorothy Zbornak.

TRACY GAMBLE: I didn't like that we were ending the show with Dorothy departing to get married, because it seemed to me that *The Golden Girls* was about single women, and the theme was that they're still vital. This ending seemed to say that a man was the answer to all Dorothy's problems. However what I did like about the finale was when Dorothy kept coming back to say goodbye—and then she doesn't come back. And suddenly, you feel her missing, and the void and the emptiness. I felt that was a great way to underscore the feeling. And if we were going to marry her off, Leslie Nielsen was a terrific choice.

BEA ARTHUR: I hated that wedding gown. It was the first and last time our costume designer, Judy Evans, ever did anything I didn't like. I had known Leslie Nielsen for years, from the Actors Studio. But I was terrified when he came on the show, because Leslie is known for that prank gadget that makes you sound like you are farting. He uses it with everyone. So I remember when he first came on to the set, I said, "Leslie please don't shake hands with me, because I really don't think that thing is funny."

I loved the bit about exiting and then running back in for another hug. I was just upset that I couldn't do it faster, that I couldn't do it so that I would leave in one door, and then instantly be back in through the next.

MITCHELL HURWITZ: Because I had spent so much time with Paul Witt and Tony Thomas, I had been privy to a very personal story from Paul's life, and I suggested that we adapt it for this last episode. Paul and Tony and Susan Harris had created their company, Witt/Thomas/Harris. Paul and Susan had dated for a while, but it was unsuccessful. And working together, the two of them had a very contentious and heated relationship, with a real intensity.

At one point, Paul and Susan heard that Tony was going on a trip to Italy with his wife, and, flush with all this money from *Soap*, they decided to pull the greatest practical joke of all time. Tony didn't know that they had access to his itinerary. So they came up with the plan to fly to Italy, and wait at the restaurant where Tony would be arriving. When he walked in, they would act surprised to see him, and tell him, "We just got married!" They anticipated he'd be shocked, so they'd tell him, "You left us alone, and passions ignited!"

So they did it. They flew to Italy, and pulled this elaborate gag—but they didn't get the reaction they expected. Instead of being shocked, Tony raised his glass and spoke at great length about

OPPOSITE:
On Dorothy's wedding day, cast, crew, and a church full of extras get ready for the big moment.
FOLLOWING PAGE:
A view from the altar inside the brand-new church set.

Photos courtesy of the EDWARD S. STEPHENSON ARCHIVE *at the* ART DIRECTORS GUILD.

how the two of them were the most wonderful people he'd ever met, and how it is so clear to everyone around them that theirs is real love, a good match. That is what the heat between them, and the fighting, is all about, he said. He'd always known this would happen someday, and that it had been merely a matter of time before Paul and Susan discovered the truth for themselves.

Well right on the heels of that, Paul and Susan now had all this time to spend together in romantic Italy. And whatever it was that Tony had said, it led them to really take each other seriously. And sure enough, they did get married!

I would never have pitched a story about Dorothy pretending to fall in love with Blanche's uncle Lucas, then doing so for real—because it's crazy. But so many times, the stories that seem the most contrived are the real ones. So when we were looking for a romantic, two-part story for

the finale, I remember saying, "I happen to know this thing about Paul Witt . . . " The finale story had to be special, and I knew all the other writers would be hard on any pitch. But I also thought to myself: "This story is so crazy I bet they approve it." And they did. It didn't all remain in the final episode, but in my first draft, Blanche even got up and spoke just as Tony had, saying, "Of course you guys got married, because you're such a great match."

For me, doing this story was a great way to pay homage to the bosses, by telling their romantic story. It came from a real place, and that made it more interesting to write. Even the last hug, where Dorothy leaves, then comes back, then leaves again—twice—was something you might do in real life. We weren't sure it would be that funny on TV, but it's the type of real, dramatic moment you'd have in saying goodbye to somebody, and that's what made it work.

FROM
KITCHEN to LANAI:
PRODUCTION & SET DESIGN

WHEN LEGENDARY PRODUCTION designer Ed Stephenson first read the script for Susan Harris's new high-profile pilot, he knew just the home he wanted to create for the *Girls*. A decades-long TV veteran and three-time Emmy winner, Ed had worked with Betty White on live TV in the fifties, and later with Bea Arthur and Rue McClanahan on *Maude*. Now as the in-house designer for all the Witt/Thomas/Harris productions, Ed had a gut feeling that *The Golden Girls* was going to be a big hit, and wanted to create a lasting environment befitting the show's four powerhouse stars.

Even before earning his credits in TV, Ed had started his career working in Florida theater. "So he knew exactly what he wanted to do," remembers Michael Hynes, *The Golden Girls*' longtime assistant art director. "He went home one weekend and designed the whole thing, and then we started making a model of the three rooms in the house the pilot called for: the living room, lanai, and Blanche's bedroom."

Right from the start, Ed envisioned a certain "Florida look" for the Girls' home's interior, explains John Shaffner, the assistant art director Ed tasked with decorating the pilot's sets. Ed wanted the look of pecky wood, a textured cypress popular in South Florida, for the house's doors, interior columns, and roofline. Then, it was time for the two to talk furniture. "We realized that each of these women was going to be bringing something into this house. It wasn't just Blanche's house now, but a little bit of everyone's," John explains. And so, although the living room was dominated by a tropical rattan-style couch, its adjoining end table or console might not match.

For the home's fabrics and decorative touches, the designers opted for a palette of pastels and softer hues, with occasional pops of brighter color. Then, as John remembers, "When it came time for the set to be installed on the stage, it was so simple. The flooring I had selected was unrolled and taped down. The set walls were put up, and painted all the colors and textures Ed had selected. Prop men moved in the furniture and hung art on the walls, and I finished dressing the set down to the coffee mugs on the kitchen counter.

"The producers came through the next day, and looked at everything, and said, 'This is wonderful. Thank you very much.' And that was it," explains John, who went on to design the iconic looks of *Friends*, *Two and a Half Men*, and *The Big Bang Theory*. "It wasn't nearly like today, where hand-wringing executives will come to check your progress every day, and say, 'Are those the throw pillows you're going to use? Are you sure about that lamp?'"

It Takes a Kitchen

◆ ◆ ◆ ◆

THEN, EVERYTHING CHANGED in a Miami minute. Not long before the actresses were scheduled to start rehearsing on the sets, Ed's team received a revised script, complete with new scenes to take place in the Girls' kitchen. "There had been no kitchen in the original script. But now, right at the last minute, we needed one," Michael remembers. Luckily, having worked on so many sitcoms, Ed had kept over 150 of his past sets in storage; the Witt/Thomas warehouses were full of rooms previously seen on such shows as *Soap*, *Benson*, and *It's a Living*. "Ed came back to the office," Michael recalls, "and said, 'What do we have in stock?'"

Perusing the company's inventory, Michael found a kitchen he convinced Ed would work, from Witt/Thomas's earlier show *It Takes Two*. "So we took what had been that show's kitchen and just spliced it right on to the *Golden Girls'* living room," he explains. "We took out the oven area and a couple of cabinets to make it a little smaller, but otherwise that was their wall paper, their shelves, and their plants." Outside the same kitchen window, instead of a scrim of the glittering Chi-

ABOVE:

Left to right: Helen Hunt, Richard Crenna, and Patty Duke in ABC's 1982–83 sitcom *It Takes Two*.

Photo courtesy of PHOTOFEST, *with permission of* DISNEY ENTERPRISES, INC.

cago skyline was now an image of sun-dappled Miami palms. And with that, the kitchen that would become iconic as the setting for *The Golden Girls'* beloved cheesecake scenes was created, recycled from the remnants of a forgotten show that had lasted merely one season.

With the Girls' new kitchen installed and ready, the show's first crisis was averted—temporarily. By their very nature, sitcoms suffer from what Michael refers to as "the proscenium theater problem": multicamera shows require three-walled sets, much like opened-up dollhouses, which still need to look convincingly like someone's home. "Life exists in 360 degrees, and theater exists in 180," Michael explains. "And yet I still have to fit everything in there: stairways, doors, the kitchen. So by their very nature, all sitcoms sets are already contorted."

Production designers usually devise ways around this issue in their blueprint or modeling stages; but here, the Girls' kitchen had been added after the fact, creating a ripple effect of other changes that made the layout of the house cease to make sense. "The kitchen created issues no one could ever solve," Michael admits. For starters, now that the room was established as being off the stage-right end of the living room, where was the access to the Girls' sleeping quarters?

The team's solution was to create an upstage hallway,

leading back to the bedrooms—but the fix created even more discrepancies. The pilot presents Blanche's bedroom as being off the upstage-left corner of the living room, and the lanai as entered from a door just to the left of the fireplace; in the series, the lanai orientation would be reversed and its access moved upstage left, with Blanche now bunking off the same hallway as her roommates. Either way, Rose's room now seems to be in the middle of the backyard. And now, the back exit of the kitchen, supposedly toward the garage, seems to lead right into the area of Dorothy and Blanche's bedrooms. "We don't know where the garage is," Michael admits with a laugh. "All we know is there were minks in there once."

As Michael remembers, "We said, 'Well, when we get through the pilot, we'll fix it'—and then we never did." And so, throughout the series, sharp-eyed fans remained confused. "We used to get letters on occasion, saying: 'It looks like when Rose goes into her bedroom, she's going into the backyard, and I don't understand,'" he reveals. "And in fact, they were right. But Ed would answer the letters by saying, 'Just keep watching the show, and you'll figure it out eventually.'"

Reduce, Reuse, Recycle

◆ ◆ ◆ ◆

DRAWING ON HIS training in 1950s live TV, Ed Stephenson favored working with "modular" sets, which could be rearranged in different configurations to create various new rooms. By the time of *The Golden Girls*, Ed was expert at minimizing set-building expenses by recycling old pieces from his previous repertoire. Thus, a teak-paneled courtroom that had appeared on *Soap*, with a little bit of redressing, now became *Golden Girls* offices, waiting rooms, and even the apartment of Sophia's ancient millionaire roommate Malcolm in the show's fifth-season episode "Twice in a Lifetime."

Set photos courtesy of the EDWARD S. STEPHENSON ARCHIVE at the ART DIRECTORS GUILD.

Conference room, season 7, "Rose: Portrait of a Woman."

Courtroom, season 7, "Ebbtide VI: The Wrath of Stan."

Psychologist waiting room, season 7, "Mother Load."

Meeting hall, season 5, "Great Expectations."

Mr. Edouardo's hair salon, season 4, "Rites of Spring."

Men's clothing store, season 4, "Love Me Tender."

French restaurant, season 7, "Ro$e Love$ Mile$."

Banquet hall for Bachelorette Auction, season 6, "Love for Sale."

Hotel ballroom, season 5, "The Mangiacavallo Curse
Makes a Lousy Wedding Present."

Banquet hall for Volunteer Vanguard Awards,
season 6, "Sisters of the Bride."

Hotel ballroom housing the East Miami High Class of '52 reunion in season 7, "Home Again, Rose."

Daughters of the Old South banquet hall, season 6, "Witness."

Because the Girls attended so many receptions and awards banquets in hotel ballrooms and restaurants, Ed also devised a set he called the Classic Interior, which would pop up on the show again and again. With a selection of French-paneled walls, arches, and Palladian windows connected by individual pilasters, the set could be assembled in various configurations. "Like LEGOs," Michael explains. So whether they were vying for the Volunteer Vanguard Awards or crashing a high school reunion, the Girls were in differing versions of the same room.

In fact, the Classic Interior proved so versatile that when *The Golden Girls*' sequel series *Golden Palace* ceased production in 1993, Michael opted to keep the set in storage. He has continued to use the set for years, and has even rented it out to other production designers for their shows, donating the pro-

ceeds to the Thomas family's beloved charity, the St. Jude Children's Research Hospital.

Plywood walls, Michael notes, "last ten years if you're lucky." And yet, still viable today, the Classic Interior—"which, in scenery years, is Jurassic"—has proven to be atypically sturdy. In 2012, Michael brought the set to the stage yet again, for an episode of *Hot in Cleveland*. For a scene in which that show's four leading ladies attended a hotel fashion show, "I painted it white and put the runway right down the middle."

Then, just as the scene was ready to go, Michael asked *Hot in Cleveland* star Betty White if the surroundings looked familiar. "When I told her where the set came from, she flipped out," he reveals. "She went up and touched it, and got very emotional" to be back again, literally in the same halls where *The Golden Girls* once stood.

GOLDEN DECOR

KITCHEN

MICHAEL HYNES: Ed had picked out the original kitchen wallpaper, beige with a very small pattern of white dots. Midway through the first season, we changed it. The new paper from Astor Wallcovering had a cross-hatch rattan pattern, then big banana leaves in a darker beige over that, with three colors of green in it as well. The reason we changed it was that in those days, cameras were more primitive than they are now, and things would "flatten out" a lot. So we always looked for wallpaper that added layers and depth.

JOHN SHAFFNER: It was very smart of the writers to make the kitchen a separate room, because it gave them private places to take stories to. The swinging kitchen door allowed the storytelling to go into this other room, where you could have a conversation that wouldn't be overheard.

MH: By adding on the kitchen, we inadvertently created this little space behind the set walls that became a Golden Girls Bermuda Triangle. It was bounded by the baker's rack on the bottom, the right side of the hallway, and the left side of the kitchen. Often the ladies would hang out there and study their lines. Plus, it often happened that after the ladies were first introduced to the audience, and the camera would sweep in for extreme close-ups, the producers upstairs would start nitpicking their makeup. So the makeup people waited back in the triangle to fix them. But usually, the ladies would just pretend to get touch-ups. Then they'd come back out, just as before, and the producers would say, "Ah, much better."

JS: In the pilot, the kitchen table was a round, glass-topped piece from

Tropitone, with matching chairs, which we got at a patio store in the San Fernando Valley. Later the chairs remained but the table was a different piece, on a pedestal. But really, post-pilot, the look was all about the tablecloths, which they would change for each episode both to switch up the look and also to complement the ladies' wardrobe.

MH: Everything in the vicinity of the kitchen table was graffitied by Estelle. She would take a permanent marker and write her lines all over. I kept waiting for her to say a line from a previous episode, but she never did.

MH: The tablecloths quickly became a big deal on the show. Ed always wanted a pattern, but then after dress rehearsal, the producers would often note that the tablecloth clashed with someone's dress. So we started collecting different options. I bought quite a few on a personal trip to Paris. We ended up with a whole rack of fifty to sixty tablecloths, which we kept right behind the refrigerator.

JS: When the four ladies were in the kitchen, one would take a seat on a stool rather than the fourth place at the table, which would have her back to the camera. Today's sitcoms sometimes can take cameras deeper into the set, put up a section of wall and do a reverse shot, so that people can sit all around the table. But I think our classic multicamera, proscenium style is more appealing to the audience, because it's more like going to see a play.

JS: The original piece here was a butcher-block table, on wheels so that it could be moved, which was later replaced with a taller butcher-block kitchen island. The way Ed had laid out the kitchen, the sink was on a diagonal looking upstage, and the refrigerator was on the side wall. It wasn't a playable kitchen in terms of actually cooking, because all the appliances forced you to face away from the audience. So the kitchen island gave the actresses an area where they could do things facing downstage.

MH: Ed liked using things like the Jell-O molds over the sink to fill the space and cover blank walls. Sometimes we'd go to a design center, and he'd fall in love with things and say, "Let's put this

in the kitchen." At one point, we added a ceramic keyholder he found, with a caged bird design on it. It was imported from France, and we put it in the space above and to the left of the phone. I still have it today.

JS: Because shows are limited on stage space, Ed had come up with a way to replace the *It Takes Two/Golden Girls* kitchen set with something else when it wasn't needed. This area behind the swinging door, where he put the baker's rack, is all you see from the living room of the kitchen when the swinging door opens, so that the rest of the set could be removed.

MH: The big secret about the *Golden Girls* kitchen was that there was no oven. The *It Takes Two* kitchen had had a built-in oven next to the refrigerator, but we'd had to take it out for lack of space. We did still have a range, downstage facing the audience, where we'd sometimes see Sophia cooking. But underneath, it was just a cabinet. We took off the doors and replaced them with a piece of plywood with a handle on it. And the ladies would have to fake like they were taking something out of the "oven."

MH: We did change the kitchen curtains a few times, but they were always so stiff and not fun. If I could go back, that's the one thing I would change. Come on, these were four ladies in Florida. At least have flowers or something!

LANAI

JS: For the lanai furnishings, I went with pieces made by Tropitone, which had a wrought iron and vintage look, with forties-era detail.

MH: The original plants on the lanai were plastic, but they were always getting bent up and dusty. So we replaced them with living plants. Ed kept many of them, and to this day, those original plants are all still thriving at his shop.

MH: The lawn beyond the lanai was of course fake grass mats, and the scenery beyond was a giant rented backdrop. It had originally been painted for Frank Sinatra's 1959 movie *A Hole in the Head*.

LIVING ROOM

JS: It's funny how people scrutinize things over time that at the beginning had no significance whatsoever. People often comment on the "exclamation mark" in the grain of the front door. All of the woodwork on the set was not actually carved, but was painted to look grained and textured. Any marks you may see on the front door were just results of the nature of the paintbrush.

MH: This chunky doorknob was a great piece. It was made to go in the middle of a door, so I had to have it rebuilt. I was worried the actresses might have trouble with it, but they never did.

MH: Having done time in Florida, Ed really wanted to capture the distinctive wormholed look of pecky cypress wood, which a scenic artist would recreate with paint. This was before the Internet, and it was hard to find pictures in California to show just what he wanted.

JS: I had done a short-lived show for Witt/Thomas/Harris called *Condo*, and had purchased this large, Chinese art deco wool rug for the WASPy family on the show. It was yellow and white, and had an asymmetrical design, with a few pink and peach flowers in two corners, and a big border. It had been expensive—about thirty-five hundred dollars in 1983—and it was all the right colors we wanted for *The Golden Girls*, so we used it again.

JS: Putting this Chinese vase just inside the front door was just a decorative way to take up that space, and to put something with color and shape in front of a flat wall. We had no idea when we put it there that it would soon become part of a plot point, as Blanche's treasured vase that Rose accidentally shoots and destroys.

MH: I had to have duplicate versions made of this vase, for the episode where Rose shoots it. It was a fairly standard shape, so we had to find a breakaway vase and paint it to look the same. And then of course the next week, the vase was back in the living room again, like nothing had happened.

JS: One of the first things you have to do on a sitcom is identify the big piece for the living room: the sofa. It helps tell you where else you can go with the room's other elements. I decided I wanted a bamboo/rattan look. So I went to Harvey's, a popular furniture store now on Beverly Boulevard in LA, which was known for carrying the Florida look, as it was being called at the time.

I chose this piece because, although most rattan couches tended to have flat arms, this one had more of a unique, fan shape, which I thought was more feminine. The couch was actually made out of sectional elements, so we had to wire them together. Then, we tested several color palettes of fabric to cover it with, and gravitated to the orange/peach color, because it also went with the paver tile linoleum floor. The couch and its two matching chairs looked great on-screen, but they did create some issues for the wardrobe department, because they clashed with so many things. So we kept a constant array of throw pillows on hand, to create more of a neutral background between the ladies' outfits and the couch.

JS: Just a few years ago, I ran into Harvey's owner, Harvey Schwartz, at an event, and said to him, "You'll never remember this, but I bought the sofa for *The Golden Girls* from you." And he said, "You have no idea how many of those I sold because of that!"

MH: Each Saturday, we'd change the sets over for the next show. One day, we were goofing around, and one of the prop guys put a lampshade on my head, and took a picture. They decided that Polaroid should go on the set, so they framed it and put it right near the sofa. It sat there for three or four seasons.

MH: The pilot had a different coffee table, a carved square piece in dark wood—but we replaced it immediately afterward with this large square rattan model.

JS: Today, any photograph, painting, or illustration you put on a set has to be legally cleared with the owner of the image. Back in 1985, we had no restrictions—but still, it was hard to find images in prop houses that worked, and that hadn't been used too much on other shows. That's where Ed Stephenson was a very clever businessman. He amassed a very large collection of two-dimensional and sometimes sculptural works, and opened a business renting works to *The Golden Girls* and many other shows. His shop, the Hollywood Studio Gallery, is still there on Cahuenga Boulevard today.

MH: Ed wanted the fireplace to capture another classic Florida look: cut coral was literally mined from reefs and cut into blocks. In our case, our scenic artist used paint to capture that same interesting natural texture.

MH: Ed Stephenson had a maxim: you must always design depth to a set, but do it in such a way that the director can't really stage anything there—because if you stage something back there, against a flat wall, there goes the depth! Ed deliberately wanted to trap the action in the downstage area, which is where all multicamera scenes happen anyway. And then he made sure there was space upstage way behind the couch with a slanted roofline and fireplace that they wouldn't be able to use.

BLANCHE'S BEDROOM

JS: Ed absolutely knew what he wanted to do with Blanche's bedroom walls, without a moment's hesitation. He asked me to find the big banana-leaf print wallpaper from the Beverly Hills Hotel. We cut it out along each leaf, and glued each individually to the wall. Then, we didn't even have a headboard made. Instead, to continue the pattern right onto the bed, we had a double-sided, reversible bedspread custom-made to match the wallpaper. That was not cheap. In 1985, the fabric cost over fifty dollars per yard, plus the labor. Between the shooting of the pilot and the series, I was nervous the expensive bedspread would get lost. So I took this bedspread home—and used it on my own bed all summer.

DOROTHY'S BEDROOM

MH: I used to go to the department store Robinsons-May's outlet store in Panorama City, California to look for cheap sofas and furniture, and that's where I found this great pair of cabinets for Dorothy's room, to put on each side of the window. They had lots of little drawers, and I got a great deal on them. I wish I had them! They ended up in the Warner Bros. prop collection, and so I've used them again on other shows since.

MH: This gray rattan desk in Dorothy's bedroom came from a big design showroom in the Pacific Design Center in Los Angeles. It cost a fortune—but by that point, the show was printing money, so the producers didn't care.

ROSE'S BEDROOM

MH: I got Rose's bedroom furniture for cheap at Wickes Furniture, a chain home furnishings store, somewhere in the San Fernando Valley. They had a lot of pieces that were a more modern take on rattan, so I bought a lot there.

SOPHIA'S BEDROOM

MH: Our general idea for Sophia's room was to make it look like some of the pieces had been in her home in New York, but had been put in storage when Dorothy put her in Shady Pines. Her bedroom was the smallest of the four in Blanche's house; Edward Stephenson figured the other three ladies had already taken all the biggest rooms before Sophia moved in. I put in some white "antiqued" finish pieces, because that was something many women of Sophia's generation bought in the 1960s and then hung on to forever. And I thought the marquetry vanity had an old-world feeling Sophia would have liked. The headboard and much of the rest of the furniture came from Wertz Brothers Used Furniture in Hollywood, a source we used often. But Sophia did have one designer touch in the room: her wallpaper, from Albert Van Luit.

Different on Outside, Same on Inside

◆ ◆ ◆ ◆

WHEN ASSEMBLING A new sitcom, choosing establishing shots—locations to photograph that represent the outsides of the characters' homes—is a task usually saved for last. It's thankless work, because by definition, no existing building's exterior will ever align perfectly with a multicamera show's three-walled sets. "There

approached the show with an idea. As the company prepared to open its MGM theme park within Disney World in Orlando, the park's designers planned one attraction to be an exterior street where sitcoms or other TV shows could be shot. After taking extensive photos of the real *Golden Girls* house in Brentwood, the company rebuilt the house in Orlando from scratch—and not just a façade, but a full, three-dimensional building.

"Disney wanted to be able to say honestly that the new house was 'as seen on TV,' on *The*

isn't a show on television where you'll ever see an exact match," Michael Hynes explains. "So you can't become overly anxious about it."

So, for the Girls' house, the production team focused on finding a structure with at least the same overall "tone:" a low-slung house, with an overhanging roofline and surrounded by lush green shrubbery. Then, after the ideal candidate was located in the Brentwood section of Los Angeles, Ed tried to match the feeling of its entryway by enclosing the Girls' front doorstep inside an alcove, covered with vines of blooming bougainvillea.

In the middle of the *Girls'* run, however, Witt/Thomas's production partner, Disney,

Golden Girls," the show's associate director Lex Passaris recalls. And so for the remainder of the show's episodes, some of the establishing shots—particularly specialized footage such as a special-effects shot of the house being pelted by hurricane-force winds and rain—were captured in Orlando. But don't go looking to park in the Girls' Florida driveway today; in 2003 the house, along with a similar structure built to represent the exterior setting for *Golden Girls* spinoff *Empty Nest*, was razed, as the MGM park knocked down its "Residential Street" in order to make room for a new arena for the extreme stunt-show attraction "Lights, Motors, Action!"

PREVIOUS SPREAD:

The Golden Girls house in Brentwood, CA, in 2014.
ABOVE: Seen here in March 2001, the replica Golden Girls house at the Disney-MGM Studios theme park at Walt Disney World featured landscaping, and even the house number 245, recreated to match the original in Brentwood, CA.

Photo courtesy of FRANK DeCARO.
Photo by JOSEPH TITIZIAN.

MIAMI, YOU'VE GOT STYLE

"Ed Stephenson did a brilliant job of making the Golden Girls *sets look interesting without overpowering the actors. My job was to consult not just the scripts, but also the producers for their concepts for the characters, and the actresses about their own personal clothing likes and dislikes. As the costume designer, you're putting a whole picture together, incorporating all those different inputs."*

—JUDY EVANS STEELE,

costume designer

DOROTHY AND ROSE once sang, "Miami, You've Got Style," and the same could be said for the residents of Richmond Street themselves. Starting the moment they premiered in 1985, the Girls became icons not just for their senses of humor, but their fashion sense, too.

Whether it's Dorothy's long tunics or Blanche's flowing negligées, credit for the *Girls'* character-defining looks goes to the show's hard-working costume designer, Judy Evans Steele. "I wanted to keep the show overall feeling like Florida: bright, with lots of prints," Judy remembers. But of course, in order to make sure the four iconic actresses always looked their best, "You do take some license," she admits. "Even though it's hot in Florida, we didn't do sleeveless shirts. And I layered clothes to be flattering, even though you might not do that if it's a hundred degrees outside." Furthermore, despite the show's frequent plot points about the Girls running short on cash, "I didn't worry about putting them in clothes it looked like they

could afford," Judy adds. "The main idea was to make them look good. We didn't want the show to be about four dowdy ladies."

Overall, the show's much-esteemed designer explains, "I wanted a sexy, soft, and flowing look for Rue, a tailored, pulled-together look for Bea, a down-home look for Betty, and comfort for Estelle." And while for Rose and Sophia's outfits, she could usually find selections "off-the-rack, with a lot of alterations to make them fit," Dorothy and Blanche's more unique looks had to be her own custom creations. Outfitting the four in such separate styles, she remembers, "amounted to a lot of shopping and sewing, because often the ladies could have seven to ten costume changes per show."

During the show's run, Judy received "a tremendous amount of fan mail" from viewers wanting to know where she got Dorothy's vest or Blanche's skirt. (And, not wanting to break their hearts with news that the items were not available in stores, she often enclosed a photocopy of her design sketch and a swatch of fabric along with her reply.) Judy was never surprised at the strong viewer response. "There are so many designs from the show that would have helped women in that age group," she agrees. Because while there may be a lack of fashionable choices even today, in the eighties, off-the-rack "clothes for mature women were pretty sad," Judy remembers. Particularly for a taller woman like Bea Arthur, "there was nothing really wonderful out there that would fit her."

Now, with the era's couture back in full force, the Girls' ensembles continue to captivate. Designer Zulema Griffin particularly admires Dorothy's wardrobe, full of cowl-neck, oversized tops, wide-leg capri bottoms, and slouchy boots, a style that she calls "unique and flattering to tall women." And although designer John Bart-

lett derides Dorothy's style as "beyond freaky," he does appreciate Blanche's excellent taste in Florida day wear.

The Golden Girls is definitely an eighties show," Judy admits. "But I think looking back, I get the 'what were we thinking?' feeling less than I would on other shows. I think a lot of those clothes you could probably get away with today.

"Yes, I definitely took chances, and remember: Bob Mackie could do the most stupendous design, and half the people will love it, half will hate it. I don't think you can get everybody to agree," Judy adds. "As a costume designer, you have a very short time to put these things together, and if you go out on a limb, you either make a wonderful statement or you end up doing something you wouldn't do again."

Fashion photos by JEFF BLANCHARD.

Betty and Rue in male golfer drag, season 4, "You Gotta Have Hope."

Photo courtesy of the ESTATE OF RUE McCLANAHAN, *estateofrue.com.*

SEASON 4, "VALENTINE'S DAY": The ladies had figures, so I couldn't always do a fitted waistline. Diagonal looks like on this blue linen tunic top are slimming. And rather than a tighter turtleneck, I like the white cowl-neck underneath because it's softer, feminine, and more flowing. Bea and Dorothy were both long skirt people, and the taupe suede boots complete the look of the skirt without looking choppy. I don't think a sandal or a flat would have worked—and Bea, who hated wearing shoes in general, would never wear heels.

SEASON 2, "ISN'T IT ROMANTIC?" Even at night, we wanted the women looking good, not matronly. This nightgown of Blanche's is made up of several layers of peach silk chiffon, edged in white lace trim and cut to different sleeve lengths to create the layered effect. It was very Rue.

SEASON 6, "THERE GOES THE BRIDE" For this nighttime ensemble for Blanche, I overlaid a white embroidered material over the bodice of a white nightgown, and then used the same embroidery as trim for her blue, green, and cream-print robe.

SEASON 2, "DIAMOND IN THE ROUGH": I sketched this formal gown for Dorothy in magenta, but made it in navy blue. I originally envisioned it as a simple column dress in jersey fabric with a drape of sequins attached at the shoulder and then crossing down below. But when working with the fabric, the sequins wouldn't drape the way I wanted, so I reversed the design. This was very simple, and very Bea—very much something she'd wear in her own life, and she did borrow this.

SEASON 2, "EMPTY NESTS" This lounging outfit is one of my favorite designs for the show, and we must have repeated Blanche wearing it umpteen times. I loved this "paw-print" fabric the moment I saw that it came in four tones—blue, beige, pink, and peach—that went so well together. It's made in many layers, a pink top with sleeves, a blue tank, and a robe in beige with blue sleeves.

SEASON 4, "YOU GOTTA HAVE HOPE" I drew this Dorothy design in red, but I found a great gold-yellow knit fabric instead. The top is on the theme of a dressed-up sweatshirt, with a white shawl collar and slimming diagonal lines. Underneath is a separate long-sleeved white shirt, over matching culottes. Separates were great because we could mix and match them again later.

SEASON 1, "NICE AND EASY" Lingerie was something we would reuse often, so this Blanche ensemble would pop up again and again. It's in two pieces: a robe over a nightgown, both in blue silk with small white polka dots. The robe is cut on the bias with a scalloped collar to make it fall a certain way. The matching trim on both pieces looks like lace, but it's a printed white silk as well. Blues and greens were great colors for the show, because they looked great against all the warm tones on the set.

SEASON 6, "HENNY PENNY—STRAIGHT, NO CHASER" Not only did these costumes have to look like the animals in the play, but they also had to show Rose, Blanche, and Dorothy's personalities at the same time. I had worked on commercials for Toys "R" Us, with their giraffe mascots, so I had experience in working with foam costumes. I sketched the Henny Penny costumes with rounded bellies almost like a pregnant woman's, and big rear ends. These were complicated to build, with foam pieces sewn into bodysuits, and then covered with glued-on feathers. Blanche wore pearls to look sexy and feminine, but Rose and Dorothy's costumes then had an additional layer, with little fabric vests fitted on top.

SEASON 4, "BANG THE DRUM, STANLEY" Betty and Rue both had great legs, so these *Cats* costumes were a great way to show them off. The arms were tight, up to a burst of fluff at the cuff, and the wide feather-trimmed shoulders helped to narrow the waist. I sketched this costume for Blanche in tiger stripe, but I ended up finding a great, stretchy leopard-print fabric. The hairdressing department pinned little matching ears into their hair, and the two actresses had so much fun with the end result.

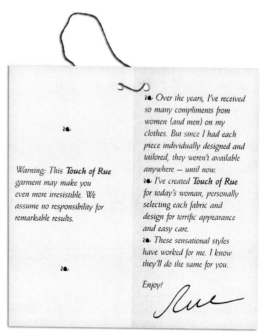

*Warning: This **Touch of Rue** garment may make you even more irresistible. We assume no responsibility for remarkable results.*

☙ Over the years, I've received so many compliments from women (and men) on my clothes. But since I had each piece individually designed and tailored, they weren't available anywhere — until now.

*☙ I've created **Touch of Rue** for today's woman, personally selecting each fabric and design for terrific appearance and easy care.*

☙ These sensational styles have worked for me. I know they'll do the same for you.

Enjoy!

A Touch of Rue

◆ ◆ ◆ ◆

AS *THE GOLDEN Girls* went off the air, Judy recalls, Betty White, Bea Arthur, and Estelle Getty were each permitted to select a small number of items from their characters' collection to keep. But not Rue McClanahan—she took them all.

"Rue used to have it built into her contracts that she got to keep all wardrobe," reveals her friend Michael J. LaRue. As evidenced by photos of the actress in her day-to-day life afterward, he adds, "She'd wear the pieces, too.

"A true clotheshorse," Michael says, Rue filled thirteen closets and several backyard storage units behind her Manhattan apartment with a lifetime worth of fashion, including her teal prom dress from 1949. A personal shopper continually supplemented the wardrobe with expensive items from Madison Avenue boutiques.

In the late 1980s, during a *Golden Girls* summer hiatus, Rue capitalized on her fashionable reputation by launching her own clothing line, Very Rue (changed to A Touch of Rue when it debuted on QVC). As she wrote in her 2007 memoir, *My First Five Husbands . . . And the Ones Who Got Away,* "I selected fabrics I loved, and designed Blanche-inspired garments with my own practical spin, making the exquisite Blanche creations wearable in real life and available at affordable prices."

With its label cheekily warning, "We bear no responsibility for remarkable results," A Touch of Rue was a hit. As Michael notes, "Rue knew what women wanted, and the pieces she personally designed would always sell out."

ABOVE:

The label for Rue McClanahan's late '80s clothing line, "A Touch of Rue."

Photo courtesy of the Estate of RUE MCCLANAHAN, estateofrue.com.

THANK YOU FOR BEING A FRIEND

ONE OF FANS' favorite parts of watching *The Golden Girls* is singing along to the show's now-famous theme song. But the historic pairing of *The Golden Girls* and Andrew Gold almost didn't happen.

As late as May 1985, the new show's producers were still pursuing use of "(You Got to Have) Friends" to play over the stock images they selected for the opening credits, such as a plane crossing the golden Miami sun. But when licensing of a one-minute snippet of Bette Midler's 1973 hit, written by Buzzy Linhart and Mark "Moogy" Klingman, proved too expensive, the producers began to brainstorm a list of other songs touching on the theme of friendship.

As the show's music coordinator, Scott Gale, remembers, "Someone in the room—it may have been Paul Witt—remembered 'Thank You for Being a Friend,' and we all agreed it just seemed to fit perfectly." Singer/songwriter Gold's recording had been a modest hit in 1978, reaching number twenty-five on the *Billboard* Hot 100 chart. But now, producers opted to create their own rendition of Gold's opening verse and chorus, with a female lead vocal to match the spirit of the Girls.

By 1985, twenty-three-year-old Cindy Fee was already one of Los Angeles's most in-demand session singers, known for performing jingles for such advertisers as Avon and Wheaties. As Scott recalls, Cindy came into a rented sound studio one summer day in 1985, improvised some tuneful lyrical "licks" over the instrumental track, and finished the entire recording session in well under an hour. "I'll never forget. She said, 'I'm really busy, so I'll do this in one take.' And she literally did. This was just one in a long list of sessions for her, and no one knew this show was going to be a big deal. So she nailed it, and was out of there. It was perfect."

Cindy, too, remembers her performance of "Thank You for Being a Friend" being, at the time, just part of a day's work. "At the time, commercial jingles were in their heyday, so I was doing about four sessions a day," she explains. "I just remember going in and thinking, 'This is cool. I like this song.' But I didn't even know what the show was about, which is often the way it works as a singer." Cindy notes that she recorded three other theme songs that same year, for pilots that never proceeded to series. "The first inkling I

ABOVE:

Singer Cindy Fee, circa 1985. OPPOSITE: Proposed shot list for the Golden Girls opening credits, 1985.

Photo courtesy of CINDY FEE. *From the collection of* LEX PASSARIS.

```
MAIN TITLE SHOTS FOR "GOLDEN GIRLS":
DADE COUNTY TOURISM TAPE
SHOTS ARE LOGGED IN THE ORDER IN WHICH THEY APPEAR

PAN UP AROUND COLUMNS WITH SUN
PLANE CROSSING THE SUN
FIRST SHOT WITH "GREATER MIAMI&BEACHES" CARD
MARINA
WATERSKIER
UNDERVIEW OF PALM TREES
EVERGLADES SHOT
HYDROPLANE THROUGH REEDS
PINK BIRD SOARING OVER REEDS
PAN UP RIVER WITH DOCKS
AERIAL HIGH DOWN MARINA
MIME WITH PUPPET
FIDDLER
GIRL DANCING IN YELLOW COSTUME
AERIAL PULL BACK HIGH SHOT OF CRUISE SHIPS
FIRST KILLER WHALE JUMPING
FRONT VIEW FLAMINGOS CHARGING CAMERA
DOGS CHARGING CAMERA
#6 YELLOW JERSEY JAI 'ALAI PLAYER
INLAND WATERWAY AND PENINSULA
COUPLE ON PARK BENCH
2ND CATAMARRAN SHOT
SAILBOAT DOCKING AT DUSK
MARINA WITH SKYLINE IN BACKGROUND (AFTER SHOT OF TWO BIRDS)


MISS UNIVERSE 1984:

AERIAL VIEW HOTEL WITH ROUND BAY
UNDERWATER SCUBA SHOT
2ND NIGHT SHOT OF CITY
```

got that *The Golden Girls* would end up being special was when, right after the show got picked up, the producers made cast T-shirts and sent me one. That was when I realized: 'This is going to be something interesting.'"

Eventually, Cindy now marvels, the quickie gig she had performed so nonchalantly in her youth would prove lucrative enough to put her two sons through college. "It never stops playing. And so even if I did nothing else, I make a pretty good living just from *The Golden Girls* alone every year." Today, the Michigan-based singer continues to record and sell albums on iTunes, and to perform live concerts. She continues to receive *Golden Girls* fan mail, and finds that "when I book a show, and do an interview with the local newspaper, a lot of people will show up because of *The Golden Girls*."

Cindy doesn't perform "Thank You for Being a Friend" at her shows—but nonetheless finds herself sometimes getting requests for it in the strangest places. On one recent summer day, she recalls, a particularly persistent fan disrupted the Zen of picking blueberries at her friend's Michigan farm. "I didn't know this girl, but she kept coming up to me and saying, 'Sing it for me!'" Cindy remembers with a laugh. "And I had to say, 'Well, I'm kind of busy right now.'"

WHICH
GOLDEN GIRL
ARE YOU, & WHY?

SOPHIA.

I have a very sharp tongue sometimes, just like Sophia with her one-liners. Estelle Getty had a gift that she could deliver a stinging one liner, but it would always be from a place of love. My family knows all about my own tendency toward zingers, and my teammates, too. I'll let my teammates tell those stories later.

—JASON COLLINS, CENTER, BROOKLYN NETS

DOROTHY.

I love a withering stare. And like her, I'm analytical, self-assured, and opinionated.

—ZACHARY QUINTO, ACTOR

ROSE.

She's seemingly naïve, but with a little twinkle in her eye.

—JONATHAN GROFF, ACTOR

I'M A BLANCHE.

As thousands of men will confirm.

—PETER PAIGE, ACTOR/ WRITER/PRODUCER

BLANCHE.

I don't think I am anymore, but I was slutty. And like Blanche, I used to be kind of delusional about how fabulous I am, and I would tell tall tales about my sex life. But really, the most brilliant thing about Blanche and the way that Rue McClanahan played her is that she seemed slutty, but she really just wanted to be loved, and appreciated and accepted. And that's really what I've always wanted, too.

—LAVERNE COX, ACTOR

ROSE,

even though people think she's a dummy. She's open minded, creative, and seems light-hearted on the surface but has an inner depth. She's a many-layered onion.

—JONATHAN ADLER, DESIGNER

SOPHIA.

Sophia, because I am a sarcastic wise ass.

—LANCE BASS, SINGER/ ACTOR/TALK SHOW HOST, SIRIUS XM OUTQ RADIO

SOPHIA.

I'm the Sophia in my group of friends. Because I'm always giving people advice, whether they want it or not.

—CHRIS COLFER, ACTOR

ROSE.

Although for a brief moment in high school, I had a perm on my bangs, and my friends told me I looked like Rue McClanahan. So I'm a little bit Blanche, too. I think it's a good mix. I'm kind of dumb and slutty.

—JAKE SHEARS, LEAD MALE SINGER OF SCISSOR SISTERS AND INTERNATIONAL DJ

DOROTHY.

Particularly as I get older, it becomes clearer. There is something about her practicality and cynicism that I really relate to. She also has this protective side and a great capacity to love that I would like to think that I share. But if you are acting like a jackass, no matter how much she loves you, Dorothy will put you in your place. I respect that.

—ANDREW RANNELLS, ACTOR

ROSE.

A little naive and constantly saying outrageous things rather inadvertently.

—REX LEE, ACTOR

BLANCHE, DUH.

She taps right into my inner Southern Slut. Every gay New York Jew has got one.

—DAN BUCATINSKY, ACTOR/ WRITER/PRODUCER

ROSE.

While it's a trait I have that has improved (and by that I mean "faded away") the longer I live, I have always been more gullible than most and, still to this day, I tend to misunderstand the point of certain conversations happening right in front of my face. I think I also identify with her optimistic view of life.

—JIM PARSONS, ACTOR

DEFINITELY DOROTHY.

I have a certain affinity with her. Bea and Dorothy were both forces of nature, and I identify with that. Dorothy was the one who was too smart for her own sake, and deserved better than the lousy husband she ended up with. She was a faithful friend, but not a silly person. And nothing makes me laugh harder than seeing a scene where Dorothy is trying to be feminine, or watching her try to flirt. It's like watching an elephant trying to sit delicately down on a flower.

— HARVEY FIERSTEIN, ACTOR/ PLAYWRIGHT

DOROTHY.

I'm usually the sane one in my group of friends -- the voice of reason. I roll my eyes a lot at the antics of my friends.

—KEVIN CHAMBERLIN, ACTOR

SOPHIA.

I'm petite, cranky, and I tend to say what's on my mind. Everyone wants to be as withering as Dorothy, as attractive as Blanche and as sweet as Rose. But I'm thinking of carrying a handbag at all times, so I'm definitely Sophia.

—ALEC MAPA, ACTOR

ROSE.

I guess my parents were pretty successful in sheltering me growing up, because there's still so much about sex and drugs and other grown-up stuff that comes as a shock to me. (What's going on there? People actually do that?!) I'm not saying I'm all that innocent, just clueless.

—MO ROCCA, JOURNALIST/ AUTHOR/ACTOR

I'M A HYBRID OF 60% ROSE

(sweet, kind and slightly dumb) and 40% Dorothy (a natural leader who can cut a bitch when pushed).

—ROSS MATHEWS, TALK SHOW HOST

SOPHIA.

I've got a snarky retort for most situations, and I keep my purse on my lap at all times.

—WENDI MCLENDON COVEY, ACTOR

DOROTHY.

I'm intuitive in figuring out people's motives and subtext. I don't miss anything that isn't being said in a room full of people. And I have a killer double/triple take.

—CHEYENNE JACKSON, ACTOR

I'M BLANCHE.

After one cocktail, I'm Blanche. Isn't everyone?

—BRUCE VILANCH, WRITER/ PERFORMER

WHEN & WITH WHOM DID YOU

FIRST WATCH

THE GOLDEN GIRLS?

...RIGHT FROM THE START.

It feels like I've always watched The Golden Girls. As to with whom, spouse, family, friends, road crew, you name it!

–JANIS IAN, SINGER

... FROM THE START,

usually with my best friend, Bruce Newberg. We loved the irreverence, the sharpness, the pop feminism and the smart, smart writing. We loved their ability to be mean and acerbic and yet still loving and caring. Their vicious insults were the indication of their intimacy – a kind of devastating affection which Bruce and I share to this day.

–SAM HARRIS, ACTOR/SINGER

...FROM THE START.

I remember when it came on; I was 7. I don't recall watching much television with my family, strangely enough. I guess they trusted me to watch it alone, because it seemed pretty innocuous, a show with a bunch of old ladies. And even though I was so young, I still found it hilarious.

–JAKE SHEARS, LEAD MALE SINGER OF SCISSOR SISTERS AND INTERNATIONAL DJ

...FROM SEASON ONE.

I remember watching the show a few times with my grandparents in Huntington, West Virginia, but they were very proper Christians, and stopped watching eventually because they found it too "tacky" and crass! That didn't stop me, though.

–SAM PANCAKE, ACTOR

...WHEN IT FIRST AIRED,

I watched with my mom and dad, which was completely awkward. With every laugh I couldn't suppress, I received a glance that said "Why did you get that joke?" The truth is, most of the time I didn't get the joke, but those actresses were so funny that even when I didn't understand what they were talking about, I found myself laughing out loud. Childhood lessons in line delivery.

–MICHAEL URIE, ACTOR

DURING ITS ORIGINAL RUN,

with my mom, who has a great sense of humor. Now I watch with my family and stepdaughter, who gets it and thinks it's the funniest thing ever. She is one of the funniest people I know, and she's 14.

–DOT-MARIE JONES, ACTOR

DURING ITS ORIGINAL RUN,

with my grandma. I remember one time, Rose referred to a female dog as a bitch – and by extension, the other three ladies in the house – and my mom asking me if I knew what that meant.

–KIRSTEN VANGSNESS, ACTOR/PLAYWRIGHT

...IN SUMMER RERUNS.

For one month out of every summer, my brother and I would get shipped off – and I say that lovingly – to stay with our grandparents upstate, in Troy, New York. There wasn't much to do there when you were a kid, other than watch TV with your grandparents – and my grandparents loved The Golden Girls. So my brother and I, my grandparents, and my aunt would all watch together. And now, when I see the show, it brings back nice memories of those times.

—JASON COLLINS, CENTER, BROOKLYN NETS

...IN RERUNS.

I was home sick from elementary school. And then started coming up with excuses why I needed to stay home so I could watch the show. Sometimes my mom would watch it with me. And I remember telling my friends at school, "There is a show called The Golden Girls, and it is funny – and you all have to watch it!" I might as well have been telling them, "I'm gay!" I think that's the first sign, isn't it?

—CHRIS COLFER, ACTOR

DURING ITS ORIGINAL RUN,

either alone or with friends. It was a wonderful catharsis between my nightly rounds, and gave me some great zingers to use at after-parties. Since then, I've watched the show nonstop in reruns. One year, there were a few months when it was off the air and I was in a severe panic. But it came back!

—MICHAEL MUSTO, COLUMNIST AND AUTHOR

...IN RERUNS.

Once I discovered the show, it became a late-night addiction, instead of the 11 PM news or the talk shows. I'd watch with my roommates when we were all starting out in New York as struggling actors.

—KEVIN CHAMBERLIN, ACTOR

...IN RERUNS.

I have a few memories of watching some episodes with my grandma when I was younger, but -- like so many people have -- I fell in love with the show by watching reruns (over and over and over and over again).

—ROSS MATHEWS, TALK SHOW HOST

...BACK IN THE '80S,

when it was first on. For me it was a way to escape from a lot of the pressures of training and of preparing for the Olympic games. I still go back and watch reruns now, and I love going back and visiting. It brings back so many good feelings.

—GREG LOUGANIS, GOLD MEDALIST IN DIVING, 1984 AND 1988 OLYMPICS.

...IN THE LATE '80S OR EARLY '90S,

with my mom. She has two sisters, and together I used to call the three of them with my grandmother "The Golden Girls." My mom was definitely the Dorothy, her sisters were Rose and Blanche, and my grandmother obviously was Sophia. We used to laugh about it all the time.

—ZACHARY QUINTO, ACTOR

DURING ITS ORIGINAL RUN,

I was in college, so it was bound to be on in someone's room. And now you can turn the TV on at any time of day, to any channel, in any country, and Dorothy, Blanche, Rose, and Sophia will be cavorting in caftans. It's one of the greatest mysteries of the universe.

—JONATHAN ADLER, DESIGNER

DURING ITS ORIGINAL RUN,

I would watch with my family, especially my sister, and I was lucky enough to get to watch with my grandma many times. I really looked forward to Saturday night prime time TV back then.

—JIM PARSONS, ACTOR

WHICH OF THE GIRLS IS
YOUR FAVORITE?

DOROTHY.

I love that she had real moments of tenderness, and could just give you that "look" – and if you're a Golden Girls fan, you know what I'm talking about.

–HEATHER MATARAZZO,
ACTOR

ROSE.

I think Betty White is hilarious. Her delivery, her timing. She plays sweet, and there's something so loveable about her.

–JASON COLLINS, CENTER,
BROOKLYN NETS

DOROTHY.

I've been a huge Bea Arthur fan my whole life, since her Maude days. Her slow burns to the camera are priceless. That woman's got comic timing to die for.

–DAN BUCATINSKY, ACTOR/
WRITER/PRODUCER

DOROTHY.

Always and forever. She was the shoulder padded, tunic-wearing heart and soul of that show. Also, probably the only one I could borrow clothes from.

–MICHAEL URIE, ACTOR

BLANCHE.

I'm from Mobile, Alabama, so I love Blanche's Southern belle thing. Blanche was a diva, and I love the way she slinked around, like she was just above everything. I even love her reverence for the Confederacy, which borders on being racist and white supremacist, and her longing for old times, and Big Daddy. Oh, Big Daddy!

–LAVERNE COX, ACTOR

DOROTHY.

She's a no-nonsense substitute teacher who lives with her mother, but she's not afraid to rock scrunch boots and giant Chanel earrings.

–JONATHAN ADLER, DESIGNER

DOROTHY.

She never fails to make me LOL. I also loved the wedding dress she wore in the finale, with the weird toilet paper roll-like details on the shoulders.

–ROSS MATHEWS,
TALK SHOW HOST

DOROTHY.

She was the most complex, with thick walls around her giant, sometimes bitter heart. I loved her intelligence and obligation to social progress. And of course the classic deadpan which spoke a thousand words. And then her words! Snapped, crackled and popped like those of a seasoned vaudevillian.

–SAM HARRIS, ACTOR/SINGER

BLANCHE,

because she seems to be having the most fun and is oblivious to getting older.

–JONATHAN DEL ARCO,
ACTOR

ROSE.

I love her relentless optimism, and her homespun logic that seems insanely wrong but often manages to be just what someone needs to hear at the end of the day.

—Peter Paige, actor/ writer/producer

SOPHIA,

of course. She calls 'em as she sees 'em, even if she doesn't see 'em too clearly.

—Bruce Vilanch, writer/ performer

DOROTHY.

Because she did more with one eyebrow than most people can do with an entire script.

—Maile Flanagan, actor

ROSE.

Because she has the most heart and was the glue that held them all together.

—Perez Hilton, blogger

DOROTHY.

Bea Arthur taught me how to land a "blow" line, do a drive-by, a one-line zinger, and most importantly, the slow burn. No one does a slow burn like Bea.

—Kevin Chamberlin, actor

ROSE.

She is so sweet and a bit thick, but always has her heart in the right place. And I love her endless and nonsensical stories about home.

—John Bartlett, designer

DOROTHY.

I think, even as a child, I both admired her ability to be "in the know" about what was going on (as opposed to Rose or myself). I really admired her timing and her dry interpretation of certain lines. I guess I'm really saying I loved Bea Arthur, which is very true -- I watched Maude in late-night reruns at the same time I watched The Golden Girls in primetime.

—Jim Parsons, actor

SOPHIA.

I just love that she just says whatever the hell she feels like saying. I aspire to that freedom and lack of inhibition. How liberating it must be to not ever care about tact.

—Rex Lee, actor

DOROTHY,

of course. She said a million words with that face. She was so tough, but also deeply caring and smart, and often misunderstood. Those other three would fall apart without her, and they all know it.

—Drew Droege, actor

DOROTHY.

All of the women on the show were consummate pros, but Bea Arthur had everything. Presence, timing, believability, heart – she was a perfect storm of every skill set a sitcom actor needs.

—Alec Mapa, actor

ROSE

is my favorite – who doesn't love Betty White? I was also a huge fan of The Mary Tyler Moore Show, and I loved the switch-up in the characters Betty played so well. When I got to direct Betty on yet another sitcom back in the day, I was keenly aware of how amazing it was to work with such a television legend. Her timing and delivery are impeccable!

—Amanda Bearse, actor/ director

SOPHIA,

because she gets to cut to the chase. It's rare that she is learning the lesson; she's mostly the one doling out the knowledge. Plus, she is the perfect combination of mean and funny.

—Andrew Rannells, actor

DOROTHY

At the end of the day I think Dorothy is my girl. But I wanna go to the rusty anchor with Blanche, be a candy striper with Rose, go to a piano bar with Dorothy and introduce Sophia to drag bingo.

—Jai Rodriguez, actor

CONCLUSION:

THE GIRLS ARE STILL GOLDEN TODAY

*"During the production of only the third or fourth episode, I was watching
a run-through with Paul Witt. I remember turning and saying to him that what these
amazing women are doing is going to be like* Lucy. *He looked at me as if to say,
'We'll see.' And I could have been wrong. But I've sat through a lot of run-throughs,
and I've never had the same feeling that the material was clearly so universal
and timeless we'll still be laughing at it thirty, forty, fifty years later."*

— TONY THOMAS

PICTURE IT: NEW York City. On a midweek afternoon, hundreds of fans crowd inside a Barnes and Noble bookstore, and hundreds more huddle outside in the rain—all hoping for a moment with three of their idols. Finally, more than six hours after the line was officially established, there they were. At first glimpse, the crowd called out passionately for them, as if they were about to take the stage and burn up their electric guitars. But no, these three women were slightly older than your typical rock stars (even Mick Jagger and Paul McCartney).

Those three women are none other than the Golden Girls themselves, Bea Arthur, Betty White, and Rue McClanahan. And you're probably also not surprised that these women have the power to elicit such a strong reaction from their fans. That November 22, 2005, as a crowd heavy on young girls and gay men filled the Barnes and Noble in Manhattan's Chelsea neighborhood, the store quickly sold out of the show's third-season DVD sets. A few of those at the front of the line had earned their spots by camping out overnight on the sidewalk, or in one case driving all night from Boston with her mother and sister. Two NYU students named Nya and Erin passed the time by leading fellow fans in a sing-along of "Thank You for Being a Friend." Then, more than an hour before the Girls' allotted signing time was to begin, bookstore employees had to cut off the queue at five hundred people. And so more fans took to the rainy street, piling five- and six-deep in front of the store's north- and east-facing windows. There, as the three-hours-long signing commenced, one young male fan scored the moment he was hoping for: Betty saw his homemade sign: I'M SERIOUS—WILL YOU SHARE CHEESECAKE WITH ME?! She made a pantomime gesture for being way too full, and the two of them shared a laugh, six feet and several inches of glass apart.

By the summer of 2006—fourteen years after *The Golden Girls* ended its original run—the show was still drawing eleven million viewers per week and thirty million per month on the Lifetime cable network, its home from 1997 to 2009. Although up against much newer sitcom competition, any given one of the show's seven daily airings still ranked among the top three "off-network" sitcoms shown by Lifetime, and among the top seven on any cable channel.

OPPOSITE:

Only a few sitcoms have been turned into Saturday morning cartoons, such kid-focused fare as *The Brady Bunch, The Partridge Family, Gilligan's Island,* and *Happy Days. The Animated Everyday Adventures of Sophia Petrillo and the Golden Gang* would have been the first to feature an animated old lady, a testament to Sophia's appeal to fans of all ages.

Illustration by KENT ZBORNAK, *courtesy of* ROBERT SPINA.

"There aren't too many shows from 1985 which hold up like that," notes television historian Tim Brooks, formerly Lifetime's Vice President of Research and the coauthor with Earle Marsh of a TV fan's bible, *The Complete Directory to Prime Time Network and Cable TV Shows: 1946–Present*. Tim explains that the steady viewership of *The Golden Girls*, barely changed from 1997 to that point in 2006, was very unusual. After all, over the course of those nine years, most of us viewers had aged into the next Nielsen age group—and some viewers, unfortunately, just plain die off. Yet, for example, the dinnertime airings of *The Golden Girls*, at 6:00 and 6:30 p.m., attracted 1.1 million viewers back in 1999, and still drew 1.1 million by 2005. So obviously, the show must have been continually attracting new fans to replace those who for one reason or another left. "That's unusual because with all the competition out there, shows of any kind usually tend to wear out," Tim says. "But *The Golden Girls* has turned out to be a long-distance runner."

The show also turned out to be a boon for Lifetime in that it attracted a wider audience than the network's typical fare. As Tim explains, whereas the typical Lifetime Original Movie tends to attract women in mostly the middle age ranges, the *Girls'* appeal is not age specific. Younger women, older women—*The Golden Girls* is one of the few shows they all share. And since the network in general pulls strong ratings among African American women, so did the *Girls*. As Tim explains, "The show has a lot of gender appeal rather than being based on race or age."

And although as of 2016, the Nielsen Corporation still does not report their viewership as its own demographic, everyone knows anecdotally that the Girls mean an awful lot to the Gays. As marketers continue to get hip to gays' fabled disposable income, a few smaller research companies are beginning to track trends in LGBT viewership. And in the preliminary data Lifetime produced during the show's tenure on that network, Tim says, *The Golden Girls* always did very well among gays; it was a top-ten cable show.

K.Z.

Saturday Morning Girls

◆ ◆ ◆ ◆

IN THE FALL of 1988, at the height of the *Girls'* powers, the show's production associate Robert Spina began to wonder, "What does Sophia do during the day while the other Girls are at work?" He answered his own question by conceiving an animated Saturday morning series, to be called *The Animated Everyday Adventures of Sophia Petrillo and the Golden Gang* and to star the voice of Estelle Getty.

"I imagined that the kids of Richmond Street would stop by to hang out with the badass grandma," Robert explains. Accompanied by *Empty Nest* neighbor Harry Weston's dog, Dreyfuss, and armed with Sophia's all-powerful, multipurpose purse, the "Gang" would "have adventures around the neighborhood." For adult viewers, each episode would feature *Golden Girls* "Easter eggs," such as regular "Picture it: Sicily" stories, references to old friends from Shady Pines, and even cameo voice appearances by the other three Girls.

Robert and stage manager Kent Zbornak presented their pitch to *Golden Girls* producers Paul Witt and Tony Thomas, who jumped on board and brought the concept to executives at Disney. As Robert recalls, the typical series of meetings, notes, and rewrites ensued—but the project never came to fruition. Still, of having gotten to step briefly inside Sophia's world, he says, "The whole experience was a blast."

Golden Shout-Outs

◆ ◆ ◆ ◆

FOR ALL THE times *The Golden Girls* presented its educated, liberal viewpoint on social issues, the show rarely got overtly political, favoring one party over another. In fact, writer Tom Whedon remembers that on the extremely rare occasion when he did slip some political commentary into a script "we got a very angry response." In Tom's season-five episode "Have Yourself a Very Little Christmas" in December 1989, a priest working at a soup kitchen refers sarcastically to Ronald Reagan's handling of the homeless situation. "When the Great Communicator talked about his vision of a 'City on a Hill,' I wonder if it included people sleeping on gratings in the street," remarks Reverend Avery (Matt McCoy). "The line slipped by the producers, or they probably wouldn't have put it in," Tom admits. "And it got more angry letters than anything that was ever on the show."

So perhaps this episode's anti-Reagan dig was still fresh on Republican senator Mitch McConnell's mind in March 2013 when he invoked *The Golden Girls* at the Conservative Political Action Conference outside Washington. The then Senate minority leader from Kentucky was trying to pay a compliment to the youthful Republican rogues' gallery of Paul Ryan, Rand Paul, and Marco Rubio as he quipped, "Don't tell me the Democrats are the party of the future, when their presidential ticket for 2016 is shaping up to look like a rerun of *The Golden Girls*." Undoubtedly McConnell meant the remark—a sexist slam aimed at Hillary Clinton, to be sure— to be disparaging. But by linking the Democrats in the minds of voters with four of America's most beloved ladies, McConnell inadvertently illustrated just another way his right-wingers are out of touch.

Despite what McConnell seems to think, America continues to cherish its *Girls*, decades after the show went off the air. Alexander Payne's 2013 film *Nebraska*, nominated for the year's Academy Award for Best Picture, contained a nod to *The Golden Girls*, as Bruce Dern's character's extended midwestern family sat silent in their living room, mesmerized by the Miami matrons on their screen. And just a month before McConnell's comment, in February 2013, an episode of NBC's short-lived, decidedly young-and-hetero sitcom *Guys with Kids* ("Gary's Idea") had built a B plot around straight, young divorced dad Chris's (Jesse Bradford) love of all things Golden. After deciding in a moment of midlife crisis to become a DJ, Chris's new career was floundering—until he played his own custom remix of "Thank You for Being a Friend" for his college-age clientele.

In fact, on the small screen, the ladies of the eighties continue to earn shout-outs on the hippest, twenty-first-century shows. In 2004, after overhearing his star Rachel Bilson talking about how she loves to watch *The Golden Girls* with her friends, writer Josh Schwartz decided to write her passion into his teen soap, *The O.C.* And so in the first-season episode "The Third Wheel," Rachel's character, Summer, bonded with her romantic rival, Anna (Samaire Armstrong), singing "Thank You for Being a Friend" in front of the ladies' room mirror at a rock concert. Two seasons later, in "The Party Favor," Anna returned to Newport Beach to reassure Summer—"You're still my Blanche, you know"—extending the *Golden Girls* reference into an extended, multiyear metaphor for female friendship.

In the last weeks of 2013, the elderly Girls were paid major homage on another youthful soap, with a plot thread on Candace Bushnell's *Sex and the City* prequel series, *The Carrie Diaries*. In 2007, Bea Arthur had appeared in a TV Land spoof, playing a geriatric Carrie Bradshaw obsessed with landing Abe Vigoda's Mr. Big. (See it on YouTube by searching "*Sex and the City*—Parody starring Bea Arthur.") But with a second-season story line on the CW network's *Carrie Diaries*, the two worlds officially collided, resulting in what can only be described as a fan's fever dream.

In the episode "The Second Time Around," teenage Carrie's high school friend Walt (Brendan Dooling), having been kicked out of his parents' house after coming out, showed up at the Bradshaws' door toting his prized box of VHS tapes full of *Golden Girls* episodes. And although Carrie's lawyer father, Tom (Matt Letscher), was initially uncomfortable with the new living arrangement, he ultimately accepted Walt into his Connecticut home as the two bonded over their appreciation for the ladies of Miami.

With her show's 1980s setting, *The Carrie Diaries* creator, Amy B. Harris, admits, "I always wanted to put *The Golden Girls* into the show somehow." Amy, who previously had written for *Sex and the City*, had always heard that show called "a younger, more modern-day version of *The Golden Girls*," and so mixing the Girls officially into the Carrie-verse "would be a really fun, meta experience."

Aware of the gay community's affection, the *Carrie* writers immediately focused on Walt as the character who would be the Girls' biggest fan. "I loved the idea of a kid who was struggling to find himself being able to find a sense of community with these older women. And not only did the show give Walt comfort, but then it also provided a surprising common ground with Tom, where he could open up to him about the difficulties in his life," Amy explains.

"I once asked my friend about how hard it was to come out. And because this was back in the eighties, when gay men didn't necessarily think they could have marriages and kids of their own, he said the hardest thing was realizing he had to give up the 'white picket fence' dreams for his life. I think that's what *The Golden Girls* was all about, too," Amy theorizes. "Like the Girls, who lost their husbands, you envision a certain life for yourself for so long, and then you don't get it. But in a way, you probably are happier—because you get something even better. That's a powerful theme that resonates for so many people, and that's what we wanted to tap into for our story line."

Girls in the Afternoon

◆ ◆ ◆ ◆

SHORTLY AFTER THE *Carrie* cast gave the *Girls* some prime time love, a very similar story line began to play out on daytime TV. In the summer of 2014, ABC's soap *General Hospital* invoked *The Golden Girls* as a device to spark romance and jealousy in the love triangle of Felix the nurse (Marc Anthony Samuel), his former patient Lucas (Ryan Carnes), and Brad the lab technician (Parry Shen), as the former two stayed up all night—shirtless, of course—drinking wine and watching their fave eighties sitcom. Later, when Lucas introduced the show to his recently discovered dad, Julian (William deVry), he was able to bond with Port Charles's tough mobster over their own mutual appreciation of *The Golden Girls*; *GH*'s episode on New Year's Day 2015 then found the father and son hanging out on the couch together, debating about whether to watch a football game or a marathon of their favorite sitcom.

As *GH*'s former head writer Ron Carlivati explains, *The Golden Girls* proved to be a useful story device not only in bringing together an otherwise disparate father and son, but also in playing out the beats of gay romance. At various points, the three gay characters played the inevitable game: Which Golden Girl Are You? But sometimes, *The Golden Girls* brought these guys a bit too close. "We had Brad, who was jealous, deliver a speech where he said, 'Oh, please—watching *The Golden Girls* is basically the equivalent of gay foreplay! The next thing you know, you'll be watching *Knots Landing*, and then heading for the altar!'"

The *Golden Girls* references have proven popular among the soap's fans, who immediately expressed their approval on Twitter. But interestingly, Ron notes, "Some of our audience was surprised, not knowing that *The Golden Girls* is something that's popular in gay culture. I had thought that the link was something well documented, so it was funny to see that a lot of our young, female fans didn't realize that." After Ron then tweeted some links to web articles about gays and *The Golden Girls*, he was happy to see the show now bringing together different demographic groups within his *GH* fan base as well. "I got a really nice response from at least one fan, who said, 'Cool, I didn't know that! You learn something new every day!'"

"Girls" Will Be Girls

◆ ◆ ◆ ◆

AT THE SAME time the Girls were bringing together daytime's men, they were also being celebrated by the queens of Logo's hit reality show *RuPaul's Drag Race*. In the main challenge at the heart of the show's sixth-season premiere in February 2014, seven contestants were assigned boxes of mystery materials themed to various TV shows and tasked to create couture. Six of the boxes related to current hits, such as *Downton Abbey*, *Game of Thrones*, and *Duck Dynasty*; *The Golden Girls* was the only classic.

The season's eventual runner-up, Adore Delano, hinted at wanting to get her hands on the *Golden* box. But it was instead given to Ben DeLaCreme, whose pastel paean to the Girls went on to triumph over tributes to pop culture flashes-in-the-pan Honey Boo Boo and the Kardashians. A Connecticut native now based in Seattle,

Ben had first begun watching *The Golden Girls* with friends while in college in Chicago, and was secretly thrilled when the Miami-themed box landed in her lap. Inside, Ben recalls, "were lots of fabrics that looked like the décor of the Girls' living room, a mix of muted pastels and then bright patterns with flowers and palm fronds." In creating the week's winning gown, Ben looked past "the surplus of flamingo memorabilia, both cardboard and stuffed," but did take advantage of one key item: an actual cheesecake.

Although much of the footage was edited out of the finished episode, Ben worked the runway, plate in hand, offering bites to the judges while sneaking some for herself. Although some of the other competitors eschewed props they found gimmicky, Ben explains, "It would have been such a missed opportunity *not* to use that cheesecake. It gave me the opportunity to create a glamorous look but also be a little silly about it, too."

A drag veteran for over a decade before entering the *Drag Race*, Ben admits that in her earliest days "my character was a bitch. I think that's the thing a lot of young queens turn to first." But later, both Ben and his alter ego began to find feminine inspiration elsewhere. In another scene cut from the season-premiere episode, Ben chatted with RuPaul in the show's workroom about the origins of his character's now sugary-sweet personality. "Right away, Ru asked which Golden Girl I thought I was," Ben remembers. "And so I said that I myself am Dorothy, definitely more cynical and pessimistic, but Ben DeLaCreme is Rose. She is willfully ditzy—smart sometimes, but 'dumb' when it serves her not to understand what's going on." Rose was "definitely a big influence on my drag persona," Ben explains. So it was no surprise when Ben DeLaCreme would eventually be named the winner of the season's Miss Congeniality crown.

ABOVE:

Ben DeLaCreme in her winning *Golden Girls* gown on the sixth-season premiere of Logo's *RuPaul's Drag Race*, February 24, 2014.

Photo courtesy of WORLD OF WONDER.

Golden Tributes

❖ ❖ ❖ ❖

AS MUCH AS the Girls continue to pop up on the TV screen, they've served as muses to several singers as well. Drag diva, comedienne, and superfan Jackie Beat was looking to honor the Girls, and knew she'd found the right base for a parody song in David Bowie's hit "Golden Years" (her 2009 version called, of course, "Golden Girls"). A year later, she tweaked Nina Simone's anthemic "Four Women." Ever since, "I often end a show with 'Four Girls,' and by the time I get to Dorothy at the end, people are usually hooting and hollering," says Jackie.

Growing up overseas, another lifelong fan, Jonny McGovern, relied on bootleg *Golden Girls* videos in Thailand, and later, episodes his stateside grandmother would record on VHS tape and mail to him in Egypt. The singer and comedian, known from his stint on Logo's *Big Gay Sketch Show* and his current Internet talk show *Hey, Qween* on theStream.tv, released in 2012 his album *The Gayest of All Time*, which included an ode to his favorite slut. "'Blanche Devereaux' was a pop song about how a boy made me feel like her," Jonny remembers. "I peppered it with as many *Golden Girls* references as I possibly could—singing at the Rusty Anchor, how I wanted a guy to come sit on my lanai, and so many other double entendres the show was famous for."

"Blanche Devereaux" proved such a success that soon after, Jonny and his producer, Adam Joseph, birthed a follow-up EP, *Songs About "The Golden Girls."* That album's song salutes to the other Girls included "Zbornak," which he calls "a new wave anthem to Dorothy and her fashion," and "Take Me to St. Olaf," the music video which depicted Jonny frolicking in a field with his beloved blonde and striding down the driveway of the Girls' "real-life" Brentwood, California, house—not necessarily with the current owners' knowledge or permission. This reverie about Rose "required the most research of all, to get all of her weird Scandinavian references right," Jonny reveals. "And I enjoyed that research enormously."

"TAKE ME TO ST. OLAF"

by Jonny McGovern

They don't understand you,
Always telling you to shut your mouth.
But I'm here to tell you true,
I love it when I hear you talk about
Petunia the pig, and Bessie the cow,
The herring circus that got shut down,
And the time that you lost out on being
Butter Queen.

Take me to St. Olaf
Right next to St. Gustav
We'll get there by toboggan
Play a game of whackanoggin
Take me to St. Olaf
We'll frolic in the snow
Take me to St. Olaf
It's where I wanna go

(Oh Rose, you and me can get together
With Ollie Neutensprinkle for a spirited game
of Googenspritzer
Then we'll run off behind the barn
And do a sock puppet retelling of
Toonder the Tiger.
Ah, I can just imagine a perfect day
in St. Olaf!)

As soon as the rooster crows
We'll meet up with Big Sven and Little Sven,
Have some eggs gerflaffelen
And pigs in a svooblaten,
See A Christmas Carol *with a*
non-chicken cast,
Play oogle and flugel until the
last person's passed,
Visit Broom Hilda, your favorite pig,
And we'll celebrate Hay Day,
Which is a day where you celebrate hay.
Hey!

Take me to St. Olaf
Right next to St. Gustav
We'll climb Mount Roosenbaden

...at some floogenflaben
Take me to St. Olaf
We'll frolic in the snow
Take me to St. Olaf
It's where I wanna go

(You know, some people don't understand
how I feel
But those people can blow it out their
tubenburbles
Like Rose said, "Geflectenflaffen, fleffen
fleuven
Va flecten flug, ger flaffen!")

In September 2014 came the latest audio-visual tribute to the Girls, titled *Out on the Lanai*; within less than a year, the weekly podcast already boasted over seventy-five thousand downloads. Each installment features writer/comedian hosts H. Alan Scott and Kerri Doherty, plus special guests such as Grace Helbig, Baron Vaughn, and *Buzzfeed*'s Louis Peitzman, offering their own comedic commentary on a particular *Golden Girls* episode. Bringing the ladies of the eighties to a twenty-first-century hipster crowd, *Out on the Lanai* recorded several of its episodes live in front of an aficionado crowd at *NerdMelt*, a comedy programming series at the Nerdist Showroom within Los Angeles's Meltdown Comics.

Golden Goods

◆ ◆ ◆ ◆

BY THE FALL of 2015, exactly thirty years after *The Golden Girls*' debut, the show's fan page on Facebook would amass over 1.6 million likes. On Twitter, over a dozen accounts tweet daily about *Golden Girls* news and quotes, with a combined follower total in the tens of thousands. But with all this contact we fans still have with the Girls in our everyday lives, it's surprising that there has never been much official *Golden*

Girls–themed merchandise available for purchase. For all these lost years, picture the pepperonis the Sophias among us could have been packing into our *Golden Girls* lunch boxes, or the wear we Blanches could have been getting out of our *Golden Girls* bedsheets! Luckily now, the Internet has again changed everything; where mass manufacturing has long neglected us, we fans have started doing it for ourselves.

These days, any random visit to the website Etsy.com yields offers of thousands of often homemade *Golden* goods, including the typical T-shirts and magnets, earrings and charm bracelets—but also greeting cards and postcards, mugs, wallets,

makeup bags, neckties, stickpins, coasters, tote bags, tutus, baby onesies, paperweights, pocket mirrors, Christmas ornaments, clocks, switch plates, nightlights, wineglass charms, lip balms, fingernail decals, oil paintings, prayer candles, and even Russian nesting dolls. A *Golden Girls* birthday party kit comes complete with invites, banners, place cards, cupcake decorations, and thank-you notes—all bearing the faces of the foursome. Supposed ads for the Rusty Anchor and Shady Pines are immortalized in cross-stitch, as is an ode to the Great Herring War. For $140, there's a silver and brass, quasi-religious medal, bearing a native of St. Olaf rather than an actual saint; the same artist offers a set of cufflinks, similarly hand carved with the image of Stan Zbornak. If you have the $210, you'd have to be a yutz not to want them.

In early 2015, New York-based toy company executive Sam Hatmaker assembled this *Golden Girls* tableau, stealing Blanche's hair from Professor Umbridge in a *Harry Potter* play set, and the house's beige bricks, an otherwise rare LEGO hue, from *Star Wars*. Soon after the forty-year-old Michigan native uploaded photos of his proposed kitchen/living room play set onto the company's "Ideas" web submission page, news of his creation went viral on Facebook and in the blogosphere. Sam's project handily scored the required ten thousand votes to proceed to official consideration, but ultimately, by the fall, LEGO declined to put the Girls into production. Still, he enthuses, "In the end I really did build it for myself, just for fun, just because I wanted it. It's still put together, and it's probably going to sit on my shelf forever. So any attention that it got after that was just icing on the cheesecake."

Photos by SAM HATMAKER

Golden Gallery

◆ ◆ ◆ ◆

IN 2013, NEW York's venerable auction house Christie's hauled in $1.9 million for John Currin's 1991 painting *Bea Arthur Naked*. (Fans thought they'd learned the identity of the anonymous telephone buyer when a week later, comedian Jeffrey Ross—who had infamously joked about Bea's body parts during the 1999 *Friars Club Roast of Jerry Stiller*, broadcast on Comedy Central—tweeted a photo of himself with the painting, with a thank-you message to his generous benefactor, Jimmy Kimmel. But Jimmy replied with a tweet denying the purchase—and so the mystery continues.)

In the summer of 2007, years before the Currin sale made national headlines, Lenora Claire was also garnering press attention for curating the erotic art show *Golden Gals Gone Wild*. Out-

lets like CNN, NPR, NBC News, the *National Enquirer*, and TMZ reported how, inspired by yet a different topless Bea Arthur painting by Chris Zimmerman that she scored for a mere $110 on eBay, the onetime performance artist brought together over forty of the day's up-and-coming artists for a four-week exhibition in the heart of Hollywood. Over two thousand curious art fans crowded the show's opening night at the World of Wonder gallery, where original works were priced between $50 and $4,000. Then in 2009, a second edition of the show, featuring all-new art, sold out at the World Erotic Art Museum in the Girls' hometown of Miami, and landed Lenora and company on the cover of the *Miami New Times*.

Today, just as the Girls continue to rack up tributes from writers and singers, they inspire today's foremost visual artists as well. And so here, in this Gallery of the Girls, is a roundup of recent works of *Golden Girls* inspiration.

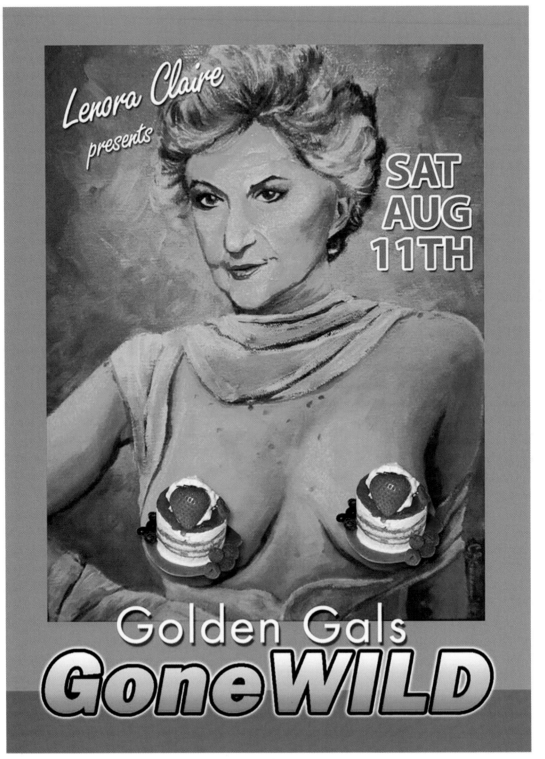

LENORA CLAIRE'S HIT EROTIC ART SHOW *GOLDEN GALS GONE WILD*

LEFT: Canadian-born artist Glen Hanson's popular 2006 *Golden Girls* caricature has been turned into T-shirts (www.huntees.com/glenhanson), mugs, greeting cards, Christmas ornaments, and even a shower curtain (www.sallyandmitch.com).

GLEN HANSON · LOS ANGELES · INK ON PAPER · 2006 · WWW.GLENHANSON.COM

BELOW: Mike Giblin, a character designer for the British network ITV's 2015 sketch show *Newzoids*, is a lifelong *Golden Girls* fan who as an artist has always admired the characters' clearly defined personalities, which lend themselves to caricature.

MIKE GIBLIN · NEWCASTLE UPON TYNE, UK · *THE GOLDEN GIRLS—THE ANIMATED SERIES* · DIGITAL · 2008 · WWW.MIKEGIBLINILLUSTRATION.COM

ABOVE: Instead of erotic art, Trevor Wayne decided to put the Girls in the world of "cos-play." "So instead of being extreme, this piece has become definitely the most popular of all my paintings," he explains.

TREVOR WAYNE · LOS ANGELES · *GOLDEN HEROES* · ACRYLIC ON CANVAS · 2014 · WWW.TREVORWAYNE.COM

ABOVE: As another sign of the show's continuing international appeal, the Girls number among the caricatures the Australian artist Erin Hunting emblazons on prints and T-shirts and then ships all around the globe.

ERIN HUNTING · MELBOURNE, AUSTRALIA · DIGITAL DRAWING · 2015 · WWW.ERINHUNTING.COM

LEFT: Originally created for a client in Canada, Barry Belcher's illustration of the Girls around their kitchen table proved so popular on the artist's website that he painted this second, almost identical work, titled *Cheesecake Roundtable*.

BARRY BELCHER · ATLANTA · *CHEESECAKE ROUNDTABLE* · ACRYLIC ON STRETCH CANVAS · 2012 · WWW.BARRYBELCHER.COM

ABOVE: Inspired by his memories of watching the show each night with a "punk as f---" roommate who owned her own record store, Jesse Beamesderfer combined *The Golden Girls* with the look of the '70s band KISS. "To me, the Golden Girls are rock and roll, and will always remind me of Stacey 'Vertigo,'" he explains.

JESSE BEAMESDERFER · PHILADELPHIA · PEN AND INK · 2012 · WWW.MOEBIUSGOLDBERG.COM

MIDDLE RIGHT: "I was going through a phase of spoofing the masters with pop culture," says Sam Carter of his mash-up of Botticelli and Bea Arthur. "This is probably one of my more shocking pieces. People either love it or hate it, but it definitely gets them to stop and look."

SAM CARTER · ORANGE COUNTY, CA · *THE BIRTH OF ZBORNAK* · ACRYLIC ON CANVAS · 2009 · WWW.SAMCARTERART.COM

RIGHT: Sarah Hedlund conceived this piece as a tribute to both the Girls and to the Czech art nouveau painter Alphonse Mucha, "combining two of my pop culture favorites," she explains. "I grew up watching *The Golden Girls* with my mom. I always wanted to create my own fan art, adding little details like the ! in the door that other super fans would appreciate."

SARAH HEDLUND · LONE TREE, IOWA · DIGITAL ILLUSTRATION · 2015 · WWW.SARAHHEDLUND.COM

In 2014, former *Golden Girls* writer/executive producer Marc Cherry commissioned this drawing from New York artist Ken Fallin, whose work has appeared in such publications as the *Wall Street Journal* and *Playbill*.

KEN FALLIN · NEW YORK · INK ON PAPER · 2014
WWW.KENFALLINARTIST.COM

A Bea a Day Allows an Artist to Play

◆ ◆ ◆ ◆

IN FEBRUARY 2013, lifelong *Golden Girls* fan Mike Denison painted a homemade birthday gift for a friend featuring the Girls. A tile installer by day who trained as an artist at the School of the Museum of Fine Arts, Boston, Mike was looking for a creative project and, partly inspired by John Currin's topless Bea Arthur painting fetching nearly two million dollars, set out to create Bea-related art every day for a year.

Mike's *Bea a Day* project, begun on his thirty- fifth birthday that September, took Bea and the rest of the Girls out of the kitchen and into more abstract settings: floating through space with a piece of cheesecake, or a Tarantino-style poster for a movie called *Kill Stan*. After brainstorming an initial list of over a hundred Bea-related ideas, "I knew the project would be sustainable, whether the works would just be straight homage to Bea, or be parodies, or even just bad puns," Mike explains. "I enjoyed getting to challenge myself — especially because as soon as the idea came to me, it also came with a set of rules that I can't explain. First of all, I had to create a new piece every single day. Second, I would never do anything tasteless. Yes, people suggested bad puns, and I'm open to that. But the idea could never be *too* much of a stretch."

Mike had sold some of his prints at a comic book convention in Portland, Maine, and scored

Girls Beneath the Skin

◆ ◆ ◆ ◆

SOME *GOLDEN GIRLS* art has been preserved on quite a different type of canvas. On an April 2015 episode of *Jimmy Kimmel Live!*, the host surprised guest Betty White with a type of tribute she'd never before seen. Courtesy of his video *Wall of America*, Jimmy introduced Betty to nine fans whose bodies bear her image. "Oh no! And you have to live with that all the time?" Betty exclaimed playfully, upon seeing a reproduction of her face with the words STAY GOLDEN upon the calf of a woman named Morgon, of Logan, West Virginia.

Los Angeles resident H. Alan Scott, host of the podcast *Out on the Lanai*, was next up to show his idol the image of all four Girls on his left arm. Then, Jimmy had a question for the then-ninety-three-year-old star, in reaction to further displays from Stephen, of Heber Springs, Arkansas; Gretchen, of Austin, Texas; Carl, of Ontario, Canada; Shawn, of Troy, New York; Maren, of Champaign, Illinois; Tiffany, of Mims, Florida; and Adrian of Houston, Texas:

"How does that make you feel?"

"It makes me feel wonderful . . . " Betty quipped. "And so glad that I'm not them."

rave reviews first from *Golden Girls* superfan Dave Rubin, formerly the face of Logo TV's weekly web series *The Golden Girls Ultimate Fan Club* and now host of Ora.tv's *The Rubin Report*, and then on the *Huffington Post*'s Arts and Culture page. Soon after, Mike made his works from *Bea a Day* available as prints and T-shirts on his store page on etsy.com (www.etsy.com/shop/BeaADay).

Since then, the iPhone game Busy Bea, which features *Bea a Day* art, has racked up over ten thousand downloads, and the illustrations have been featured on the web's hippest news and culture sites. But the best part of his newfound fame, Mike avows, has been "the fan community I've fallen into. You've heard of the 'Bronies.' Well, I'm calling this group my fellow Broldens."

ABOVE:
Painted as a birthday gift for a friend, this "take on a classic *Star Wars* movie poster" became the inspiration for Mike Denison's eventual *Bea a Day* and *Betty a Day* art projects. RIGHT: Writer/comedian Eliot Glazer shows off his Bea Arthur "Thank You For Being a Friend" tattoo. OPPOSITE TOP: Bea Arthur is on the menu at the Big Gay Ice Cream shop. OPPOSITE BOTTOM: Artist Jason O'Malley's rendition of Sophia in Big Gay Ice Cream's shop in New York City's West Village.

Photo by ELIOT GLAZER. Photos by DOUG QUINT.

Golden Dessert

• • • •

THEY'VE BEEN MUSES to artists, and their likenesses have graced every product from baseball hats to bangle bracelets. But ever since 2010, several of the cheesecake-loving Girls have also been the inspirations for their own desserts.

A year after Doug Quint and Bryan Petroff began driving their Big Gay Ice Cream truck around the streets of Manhattan in 2009, the two consulted with the Twitter-verse to come up with catchy names for the company's signature confections. For one particular menu item—a golden-yellow cone filled with golden vanilla ice cream, drizzled with brownish-gold *dulce de leche*, and topped with golden Nilla wafer crumbs—one fan suggested the "Golden Girl." At just that moment, Doug remembers, Bea Arthur's historic bequest to New York's Ali Forney Center was announced in the press. And so they dubbed the "Bea Arthur" in her honor, with some proceeds going to the charity providing housing for homeless LGBT youth.

Sales immediately jumped—and so in 2011, as the entrepreneurial duo opened their first brick-and-mortar store in New York's East Village, they prevailed again on the power of the Girls. "We don't normally start with a name and then come up with the recipe after," Doug admits. "We would never set out to make a Lady Gaga cone and *then* figure out what should go in it." But for the Rue McClanahan, the Big Gay owners made an exception. "We knew we wanted to come up with something

that Blanche might have served to Big Daddy," Doug explains. And with that, bourbon came to mind. "It was as if we channeled Blanche, and could hear her in our heads describing in her Southern accent the ingredients of this ice-cream sandwich: praline-pecan cookies and bourbon ice cream."

The Bea Arthur has since been featured on the Food Network, and the Rue McClanahan has become the three Big Gay Ice Cream shops' top-selling ice-cream sandwich. But, Doug notes, the other two Girls are not to be neglected. The company, whose policy is to name its treats after only the deceased, opted to honor Betty White by commissioning artist Jason O'Malley to create a five-foot-by-five-foot Warhol-esque portrait for its Philadelphia store. Jason's smaller, similar depictions of Estelle Getty hang in both Philly and New York—and an Estelle-themed frozen dessert, some form of ice-cream-filled cannoli, is being concocted.

Even in the company's earliest days, as Doug manned the window of its first truck, he would make sure the beloved icon got her propers. "Not very often, but occasionally, someone would have waited in line for half an hour, and then would get to the window and ask for the 'BEE-ya' Arthur or the 'BAY-ya' Arthur," Doug remembers. "And a couple of those times, I made the person go to the back of the line and research her on his phone, so that by the time he got to the window again he could give me a three-sentence dissertation on Bea Arthur and who she was." But more often on such occasions, Doug notes, "When someone would order the Bea Arthur by the wrong pronunciation, I could just stand back and laugh. Because anyone who didn't know who Bea was was chastised and taught a lesson by the other customers. People wouldn't have it. They really took this cone to heart, because they wanted to remember Bea Arthur and make sure she was always respected."

Girls Across the Water

◆ ◆ ◆ ◆

FOR DECADES, AMERICAN TV has borrowed concepts liberally from abroad and turned them into stateside hits; that's how England's *Till Death Do Us Part*, *Man About the House*, and *The Office* became CBS's *All in the Family*, ABC's *Three's Company*, and NBC's . . . *The Office*. In recent years, the process has worked in the other direction as well, with countries like Spain, Argentina, Russia, and Turkey cooking up their own versions of *The Nanny*, *Married with Children*, and *Everybody Loves Raymond*.

The *Golden Girls* was way ahead of this reversal of trend, with foreign adaptations based on Susan Harris's concept popping up as early as 1993 with Britain's similarly seaside- set *Brighton Belles*. The original *Golden Girls* had been such a hit in the UK that they'd performed for their fan the Queen Mum at the Royal Variety Performance in 1988; but not long after, the *Brighton Belles* were a surprising outright ratings flop. Since then, adaptations have continued to pop up around the world. But as they've debuted throughout the nineties and up to the present day, vernacular versions of *The Golden Girls* in Russia, the Philippines, Turkey, and Spain have been unable to last past a single season. And it's too soon to tell the fates of the particularly faithful adaptations that have premiered in Greece and the Netherlands in just the last few years.

Of course, none of those foreign productions has benefitted from the special magic bestowed by Bea, Betty, Rue, and Estelle—how could they?—which probably accounts for the middling results. But recently, two young writers in Australia—where *The Golden Girls* still airs every day as well—may have found a workaround to the problem. In 2012, Jonathan Worsley and Thomas Duncan-Watt presented the stage show they penned, *Thank You for Being a Friend*, at Sydney's Darlinghurst Theatre to a late-night, predominantly gay and lesbian crowd. Their original episode featuring the *Girls* was acted à la the off-Broadway hit *Avenue Q*—that is, by puppet likenesses of our beloved American leading ladies, with their corresponding humans in full view.

When the producing team of Neil Gooding and Matthew Henderson then came aboard the show, they toned down its risqué humor to broaden its appeal to a more mainstream crowd, and most importantly, requested a key bit of recasting. After witnessing the actress playing Dorothy "spending her entire night trying to force her voice down into the bottom of her shoes," Neil remembers, the two producers had an idea: why not just cast a man? "I know some audiences laugh, and think we're going for camp," he explains.

OPPOSITE:

The original Australian cast of *Thank You for Being a Friend*, with Julia Billington as Rose, Donna Lee as Sophia, Darren Mapes as Dorothy, and Chrystal de Grussa as Blanche.

Photo by MATTHEW MANAGEMENT *and* NEIL GOODING PRODUCTIONS.

"But really, having a male actor produces probably a better representation of Bea Arthur than having a female trying to re-create her voice. Bea had such a unique tool, and there aren't too many women who can find that same droll depth of voice."

Thank You for Being a Friend starts with its puppets reenacting *The Golden Girls'* opening credits, and proceeds through Dorothy's battle to get Sophia to the doctor, Rose's attempt to write a song, and Blanche's struggle to accept her gay son's baby via an Asian surrogate. The revised eighty-five-minute show debuted in February 2014 at Melbourne's Theatre Works as part of the city's gay and lesbian Midsumma Festival, then proceeded to the Seymour Centre during the Sydney Gay and Lesbian Mardi Gras. The fall of 2015 brought a revival that toured the eastern cities of Sydney, Brisbane, Tamworth, Port Macquarie, and Canberra; then, for the latter half of 2016, the producers plan on touring the show around the United States.

Golden Girls Forever
◆ ◆ ◆ ◆

"Right from the beginning, young people liked the show. I thought and thought about why and I finally realized it is because the show may have been about older ladies, but it was still very antiestablishment."

—BEA ARTHUR

ON JUNE 2, 2003, Lifetime aired *The Golden Girls Reunion*, which drew 4.2 million viewers to become the network's highest-rated special ever in total viewers. Among both the Women 18–49 and Women 25–54 demos, it was the top-rated cable program of the night, and among all Adults 18–49, it was the night's number four cable show, behind only such male-dominated fare as two editions of *WWE Wrestling* on Spike and an episode of *American Chopper*. Among twentysomething Americans that evening, the now-seventysomething Girls were more popular than anything airing on MTV.

Until 2007, Nielsen did not take into account any viewership by dormitory-dwelling students; but even back in the show's days on Lifetime, the network knew from their feedback that college kids are yet another niche audience, watching in huge numbers. Back then, Tim Brooks estimated that of the 250 to 300 e-mails the network received per month about the show, about 30 percent were from people in college or college age. And Betty White corroborates that pattern, explaining that to this day 70 percent of the mail she receives about *The Golden Girls* is from fans under age twenty-five.

Now, in the latter half of the 2010s, a sizable chunk of TV viewers, particularly those in the youngest, tech-savviest age demographics, has shifted to downloading and streaming their shows via the Internet or mobile devices, making tracking their consumption of any particular series much more challenging. But even as some networks are witnessing declines in their viewership on our traditional TV screens, today not one but three different cable channels are finding success by airing the *Girls*—each multiple times per day. After exiting Lifetime in 2009, and a brief run on WE from 2009 to 2013, the indefatigable Golden ladies have now set up shop at Hallmark, TV Land, and Logo, with each network proclaiming its positive and youth-affirming results.

Since acquiring *The Golden Girls* in 2009, Hallmark has aired the show multiple times per day, every day—except from early November through the end of each year, when the channel's programming switches exclusively to Christmas movies (and its executives hear lots of complaints from *Golden Girls* fans looking for their fix). The show, explains Hallmark's VP of Program Planning and Scheduling, Darren Melameth, "continues to deliver, wherever we put it." In the age of the DVR and other forms of on-demand viewing, the show scores some of Hallmark's strongest live viewership numbers of the day, particularly in its two-hour late-night block from 11:00 p.m. to 1:00 a.m. "It's pretty amazing," Darren adds, "that the last episode at twelve thirty does even better than the first at eleven. The show continues to build on itself. I want to meet these women who at midnight and twelve thirty are watching *The Golden Girls*. These are my friends."

Although Hallmark overall "does speak to a slightly older audience," Darren notes, "[*The Golden Girls*] drops our median age ten years from the rest of our schedule." And the lower age number doesn't just mean that more slightly younger people are watching, the programmer explains. Mathematically, "the only way you can get a median age down into the high forties or low fifties is to have college-age people or younger watching the show."

Hallmark might seem like an unusual choice for these youngest viewers—and an even more unusual home for a series where Blanche is wont to boast about her bedroom gyrations. And as Darren does admit, the network had to make some concessions: "'Slut' for Hallmark is usually a dirty word, but we let *The Golden Girls* get away with it." Thematically, though, *The Golden Girls* fits perfectly at Hallmark, he avows, because "the show is 'safe,' and what I mean by that is you know it's going to work out. Whatever conflicts they have, you know they're going to figure it out, and together they're going to make it."

Actually, there is only one thing about *The Golden Girls* that Hallmark does have to change, slightly: each episode's running time, from the original nearly twenty-four minutes down to cable's typical twenty-two. But luckily, Darren says, technology has progressed to the point where "time tailoring"—i.e., subtly speeding up some scenes—allows a network nowadays to keep as much content as possible and still air a shorter show. "Of course, that's just to a point," he warns. "A good, long stare from Bea Arthur is important. You don't want to speed that up."

In 2013, *The Golden Girls* started airing on two different Viacom-owned networks as well—TV Land and Logo. "There are some acquisitions that are no-brainers, and this was one of them," remembers TV Land's SVP of Programming and

Acquisitions, Jaclyn Cohen. "*The Golden Girls* felt like it was going to be something that made everybody happy—those who came to us for nostalgia, and those who came for originals like *Hot in Cleveland.*

"*The Golden Girls* is an evergreen, and doesn't require a lot of work on our end to launch it," Jaclyn explains. "It doesn't require a lot of explaining, so we can save the explaining for our original programming." In fact, the network is able to use *The Golden Girls* as its secret weapon, whipping up its loyal female audience to deliver to one of those original sitcoms. And the *Girls* have indeed delivered, with twenty-one million viewers watching on TV Land each month. And just as on Hallmark, Jaclyn adds, the show does particularly well on her network when it's placed in a "stack." On Sunday nights, TV Land airs a block of *The Golden Girls* "through the prime time hours, and the show builds and builds," she says. "We like to call it our Potato Chip Strategy. You're sitting down and enjoying the show, and the next thing you know, you're on your third episode and you're not going anywhere."

TV Land's sister station, Logo, celebrated the second quarter of 2015 as its highest-rated ever, thanks partly to *The Golden Girls*, one of its top-rated acquisitions. The show is one of the reliable "tentpoles" propping up Logo's schedule, a perfect match because, with the network's LGBT target audience, "We can embrace the irreverent humor, and our brand really speaks to some of the same tenets," says Pam Post, SVP of Original Programming and Series Development. "We like to be inclusive and progressive, and *The Golden Girls* really represents that."

Much as NBC originally found success by grouping *The Golden Girls* with its Saturday night neighbors for a hurricane- or moonlight madness–themed stunt, Pam notes that Logo has also fared well by scheduling the show with a creative flair. For Valentine's Day 2015, as cinema audiences awaited the movie adaptation of the novel *Fifty Shades of Grey*, Logo presented its own marathon: "Four Shades of Grey." On Grammy weekend, Logo once coun-

terprogrammed with the "Grannies." For the holidays—when Hallmark sends the Girls off packing presumably to St. Olaf—Logo has celebrated "A Betty White Christmas." And in September 2015, to celebrate the thirtieth anniversary of *The Golden Girls*' NBC debut, Logo cast *RuPaul's Drag Race* queens Delta Work, Willam, Pandora Boxx, and Shangela as Dorothy, Blanche, Rose, and Sophia to host a thirty-episode marathon titled "30 Isn't a Drag."

However the episodes are stacked or sorted, TV Land's Jaclyn Cohen enthuses, *The Golden Girls* will continue to score new fans simply because "it's laugh-out-loud funny every time. The show was always a good experience for everybody." Whereas a smarty-pants show like *Frasier* might not be fun to cuddle up with before bedtime, "*The Golden Girls* has smart writing that's not too heady. You get the escape that you want. And you don't have to take notes."

By analyzing *The Golden Girls*' previous ratings results on Lifetime, Jaclyn adds, her team already knew just how popular the show was with varying ages of women. "There was a lot of discussion around college women finding the show and loving it," she remembers.

In fact, *The Golden Girls* has become one of the rare shows to develop this whole new generation of devotees—a critical achievement, because nostalgia can only carry a show so far. After all, older fans eventually die off or just move on to something else. This is the reason, TV historian Tim Brooks says, why today we don't see too many repeats—aside from *I Love Lucy*—of anything from the 1950s. Ultimately, Tim explains, the shows that stick around are the ones, from any era, that continue to touch and tickle new people—and that's why he predicts that *The Golden Girls* will still be golden twenty years from now, just like *Lucy*. "Shows that remain very popular are not specific to their times. They're just well written, about funny people. These are happy comedies for the middle of the night when you want to go to bed with your head clear. Like *The Golden Girls*, they're easy-to-watch television."

THANK YOU FOR BEING A FRIEND

My husband, Frank DeCaro, without whose continued love and support this book would not be possible.

Susan Harris, Paul Junger Witt, and Tony Thomas, for creating a show that has inspired lives, never mind this book.

Some true Disney heroes, including Robert Iger, Zenia Mucha, Kevin Brockman, Ann Limongello, Liana C. Yamasaki, Dan Kilgore, and Margaret Adamic.

Rebecca Hunt and the amazing team at Harper Design.

Foundry Communications and specifically Brandi Bowles and Richie Kern, who are not just visionary agents but fellow fans.

Friends at CBS, particularly Jeremy Murphy and Chris Ender, for their invaluable help behind the scenes.

Wayne Williams, Kari Hendler, Robert Spina, Lex Passaris, Tara Stephenson-Fong, David Lombard and the CBS Photo Archives, Michael Hynes, Judy Evans-Steele and Jeff Blanchard, Michael J. LaRue and the Estate of Rue McClanahan, Rosemarie Knopka and the Art Directors Guild, and everyone else who dug deep into his or her own archives to produce photo and illustration treasures.

The artists who graciously provided their original works: Jesse Beamesderfer, Barry Belcher, Sam Carter, Lenora Claire, Mike Denison, Ken Fallin, Mike Giblin, Glen Hanson, Sarah Hedlund, Erin Hunting, Ricky Kwong, Andre Mello, Jason O'Malley, Trevor Wayne, Richard Weinstein, and Jim Winters.

MY INTERVIEWEES: Kevin Abbott, Rhonda Aldrich, Garth Ancier, Bea Arthur, Barbara Babcock, Doug Ballard, Bonnie Bartlett, Jackie Beat, Susan Beavers, Doris Belack, James Berg, Ken Berry, Valerie Bertinelli, Peter D. Beyt, Raye Birk, Barry Bostwick, John Bowab, Randy Brenner, Tim Brooks, Robert Bruce, Zane Buzby, Ron Carlivati, Paul Chapdelaine, Don Cheadle, Marc Cherry, Margaret Cho, Eric Cohen, Jaclyn Cohen, R. J. Colleary, Anderson Cooper, Rick Copp, Sondra Currie, Bill Dana, Henry Darrow, Michael Denison, Jo DeWinter, Matthew Diamond, Dena Dietrich, Flo DiRe, Elinor Donahue, Ellen Albertini Dow, Jim Drake, Drew Droege, Ja'Net DuBois, Helen Duffy, Lena Dunham, Jeffrey Duteil, Rachel Ehrenberg, Debra Engle, Michael Ensign, Barry Fanaro, Cindy Fee, Jeffrey Ferro, Harvey Fierstein, Lucy Lee Flippin, Deena Freeman, Tracy Gamble, Lee Garlington, Betty Garrett, Carl Gettleman, Billy Goldenberg, Pamela Golum, Neil Gooding, David A. Goodman, Harold Gould, Beth Grant, Juliet Green, Lyn Greene, Max Greenfield, Simone Griffeth, Terry Grossman, Molly Hagan, Jerry Hardin, Amy B. Harris, Susan Harris, Sam Hatmaker, Dave Heckman, Tippi Hedren, Heklina, Sandy and Harriet Helberg, Richard Herd, Winifred Hervey, John Hoffman, Ken Howard, Terry Hughes, Mitchell Hurwitz, Michael Hynes, Allison Jones, Jeffrey Jones, Stephen Jones, Leslie Jordan, Bruce Eric Kaplan, Leila Kenzle, Ken Kercheval, Monte Landis, Michael Lannan, Philip Jayson Lasker, Jane Leeves, Nancy Lenehan, Charles Levin, Hal Linden, Warren Littlefield, Christopher Lloyd, Mario Lopez, Jessica Lundy, John and Peter Mac, Wendie Malick, Robert Mandan, Dinah Manoff, Russell Marcus, Cheech Marin, Monte Markham, Suzanne Martin, Michael Matthews, Rue McClanahan, Edie McClurg, Jonny McGovern, Sam McMurray, Darren Melameth,

Ellen Meyer, Rita Moreno, Mort Nathan, Lois Nettleton, David Nichols, Michael Orland, Sam Pancake, Gail Parent, Lex Passaris, Marco Pennette, Lisa Jane Persky, Miss Coco Peru, Jerry Perzigian, Judy Pioli Askins, Patrik-Ian Polk, Julie Poll, Peggy Pope, Pam Post, Lonny Price, Paul Provenza, Doug Quint, Alan Rachins, Joe Regalbuto, Debbie Reynolds, Doris Roberts, Bob Rosenfarb, Casey Sander, Jay Sandrich, Shawn Schepps, Jonathan Schmock, John Schuck, Josh Schwartz, Don Seigel, John Shaffner, Patt Shea, Michael Shepperd, Trenton Shine, Marc Sotkin, Kathy Speer, Robert Spina, Judy Evans Steele, Maurice Stein, David Steinberg, Tara Stephenson, Lynne Marie Stewart, Ken Stovitz, Elaine Stritch, Billy L. Sullivan, Jackie Swanson, Inga Swenson, Jeffrey Tambor, Quentin Tarantino, Jay Thomas, Tony Thomas, Tim Thomerson, Joel Thurm, Doug Tobin, Hallie Todd, Alex Trebek, Nick Ullett, Brenda Vaccaro, Richard Vaczy, Jim Vallely, Chick Vennera, Sherry Vine, Lyle Waggoner, Nina Wass, Tom Watson, Richard Weaver, Joss Whedon, Tom Whedon, Betty White, Fred Willard, Marsha Posner Williams, Paul Willson, Paul Junger Witt, Lenny Wolpe, Don Woodard, Jamie Wooten, George Wyner, Kent Zbornak, and Stan Zimmerman.

MY SURVEY RESPONDENTS: Jonathan Adler, ANT, John Bartlett, Murray Bartlett, Lance Bass, Bryan Batt, Douglas Carter Beane, Amanda Bearse, Jackie Beat, Willam Belli, Tom Bianchi, Keith Boykin, Dan Bucatinsky, Ann Hampton Callaway, Ted Casablanca, Candis Cayne, Kevin Chamberlin, Craig Chester, Jaffe Cohen, Chris Colfer, Jason Collins, Laverne Cox, Bruce Daniels, Frank DeCaro, Jonathan Del Arco, Ben DeLaCreme, Drew Droege, Harvey Fierstein, Josh Flagg, Maile Flanagan, Malcolm Gets, Ari Gold, Judy Gold, Nathan Lee Graham, Zulema Griffin, Jonathan Groff, Stephen Guarino, Sam Harris, Derek Hartley, Dennis Hensley, Jeff Hiller, Perez Hilton, Janis Ian, Cheyenne Jackson, Geri Jewell,

Ben Patrick Johnson, Dot-Marie Jones, Randy Jones, Ellie Kemper, Rex Lee, Greg Louganis, Mark Lund, Alec Mapa, Billy Masters, Heather Matarazzo, Dan Mathews, Ross Mathews, Brini Maxwell, Jonny McGovern, Wendi McLendon-Covey, Varla Jean Merman, Tammy Lynn Michaels, Eric Millegan, Jackie Monahan, Michael Musto, Scott Nevins, Peter Paige, Jim Parsons, Miss Coco Peru, Zachary Quinto, Andrew Rannells, Mo Rocca, Jai Rodriguez, Felipe Rose, Dave Rubin, Tony Sepulveda, Michael Serrato, Jake Shears, Del Shores, Bob Smith, Doug Spearman, Nicole Sullivan, Jermaine Taylor, Jonathan Tolins, Tony Tripoli, Michael Urie, Kirsten Vangsness, Jane Velez-Mitchell, Robert Verdi, Bruce Vilanch, Sherry Vine, Max von Essen, Stephen Wallem, Suzanne Westenhoefer, Paul J. Williams, Jeff Zarrillo, and Cyd Zeigler.

AND SPECIAL THANKS TO: Kim Abend; Alyssa Adams, Jean Curnyn and Angel Gonzalez at *TV Guide* magazine; Raji Ahsan; Angela Allen; Harry Althaus; Pat Altomare; Emily Anton; David Axlerod; Fran Bascom; Ellen Benjamin; Erica Berger; Greg Berlanti; Justin Berns; Doria Biddle; Kevin Biegel; Tammara Billik; Steve Bluestein; Liane Bonin Starr; Adam Bonnett; Judy Bradley; Howard Bragman; Robyn Burt; Julie Bush; Max Calne; Kassie Canter; Maj Canton; Frank Carabineris; Curtis Chin and Jeff Kim; Pamela Gee Chowayou; Heidi Clements; Angelo, Mary Kate, Tom, Joe, Alison, Madelyn, Kate, and Alyssa Colucci; Marty Colucci and John Volland; Tom Craig; Allen Crowe; Janet Daily; Janine Damura; Beverly D'Angelo; Patti D'Arbanville; Bill and Evelyn Shular Dana; Bonnie Datt and Chris Lowe; Frank Sr. and Marian DeCaro; Jack Degerlia; Louisa Dette; Wendy Diamond; Mike DiGaetano; Lisa Donahey and Dexter Warren; Lois Draegin; Chip Duckett; Catherine Dunn; Scott Edwards; Rachel Ehrenberg; Donna Ellerbusch; Jeanette Eliot; Anne Kissel Elliot; Kiel Elliott; Ramin Fathie; Marianne Fleschman; Fredrick Ford; Dan

Fortune; Rusty Frank; Marlene Fuentes; Bill Funt; Dwight Garcia; Yfat Reiss Gendel; Eliot Glazer; John Glines; Steve Gonzalez; Jennifer Good; Gerry Goodstein; Dave Gorab; Robert Graves; Annabelle Gurwitch; Barbara Haigh; Geoff Hansen; John Harper; Steve Hasley; Chris Haston; Sean Hayes; Karen and Eric Herman; Joel Hornstock; Todd Jackson and Danielle Perez; Tom Jacobson and Ramone Muñoz; Bonnie Johanson; Jocelyn Jones; Larry Jones; Hollis Jordan; Marion and August Kammer; Phyllis Katz; Serena Kodila; Jay Kogen; Jenni Konner; Sean Lambert; Lisa Lampanelli; Jennifer Lang; Karen, Rick, Jake, and Elyssa Langberg; Suze Lanier-Bramlett; Robert Laurita and Don Carroll; Barbara Lawrence; Steve LeGrice; Samara Lenga; Michael Levitt and Marc Loren; David Logan; Jim Marden; Pat McDonough; Cathryn Michon; Todd Milliner; Sara Moskowitz; April Neale; Allan Neuwirth; Sharon Packer; Dan Pasternack; Romaine Patterson; Melissa Peterman; Joseph Pittman; Keith Price; Rosalina Primiano; Erin Quill; Larry Raab; Tanya Ropella; Don Robert; Andria and Daniel Roling; Todd Rosentover and Alycia Weinberger; Barbara Roy; Mark Rupp; Greg and Dawn Sahakian; Richard Samson; Christine Sanchez-Bixler; Rachel Sandler; Rich Sands; Frank Santopadre; Andi Schechter; H. Alan Scott and Kerri Doherty; Lauren Shaham; James Sie and Douglas Wood; Mike and Suzanne Sievert; Michelangelo Signorile; Pam Slay and the Hallmark Channel; Jordan and Melissa Sonnenblick; Tracy Speed; Caissie St. Onge; Sally Starin and June Ploch; Michael Stern; Tristan Svare; Kent Taylor; Rouhi Taylor; Joseph Titizian; Eric van der Werff; Michael von Redlich; Marcia Wallace; Gene Walsh; A. Chandler Warren; Tom Watson; Ken Werther; Morrow Wilson; Lizz Winstead; Steven Wishnoff; Marc Wolf; Don Woodard; World of Wonder; Eric and Elaine Yu; the crew of the Frank DeCaro Show on Sirius XM Radio OutQ; the Knops, Skaggs, Harbaugh, Bylsma, Simonetty, Colucci, Vanas, Dige, Thomas, Decman, Dattilo, and Mastrangelo families.

ABOUT THE AUTHOR

JIM COLUCCI IS a freelance entertainment writer whose work has appeared in such publications as *TV Guide, Inside TV, Quick and Simple, The Advocate, Next,* and *CBS's Watch!* magazine, where he serves as a deputy editor. Jim also delivers a weekly on-air report, *Must Hear TV,* as a correspondent for *The Frank DeCaro Show* on SiriusXM satellite radio. In 2004 he wrote the authorized companion book *Will & Grace: Fabulously Uncensored.*

Originally from Wayne, New Jersey, Jim now lives in Los Angeles with his husband, Frank DeCaro, and their mischievous Boston terrier, Gabby.